**On Descartes' Passive Thought**

**On Descartes' Passive Thought**
**The Myth of Cartesian Dualism**

**Jean-Luc Marion**
Translated by Christina M. Gschwandtner

The University of Chicago Press :: Chicago and London

The University of Chicago Press, Chicago 60637
The University of Chicago Press, Ltd., London
© 2018 by The University of Chicago
All rights reserved. No part of this book may be used or reproduced
in any manner whatsoever without written permission, except in
the case of brief quotations in critical articles and reviews. For more
information, contact the University of Chicago Press, 1427 E. 60th St.,
Chicago, IL 60637.
Published 2018
Printed in the United States of America

27 26 25 24 23 22 21 20 19 18     1 2 3 4 5

ISBN-13: 978-0-226-19258-1 (cloth)
ISBN-13: 978-0-226-19261-1 (e-book)
DOI: https://doi.org/10.7208/chicago/9780226192611.001.0001

Originally published as *Sur la pensée passive de Descartes*. © Presses
Universitaires de France, 2013.

Library of Congress Cataloging-in-Publication Data

Names: Marion, Jean-Luc, 1946– author. | Gschwandtner, Christina M.,
    1974– translator.
Title: On Descartes' passive thought : the myth of Cartesian dualism /
    Jean-Luc Marion ; translated by Christina M. Gschwandtner.
Other titles: Sur la pensée passive de Descartes. English
Description: Chicago : The University of Chicago Press, 2018. | Includes
    bibliographical references and index.
Identifiers: LCCN 2017035328 | ISBN 9780226192581 (cloth : alk. paper) |
    ISBN 9780226192611 (e-book)
Subjects: LCSH: Descartes, René, 1596–1650. | Mind and body—
    Philosophy. | Philosophy, French—17th century.
    Classification: LCC B1875 .M336613 2018 | DDC 194—dc23 LC record
    available at https://lccn.loc.gov/2017035328

♾ This paper meets the requirements of ANSI/NISO Z39.48–1992
(Permanence of Paper).

*To all my students, who have helped me,*
*followed me, and often preceded me*

There are two facts about the human soul on which all the knowledge we can have of its nature depends. The first is that it thinks, the second is that, being united to the body, it can act and be acted upon along with it.

TO ELIZABETH, 21 May 1643 (AT III: 664, 23–27; CSMK: 217–18; trans. lightly modified)

I think the healthy thing for man—for reflective nature—is to think with his whole body; then you get a full harmonious thought, like violin strings vibrating in unison with the hollow wooden box.

MALLARMÉ TO EUGÈNE LEFÉBURE, 17 May 1867[1]

1. Stéphane Mallarmé, *Selected Prose Poems, Essays, and Letters*, trans. Bradford Cook (Baltimore: John Hopkins University Press, 1956), 95.

# Contents

## Translator's Introduction

Why should we still read Descartes today? Jean-Luc Marion responds to this question by claiming that "the way Descartes is interpreted during a particular period appears to correspond to the broader state of French philosophy at that time . . . in short, tell me who Descartes is, and I will tell you the state of philosophy in the era in which you work."[1] He goes on to elaborate the various ways in which Descartes was discussed in subsequent philosophical history and to show how the respective interpretation of Descartes was reflective of the larger questions asked during that particular period. While this is obviously a comment on the history of Descartes interpretation, it might just as well be applied to Marion's own extensive reading of Descartes. Who is Descartes today? What does that tell us about the "state of philosophy" and—maybe even more interestingly—what does it tell us about Marion as an interpreter of Descartes but also as an important contributor to contemporary philosophy in his own right? How does Marion's work on Descartes interact with his work in phenomenology? This "final"

---

1. Jean-Luc Marion, *La rigueur des choses. Entretiens avec Dan Arbib* (Paris: Flammarion, 2012), 71, 72, trans. as *The Rigor of Things: Conversations with Dan Arbib* (New York: Fordham University Press, 2017), 41.

book on Descartes[2] constitutes not only the culmination of Marion's work on Descartes specifically, but also the fullest interaction between these two "sides" of Marion's philosophical interests: Descartes studies and contemporary phenomenology.

*On Descartes' Passive Thought* is certainly the pinnacle of the conversation between Descartes and phenomenology in Marion's work. His reading of Descartes on the body and on the distinction or relationship between soul and body is not only deeply informed by phenomenological considerations of the flesh-body distinction and phenomenological analyses of affectivity, but—not surprisingly in light of Marion's earlier Descartes interpretations—he recovers aspects of Descartes in his reading that he contends still have something to teach us today, and precisely on phenomenological terms.[3] This introduction will try to point to some of the ways in which this book is crucial in both respects.

## I. Descartes' Passive Thought

The central concern in this book is a reading of the Sixth Meditation, supplemented by *The Passions of the Soul*, the letters to Elizabeth (and others), and to some extent the entire rest of Descartes' extensive work.[4] Marion first works out the aporia of the Sixth Meditation, which he

2. Marion claims in the preface that it is the final one that "ends" his work on Descartes.

3. In this he is followed even more strongly by his student Emmanuel Falque who consistently reads medieval and patristic thinkers phenomenologically and argues that they can help solve phenomenological problems. In his *God, the Flesh, and the Other*, written under Marion's supervision, he draws on six different medieval and patristic thinkers to push phenomenological thinking on these three topics further, calling it a "phenomenological practice of medieval philosophy" and arguing that medieval philosophy not only treats phenomenological concepts (like God, flesh, and other), but also is able to "renew" them. Emmanuel Falque, *Dieu, la chair, et l'autre. D'Irénée à Duns Scot* (Paris: PUF, 2008), 12; translated by William Christian Hackett as *God, the Flesh, and the Other: From Irenaeus to Duns Scotus* (Evanston, IL: Northwestern University Press, 2015), xxii. He works this out even more fully in his *Passer le Rubicon. Philosophie et théologie: Essai sur les frontières* (Paris: Lessius, 2013), translated by Reuben Shank as *Crossing the Rubicon* (New York: Fordham University Press, 2016).

4. Marion's reading ranges over Descartes' entire oeuvre, often tracing developments of the shades of meanings of particular terms in their specific contexts in Descartes' development, drawing on letters and obscure remarks in minor texts, as much as the main texts such as the *Meditations*. He also comes full circle by connecting the reading of Descartes' final work, *The Passions of the*

suggests is interested not only in the distinction between soul and body, but also in the relationship between them, besides the quite separate question of the existence of material things. The issue at stake, then, is not just the relationship between soul and body in some general sense, but the relationship of my soul or mind to *my* body, that is to say, *my flesh*, which, Marion argues, is a different "body" from the "bodies" of material things. The Sixth Meditation, in Marion's view, advances a distinction between bodies as "external bodies" (*alia corpora*) and my body (*meum corpus*) as self-affected flesh, although Descartes obviously does not use the phenomenological terminology that distinguishes more clearly between body (*Körper*) and flesh (*Leib*, translated into French as *chair*).

Marion uncovers several aspects of Descartes' argument concerning "my body" or flesh, which becomes "the body, which I regarded as part of myself, or perhaps even as my whole self."[5] First of all, contrary to popular perception, Descartes does not try to prove that I have a body. While he certainly does attempt to prove the existence of external, material things, of *other* bodies, he presupposes "my body" as self-affected flesh to be a given that requires no proof, because it is so intimately experienced that it would be absurd to doubt it. For example, Descartes says: "That the mind, which is incorporeal, can set the body in motion is something which is shown to us not by any reasoning or comparison with other matters, but by the surest and plainest everyday experience. It is one of those self-evident things which we only make obscure when we try to explain them in terms of other things."[6] Accordingly, Marion suggests that on the one hand Descartes makes an important distinction between my body/flesh and other bodies and on the other hand Descartes recognizes that my flesh is so intimate it cannot be doubted and does not require proof. Beyond this he also maintains that Descartes articulates a distinction between types of knowledge appropriate to particular kinds of investigation; thus the method of certainty (clarity and distinction) he imposes as absolute parameter for knowledge in the *Regulae* does not, in fact, apply to and is not appropriate for the knowledge of my body, which comes to me from affectivity rather than from mental deduction based on mathematical calculation (i.e., it is not

---

Soul, with Descartes' earliest text, the *Regulae ad directionem ingenii* (Rules for the Direction of the Mind).

5. CSM II: 52, cited repeatedly by Marion in the book.

6. To Arnauld, 29 July 1648, CSMK: 358. Marion adduces many other passages of this sort, including some where Descartes judges it "insane" that anyone would doubt the body united with the soul in sensing (esp. the passions).

subject to the *mathesis universalis*). This, in Marion's view, is neither arbitrary nor inconsistent on Descartes' part, but follows his earlier work of recognizing different modes of reasoning for different topics.

Marion goes on to show that "sensing" and thus the self-affectivity of the body becomes in the Sixth Meditation a mode of thought. As already the Third Meditation affirms, the ego is "a thing that thinks, that is, a thing that doubts, affirms, denies, understands . . . is willing, is unwilling, and also which imagines and *senses*."[7] Marion interprets this to mean that the flesh *thinks by being affected* in its sensory experience. This flesh of *meum corpus* is irrevocably and intimately linked to the sensing *mens*, as is particularly evident in the experience of pain, in which I suffer my own affective corporeality. Marion draws on Husserl's distinction between *Leib* and *Körper* to show how the self-affectivity of Descartes' notion of *meum corpus* anticipates Husserl's explication. In both Husserl and Descartes this self-affectivity becomes a "passive knowledge" that "opens on a field of sensation, hence of experience of the world" in terms of the receptivity of the flesh to what is given in sensory/affective experience (§9).[8] This receptivity, according to Marion, is a knowledge of *Zuhandenheit* (utility) in Heidegger's sense, rather than the *Vorhandenheit* (objective presence) that "clear and distinct perception" would reach. And it is not some sort of abstract knowledge or information, but a knowledge that is *suffered*, that is experienced in the intimacy of the passive flesh undergoing (especially, but not only) pain. Unlike imaginations or the thoughts coming from the encounter with objects in the world, the "passive" thoughts of the "passions" are real and indubitable even in sleep or even if they are the result of deception by an evil genius. If I am sad or joyful in a dream, I am indeed sad or joyful, regardless of whether the objects presented in my dream exist and evaporate upon waking. And yet I do not generate this joy or sadness, but it comes to me out of its own accord; it affects me. Furthermore, not only does my body affect me as an exterior object that touches me, but it is self-affected, it affects me within myself. The

7. CSM II: 24; trans. lightly modified; emphasis added. Note also that it is only the final mode, that of sensing, that is passive and requires "my body." The others (doubting, imagining, etc.) are active modes and can be engaged by the mind or soul alone and on its own terms. Indeed, insofar as it senses, the mind can be said to be "corporeal."

8. The following section of the chapter (chapter 2) employs Heidegger's distinction between *vorhanden* and *zuhanden* heavily to read Descartes' *commoda* and *incommoda*, i.e., "convenient" and "inconvenient" stimuli (as specific to sensory experience and hence *zuhanden*, not *vorhanden*).

human ego is unique, inasmuch as it is a mind (i.e., a flesh) that senses corporeally and hence thinks also passively (in contrast to animals or angels): "not only does all sensing imply an *ego [cogito] sum*, but any performance of the *ego [cogito] sum* implies a primordial sensing, thus the *meum corpus* as ultimate shape of the ego."[9]

Marion argues that the union of *mens* and *meum corpus* becomes a third primitive notion.[10] While the soul or intellect alone is characterized by thought and material bodies by extension, the union of "my body" thinks passively through affectivity, where the ego experiences itself as affected. This is not a combination of the other two, but actually a more fundamental and more primordial notion, which has to be thought from the union itself. The union of soul and body in my flesh is a matter not of mere extension or just of thought, but of "passive" thought. Marion shows how Descartes vigorously disagrees with Regius, who presented the union as a composition of two substances and as a mere accident. Descartes instead insists that the whole human being (soul and body as *meum corpus*) is a being *per se*, not *per accidens*. The union is essential to us and defines us most fundamentally. This, so Marion suggests, is what allows Descartes to proceed beyond the previous metaphysical definitions and to inaugurate a new (non-scholastic) way of thinking (e.g., by dispensing with the terminology of "substantial form" and "principal attribute"). Rather than inventing a new substance (of union), Descartes' notion of the flesh envisions the mind as *cogitatio*, open to receiving (rather than merely producing) certain thoughts, thus thinking also in a passive mode. This does not create a new or composite substance, but rather indicates a primordial mode of being and thinking for the mind.

In sum, the self cannot think without a body, or more correctly, it can only think "actively" as "soul" through the understanding, the will, or the imagination. Its intimate connection to its own body allows it also to think "passively," that is, to think by being affected, through the senses. Sensory experience hence is a kind of "thinking," and it is the only kind that thoroughly mingles soul and "my body." This union is not a composite of two substances, but stands on its own, as a whole. Thinking only actively (only through the mind) is an impoverished sort of thought. Hence, we must also think passively, through the senses, that

9. See below, 118 (the square brackets in the quote are Marion's).

10. This is terminology first articulated in Descartes' early *Regulae ad directionem ingenii*. Marion examines it in detail in his first doctoral thesis that became *Ontologie grise*.

is, through the flesh of my body. This is why Descartes in the end turns to the passions (such as gratitude) explicitly. They designate precisely those thoughts, feelings, or experiences that come to me without myself, affect me, cause me to "suffer" them. They come to me as events that happen to me, uncaused, unpredictable, and yet affect me intimately. They hence put the self in a position of receptivity.

This account has, of course, profound parallels with Marion's phenomenological work. On the one hand it draws on the phenomenological distinction between body and flesh in order to argue for a phenomenology of "my body" as flesh in Descartes that relies heavily on a phenomenological framework, albeit supported by extensive citations from Descartes' letters and his treatise on the *Passions of the Soul*. Marion discovers a distinctive account of the sentient body of the thinking self in Descartes, which is able to bypass the traditional mind-body dualism by showing that my own body is always already experienced as thinking and that my thinking is always already embodied in a way that renders them inseparable. On the other hand, this account of the body provides an account of the passions that reads them as phenomenological events, as what comes to affect me patterned on Marion's prior phenomenological work. This interpretation of Descartes' account of the passions displays all the characteristics of the saturated phenomenon, as Marion has outlined it in other places: it happens as an event, is unpredictable, overwhelms me, comes to me from outside myself, renders me passive when confronted with this overwhelming and bedazzling event, reduced to pure receptivity.

Yet we can also already note a broader shift. While Marion's earlier treatments often drew on isolated aspects of phenomenology in order to advance a novel and more fruitful interpretation of Descartes, primarily to enhance our understanding of Descartes, the present work advances a reading of Descartes in order also to broaden and deepen our understanding of and work in contemporary phenomenology. Indeed, Marion claims that maybe in the end Descartes is the better phenomenologist and calls him a *phenomenologus larvatus prodeo*, a phenomenologist who proceeds masked.[11] This text is no longer just an employment of

---

11. See below, chapter 2, final section, 76. This takes up a claim Marion had made in a different way at the end of the *Metaphysical Prism*: "And if the Cartesian names of God are organized in a confused complex of contradictions, this is not because Descartes lacked conceptual power or conceptual rigor; on the contrary, it is because he dared face up to the contradiction that is necessarily imposed on the finite by the infinite advancing upon it—and to which, perhaps, only a certain conceptual madness can testify without being unworthy of it.

certain aspects of Heidegger's and Husserl's philosophy applied to historical sources, but now Descartes becomes much more fully a *contemporary* philosopher engaged in our existential questions today, with real insight into the fundamental questions we raise about our being in the world, our being with others, and our being in our own body and *as* our flesh.[12] Descartes emerges in this reading as an immensely cohesive, amazingly creative, thoroughly unsettling, and deeply phenomenological thinker.

## II. Descartes and Phenomenology

Marion has written far more extensively on Descartes than many English-speaking readers realize. All of his early work was on Descartes' thought, and he has continued to publish in this field throughout his career. Not only did he not begin with *God without Being* as many people continue to think, but he also did not abandon his interests in Descartes and commitment to Cartesian studies after turning to phenomenology more explicitly. Besides his own extensive writing on Descartes (to date, six books, a translation of Descartes' early treatise *Rules for the Direction of the Mind*, a concordance, and many articles), he was also instrumental in the formation of the Centre d'études cartésiennes, the Center for Cartesian Studies, at the Sorbonne, which brings together Descartes

---

Before God, reverentially, and as a rarity among the metaphysicians, Descartes stands hidden—he does not keep secrets, nor does he sneak away, but hides his face before that of the infinite—*larvatus pro Deo.*" *On Descartes' Metaphysical Prism: The Constitution and the Limits of Onto-theo-logy in Cartesian Thought*, trans. Jeffrey L. Kosky (Chicago: University of Chicago Press, 1986), 276.

12. Marion justifies the confrontation of Descartes with later thinkers—without necessarily considering all the intervening work and dealing with all the secondary sources (although in this particular book he engages the secondary material extensively)—in his interview with Dan Arbib, arguing that sometimes one must think from mountain top to mountain top rather than just laboring in the valleys below, that the great thinkers were often closer to each other than they were to their contemporaries. He also speaks of phenomenology as an ongoing activity to which each thinker adds something as part of a larger project. Marion justifies his turn to phenomenology with the need to "do philosophy" and not just "history of philosophy"—i.e., not merely to comment on past historical thought, but actually to work philosophically today. He sees only two predominant modes of doing so available today: the analytical and the phenomenological one, judging the phenomenological far more productive because it works on a joint and continuous project where real progress is possible. See *The Rigor of Things*, 72–73 and 141–46.

scholars from all over the world and has led to extensive collaboration and cross-fertilization. It has truly opened French work on their
own philosopher—*the* French philosopher par excellence—to an international dialogue.[13] Marion's own contributions to Cartesian studies
have been continually tested in this larger conversation and confirmed
through the work of other scholars.

This work on Descartes has from the very beginning been informed
by phenomenological concerns at least to some extent. Already in his
first book, *Sur l'ontologie grise de Descartes*,[14] based on his doctoral
dissertation under the prominent Descartes scholar Ferdinand Alquié,
Marion had suggested that Heidegger's definition of onto-theo-logy
might prove enlightening for understanding Descartes' metaphysics and
also employed the Heideggerian distinctions between various senses of
being and his notion of the "forgetting of being" to evaluate Cartesian ontology throughout the book.[15] Furthermore, his methodology
of reading Descartes as in direct conversation with Aristotle, skipping
over the intermediary discussion between the two thinkers, he attributes
to a Heideggerian reading of the history of philosophy that he learned
from Jean Beaufret in his student days at the Lycée Condorcet and justifies in the introduction to *L'ontologie grise*.[16] A similar employment of
Heideggerian notions of ontology and onto-theo-logy marks his treat-

13. Marion describes it as follows: "The Center for Cartesian Studies was
international from the beginning, because even before its founding we worked
with the 'Lessico intellettuele europeo' at the University of 'La Sapienza' in
Rome, a celebrated research center directed by Tullio Gregory. Then there were
relations with Giulia Belgioioso and the Center for Studies on Descartes and the
Seventeenth Century at Lecce, with Daniel Garber and his important American
network (at Chicago, then at Princeton), with the Dutch in Utrecht gathered
around Theo Verbeek, then the Germans, the Spanish, the Japanese. This inter-
nationalization also allowed to test out a great many hypotheses, including my
own, on very exact philological grounds owing to the translations, editions, and
concordances, already published or in the process of being worked out, during
the conferences that we organized once or twice a year always on very specific
topics. In this way an uninterrupted process of validating and verifying each
other's work occurred." Marion, *The Rigor of Things*, 62–63.

14. Marion, *Sur l'ontologie grise de Descartes* (Paris: Vrin, 1975, 4th ed.
2000).

15. The newest edition includes a 1976 essay on the doubled nature of Cartesian metaphysics, read as two "onto-theo-logies," one based on "ousia" (associated with the *ego cogito* as ultimate founding principle) and one based on
"causa" (associated with God as ultimate founding principle in the form of the
*causa sui*).

16. See *The Rigor of Things*, 46; *Sur l'ontologie grise*, 23.

ment of the creation of the eternal truths and his account of the demise
of notions of analogy in the late medieval and early modern context in
*Théologie blanche.*[17]

This metaphysical framework becomes again a central and far more
extensive guiding factor in *On Descartes' Metaphysical Prism*, where
Marion uses it explicitly in order to evaluate what he calls the "constitution and limits of onto-theo-logy in Cartesian thought," spelling out
how he sees the "doubled" onto-theo-logy functioning in Descartes.[18]
Marion shows that in Descartes' earlier work (especially in the *Discourse on Method*), the ego cogito serves as a grounding figure for a
metaphysics of thought (or onto-theo-logy of the *cogitatio*).[19] That is
to say, all being as cognized (*cogitatum*) depends on the being of the
ego that cognizes and thinks them. Descartes' early philosophy can be
understood as metaphysical in character by virtue of these claims about
the being of objects grounded in the knowledge of a subject. These two
groundings are reciprocally related: the ego serves as first being on
which all other beings as *cogitata* are dependent, and the very nature
of ontology is epistemological in character: being depends on knowing
or thought. Marion then contends that this metaphysical structure does
not characterize all of Descartes' texts, but that a different structure
emerges in his later writings, starting with the Third Meditation. This
meditation raises the question of whether the ego can truly ground itself
in the way in which the *Discourse* supposed: what happens to the ego
when it is sleeping or not thinking? The Third Meditation therefore
posits an omnipotent God as ultimate ground of all being, including
the being of the ego. A different metaphysical grounding is achieved in
which the divine functions as the supreme being grounding the being of

17. Marion, *Sur la théologie blanche de Descartes* (Paris: PUF, 1981, 2nd ed.
1991).

18. Marion, *Sur le prisme métaphysique de Descartes* (Paris: PUF, 1986),
translated by Jeffrey L. Kosky as *On Descartes' Metaphysical Prism*. Many of
his individual essays on Descartes, collected in the two volumes of "Cartesian
Questions," also employ phenomenological tools for reading Descartes on various topics, especially methodology, metaphysics, questions of self and other,
and God: *Questions cartésiennes. Méthode et métaphysique* (Paris: PUF, 1991),
translated as *Cartesian Questions: Method and Metaphysics* (Chicago: University of Chicago Press, 1999); *Questions cartésiennes II. Sur l'ego et sur Dieu*
(Paris: PUF, 1996, 2002), partially translated as *On the Ego and on God: Further Cartesian Questions* (New York: Fordham University Press, 2007.

19. See "What Is the Metaphysics within the Method? The Metaphysical
Situation of the Discourse on the Method," chapter 2 in *Cartesian Questions*,
20–42.

all other beings, including the ego, by serving as their ultimate cause (the onto-theo-logy of causality).

In *On Descartes' Metaphysical Prism* and several related articles Marion mostly posits these two systems or structures and shows that they are present and probably related, but he does not yet fully explain how one might ground the other, apart from a kind of reinforcement of the metaphysical structure.[20] In the present book he takes this final step, arguing that Descartes' "third sailing" in the Sixth Meditation and the *Passions of the Soul* enables him to reconcile and bring together the two metaphysical structures. The fourth chapter in particular lays out how "my body" does not serve as a separate third grounding principle or a third substance, but rather manages to bring together the other two, just as it also brings together thought and extension by allowing them to bleed into and color each other. A third posture of the ego as self-affected flesh comes to bring together the previous two postures of the ego associated with two onto-theo-logical structures. This book hence serves as the culmination of Marion's argument about the nature of metaphysics in Descartes.

This is the case also for the related notion of the *causa sui*. Marion explored this concept, which he associates with Descartes' third proof for God's existence as given in the *Replies* to the objections to the *Meditations*, already in several earlier discussions.[21] In *Théologie blanche* the argument about the demise of the doctrines of analogy in the late medieval thinkers, which makes it impossible for Descartes to have recourse to them, and the connected argument about the code at work in Descartes' early work, culminates in a chapter on the *causa sui*, which is crucial to the argument. For Descartes, the human comes to imitate the divine autarchy by grounding the code of the simple natures, and this grounding functions univocally for human and divine.[22] Through free will and the ethical self-sufficiency it implies, the human imitates the divine and the *causa sui* ends up working a kind of analogy, replacing the medieval notions of analogy no longer available to Descartes: "The

20. I.e, he says that "this doubling strengthens the onto-theo-logical constitution" (*Descartes' Metaphysical Prism*, 122) and firmly establishes "the precisely metaphysical dignity of Cartesian thought" (127). In the remainder of the book he turns to an examination "of the two privileged beings put into play in each of them—the ego and God" (ibid.).

21. In a chapter in *Questions cartésiennes II* he argues that Descartes is the first to use the *causa sui* and shows its precise connection to the Cartesian metaphysical system. *On the Ego and on God*, 139–60.

22. *Théologie blanche*, 427–28.

Replies [to the *Meditations*] use analogy only in order to reduce the essence of God to the general rule that governs finite beings—namely, causality. That is why far from decreasing this tendency to univocity, this kind of analogy increases it."[23] Consequently, Descartes subjects God to causality: "one could not underline more clearly that it is the efficient cause that becomes aware of the divine essence in the analogy."[24] Thus, although most of the book has served to show that via the insistence on the creation of the eternal truths Descartes escapes the late medieval and early modern move to univocity, he ultimately also succumbs to it by thinking God under a univocal concept. At the same time, the *causa sui* is different from ordinary causality and hence still maintains a certain measure of incomprehensibility in regard to the divine.[25] The disappearance of analogy is wrapped up with the appearance of the *causa sui*. This argument returns in a different form in *Descartes' Metaphysical Prism* when Marion considers the three proofs for God's existence set forth in the *Meditations* and suggests that they take up in veiled fashion the discussion of the divine names in apophatic or mystical theology as drawn from Western appropriations of the early sixth-century thinker Dionysius the Areopagite.

While the possible link to mystical theology recedes in the present book (indeed, there is hardly any mention of God or "theological" questions), the *causa sui* again emerges as significant. Marion argues that the *causa sui* not merely is a notion—the idea of a self-caused cause as applied to the divine—but functions methodologically. Although the ego is not per se called a *causa sui*, there is a way in which it functions as a quasi *causa sui*, by taking up the kind of productive work the *causa sui* does. Here it is no longer just the self-sufficient will but more specifically the capacity for generosity and love that establishes the parallel between divine and human. The third posture of the ego in some form is both cause and caused: in its active use of the will, it functions in some way as a *causa sui*, while in its passive reception of thoughts by the flesh it is caused by something other than itself. On the one hand, this shows how

23. Ibid., 428.

24. Ibid., 434.

25. The *causa sui* does not subject God to ordinary causality, "but rather shows his radical strangeness from other beings" (*Théologie blanche*, 438); thus "the existence of God becomes causally intelligible only on the condition of his essence appearing intrinsically incomprehensible" (438). Marion concludes: "If God, finally, must admit as first divine name that of the *causa sui*, it is because in this way he responds to the question of his *causa sive ratio*, in short that his own proper essence becomes for him a grounding" (454).

the notion of the *causa sui* and Marion's convictions about how it functions are crucial to his overall presentation and evaluation of Descartes' work. On the other hand, it points to further parallels between Marion's work on Descartes and his phenomenological project.

Not only does Marion appropriate Heidegger's definition of the onto-theo-logical character of metaphysics and apply its various aspects to what he interprets as Descartes' successive attempts to ground the being of all beings on either the constituting ego in his earlier work or on the divine as *causa sui* in his later discussions (from the Third Meditation onward), but when Marion begins to write about phenomenology more explicitly in *Reduction and Givenness*, one of the chapters investigates the relationship between Heidegger's Dasein and the Cartesian ego in detail, arguing that they mirror each other and are considerably closer than Heidegger is willing to admit—an argument he pursues in the present work by employing Heidegger's terminology of *zuhanden/ vorhanden* and showing how it is already operative in Descartes.[26] When Marion begins to work out his own phenomenological proposal, he again relies heavily on Descartes. In *Being Given* he draws on Descartes at several crucial points in order to articulate his notion of givenness, appealing especially to the Cartesian notion of God as the infinite as an example of a saturated phenomenon that transcends the categories of cognition.[27] This becomes even more evident in the first chapter of *In Excess*, where he articulates the need for a new "first philosophy," drawing explicitly on Descartes and Husserl (among others) in order to arrive at the conclusion that "none of the types of primacy that metaphysics has ever been able to propose . . . can assure, today and for us, the legitimacy of any philosophy, in short, of a 'first philosophy.'"[28]

26. Marion, *Reduction et donation. Recherches sur Husserl, Heidegger et la phénoménologie* (Paris: PUF, 1989), 119–161, translated by Thomas A. Carlson as *Reduction and Givenness: Investigations of Husserl, Heidegger, and Phenomenology* (Evanston, IL: Northwestern University Press, 1998), 77–107.

27. Marion, *Étant donné. Essai d'une phénoménologie de la donation* (Paris: PUF, 1997), translated by Jeffrey L. Kosky as *Being Given: Toward a Phenomenology of Givenness* (Stanford: Stanford University Press, 2002), 219. Indeed, Descartes is the fourth-most-cited figure in the book, after Heidegger, Husserl, and Kant.

28. Marion, *De surcroît. Études sur les phénomènes saturés* (Paris: PUF, 2001), 1–34, translated by Robyn Horner and Vincent Berraud as *In Excess: Studies of Saturated Phenomena* (New York: Fordham University Press, 2002), 1–29, quoting page 13. Marion has investigated the notion of "first philosophy" in Descartes (stressing his use of that expression rather than "metaphysics") in

Here Descartes is explicitly used as a paradigm for first philosophy that can be imitated and also overcome in a phenomenological "final" philosophy that takes up the same stakes in a different mode.

Indeed, Marion often appeals to Descartes in his phenomenological discussions. *The Erotic Phenomenon* is explicitly posited as "six meditations" to face the Cartesian *Meditations*, complete with radical, systematic doubt.[29] Unfortunately, the English translation omits the French subtitle "six meditations," but Marion is also clear in the text itself about the continuity with (and opposition to) Descartes. After a brief review of the ego as *res cogitans* (and pointing out that the French translator adds "which loves, which hates" to the ego's "definition"), he concludes about his own project in the book: "In short, it will be necessary to substitute erotic meditations for the metaphysical ones."[30] Our search for assurance, for an affirmation that someone loves us, is explicitly patterned on the Cartesian search for certainty, while also challenging it as the most basic and most primordial question. Love concerns us more profoundly than knowledge and can function as an alternative form of knowledge.

In a quite different vein, Marion's even more recent proposal of "negative certainties" is clearly informed by Descartes' search for certainty, arguing that there are phenomena for which Cartesian-style certainty (in terms of clarity and distinction) will always be impossible because they defy it by their very nature—and that we can be "certain" about this, so that it constitutes a real increase of knowledge.[31] Here even more fully Marion develops the notion of a phenomenological kind of knowledge that would not be a metaphysical knowledge of objects and

several other places in his work. See, for example, *Metaphysical Prism*, 31–40, and "On Descartes' Constitution of Metaphysics," *Graduate Faculty Philosophy Journal* 11 (1986): 21–33.

29. Marion, *Le phénomène érotique. Six méditations* (Paris: Grasset, 2003), translated by Stephen E. Lewis as *The Erotic Phenomenon* (Chicago: University of Chicago Press, 2007).

30. *Erotic Phenomenon*, 8, trans. lightly modified.

31. Marion, *Certitudes négatives* (Paris: Grasset, 2010), translated by Stephen E. Lewis as *Negative Certainties* (Chicago: University of Chicago Press, 2015). There are far more references to Descartes in this (purely phenomenological) book than to any other thinker, historical or contemporary. The only two who come close are Kant and Heidegger (interestingly, not Husserl, to whose work there are far fewer references even than to Heidegger's). Besides the epistemological question, this book also reiterates the close association between human and divine that Marion highlights for the will in Descartes' work.

yet give us valid insights on its own parameters. This concern, as we have seen above, is continued in a somewhat different mode in the discussion of Descartes' passive thought.

Marion already explored alternative models of knowing in his earlier work on Descartes, usually associating these with a Pascalian challenge to Descartes, as in the fourth chapter of *On the Ego and On God* and in a different form at the end of *On Descartes' Metaphysical Prism*.[32] Pascal's third order of charity is a form of knowing that challenges the second order of the mind, associated with the Cartesian search for certainty. In the present book Marion argues much more fully that such an alternative can actually be found in Descartes himself. He shows that there is a way in which Descartes argues against Descartes: while there are modes of knowing distinguished by clarity and distinction leading to certainty, there are other ways of knowing—which also concern other realms of knowledge—for which these methods are inadequate or inappropriate. This is maybe the most important contribution of the present work, indicated also by the fact that it is used in the title: "passive thought" is an important and valid element of thought. A thinking that would operate only actively is an impoverished thinking. To think passively, namely, by being affected, is to take advantage of the entire range of possibilities for the self, including the knowledge given it by its flesh and its various modes of affectivity. This not only gives us a far more nuanced interpretation of Descartes and the Cartesian legacy but enables us to advocate for taking seriously other modes of knowing that might not confer certainty in quite the same stereotypically "Cartesian" fashion. This is, of course, what Marion himself has tried to do throughout his work by positing love as an alternative form of knowing or a "knowledge of the heart," from early theological articles in *Communio* (collected in *Prolegomena to Charity*, *The Visible and the Revealed*, and *Believing in Order to See*) to *The Erotic Phenomenon* and *Negative Certainties*. Here Marion gives this project further support by showing that such an alternative kind of thinking—passive or, more precisely, receptive—is already suggested by Descartes.

32. It is striking that Pascal is not mentioned even once in the whole book, considering what a large role he has played in all of Marion's previous readings of Descartes, often precisely as the quasi-phenomenological "good guy" against any instances where Descartes becomes irredeemably "metaphysical." For a more detailed exploration of the claim above, see my "Marion and Negative Certainty: Epistemological Dimensions of the Phenomenology of Givenness," *Philosophy Today* 56.3 (2012): 363–70.

## Conclusion

What does Marion's phenomenological reading of Descartes then have to say about contemporary philosophy, that is to say, about phenomenology? While I can address that question only very briefly here, let me offer a couple of concluding comments about possible further avenues of exploration. On the most basic level, as already indicated, this treatment recovers Descartes as a contemporary thinker, whose insights are still useful for phenomenology. It also shows the continued importance of the critical appropriation of past thinkers for contemporary phenomenological work more broadly. Reading past thinkers carefully, generously, critically but also hospitably, offers productive and creative insight for contemporary debates. And approaching past thinkers with contemporary questions can also show their texts to be newly illuminating. Marion is surely right that Descartes (and Kant, Husserl, Heidegger, etc.) still have something to teach us that is not merely of historical but of genuinely *philosophical* interest.[33]

On another level this reading—as is true for much of Marion's work on Descartes—reveals Descartes as a much more complex thinker than the usual image we have of him as the first modern philosopher. It reads Descartes in his late medieval context, shows him in conversation with many other thinkers, reveals the ways in which his thought shifts in conversation, and highlights the manner in which some of his philosophy is far more careful, more subtle, and also more ambivalent than usually assumed. Maybe most importantly, it demonstrates—as Marion said at a recent conference—that Descartes was not always Cartesian, but often critical of positions that later become associated with Cartesianism. This constitutes also a continual but productive ambivalence in Marion's own treatment of Descartes' work. On the one hand, he often points to serious shortcomings and problems in Descartes' philosophy and occasionally severely criticizes him, even using him as a foil for a "Cartesian" position we must overcome. On the other hand, he consistently singles him out as someone who escaped certain late medieval or early modern traps, showing how he argues against a larger metaphysical consensus (especially apparent in his defense of the creation of the eternal truths),

---

33. On this see also his discussion in *The Rigor of Things* about the distinction between reading historical texts for purely historical interest and reading them for genuine philosophical engagement with them, i.e., "history of philosophy" vs. "philosophy of history" (134–44).

and highlights all the ways in which Descartes not only can still inspire us, but indeed often is not at all "Cartesian," defying the stereotypes we have about his work. This fruitful ambivalence—defying any easy reading or positioning of Descartes—also characterizes Marion's appropriation of Descartes for phenomenological questions. Again, we can still learn not only about Descartes, but also from Descartes.

More specifically, the investigation of flesh and body in Descartes may well allow us to approach contemporary phenomenological discussions of flesh/body and possibly also of inter-subjectivity in a new way or to come at them from a different angle.[34] Marion develops an account of passivity and self-affectivity in this book that—despite the language of "passivity"—is actually an account of receptivity.[35] It is not passivity in the sense that the self now becomes the "object" of the phenomenon as subject (as Marion's phenomenology of givenness and the saturated phenomenon is often misread), but passivity in the mode of self-affectivity, of feeling and sensing. In his analysis of Descartes' accounts of dreaming, imagining, believing, and sensing, he opens new possibilities for analyses of noetic acts and their deep rootedness in our experiencing as flesh (and the ways in which the flesh is "conscious,"

34. Besides his brief review of Husserl's distinction between *Leib* and *Körper* Marion himself does not explicitly engage twentieth-century or contemporary texts. Merleau-Ponty is not mentioned in the book itself, although the final lines of the book are a quotation from *The Visible and the Invisible*, which Marion presents as confirming his insights about the Cartesian insistence on the union of soul and body (below, 249). Didier Franck's important work on the flesh is mentioned once in a footnote as a secondary source for Husserl's distinction (below, 56, note 28). Jean-Luc Nancy is also mentioned only once as a secondary source in a footnote (below, 142, note 41). Marion does not engage recent work on transhumanism or plasticity (e.g., Malabou), yet his phenomenological explication may well have something to contribute to these discussions. Emmanuel Falque has recently criticized the phenomenological distinction between flesh and body prevalent in the French literature as merely reinstituting the Cartesian distinction between soul and body in problematic fashion. It is hence unable to address the deeper divide this represents, which Falque himself seeks to overcome with his notion of the "spread" body (*corps épandu*), one deeply involved in the organicity of our passions and impulses. See his *Les noces de l'agneau. Essai philosophique sur le corps et l'eucharistie* (Paris: Cerf, 2011), translated by Georges Hughes as *The Wedding Feast of the Lamb* (New York: Fordham University Press, 2016), where he develops this argument in detail.

35. See also his important article on this issue in Descartes, "What Is the Ego Capable of? Divinization and Domination: *Capable/Capax*" (chapter 4 of *Cartesian Questions*).

though maybe not always in a straightforward "intentional" manner). Marion's discussion of self-affectivity in the intimacy of my sensory flesh employs much of the language of Michel Henry's phenomenology of the flesh, but without the somewhat problematic assumptions about the "Truth" of "Life," generating us as "sons" within the eternal source of Life (God) via the "Arch-Son."[36] It is a "fleshly" and "affective" phenomenology, albeit not necessarily a "material" one in Henry's sense of that term. Marion's reading of affectivity is also not riddled by the same absolute and binary distinctions that govern Henry's work and thus may well evade some of the difficulties these create for Henry's account of the flesh.[37] The fact that both Henry's *Incarnation* and Didier Franck's

36. It is interesting that Henry is hardly mentioned in this book on flesh, passivity, and affectivity, especially considering how deeply Marion is influenced by him. Marion once briefly refers to Henry in a footnote, as having pointed out the problem of the mode of thought that validates the ego (see below, 115, note 58; the reference is to Henry's *Genealogy of Psychoanalysis*), and to his own treatment of Henry's discussion of Descartes on the topic of affectivity in *Cartesian Questions I* (chapter 5). He does not mention Henry's extensive engagement with Descartes in *Incarnation. Une philosophie de la chair* (Paris: Seuil, 2000), translated by Karl Hefty as *Incarnation: A Philosophy of the Flesh* (Evanston, IL: Northwestern University Press, 2015) or his somewhat briefer but still trenchant discussion in *C'est moi la vérité. Pour une philosophie du christianisme* (Paris: Seuil, 1996), translated by Susan Emanuel as *I Am the Truth: Toward a Philosophy of Christianity* (Stanford, CA: Stanford University Press, 2003). This lack of engagement with his work is surprising in a book that is essentially concerned with the topics crucial for Henry: the flesh and affectivity. In the discussion of affectivity in *Cartesian Questions*, Marion focuses primarily on Descartes' notion of generosity as the first passion that might open a path for self-affectivity in Henry's sense and thus judges Henry's line of questioning productive for Cartesian research (he does not yet, here, suggest the reverse, that a particular reading of Descartes might be productive *for phenomenology*). For a much fuller account see his two other essays on Michel Henry: "The Invisible and the Phenomenon," in *Michel Henry: The Affects of Thought*, ed. Jeffrey Hanson and Michael R. Kelly (New York/London: Continuum, 2012), 19–39, and "The Question of the Reduction" in *Breached Horizons: The Philosophy of Jean-Luc Marion*, ed. Rachel Bath, Kathryn Lawson, Stephen G. Lofts, and Antonio Calcagno (London, UK: Rowman and Littlefield International, 2018).

37. I.e., Henry's absolute distinctions between the (false and lying) "truth" of the "world" and the "Truth" of "Life" (which has nothing at all to do with the "world" or its "truth"), between the "barbarism" of contemporary culture and the invisible truth of Kandinsky's painting, and so forth. Henry struggles to explain how the "sons" of life can both have "forgotten" and denied this life and yet be always already within it and thus recover it simply by "realizing" what has been true all along (and yet this is a radical "conversion" that completely

*Flesh and Body* have recently been published in translation[38] can fertilize this conversation on the flesh also for the English-speaking world.

Indeed, Marion's work not only is significant for a "French" discussion, but opens possibilities for illuminating conversation with other contemporary phenomenological work, such as that of Anthony Steinbock on the moral emotions,[39] that of Edward Casey on the body in place,[40] or that of Richard Kearney and others on "carnal hermeneutics."[41] Steinbock, for example, undertakes careful phenomenological analyses of such emotions as pride, shame, guilt, despair, hope, and love, arguing that their givenness provides evidence for them and reveals dimensions of personhood and knowledge that previous epistemological accounts ignore. While Steinbock's reading of Husserl is quite different from Marion's (although both use language of "givenness" heavily), his account of affectivity in this particular book covers territory similar to that of Marion's Descartes book. Both are deeply invested in recovering a philosophical account of love and both end their respective books with a brief discussion of the implications of their work on emotions and affectivity for morality, inter-subjectivity, and the crisis of modernity (although Steinbock does so more explicitly and more extensively than Marion). Reading these two very different phenomenological accounts together might give us much broader insight into the functioning of human emotion and the peculiar affectivity of our flesh.

---

turns upside down [the very strong "bouleverser" is his favorite word for this] all our prior conceptions and relationships).

38. Didier Franck, *Flesh and Body: On the Phenomenology of Husserl*, trans. Scott Davidson (London: Bloomsbury, 2014). For *Incarnation*, see note 36 above.

39. Marion does not mention Steinbock nor does Steinbock mention Marion in this particular text. His *Phenomenology and Mysticism* (Bloomington: Indiana University Press, 2007) does refer to Marion's work on a couple of occasions, but *Home and Beyond* (Evanston, IL: Northwestern University Press, 1985) and *Moral Emotions: Reclaiming the Evidence of the Heart* (Evanston, IL: Northwestern University Press, 2014) do not list any of Marion's texts even in the respective bibliographies, although Steinbock does use other French thinkers, such as Levinas.

40. Edward S. Casey, *Getting Back into Place: Toward a Renewed Understanding of the Place-World* (Bloomington: Indiana University Press, 1993, 2009), *The World at a Glance* (Bloomington: Indiana University Press, 2007), and other texts.

41. Richard Kearney and Brian Treanor, eds., *Carnal Hermeneutics* (New York: Fordham University Press, 2015). A brief excerpt from Marion's essay on Henry, "The Invisible and the Phenomenon" (cf. note 36 above) is included in this collection.

Similarly, there is an interesting conversation that could be had with Kearney's work on carnal hermeneutics. Although Marion's writings on hermeneutics are reluctant and highly qualified, this reading of Descartes on the body and the flesh is, after all, a profoundly hermeneutic exercise.[42] And his contention that Descartes' account of the passions and of the sentience of the flesh might provide an alternative kind of knowledge, a way of thinking that is "passive" and "receptive" rather than "active" and "controlling," may well open avenues of fruitful conversation with the sort of reading of the body or a hermeneutics that "goes all the way down" that Kearney advocates. In Marion's reading we encounter a Descartes who does go all the way down or maybe better all the way "in," to our innermost and most intimate knowledge of ourselves, which we ultimately discover to be given to us, to come to us as gift.

Finally, and this is probably the least developed of these implications of Marion's analysis of Descartes, he suggests that it opens a new way to talk about morality, that there is a moral dimension to Descartes' account of the passions that does not get caught in the Kantian version of morality rejected so forcefully by Nietzsche. A morality based in the passions, in the sense of wonder and admiration, might open new avenues of conversation on a topic on which Marion has so far not said very much (as has been repeatedly pointed out by some critics, such as Kevin Hart). Although Marion's account of Descartes here ends in charity, especially love for God, as do so many of his other accounts, he at least suggests that this charity might function as a moral passion, as a supreme virtue. Again, on this point also interesting parallels and connections with Steinbock's work on the moral emotions might become possible.

There are, then, many fruitful avenues of further exploration and dialogue opened by this text. Above all, however, this book might also again remind us not simply to dismiss Marion as a crypto-theologian but to take him seriously as a genuinely *phenomenological* thinker.

*   *   *

I would like to thank my graduate assistant, Ela Tokay, for her diligent work in helping me track down existing English translations of various obscure medieval authors and for proofreading some parts of the

---

42. See also his more recent *Reprise du donné* (Paris: PUF, 2016), especially chapter 2.

manuscript. I am grateful to Stephen Lewis for his advice about some translation choices and a couple of particularly convoluted sentences. I also thank Jay Boggis, who translated the Latin citations for which no English translation existed, and Susan Tarcov for her fantastic copyediting (and for catching any number of embarrassing mistakes). My special gratitude goes to Dylan Montanari from the University of Chicago Press, who helped in manifold ways and tirelessly responded to my countless questions with incomparable speed, patience, and charity. It was a genuine pleasure to work with both Dylan and Susan. An anonymous reviewer also provided useful comments which I have adopted almost without exception. Any remaining mistakes are obviously my own. This is the fifth of Marion's books I have translated—I began with one of his Descartes books and am ending with one. As he says in the preface to this book regarding his writing on Descartes, I hope to *end* here without being *done* with his work.

## Preface

The study of Descartes has attracted, engaged, and occupied me ceaselessly for more than forty years. All the other research I have been able to conduct during these years had to compose its phrases and themes with this underlying basso continuo and ostinato. My repeated and ongoing reading of Descartes has allowed me to enter, through him, into the questions of thought or at least into what I was able to glimpse of them: the theory of the science of the object, the history of *metaphysica*, the constitution of onto-theo-logy, the *différend* between philosophy and theology, the ambivalence of the visible, and even the logic of love. This is indeed the case because Descartes' rhythm of thought contains the sort of sharpness and rigor, frankness and probity, that leads him to face up to the questions at stake without any fabrication or the least affectation. And when he does not find any answers, he turns the questions into aporiae that are sometimes more enlightening than all the misleading subtleties that have been suggested subsequently as refutations or solutions. "Descartes, a venerable, humble and honest thinker, whose writings surely no one can read without the deepest emotion . . . He did not cry, 'Fire!' nor did he make it a duty for everyone to doubt; for Descartes was a quiet and solitary thinker, not a bellowing night-watchman; he modestly admitted that his method had importance for him alone and was justified in part by the bungled knowledge of his earlier years. . . . What those ancient Greeks (who also had some understanding of philosophy) regarded as a task for a whole lifetime, seeing that dexterity in doubting is not acquired in a few days or weeks, what the veteran combatant attained when he had preserved the equilibrium of doubt through all the pitfalls he encountered, who intrepidly denied the certainty of sense-perception and the certainty of the processes of thought, incorruptibly defied the apprehensions of self-love and the insinuations of sympathy—that is where everybody begins in our time."[1] I began with Descartes and today I will try to end with him.

Of course, ending with him is not a matter of being *done with* him. The crowd of minor thinkers attempts this in every generation and truly every time in vain; whereas the great thinkers—from Kant to Heidegger, from Nietzsche to Wittgenstein—have always tried to go back to Descartes, to his questions, his answers, and his aporiae, in order to discover their own path of thought. One must go all the way with him, follow him to the furthest reaches of his investigations. And, as a matter of fact, from the start Descartes had mentioned this final place, the abode of morality, the attitude of *praxis*, the "world of life"—albeit always with worrisome reservations: The *Regulae* open by challenging the idea that the *vitae commoda* (AT X: 364, 4) could justify the study of the sciences, and the first of the *Meditations* still impugns the *cura omnia* (AT VII: 17, 14—18, 1) in order to initiate a scrupulously theoretical doubt. Even so, at the very moment that the *Discourse on Method* establishes precisely both the doubt and the method that creates the sciences, it revisits this negative condition in order to devote a whole third part to it. All the same, in that case it is just a matter of "providing materials" (AT VI: 22, 18) for the purpose of a "provisional morality" (22, 27–28) that could undertake just actions when one is unsure about what to do, namely, implement "judgments" (22, 25). One cannot help but wonder: Does philosophy let the "world of life" lie fallow or does it end up retrieving it and thinking it within the coherence of its apparently purely theoretical logic? Reading Descartes seriously requires responding to this primordial question: Can a place be found for morality and more generally for the attitude of *praxis* within the entirety of

1. Søren Kierkegaard, *Fear and Trembling and The Sickness unto Death*, trans. Walter Lowrie (Princeton: Princeton University Press, 2013), 31–33. Kierkegaard owned a copy of the edition of Descartes' *Opera philosophica* (Amsterdam: Typographia Blaviani, 1692).

the journey of the search for truth? Or is it always just a matter of the search for truth *in the sciences*?

The experience of interpreting Cartesian texts and the repeated consultation of commentaries about them quickly show how rare the readings are that manage to hold all the stages and dimensions of the Cartesian search for truth together. Yet the question "*Quod* vitae *sectabor iter?*—What way *of life* shall I follow?" (AT X: 183, 3) really does concern *life* and really does demand that one finally respond to the question of *praxis*. After having identified a gray ontology, a white theology, and the metaphysical prism that breaks down their light, I must therefore respond to this all-decisive question. That is what it means to end with Descartes.

Paris and Chicago, 3 July 2012[2]

2. I thank Olivier Dubouclez for helping me avoid making too many mistakes in this text.

## Bibliographic Note

References to Descartes are always given according to the edition by Charles Adam and Paul Tannery, *Œuvres de Descartes* (in the new edition by Joseph Beaude, Pierre Costabel, Alan Gabbey, and Bernard Rochot; Paris: J. Vrin-CNRS, 1964–74), 11 volumes (in 13 books). This will be abbreviated by AT, followed by the volume number in Latin numerals, the page and the line number. AT is often omitted when the reference is obvious; the volume number is also mentioned only when a series of references moves from one to another volume.

[English references are given for the three-volume edition of *The Philosophical Writings of Descartes*, translated by John Cottingham, Robert Stoothoff, and Dugald Murdoch (for the third volume also by Anthony Kenny) (Cambridge: Cambridge University Press, 1984–91), abbreviated by CSM I, CSM II, and CSMK, respectively, followed by English pagination. Marion usually cites both Latin and French in his text, occasionally pointing to differences between them. This creates some difficulties, because the English translation—especially for the *Meditations*—usually relies on the Latin text rather than the French translation. Consequently, the existing English translation will on occasion be amended as necessary to reflect the French text and to retain the nuances Marion emphasizes. I have also occasionally added AT and the volume number to distinguish the Adam-Tannery references more clearly from the extra English translation references. Finally, as customary in English-language publications, first names of authors have been supplied rather than just initials, and page ranges and other publication information are added where they are missing in the French.—Trans.]

I depend on the bibliography of the *Bulletin cartésien* [Cartesian report], published by the Centre d'études cartésiennes [Center for Cartesian Studies] (University of Paris-Sorbonne) in the *Archives de philosophie* since 1971 and the volume based on them: Jean-Robert Armogathe and Vincent Carraud (with the collaboration of Michaël Devaux and Massimiliano Savini), *Bibliographie cartésienne (1960–1996)* (Lecce: Conte Editore, 2003). I have often consulted the edition that appeared in three thick volumes from the Bompiani press under the direction of Giulia Belgioioso: *René Descartes. Tutte le Lettere, testo francese, latino e olandese a fronte* (Milan: Bompiani, 2005 and 2009); *René Descartes. Opere 1637–1650, testo francese e latino a fronte* (Milan: Bompiani, 2009); and *René Descartes. Opere postume 1650–2009* (Milan: Bompiani, 2009).

I hope that the somewhat too numerous references to my prior works will be forgiven. It is really just a matter of being concerned about conciseness: I refer to old analyses either to avoid redoing a long demonstration that is presupposed by a new formulation or to correct an old conclusion with a new argument.

# Introduction

## §1. The Delay of Interpretations

*Sentire?*
*Nempe etiam hoc non sit sine corpore.*
**AT VII: 27, 5–6**

Sensing?
This surely does not occur without a body.
**CMS II: 18; trans. modified**

Descartes remained an inaugural thinker to the very end of his career. In fact, up to his final work, *The Passions of the Soul,* he opened questions (even more than answers to these questions) that had never been asked up to this point. In this way, after having established in the *Regulae* the precedence of method over truth itself, after having initiated in the *Meditations* the ego's anteriority as much in existence as in intelligibility, he ended in 1647 by claiming a third priority: "primus *enim* sum *qui cogitationem, tanquam praecipuum attributum substantiae incorporeae, et extensionem, tanquam praecipuum corporeae, consideravi.—I am the first* to have regarded thought as the principal attribute of an incorporeal substance, and an extension as the principal attribute of a corporeal substance."[1] Even so, this final priority gives rise to other difficulties than the former two. These difficulties do have bearing not only on what the thesis leads to but on its very formulation. For the *distinction* of two types of substances, such as predominates in *almost* all of the *Meditations*, results nonetheless in enforcing the *union* of soul and body on all of metaphysics from the second part of the Sixth Meditation onward. It does so with difficulty but definitively. And, in fact, this culminates in leading us to a third "primitive notion," namely that of "the union" of "soul and body together."[2] One cannot fail to be surprised that the supposedly unprecedented discovery of the distinction could (and *must*) lead to what at least apparently contradicts it, namely the union of soul and body. What kind of logic—possibly quite concealed— would allow us to continue to safeguard the coherence of the Cartesian advance? Or is this a matter of definitive incoherence? Besides, what connection should one establish between this difficulty and the thematic of his final work *The Passions of the Soul*? Finally, what link should be maintained between the description and enumeration of the passions and the (definitive or provisional) completion of the ethics that was delayed up to this point? Descartes seems perfectly aware of how serious these questions are because he admits from the outset that he finds himself in an unprecedented situation that forces him to take all the difficulties up again from a point of departure still to be discovered and thus also to have to "write just as if I were considering a matter that no one had dealt with before me."[3]

What is the advance at stake here and in regard to what "matter"? Of course, Descartes had already laid claim to other kinds of progress, that of having been "*primus*—the first" to establish the distinction of substances by their principal attributes and also the fact that "*nemo ante me*—no one before me" had proved that God cannot deceive, and finally that "*a nemine ante me*—never before me" had anyone established the existence of God and the immortality of the soul against the skeptics.[4] But these claims all bore on certainties that are in principle known. Here the priority to which Descartes lays claim bears instead on a difficulty (the inadequacy of the passions in the ancients) or even on

1. *Comments on a Certain Broadsheet*, AT VIII-2: 348, 15–17; CSM I: 297.
2. To Elizabeth, 21 May 1643, II: 665, 21–22 and 10; CSMK: 218. See below, chapter IV, §17.
3. *Passions of the Soul*, §1, XI: 328, 3–5; CSM I: 328; trans. lightly modified.
4. To the Curators of Leiden University, 4 May 1647, AT V: 9, 16; CSMK: 317 and Seventh Set of Replies, VII: 549, 20–21; CSM II: 375, respectively.

a more general aporia ("and incidentally the whole nature of man").[5] Furthermore, while the *Discourse on Method*, the *Meditations*, and obviously the *Principles of Philosophy* certainly know how to reach a precise target with a deliberate aim (the practitioners of the new sciences or the department of theology at the Sorbonne and besides them either the Jesuit colleges or the Oratory, etc.), with the firm hope of convincing or even of mobilizing them, the final work (and without doubt all the writings that prepare it) not only renounces that aspiration but even seems to expect a failure, if not in its demonstration, at least in its reception: "I foresee that this treatise will fare less well than my other writings. Though more people may perhaps be drawn by its title to read it, yet only those who take the trouble to study it with care can possibly be satisfied with it."[6] And, actually, Descartes' final advance was understood neither at the time when he accomplished it, nor at the time of its first reception, nor most probably by its modern interpretation. The "careful" examination, for the most part, still remains to be done. Not that speculative efforts would have been missing or that there was a lack of historical inquiries. To the contrary, it may be that their very number and their vigor had too quickly settled or at least been taken to have settled the preliminary questions that were more essential than their replies acquired from the outset.

Even so, a first pattern should have prompted greater prudence: the sequence that opens with the Sixth Meditation (and especially its second part) and concludes with *The Passions of the Soul* is characterized by an extreme heterogeneity that applies equally to its interlocutors, its polemical contexts, and the vocabularies in which the discussion takes place each time, to the point where it seems to be a matter of several debates that are linked by nothing or almost nothing.

(a) Thus, in 1641 the point is to achieve a metaphysics of nature (a kind of *cosmologia rationalis*) that takes up the essence and the existence of material bodies into the metaphysical grounding of being in general. In this case, the point of view and the vocabulary remain resolutely metaphysical. In a similar way, the immediate reception of the Cartesian theses by the objectors (Hobbes, Arnauld, and Gassendi, soon also Regius) is overwhelmingly made according to the guiding principle of the *substantia*. They do so by privileging the supposed parallelism of soul and body, hence accentuating the confusion between bod*ies* and my body, at

---

5. *Passions of the Soul*, subtitle of the first part, XI: 327, 5; CSM I: 328.

6. *Passions of the Soul*, Preface, "Reply to the Second Letter," XI: 326, 15–20; CSM I: 327.

the very moment when the irreducibility of *my* body to other bodies tries to emerge. And, besides, the limits of the order of reasoning also constrain Descartes successively to undo the distinction of thought from extension and the union of my soul with *my* body, so that they are instead articulated organically and simultaneously. In this way a central core (the link between distinction and union) is dissolved and thus the question for which it serves as symptom is also obscured (chapters 1 and 2).

(b) It even seems that Descartes himself compromises his own theoretical advance. From the very beginning, but especially in its second part, the Sixth Meditation clearly captures the primordial status of my body (*meum corpus*) as irreducible to the other bodies of extension. It does so not only against the indecisiveness of the *Search for Truth* (in 1632) and the *Discourse on Method* (in 1637), but also against the rhetorical excess of the first two Meditations. For they suppose that they are strengthening the certainty of the *ego sum, ego existo* by making it triumph over a doubt that disqualifies even my body (*meum corpus*), yet the hyperbole of this doubt is in fact and by right never accomplished. Here also the progress toward a *corpus meum* is held back, if not obscured, in a different sense (chapter 3).

(c) The confusion over Descartes' very theses will be accentuated by the polemics that Regius first provoked in 1647 and to which he was then subject (coming from Voetius and his lot). Not only does the irrepressible primacy of the semantics of *substantia* compel privileging the distinction over the union, not only does it transform the distinction into a causal aporia that its qualification as occasionalism does not resolve but ossifies in a word; but this semantics forces Descartes himself to retranslate into a useless and uncertain language what he had discovered under the new title *meum corpus* while trying to resist its nevertheless almost inevitable disfigurement. Strange compromises result from this, for example that of a final *forma substantialis*, corresponding to what nevertheless does *not* constitute a third substance (chapter 5).

(d) One can then consider the French vocabulary that he elaborated from 1643 onward in order to respond to the Palatine Princess Elizabeth and to Christina, Queen of Sweden[7] (as also to Chanut and some others) as a resistance to and a discrepancy from the corruption and the deformation that are provoked and maintained by the metaphysical vocabulary of *substantia* and of *causa efficiens*, which the academic

---

7. [I have adopted the Anglicized spellings employed by the English translation *The Philosophical Works*, rather than "Elisabeth" and "Christine" (the French spelling employed by AT) or "Kristina" (the original Swedish).—Trans.]

objectors use exclusively. In this way Descartes attempts a high-stakes recovery of the concepts adapted to what he had sought to think since 1641: the third "primitive notion" and its paradoxical properties (at least in regard to the metaphysical device of the *substantiae*). Yet even there, Descartes' profound speculative intention finds itself compromised or at least distorted by the dialogical context in which it must be displayed. From Elizabeth's (and Christina's) point of view everything takes place within the horizon of morality in the strictest sense: virtue, the highest good, beatitude, autarchy, and self-control (chapter 4). In a sense, Descartes accepts their decision and restricts to this horizon even those aspects of his research that aim elsewhere and further.

In fact, a last movement finally brings to light what already urgently dawned under different forms or concepts: the passivity of thought. For *The Passions of the Soul* do not first of all or only impose a treatise of physiology (except in the first part) or of morality (except in the second part) or even an exhortation to virtue (maybe with the third part); the treatise searches for something else that it enables by accomplishing all of this: namely, to think the *cogitatio* even in its passivity and to think this passivity as a mode of thought as essential as any other. The study of the passions forms only the most obvious manner of a more radical undertaking, one that is not limited to either morality or physiology. It establishes or even reestablishes passivity in the exercise of thought (chapter 6).

Consequently my hypothesis will consist in distinguishing the registers of the concepts, the levels of language, and the contexts of debate or polemic in order to allow the emergence of the "matter that no one before me" had ever attained or formulated—especially not the objectors determined to substitute the problems they do understand (their own) for Descartes' questions (and answers) that they do not understand. Only in this way would one maybe be able to take "the trouble" and provide the "care"[8] that Descartes demands in order to allow the real questions to surface. In order to do this one must begin by *not* raising the problem of the supposed "Cartesian dualism"; even if, as one criticizes it, it does not cease to be reborn in a derived form or in its ancient absurdity. Actually, this "dualism" tries to resolve a question that Descartes takes to be already resolved *in fact*: experience proves to us that soul and body, at least *my* soul and body, are so closely united that certain thoughts modify certain movements, and do so reciprocally. This fact takes the very status of a *factum rationis*, of a fact of

8. *Passions of the Soul*, Preface, "Reply to the Second Letter," XI: 326, 19; CSM I: 327.

reason, because (like others, for example freedom) it is experienced, even though it cannot be comprehended: "*Quod autem mens, quae incorporea est, corpus possit impellere, nulla quidem ratiocinatio vel comparatio ab aliis rebus petita, sed certissima et evidentissima experientia quotidie nobis ostendit; haec enim una est ex rebus per se notis, quas, cum volumus per alias explicare, obscuramus.*—That the mind, which is incorporeal, can set the body in motion is something which is shown to us not by any reasoning or comparison with other matters, but by the surest and plainest everyday experience. It is one of those self-evident things which we only make obscure when we try to explain them in terms of other things."[9] His undertaking thus never aims at explaining an inexplicable correlation. It is, moreover, explicably inexplicable because (like the experience of my freedom of choice in the face of divine omniscience and omnipotence) it puts into play God's infinity, which is by definition incomprehensible to a finite mind. His undertaking tries to find out when to implement this combination and how to use it advisedly. The first point concerns the physiology of *my* body, the second morality. But these two points themselves follow from a third that ends up by appearing as the first: my mind can receive thoughts passively. As to wondering about the supposedly causal relationship between ideas and extended things in general or that between ideas from a supposedly purely sensible origin and those supposedly purely innate (actually the entirely different doctrine of the *code*),[10] or in regard to the inclusion of sensibility itself in representation, these are not Descartes' questions, even if they become very early (most probably from 1641 onward, in any case from 1647) those of his readers, both critical and approving. The at times a bit surprising consensus of the neo-Thomist, empirical, "analytical," and all the other positivist traditions that want to attribute aporiae to Descartes in replies that he did not make to questions that he did not raise does not change anything in the need for a truly cautious reading of his final texts.

I will take up only two hypotheses: First that throughout the diver-

9. To Arnauld, 29 July 1648, AT V: 222, 15–20; CSMK: 358. See, for once, Burman's Conversation with Descartes: "*Hoc explicatu difficillimum; sed sufficit hic experientia, quae hic adeo clara est, ut negari nullo modo possit, ut illud in passionibus etc., apparet.*—This is very difficult to explain; but here our experience is sufficient, since it is so clear on this point that it just cannot be gainsaid. This is evident in the case of the passions, and so on" (16 April 1648, §44, V: 163; CSMK: 346). See below, chapter 3, §16.

10. See my study *Sur la théologie blanche de Descartes. Analogie, création des vérités éternelles et fondement* (Paris: PUF, 1981/2009), §12, 231ff.

sity of the polemics and of the vocabularies in the final period of his work, Descartes pursued in the end only a single issue: to think passivity as the full mode of the *res cogitans*, probably the most difficult mode to define precisely in virtue of its exception in regard to others— that is, its passivity. Here is the definition of the thinking thing, as of yet without substantiality but modeled from the outset: "*Res cogitans. Quid est hoc? Nempe dubitans, intelligens, affirmans, negans, volens, nolens, imaginans, quoque et sentiens.*—A thing that thinks. What is that? A thing that doubts, understands, affirms, denies, is willing, is unwilling, and also imagines and senses." Or: "*Ego sum res cogitans, id est dubitans, affirmans, negans, pauca intelligens, multa ignorans, volens, nolens, imaginans etiam et sentiens.*—I am a thing that thinks: that is, a thing that doubts, affirms, denies, understands a few things, is ignorant of many things, is willing, is unwilling, and also which imagines and senses."[11] One immediately notices especially that the thinking thing never appears only as thinking, neutrally, but always already *in a mode* (just as the extended thing never appears as simply and purely extended, but always as an extension *modified* by some figure or movement): "*Per cogitationem igitur non intelligo universale quid, omnes cogitandi modos comprehendes, sed naturam particularem, quae recipit omnes illos modos, ut etiam extensio est natura, quae recipit omnes figuras.*—So by 'thought' I do not mean some universal which includes all modes of thinking, but a particular nature, which takes on those modes, just as extension is a nature which takes on all shapes."[12] My hypothesis fol-

11. *Meditations*, AT VII: 28, 20–22 and 34, 18–21; CSM II: 19 and 24, trans. lightly modified [replacing "has sensory perception" with the verb "senses" to translate the verbal form *sentiens*].

12. To Arnauld, 29 July 1648, AT V: 221, 21–25; CSMK: 357. An argument that is not anywhere near as clear precedes this affirmation: "I tried to remove the ambiguity of the word 'thought' in articles 63 and 64 of Part One of the *Principles*. Just as extension, which constitutes the nature of body, differs greatly from the various shapes or modes of extension which it assumes, so thought, or a thinking nature, which I think constitutes the essence of the human mind, is very different from any particular act of thinking. It depends on the mind itself whether it produces this or that particular act of thinking, but not that it is a thinking thing; just as it depends on a flame, as an efficient cause, whether it turns to this side or that, but not that it is an extended thing" (221, 10–21; CSMK: 357). One must understand that the *res cogitans* is not a neutral thought that subsequently is diversified into successive individuations, because it is not directly an *as such* thinking *thing* (no more than the extended thing is a thing that is by nature and as such extended), except by being modeled straightaway entirely and without remainder in one of its modes: there is no *natura cogitans*

lows from this: Passive thought makes it possible to reunite the question of union (flesh, *meum corpus*) and the survey of the passions and to prolong this latter into a doctrine of the virtues. The final mode of the *res cogitans* is accomplished in this way.

Finally, I will assume that not only does passive thought ensure the cohesion of the last moment of Cartesian thought (from 1641 to 1650), but also and above all that this last moment, precisely because it is limited to unfolding the final mode of the *cogitatio*—though in its grandest and most radical form—protects and sanctions the unity of Descartes' entire philosophical path. In other words, with this final book I aspire to provide one of the very rare overall interpretations of Descartes' sole and constant *instauratio magna* of metaphysics from the *Regulae* to the *Passions of the Soul,* and to do this by no longer choosing a period or a privileged moment for it.

---

without already a mode, just as there is no *natura extensa* that does not already offer a particular shape. See Leslie J. Beck, "Cogitatio in Descartes," *Rivista di filosofia neo-scolastica*, Suppl. Vol. XXIX, *Cartesio nel terzo centenario del "Discorso del metodo"* (July 1937): 41–52.

# 1

## The Existence of Material Things or the "Scandal of Philosophy"

### §2. The Sixth Meditation as Aporia

The extreme difficulty of the Sixth Meditation strikes or should strike any reader, whether attentive or uninformed. Moreover, even Martial Gueroult, one of Descartes' most fastidious interpreters and also someone very convinced about the perfect coherence of the Cartesian arguments, admits, a bit despite himself, that "Meditation VI completes the unfolding of the chain of reasons. It also presents the maximum of complexity; this is something natural for a final reason, which is necessarily the most composite and most difficult of all the reasons."[1] We will see that this is a correct diagnosis but a very surprising explanation; for it is not at all obvious that the final argument would have to present the greatest complexity, because in contrast Descartes makes clear in 1627, "while our experiences of things are often decep-

1. Martial Gueroult, *Descartes selon l'ordre des raisons*, vol. II, *L'Âme et le Corps* (Paris: Aubier, 1953, 2nd ed. 1968), 7, trans. by Roger Ariew as *Descartes' Philosophy Interpreted According to the Order of Reasons*, vol. II, *The Soul and the Body* (Minneapolis: University of Minnesota Press, 1985), 3. In other words, the "demonstration of the Sixth Meditation consequently becomes very dense." Geneviève Rodis-Lewis, *L'Œuvres de Descartes* (Paris: Vrin, 1970), 347.

tive, the deduction or pure inference of one thing from another can never be performed wrongly by an intellect which is in the least degree rational."[2] Should one not actually expect instead that the final Meditation would benefit from the more solid deductive evidence that all the previously demonstrated truths would in principle assure it? And does not Descartes himself at times at least venture to claim that he has demonstrated the union of soul and body by "arguments . . . as strong as any I can remember ever having read"?[3] Now the immense difficulty of the Sixth Meditation cannot be denied if only because it demands from one canonical commentator [namely, Gueroult] all by itself an explanation as long as that of the first five, as if the final move to the last question, that of corporeality, would alter the entire scheme not only of the *Meditations* but of the entire Cartesian cartage. It is even more surprising that this extreme and intensified particularity has not been taken into account inasmuch as Descartes in his customary frankness did not fail to admit it or even to underline it by any number of quite obvious hints.

Thus he admits that one would gain no benefit from reading the *Meditations* "if one does not dedicate whole days and even weeks of meditating on the same matters that I have treated." As such a requirement may seem "quite awful," Descartes immediately qualifies the assumption of such a rigorous timeframe: "I would say: if one does not take at least the trouble to read the first five Meditations in one breath with my literal response at the end and come up with a summary of the main conclusions in order to be able better to notice what follows."[4] Negatively speaking, corporeality also sometimes seems excluded from what the *Meditations* demonstrate: "For I draw a comparison between my work in this area [i.e., in metaphysics] and the demonstrations of Apollonius. Everything in the latter is really very clear and certain, when each point is considered separately; but because the proofs are rather long, and one cannot see the necessity of the conclusion unless one remembers exactly everything that has gone before, you will hardly find a single person in an entire country who is capable of understanding them. Nevertheless, because those few who do understand them vouch

2. Regula II: "*Notandum insuper, experientias rerum saepe esse fallaces, deductionem vero, sive illationem puram unius ab altero, posse quidem omitti, si non videatur, sed nunquam male fieri ab intellectu vel minimum rationali*" (AT X: 365, 2–6; CSM I: 12).

3. "*ususque sum rationibus, quibus non memini me ullas ad idem probandum fortiores alibi legisse*" (AT VII: 228, 3–5; CSM II: 160).

4. To Huygens, 12 November 1640, AT III: 241, 12—242, 6; untranslated in CSMK.

for their truth, everyone believes them. Similarly, I think that I have fully demonstrated the existence of God and the non-material nature of the human soul."[5] This is a curious omission: Why treat the first five Meditations and the Replies to the Objections as a whole (we know that these were in fact printed and sent to the other objectors together with the *Meditations* themselves) but leave out the last one, although it was also printed, along with the question of the existence of corporeality?[6] And, more generally, why does the title of the *Meditations* mention only two poles (the *mens*/mind and God), even though the commentators concur in recognizing three: "three kinds of fundamental existences . . . : the existence of my mind (in Meditation II), the existence of God (in Meditation III), and the existence of bodies (in Meditation VI)"?[7] Does the Sixth Meditation have a special status? Must it be excluded from the concise reading of the order of reasoning, from the *motus cogitationis* that deploys and maintains a sole gaze (a single *intuitus*) across the deduction of arguments that it brings back to a sole certainty by dint of meditative repetitions? And in this case how will it connect with the first five Meditations? Or is it despite everything instead in line with one continuous argument?[8]

5. To Huygens, 31 July 1640, AT III: 751, 22—752, 3; CSMK: 150.

6. See To Mersenne, 24 December 1640: "But I am astonished that you promise me the objections of various theologians [the future Second Set of Replies, which were actually edited by Mersenne himself] within a week, because I was sure that it would take longer to take note of all the contents. This was also the opinion of the man who made the objections at the end [Caterus, First Set of Replies]. . . . You should also please warn the printer to alter the numbers in his objections by which the pages of the *Meditations* are cited, to make them agree with the printed pages" (AT III: 265, 16–27; CSMK: 163). And: "So I have put Caterus' objections at the end, to show where any others which come might be placed." (267, 8–10; CSMK: 164.)

7. Gueroult, *Descartes' Philosophy*, II: 3, trans. lightly modified.

8. A different argument in favor of a rupture or at least of a suspension of the order of reasoning *before* the demonstration of material things could be read in the *Discourse on Method*. At the point of beginning the fifth part and without having provided metaphysical certainty of this existence in the fourth (as has often been pointed out), Descartes justifies himself precisely via the interruption of the order of reasoning due to the order of the subject-matter: "I would gladly go on and reveal the whole chain of other truths that I deduced from these first ones. But in order to do this I would have to discuss many *questions that are being debated among the learned*, and I do not wish to quarrel with them" (AT VI: 40, 21–27; CSM I: 131). Étienne Gilson comments by citing a remark that actually means the opposite and through this contrast underlines the abrupt change of order in 1637: "But the difficulties of physics . . . are all so linked and

In fact, Descartes offers at least one hypothesis in order to explain this fracture between the first Meditations and the last. In order to justify that the Second Meditation does not prove that "the soul is really distinct from the body," but is limited to showing that one can "conceive it without the body," he underlines that the distinction relies on a conclusion for which the premises are found only "in the Sixth Meditation." Now, immediately after this comment, he introduces the maybe too celebrated distinction of the two orders of philosophical thought. Moreover, this functions as a hapax legomenon for the entire work: "It should be noted that throughout the work the order I follow is not the order of the subject-matter, but the order of the reasoning. This means that I do not attempt to say in a single place everything relevant to a given subject, because it would be impossible for me to provide proper proofs, since my supporting reasons would have to be drawn in some cases from considerably more distant sources than in others. Instead I reason in an orderly way from what is easier to what is harder (*a facilioribus ad difficiliora*), making what deductions I can, now on one subject, now on another."[9] Two insights can be drawn from this. First, that according to the order of reasoning the final Meditation offers the exemplary case of *difficiliora*, of truths that are more difficult to discover, the truths one finds only in the end, despite the fact that or rather *because* they manifest in turn the final truth at which the entire chain of arguments aims. Second, and especially, that the deduction of these *difficiliora* can alternatively concern several "matters" and not only one of them. That seems paradigmatically the case in the Sixth Meditation, which in fact treats two quite distinct questions, "the existence of material things and the real distinction between mind and body."[10]

A very strange situation indeed is that of the Sixth Meditation, which is defined as an apparently (and maybe really) incoherent project, for

---

interdependent that it would be impossible for me to give the solution to one without giving the solution to all" (To Mersenne, 15 April 1630, AT I: 140, 24–28; CSMK: 22). As to the *Principles of Philosophy*, the question of their splitting of the two orders is raised in such a radical manner (and has been discussed for a long time) that it is almost useless to insist on it: the existence of material things finds itself reported in the second part, in a break from the repetition of the order in the *Meditations*, which according to the most benign hypothesis is itself interrupted already in the first part, most probably by the treatise on substance (I, §50ff.) and surely by the theory of distinctions (I, §60ff.).

9. To Mersenne, 24 December 1640, AT III: 266, 9–25; CSMK: 163.

10. The doubling of titles (that one "should notice") in the *Meditations* is confirmed by the Letter to Mersenne, 28 January 1641, AT III: 297, 19–30; CSMK: 172.

even its title announces an obvious duality: "*De rerum materialium existentia et reali mentis a corpore distinctione*—The existence of material things and the real distinction between mind and body."[11] But it is actually not simply a matter of a title here (as in the First and Fourth Meditations) or of a title that is doubled in order to be explained (as in the Second Meditation, where the nature of the human mind is explained by the fact that its knowledge precedes that of the body, and the Third Meditation, where existence works out a perfection of God's essence), or even of a double development "sometimes for one matter, sometimes for another" (as in the Fifth Meditation, which inserts the a priori demonstration of the existence of God in the middle of the consideration of the essence of material things, following a double chiasmus of God with matter and of essence with existence). There is an exclusive duality at stake, a contradiction of something that "is absurd,"[12] opposing the existence of material things to the real distinction of body and soul. The title or possibly even the body of the text, as we will see, never notes the link between these two questions, or at least never explicitly. This inexplicable juxtaposition all the more raises several questions from the outset.

First, do the "material things" include the "body" or not? Does the body in question, this body that is so specific that what is at stake is in fact and *by right* nothing less than *my* body, belong to the realm of "material things" like a little territory in a much larger province, or does it constitute a domain that is irreducibly other and obeys different principles? In short, does *this* body, *my* body, count among the "material things" or not? Second, does the first question (the existence of material things) explain the following one (the real distinction between my mind and my body) as a consequence or particular application, or does it instead depend on it, presuppose it, and find its solution only with this latter question? Moreover, one finds an obvious symptom of such an indecisiveness regarding order (anyway, is it *in this case* a matter of the order of the subject-matter or that of reasoning?) of the Sixth Meditation (and its title) in the summary that the Synopsis gives of it: in the body of the text the existence of material things[13] *precedes* the

11. AT VII: 71, 11–12; CSM II: 50.

12. To Elizabeth, 28 June 1643: "It does not seem to me that the human mind is capable of forming a very distinct conception of both the distinction between the soul and the body and their union; for to do this it is necessary to conceive them as a single thing and at the same time to conceive them as two things; and this is absurd." AT III: 693, 21–26; CSMK: 227.

13. Developed in AT VII: 71, 13—80, 10; CSM II: 50–55.

consideration of the relationship between mind and body,[14] while in the summary everything is reversed, because it indicates first the relationship between mind and body (*"In sexta denique . . . mentem realiter a corpore distingui probatur*—in the Sixth Meditation . . . the mind is proved to be really distinct from the body") and then, clearly *afterward*, the existence of material things (*"et denique rationes omnes ex quibus rerum materialium existentia possit concludi, afferuntur*—and, *lastly*, there is a presentation of all the arguments which enable the existence of material things to be inferred").[15] In short, one cannot avoid wondering whether the existence of corporeal things is shown after my body in connection with my mind or whether this connection takes its place in the corporeal things that already exist without it? What order, or rather orders, are at stake here, that of reasoning or that of subject-matter?

Yet there is more: After these two ambiguities regarding the connection between the two questions broached by the Sixth Meditation, there are two other uncertainties, each concerning one of the two terms and producing two further difficulties. The third difficulty concerns the relationship of mind to body: Is the issue one of establishing their distinction or rather their union? For the texts seem to limit themselves to juxtaposing one and the other without any transition: *"mentem realiter a corpore* distingui *probatur; eandum* nihilominus *tam arcte ille esse* conjunctam, *ut unum quid cum ipsa componat, ostenditur*—the mind is proved to be really *distinct* from the body, but is shown, *notwithstanding*, to be so closely *joined* to it that the mind and the body make up a kind of unity."[16] Besides, it is not a question only of comprehend-

14. Developed in AT VII: 80, 11—90, 16; CSM II: 56–62.

15. AT VII: 15, 20–22 and 15, 26–27, respectively; CSM II: 11. (Gueroult mentions the text of the Synopsis without becoming aware of the fact that it inverts the order of the title in the body of the Sixth Meditation. Gueroult, *Descartes selon l'ordre des raisons*, II: 8, note 7; *Descartes' Philosophy*, II: 265, note 7.)

16. Synopsis, AT VII: 15, 21–24 = AT IX-1: 11–12; CSM II: 11. This "notwithstanding" explicates the enigma of "at the same time/*simul*" employed elsewhere: *"Nam in eadem sexta Meditatione, in qua egi de distinctione mentis a corpore,* simul *etiam probavi substantialiter illi esse unitam; ususque sum rationibus, quibus non memini me ullas ad idem probandum fortiores alibi legisse—*For in the Sixth Meditation, where I dealt with the distinction between the mind and the body, I also proved *at the same time* that the mind is substantially united with the body. And the arguments which I used to prove this are as strong as any I can remember ever having read" (*Fourth Replies*, AT VII: 227, 25—228, 5; CSM II: 160). Let me point out that this juxtaposition of contraries corrects the repetition of the title of the Sixth Meditation: *"De reali* mentis *a* corpore

ing how (or *whether*) the distinction agrees with the union, but whether Descartes attempts to establish the same thing with the distinction that governs the Sixth Meditation as what he will definitely call the "union of the soul with the body" in 1643.[17] In short, is the point to establish a distinction between soul and body (subject to determining whether it arises from material things or not) or rather a union? And if both have to be maintained, what union and what distinction can one establish between the union and the distinction of the soul and the body?[18]

The fourth difficulty amounts to demanding whether the proof for the existence of material things really has true value as proof in Descartes' eyes, in the sense in which the Second and Third Meditations (reinforced by the Fifth) had demonstrably established the ego's and God's existence. In fact, the Synopsis uses an entirely surprising and ambiguous formulation: "And, lastly, there is a presentation of all the arguments which enable the existence of material things to be inferred. The great benefit of these arguments is not, in my view, that they prove what they establish—namely that there really is a world, and that human beings have bodies and so on—since no sane person has ever seriously doubted these things. The point is that in considering these arguments we come to realize that they are not as solid or as transparent (*perspicuas*) as the arguments which lead us to knowledge of our own

---

*distinctione, quam demum in sexta Meditatione perfeci*—that there is a real distinction between *the mind* and *the body*, which I finally established in the Sixth Meditation" (226, 25-26; CSM II: 159). The *three* (rather than two) titles that Gueroult attributes to the Sixth Meditation only reinforce the difficulty, far from resolving it or even confronting it: "We must first consider, as the title of the Meditation indicates, that the Meditation intends to prove the existence of material things. . . . We must then recognize—and the title of the Meditation also indicates this—that the Meditation intends to prove the real distinction of body and soul. . . . We must finally recognize—*even though the title does not mention this*—that the Meditation intends to establish the substantial union of soul and body . . ." (*Descartes' Philosophy*, II: 3-4; emphasis added). Yet why justify three questions, two of which apparently contradict each other, when the title mentions only two?

17. To Elizabeth, 21 May 1643, AT III: 666, 21; CSMK: 218.

18. On this point I am following Thierry Gontier's excellent diagnosis: "We start from a paradox: It is in the same movement of demonstration that the Sixth Meditation establishes two truths that are apparently contradictory, namely the distinction between soul and body and their union," in Delphine Kolesnik-Antoine, ed., *Union et distinction de l'âme et du corps. Lectures de la VIe Méditation* (Paris: Kimé, 1998), 83.

minds and of God."[19] One can probably underplay the surprise by reflecting on the fact that already in the Second Meditation it is only a
matter of establishing that the existence (and the essence) of the mind is
known better (*notior*) than that of the body; and that in the Third Meditation it is a matter of establishing that the perception of the infinite
precedes (*prior quodammodo in me*) my own. All the same, nowhere
else did Descartes ever declare one of his proofs (and what is more, the
proof of existence) to lack in evidence and certainty or even to be use-

19. Synopsis, AT IX-1: 12 = AT VII: 15, 26—16, 5; CSM II: 11. "*Et denique
rationes omnes ex quibus rerum materialium existentia possit concludi, afferuntur: non quod eas valde utiles esse putarim ad probandum id ipsum quod
probunt, nempe revera esse aliquem mundum, et homines habere corpora, et
similia, de quibus nemo unquam sanae mentis serio dubitavit; sed quia, illas
considerando, agnoscitur non esse tam firmas nec tam perspicuas quam sunt
eae, per quas in mentis nostrae et Dei cognitionem devenimus.*" Moreover, what
link should one establish between this "nemo sanae mentis" and the "amentes"
of the First Meditation (AT VII: 19, 5; CSM II: 13, a question raised by the letter
to Hyperaspistes, August 1641, AT III: 423, 1; untranslated in CSMK)? Other
texts confirm the same reservation about the import of this demonstration of
existence. For example in 1637: "Finally, if there are still people who are not
sufficiently convinced of the existence of God and of their soul by the arguments I have proposed I would have them know that everything else of which
they may think themselves more sure—such as their having a body, there being
stars and an earth, and the like—is less certain. For although we have a moral
certainty about these things, so that it seems we cannot doubt them without being extravagant, nevertheless when it is a question of metaphysical certainty, we
cannot reasonably deny that there are adequate grounds for not being entirely
sure about them. We need only observe that in sleep we may imagine in the same
way that we have a different body and see different stars and a different earth,
without there being any of these things" (AT VI: 37, 24—38, 9; CSM I: 129-30;
a distinction that is confirmed by AT VII: 459, 25—460, 12; CSM II: 308). In
1641, the *Fifth Replies* comment on exactly the same passage in the Synopsis:
"*Sed advertenda est distinctio, variis in locis a me inculcata, inter actiones vitae
et inquisitionem veritatis; cum enim de regenda vita quaestio est, ineptum sane
esset sensibus non credere, planeque ridendi fuerunt illi Sceptici qui res humanas
eo usque negligebant, ut, ne se in praecipitia conjicerent, de amicis deberent as-
servari; atque idcirco alicubi* [AT VII: 16, 2-3] *admonui, neminem sanae mentis
de talibus serio dubitare.*—However, we must note the distinction which I have
insisted on in several passages, between the actions of life and the investigation
of the truth. For when it is a question of organizing our life, it would, of course,
be foolish not to trust the senses, and the skeptics who neglected human affairs
to the point where friends had to stop them falling off precipices deserved to be
laughed at. Hence I pointed out in one passage [namely CSM II: 11] that *no sane
person ever seriously doubts such things.*" AT VII: 350, 21—351, 6; CSM II:
243; emphasis added.

less: there are thus not three proofs of existence that are equal or three proofs of an equal existence. Is this a rhetorical precaution of apparent modesty, of negligence in a last-minute text? Or does Descartes here, frank as he almost always is, say exactly what he wants to say and really thinks? And in that case, in what sense does the final demonstration of existence, that of "material things," really suffer from a theoretical weakness? And what sort of weakness?

The longest and subtlest expositions of the Sixth Meditation, even the masterpieces that are the most systematic (Gueroult) or analytical (Ryle and innumerable others following him), do not lead to anything, but aggravate the confusion, because they do not seriously identify these difficulties and do not confront them: namely, (a) the equivocal nature of *body*, (b) the order between the question of the existence of the world and that of the connection between my body and my mind, (c) the distinction or the union of the union and the distinction, and, finally, (d) the certainty of the proof of the existence of material things. I will here attempt to name them so as possibly to manage to think them.

## §3. Kant's Critique

The final difficulty of all the ones just enumerated, which in retrospect garners the greatest attention, is the one that concerns the certainty of the proof of the existence of material things. Strangely enough, it raises no serious objection from the main examiners of the *Meditations*, who instead focus on the distinction between mind and body. In a sense, after the Sixth Elucidation that Malebranche added to the second edition of his *Search After Truth* (in 1678), one must wait quite a bit, namely, for more than a century, for someone to call this into question. In a famous note in the Preface to the *Critique of Pure Reason* (1787), Kant calls the proof for the existence of material things "outside of us"—as Descartes was most probably the first to formulate it—into question explicitly.

First of all it is an indirect questioning that occurs within a larger framework of a "new refutation of psychological idealism, and a strict proof (the only possible one, I believe) of the objective reality of outer intuition. No matter how innocent idealism may be held to be as regards the essential ends of metaphysics (though in fact it is not so innocent), it always remains a scandal of philosophy and universal human reason that the existence (*Dasein*) of things outside us (from which we after all get the whole matter for our cognitions, even for our inner sense) should have to be assumed merely on *faith*, and that if it occurs to anyone to doubt it, we should be unable to answer him with a satisfactory proof."[20] Yet this calling into question quickly becomes direct when in the "Refutation of Idealism," which already in the second edition of the *Critique* interrupts the course of the "Postulates of Empirical Thinking in General," Kant clarifies: "Idealism (I mean *material* idealism) is the theory that declares the existence (*Dasein*) of objects in space outside us to be either merely doubtful and *indemonstrable*, or else false and *impossible*; the *former* is the *problematic* idealism of Descartes [*Cartesius*], who declares only one empirical assertion (*assertio*), namely *I am*, to be indubitable; the latter is the *dogmatic* idealism of *Berkeley*, who declares space, together with all the things to which it is attached as an inseparable condition, to be something that is impossible in itself, and who therefore also declares things in space to be merely imaginary."[21]

Should this refutation occupy the attention of a rigorous historian of Cartesian philosophy or does it have importance only within Kantian criticism as one of its negative consequences? We will examine this. Yet from the outset we can assume that Kant was perfectly right to denounce the Cartesian "scandal" because his objection is found as if reinforced by a real tradition up to and including Husserl: "The being of the world, by reason of the evidence of natural experience, must no longer be for us an obvious matter of fact; it too must be for us, henceforth, only an acceptance-phenomenon."[22] In this sense phenomenology sanc-

20. Kant, *Kritik der reinen Vernunft*, B xxxix, trans. Paul Guyer as *Critique of Pure Reason* (Cambridge: Cambridge University Press, 1998), 121; henceforth page numbers refer to the German original, followed by the English translation. On this "scandal" for Kant, see Luigi Caranti, *Kant and the Scandal of Philosophy: The Kantian Critique of Cartesian Skepticism* (Toronto: University of Toronto Press, 2007), and Rolf Zimmermann, *Der "Skandal der Philosophie" und die Semantik: Kritische und systematische Untersuchungen zur analytischen Ontologie und Erfahrungstheorie* (Freiburg: K. Alber, 1981). Neither pays any attention at all to Descartes' own thesis.

21. Kant, *Critique of Pure Reason*, B 274; 326. Regarding this Kantian polemic against Descartes, see the valuable information provided by Vincent Carraud, "L'esistenza dei corpi è un principio della fisica cartesiana?" in Jean-Robert Armogathe, Giulia Belgioioso, eds., *Descartes: Principia philosophiae (1644–1994)* (Naples: Vivarium, 1996), 160ff.

22. Edmund Husserl, *Cartesianische Meditationen*, §7, *Husserliana. Gesammelte Werke*, vol. I (The Hague: Nijhoff, 1950), 58, henceforth abbreviated as *Hua*, trans. Dorion Cairns as *Cartesian Meditations* (The Hague: Martinus Nijhoff, 1960), 18. The title of §7 "The evidence for the factual existence of the world not apodictic; its inclusion in the Cartesian overthrow" shows that this is an explicit reference to Descartes. This question can be found again in the final "Cartesian" moment of the *Meditations*, §42, *Hua* 121; 89. (This text will be studied further below, §9, 55.)

tions Kant's objection by conferring on it a role that is much more than just a corollary of the critique of dogmatism. It acknowledges it as the symptom of a general and crucial failure of all of classical metaphysics, namely, its incapacity to envision the problem of the world and its way of being in opposition to the way of being of the realm of consciousness. The 1913 idealist turn in phenomenology has the precise function of raising the hypothesis of metaphysical idealism (whether it is problematic or dogmatic—the difference matters little in the end). One could even say that a large part of the development of post-Husserlian phenomenology can be explained as resuming and overcoming the solution that Husserl himself proposed and that was quickly judged insufficient, as if it were a false Cartesian demonstration, itself raised by a radically insufficient approach to the problem of the world: The connection of the subject (whether transcendental or not) to the external world proceeds not through the efficient causality of mental representations but via intentionality, which is itself unfolded via passive synthesis, being in the world or "the flesh of the world." Once more, all proceeds from one of "Descartes' mistakes."[23]

Even so, another comment needs to be added: Kant—and hence all who take up his quarrel—could denounce the "scandal" of the insufficiency of the Cartesian proof of the existence of material things "outside of us" only by admitting Descartes' own presupposition, namely, that the existence of material things "outside of us" is precisely what needs to be demonstrated, thus that it is not imposed by itself and by the things themselves, but must come from the supposed "interior" of the *I* or the thinking ego, alone really able to deduce them. In this sense Kant lacks at least the phenomenon of the world, the world as phenomenon,

23. This very formulation is taken up again for a different question, that of the *commercium mentis et corporis* by Robert Richardson, who anticipates my conclusion: "The only scandal in this whole matter is the failure of commentators to see the force of Descartes' reply." "The 'Scandal' of Cartesian Interactionism," *Mind* 91 (1982): 268 (see below, 78, note 67). In contrast, Anthony Kenny in *Descartes: A Study of His Philosophy* (New York: Random House, 1968), 224, and Bernard Williams, who speaks of "the scandal of Cartesian interactionism" in his *Descartes: The Project of Pure Enquiry* (London/New York: Routledge, 1978 and 2005), 273, do not hesitate to take up the antinomy. Must one go back all the way to Hume, who already speaks of the "monstrous offspring of two principles which are contradictory to each other," of an "absurdity," and of "a kind of indignity to philosophy," in *A Treatise of Human Nature*, ed. Sir Lewis Amherst Selby-Bigge with text revisions by Peter Harold Nidditch (Oxford: Clarendon, 1978), Book I, Part IV, Section 2, 205 and 188, then Book I, Part IV, Section 5, 250. [All citations given in English in the original.]

as much as Descartes, because they share the intention and the concern to demonstrate their existence *from outside of them* under the figure of the existence of "*external* things." To what are these things posited as external, if not more essentially external to themselves, in opposition to the I or the ego, which is alone in itself and hence internal to itself? And therefore another question emerges from behind the obvious difficulty that the polemic between these two privileges, one that is crucial for the two protagonists: How is the *interior* defined (maybe in an internal sense—obviously in several senses) in regard to which the exterior of the existence of things that are reputedly external could be conceived? And one can thus anticipate that it is not self-evident that Kant achieves this as successfully as Descartes does.

## §4. Three Weaknesses in the Demonstration of the Existence of Material Things

In what, then, does this "scandal" consist? By right, there would not have been any scandal if Descartes had just admitted the "doubtful and *unprovable*" character of the existence of material things. The entire skeptical approach not only admits but proclaims that we have no sure knowledge of the essence of things or even of their simple existence. It is enough to refer to Hume here, who limited himself to noting this doubled weakness as a fact without seeing or denouncing any scandal in it: "Thus the skeptic continues to reason and believe, even tho' he asserts, that he cannot defend his reason by reason; and by the same rule he must assent to the principle concerning the existence of body, tho' he cannot pretend by any arguments of philosophy to maintain its veracity. . . . We may well ask, *What causes induce us to believe in the existence of body?* but 'tis in vain to ask, *Whether there be a body or not?* That is a point, which we must take for granted in all our reasonings."[24] Such an acknowledgment can disappoint or dishearten but there is nothing scandalous about it, at least not for Hume. If Kant is scandalized by it, it must be because he is thinking of a completely different weakness. And, actually, if the Cartesian proof can scandalize legitimately, it is not at all because it fails but to the contrary because it claims to have succeeded, that is to say, to have provided a certain argument in support of the existence of the things of the external world, at the very moment when its failure stands out in multiple quite obvious ways. Leibniz' harsh diagnosis cuts to the chase here: "The argument by which Descartes seeks to

24. Hume, *Treatise of Human Nature*, Book I, Part IV, Section 2, 187.

demonstrate that material things exist is weak; it were better therefore not to try."[25] Before claiming to judge the relevance of Kant's critique, we must therefore first clearly uncover the motives for this "scandal," that is, to show no fewer than three entirely obvious weaknesses in the supposed demonstration Descartes puts forward.

Here is the actual argument: The ideas of material things come to the mind via a passive faculty that senses them, which thus presupposes an active faculty that produces them, one that in turn can only consist in the action of a substance exercising an efficient causality: "*quaedam activa . . . facultas istas ideas producendi vel efficiendi*—also an active faculty . . . which produced or brought about these ideas" (AT VII: 79, 10–11 = AT IX-1: 63; CSM II: 55). One still needs to identify the one that best suits the effects in question, that is, sensible ideas (sensations) representing material things (AT VII: 78, 21—79, 11; CSM II: 54–55). In order to decide between the candidates, the presumed demonstration chooses *to reason by a process of elimination*—that is the first weakness. In fact, it begins by envisioning three (and only three) hypotheses: either a faculty in me but unknown to me, or God directly, or, finally, "*corpus, sive natura corporea*—a body or a corporeal nature" (VII: 79, 19 = IX-1: 63; CSM II: 55; trans. modified). Then it eliminates the first two in order to validate the third: the ideas of corporeal things are caused in us by corporeal things. This type of reasoning must be confronted with three objections: (a) It reaches its presumed result only indirectly[26] without ever positively giving the least evidence for this final existence, in contrast to what is accomplished for the evidence for the ego (supported by the action of my *cogitatio*) and for that of God (supported by the idea of the infinite in me). Thus, strictly speaking, the proof for the existence of corporeal things does not *demonstrate* any existence, but is limited to inferring it without making it manifest

25. "*Infirmum est argumentum quo Cartesius demonstrare conatur res materiales existere; praestabat igitur non tentare.*" Leibniz, *Animadversiones in partem generalem Principiorum Cartesianorum*, Ad II, §1, in *Die philosophischen Schriften*, ed. Carl J. Gerhardt (Berlin: Weidmannsche Buchhandlung, 1880; Hildesheim: Olms, 1965), IV: 366, trans. George Martin Duncan in *The Philosophical Works of Leibnitz* (New Haven: Tuttle, Morehouse and Taylor, 1890), 58.

26. Gilson underlines this clearly: "And one sees at the same time what *indirect* certainty we obtain of its existence [i.e., that of the external world] and what complete absence of a guarantee, when one takes it on its own terms, the simple memory of such a certainty [i.e., of divine veracity] presents." *Études sur le rôle de la pensée médiévale dans la formation du système cartésien* (Paris: Vrin, 1930/1967), 242.

or producing the least evidence for it. It therefore does not attain the level of certainty of the two first demonstrations of existence and does not lead to a clear and distinct idea. Assuming that one would finally admit the existence of material things, one would all the same never see it directly. In this way this supposed third proof of existence thus suffers from a radical epistemological degradation in comparison to the first two. It is a matter of "shaky reasoning," as in the case of the Greeks for reaching matter, not at all of certain and evident knowledge, i.e., certain *through evidence*. The most positive reply to the Cartesian argument thus already and definitely implies that the result it assumes it has achieved is deficient in certainty. In order to experience the difficulty of the Sixth Meditation there is hence no need to contest its conclusion: it is enough to *admit* it.

But there is a further objection: (b) This reasoning assumes three hypotheses and comes to a conclusion by the elimination of the first two. Now, even if one were to admit this indirect, blind, and corrupt conclusion, a different mistake would discredit it: How does one know that there are only three hypotheses, neither more nor less? Leibniz points to this flaw: "it ought to have been shown that the enumeration is sufficient."[27] First, Descartes himself suggests a fourth substance in other places, which exercises the faculty producing ideas: "*vel aliqua creatura corpore nobilior*—or some creature more noble than a body" (VII: 79, 21 = IX-1: 63, 16–17; CSM II: 55), in this case, an angel, an intermediary between God and myself. Yet, even if one does not insist on this supplemental hypothesis, why set aside the hypothesis of a reality that would be neither me nor a transcendent God nor a sensing or extended body (as for Gassendi and Hobbes), but a cause that would be neither extended nor thinking? And, anyway, was this final solution not that of Spinoza, for whom *substantia* goes beyond the two attributes that are known to us? Only the exhaustiveness of the hypotheses would make selecting by elimination logically correct, and such exhaustiveness is never proved or even evoked.[28] (c) Finally, the argument quickly and without genuine discussion eliminates the hypotheses according to which I myself or God would be the cause. Now is it self-evident that they could not be defended and are obviously absurd? Did not Leibniz choose the solution that the ego could spontaneously cause its perceptions of external bodies without deception, with neither doors

---

27. "*Sed ostendendum erat enumerationem esse sufficientem*." Leibniz, *Animadversiones*, Ad. II, §4, 367; *Philosophical Works*, 59.

28. Gueroult seems to suspect this difficulty in *Descartes' Philosophy*, II: 73.

nor windows?[29] Did not Berkeley maintain that God could cause the ideas of material things directly in the human mind without deception or existing matter? These two hypotheses do not simply fall of their own accord. Quite the opposite, they can be confirmed by conceptual systems of the greatest rigor. Their perfunctory elimination by the Sixth Meditation is thus not self-evident.

A second weakness then appears in the very effort of the demonstration to justify the privilege of the final hypothesis (of *res corporae* causing the ideas of corporeal things) by one (and only one) positive argument, namely, our *"magna propensio*—very great inclination" (VII: 79, 28–29 = IX-1: 63; CSM II: 55; trans. modified) to believe accordingly that only corporeal things can and must cause the ideas of these things. But what epistemological validity can one admit for this *propensio*? By what right can one set it up as a clear and distinct idea and thus give it a place in the order of reasoning? If one sticks with Descartes' own uses of this notion (if not of this concept), one would have to disqualify it. (a) If I note *"quam* prona *sit mea mens in errores*—how my mind has weaknesses and tendencies that carry it unawares into error" (VII: 31, 29 = IX-1: 25; CSM II: 21, trans. altered to correspond to the French), I must conclude from this that this inclination first of all prompts to error. (b) Besides, the propensity is clearly opposed to clarity and distinctness as an impulse is opposed to a judgment: *"me non hactenus ex certo judicio, sed tantum ex caeco aliquo impulsu, credidisse res quasdam a me diversas existere*—that it is not a reliable judgement but merely some blind impulse that has made me believe up till now that there exist things distinct from myself" (VII: 39, 30—40, 2 = IX-1: 31; CSM II: 27). The impulse (of the *propensio*) thus is here a matter of belief and, let me emphasize this, especially of the belief in the existence of corporeal things.[30] It has no argumentative value at all for establishing this

29. Descartes himself seems to envision this possibility at least once in the course of the a posteriori demonstration of the existence of God: *"Caetera autem omnia ex quibus rerum corporearum ideae conflantur, nempe extensio, figura, situs et motus, in me quidem, cum nihil aliud sim quam res cogitans, formaliter non continentur; sed quia sunt tantum modi quidam substantiae, ego autem substantia, videntur in me contineri posse eminenter.*—As for all the other elements which make up the ideas of corporeal things, namely extension, shape, position and movement, these are not formally contained in me, since I am nothing but a thinking thing; but since they are merely modes of a substance, and I am a substance, it seems possible that they are contained in me eminently" (VII: 45, 3–8 = IX-1: 35; CSM II: 31).

30. See: *"Cum hic dico me ita doctum esse a natura, intelligo tantum* spontaneo quodam impetu *me ferri ad hoc credendum, non lumine aliquo naturali*

thesis. (c) But could one not for the benefit of the propensity invoke the rule that "*ex magna luce in intellectu magna consequuta est* propensio *in voluntate*—a great light in the intellect was followed by a great inclination in the will" (VII: 59, 1–3 = IX-1: 47; CSM II: 41)? Would not the inclination in this conjunction, where the *propensio* goes together with the *intellectus*, take on a more reliable epistemological dignity? This is obviously not the case, because in contrast the *propensio* is distinguished all the more clearly from the *intellectus* as it should in principle ensue from it: Actually at stake is not the light of the understanding but an inclination of the will. Now this pure power of choice taken as such (*"in se formaliter et praecise"*) and without considering the *ratio cognitionis* (VII: 57, 20) can justly (or *un*justly) also *not* follow the light of the understanding to the point of sometimes contradicting even present evidence under certain conditions.[31] (d) Furthermore, in order to alleviate any ambiguity, it is enough to note that the *corporeae propensiones* do not provoke clear and distinct ideas, but passions (like cheerfulness, sadness, anger, etc., VII: 74, 26; CSM II: 52). For these reasons at least, the *propensio* cannot assume the function of an indisputable argument according to Descartes' own meaning and purposes.[32]

---

*mihi ostendi esse verum*—all I mean is that a spontaneous impulse leads me to believe it, not that its truth has been revealed to me by some natural light" (VII: 38, 23–27; CSM II: 26–27). But immediately thereafter, the condemnation is broadened to all the *"impetus naturales*—natural impulses" (39, 1–2; CSM II: 27), which I may "in no way" trust.

31. See To Mesland, 2 May 1644 and 9 February 1645 (AT IV: 116, 6–15; CSMK: 234 and 173, 20–23; CSMK 245, respectively), where the *propensio* seems to be taken over from the *"potestatis . . . sequendi deteriora, quamvis meliora videamus*—the positive power which we have of following the worse although we see the better" (174, 10–12; CSMK: 245). Besides, the will itself is opposed to the *propensio* in the sense of the Sixth Meditation, because it is exercised without our sensing any external constraint in it (*"ita feramus, ut a nulla vi externa nos ad id determinari sentiamus*—our inclinations are such that we do not feel that we are determined by any external force," VII: 57, 26–27; CSM II: 40), other than the one that is "given" (VII: 79, 28; CSM II: 55) by God to my passive faculty (VII: 79, 7; CSM II: 55) or even against my will (*"me non cooperante, sed saepe etiam invito*—without my cooperation and often even against my will," VII: 79, 13–14; CSM II: 55).

32. Yet could one invoke the doctrine of the *impulsus* outlined in Regula XII (X: 424, 1–18; CSM I: 47–48) in order to maintain the epistemological validity of the *propensio* in the *Meditations*? This seems very difficult, even if one brackets the disputed question of the compatibility of these two texts. In fact, when the *impetus* is being defined in opposition to the *conjectura* (which obtains only the probable) and to the *deductio* (which alone composes the simple natures

Finally, the demonstration shows a third weakness by using a final argument: If the cause of the ideas of corporeal things did not go back to really existing corporeal things, God would be a deceiver. Yet why should that be so? Because in this case the cause would not correspond *"formaliter"* to the effect.[33] "Formally" here means that the same form

---

with certainty), it can be understood in only three ways. (a) Either beginning from a *potentia superior*, and it is never mistaken. (b) Or from a *propria libertas*, where it is only sometimes mistaken. (c) Or finally starting from the *phantasiae dispositio*, and it is always mistaken. The entire question thus comes down to deciding what sort of *impulsus* best relates to the *propensio*. Now it seems that in the *Regulae* (for example in the Third Regula, 370, 19–25; CSM I: 15), the *impulsus* by *potentia superior* concerns the truths of faith (*fides*, 370, 21) and them alone (see my study in *René Descartes. Règles utiles et claires*, 245ff.); but the *propensio* in the Sixth Meditation is absolutely not a matter of articles of faith. In the best case, it seems rather linked to *"in me facultates specialibus quisbusdam modis cogitandi, puta facultates imaginandi et sentiendi*—faculties in myself for certain special modes of thinking, namely imagination and sensory perception" (VII: 78, 21–23; CSM II: 54). Could one reasonably envision that God would validate, like an article of faith, a quasi-*impulsus*, which nevertheless would here fall under the *phantasia* that always deceive? It remains completely foreign to Descartes to pass in this way from the natural realm to the supernatural realm and is forbidden by him. To argue here that "divine veracity has a universal range" is no solution but expresses the difficulty well. Gueroult, *Descartes' Philosophy*, II: 76.

33. See, among other occurrences: Sixth Meditation, AT VII: 79, 16, 20 and 26; CSM II: 55. In his quite excellent commentary, Clauberg insisted on this resemblance according to form: *"Sensus a rebus ipsis corporeis in nobis excitari, in quibus* formaliter *illa continentur, quae sensibus distincte repraesentantur*—A sense is stimulated in us by bodily things in which they are *formally* contained, which are represented distinctly by the senses." Similarly, where Descartes limits himself to saying *"non video qua ratione posset intelligi ipsum [i.e., Deum] non esse fallacem, si* aliunde quam a rebus corporeis *emitterentur [i.e., idea]*—So I do not see how God could be anything but a deceiver if the ideas were transmitted from a source other than corporeal things" (VII: 80, 2–4; CSM II: 55), he goes explicitly back to the argument from similitude and in this case without the least reservation: *"Falleret autem maxime, si* talem *se nobis ostenderet, qualis tamen nec est, nec esse potest*—He would be very deceptive if he were to show himself to us as something he is not and cannot be." *Paraphrasis in Renati Des Cartes Meditationes*, VI, §136 and 133, in *Opera philosophica omnia* (Amsterdam: Adriani Wyngaerden, 1691; Hildesheim: Olms, 1968), I: 468. Pierre-Sylvain Regis similarly insists on the formality in resuming the Cartesian argument: "I ask first on what basis this idea represents extension to me in length, size, and depth rather than something else; for it must have that property from some cause. . . . Now, this can come only from myself or from extension; for as of yet I know no other thing, but it cannot come from me because I conceive by natural light that

is shared between the cause (the corporeal thing) and its effect (the idea in me of this corporeal thing), which thus remains "*omnino similis*— entirely similar" (VIII-1: 41, 7 = IX-2: 64, 9) to it. The similarity intervenes as an all the more decisive criterion as Descartes maintains its principle even when he must concede that it is not perfect: "*res corporeae existunt. Non tamen forte omnes tales omnino existunt,* quales *illas sensu comprehendo*—It follows that corporeal things exist. They may not all exist in a way that exactly corresponds with my sensory grasp of them."[34]

Yet why this reservation, this cushioning? Obviously because the similarity between the idea and its (corporeal) cause that is invoked here has been firmly criticized multiple times by Descartes himself from the *Optics*[35] all the way to the *Meditations*. Thus, for example, in the Third

---

the cause of the idea of extension must *formally* contain all the properties that this idea represents; and I know very certainly that my mind does not contain any. Thus, extension itself must be the cause of the property that my idea has of representing it." Or also: "Second, considering that the only reason I have for concluding that the body exists is that the idea I have of extension must have an *exemplary* cause and that this cause must *really and formally* contain all the perfections that my idea represents." *Système de philosophie. De la métaphysique ou de la connaissance des substances intelligentes,* I.1, 3 (Lyons: Anisson, Posuel & Rigaud, 1690), I: 74–76.

34. AT VII: 80, 4–6 = IX-1: 63; CSM II: 55. This principle of resemblance is attested at least once more elsewhere: "*Nam axioma est commune et verum: effectus similis est causae*—It is a common axiom and a true one that *the effect is like the cause.*" Conversation with Burman, §24, AT V: 156; CSMK: 339–40. But, besides the fact that here this axiom is valid only for the case of a *causa totalis ipsius esse* (i.e., God, as in AT I: 152, 2), one can, and must, always take this only indirectly Cartesian text with precaution.

35. Especially: "there is no need to suppose that something material passes from objects to our eyes to make us see colours and light, or even that there is something in the objects which *resembles* the ideas or sensations that we have of them. . . . the resistance or movement of the bodies, which is the sole cause of the sensations that he has of them, is nothing *like* the ideas he forms of them" (*Optics* I, AT VI: 85, 14–24; CSM I: 153). Or: "in no case does an image have to *resemble* the object it represents in all respects, for otherwise there would be no distinction between the object and its image. It is enough that the image *resembles* its object in a few respects. Indeed the perfection of an image often depends on its not *resembling* its object as much as it might" (*Optics* IV, AT VI: 113, 2–9; CSM I: 165). This rejection of similarity actually goes back to Regula XII: "*Nec denique res externas tales semper esse quales apparent*—[it must not judge] that external things always are just as they appear to be" (X: 423, 6–7; CSM I: 47). On this contradiction (and the three failings of the proof), see *Sur la théologie blanche de Descartes,* §15, 347–70.

Meditation the conviction that "*res quasdam extra me esse, a quibus ideae istae procedebant et quibus omnino* similes *erant*—there were things outside me which were the sources of my ideas and which *resembled* them *in all respects*" results simply in a habit of believing ("*consuetudinem credendi*—through habitual belief"; AT VII: 35, 24–27 = IX-1: 28; CSM II: 24). Similarly, to judge whether "*ideas, quae in me sunt, . . . rebus quibusdam extra me positis* similes *esse sive* conformes—the ideas which are in me resemble, or conform to, things located outside of me" constitutes "the chief and most common mistake—*praecipuus error et frequentissimus*" of the natural attitude.[36] In fact—and that is one of the essential assets of the Cartesian doctrine of knowledge—ever since such a similarity between the thing outside me and its idea within me was assimilated to the relation of efficient causality, knowledge is from now on exerted as if [it operated] between a cause (thing) and an effect (idea) no longer linked by any resemblance or conformity. The cause has no need to share the same *forma* with its effect in order to produce it or make it intelligible. For efficient causality is distinguished from formal causality in that very respect and owes its extraordinary privilege—both ontic and epistemological—to it alone. There is no choice but to accept that in invoking the criterion of resemblance in order to decide between the three possible identities of a sole and same efficient cause, not only is the Sixth Meditation unable to demonstrate its conclusion (the corporeal thing exists because it causes the idea of the sensible), but Descartes himself comes to contradict one of his fundamental theses.

Moreover, the demonstration of the Sixth Meditation marks a reluctance in regard to its own and final argument. First, because immediately after having appealed to similarity, it adds, as we have seen: "Non *tamen*

36. AT VII: 37, 22–25 = IX-1: 29; CSM II: 26. Against this "supposed resemblance [i.e., of the ideas] to material things" (Gueroult, *Descartes' Philosophy*, II: 73), see also the explicit declaration in the Third Meditation: "*quamvis a rebus a me diversis procederent [i.e., ideae], non inde sequitur illas rebus istis similes esse debere*—even if these ideas come from things other than myself, it would not follow that they must resemble those things" (VII: 39, 15–18; CSM II: 27); in the Fifth Meditation: "*nulla profecto ratio est quae suadeat in igne aliquid esse* simile *isti calori, ut neque etiam isti dolori, sed tantummodo in eo aliquid esse,* quodcunque demum sit, *quod istos in nobis sensus caloris vel doloris* efficiat—there is no convincing argument for supposing that there is something in the fire which *resembles* the heat, any more than for supposing that there is something which resembles the pain. There is simply reason to suppose that there is something in the fire, *whatever it may eventually turn out to be*, which *produces* in us the feeling of heat or pain" (VII: 83, 8–12; CSM II: 57), and in the *Principles of Philosophy* I, §46 and §48.

*forte omnes* tales omnino *existunt,* quales *illas sensu comprehendo.*— They may not all exist *in a way that exactly corresponds* with my sensory grasp of them" (AT VII: 80, 4–6 = IX-1: 66; CSM II: 55). Then, when it insists on the fact that the pain that the heat of the fire produces by efficiency (*"efficiat"*) does not count as a reason that would persuade us of the least resemblance between the fire and this pain (*"nulla profecto ratio . . . quae suadeat in igne aliquid esse simile isti calori—*there is no convincing argument that there is something in the fire which resembles the heat"; AT VII: 83, 8–12 = IX-1: 66; CSM II: 57). The efficiency exempts from the resemblance; hence there is no reason to prefer really material things as the efficient cause of the ideas of material things, rather than myself or God. The final Cartesian argument relies on the concept of similarity and resemblance, which presupposes a comprehension of the *forma* that the Cartesian doctrine of science has clearly made obsolete. In short, on this specific point, for a while, Descartes does not measure up to himself. And the critics stress this very quickly and very clearly: Thus Desgabets and Foucher, who are opposed by the others, advance more or less the same objection. Desgabets remarks, "a fault in this reasoning inasmuch as it is in no way necessary for the cause that stimulates an idea to *resemble* the idea nor for it to be its object. The body gives an infinite number of ideas to the soul itself of which the soul is sole object and subject, without its knowing via this idea the body that provided it. Consequently, it is not impossible that another agent than the body gives us an idea of the body. From this follows that one cannot conclude by reasoning from the cause to the effect that there are bodies existing outside of us, based only on the single rationale that there is some external agent that gives the idea to us."[37] Foucher says the same thing: "They [i.e., Descartes' reasons] consist in his claim that experience shows us things that *represent* and that are not *like* what they represent." One must conclude from this that "as these ways of being are not *like* these things, following the acknowledgment of these philosophers, these ideas would not represent these things, but represent only their effects."[38] One must choose between a relationship

37. Robert Desgabets, *Supplément à la philosophie de Descartes,* vol. II, chap. XI, s. 5, ed. Joseph Beaude, in *Œuvres philosophiques inédites,* ed. Geneviève Rodis-Lewis, fasc. 6 (Amsterdam: Quadrature, 1985), 266f.

38. Simon Foucher, *Critique de la "Recherche de la Vérité" où l'on examine en même temps une partie de "Principes" de Mr Descartes* (1675), reprinted by Richard A. Watson (New York/London: Johnson, 1969), 56 and 53, trans. Richard A. Watson and Marjorie Grene, *Malebranche's First and Last Critics* (Carbondale: Southern Illinois University Press, 1995), 33, 32.

of efficient causality between the object and the idea and a relationship of similarity. And the demonstration of the Sixth Meditation hearkens back to the 1637 teaching and the Third and Fifth Meditations.

Based on these three weaknesses we can thus conclude that the Sixth Meditation does not demonstrate what it claims to establish. And we can then also conclude that the *Meditations* as a whole come to a close without having reestablished the existence of the external world that the First Meditation had put into doubt. Or at least that in the end they do not reestablish the existence of the *same* world that had been placed in doubt at the beginning of the meditative path. Instead, and in place of a world of bodies that are both material and sensory, which would exist in conformity with the form that our senses perceive in them, only an efficient cause of sensations exists that is twice removed from them. First, because the essence of the bodies that are supposed to produce that form is displayed in terms of simple material natures, that is to say, mathematical ideas that are consequently not about sensation. Second, because the existence of these bodies depends on efficiency as sole symptom; they appear as its effect, actively affecting our passive perception. Thus matter becomes a simple or actually metaphorical name for identifying the active effect of the insensible cause (remaining anonymous behind the dissimilarity of efficiency) that is practiced on passive sensibility. The body of the thing is summed up in a resistance—itself anonymous—of my perception to the spontaneity of the understanding and the will. I can say that there are causes for some of my ideas that do not depend on me, I can call these causes bodies or material things, but I have no access whatsoever either to their presumed matter or to their corporeality, except via features and movements reconstituted on the basis of extension. The result of the demonstration of the existence of material things by the Sixth Meditation—the vagueness regarding the three causes left in competition in order to produce the passive ideas that come to the ego—thus places in question not so much the *existence* of material things, as Kant criticized it, but the *materiality of their existence*, because in fact, as Descartes' successors will show, one can comprehend this existence perfectly without assigning it any cause in matter. Or, and this amounts to the same thing, matter defines an effect on the mind from an essentially immaterial cause (even if it is a matter of extension that one would hence call *intelligible*).

Descartes' skepticism thus remains just one of method, because it seems to result in the solipsism of an ego that is not directed toward any world in the strict sense, that is, one that is at the same time sensory and external. Henceforth matter remains intelligible by dint of the simple material natures, while the sensory is a matter of thought via clear and confused ideas. More than a solipsism (which will most probably never be literally encountered in this line of thought), it is a matter of a brutal and strictly speaking staggering chiasmus: material things are no longer sensory, the sensory is no longer material. In this sense, this chiasmus and this reversal hence can certainly be called "a scandal."

§5. *The Historical Confirmation of the "Scandal" by Descartes' Successors*

One solid fact cannot be stressed too much: the great majority of Descartes' successors, both near and far, disciples as much as opponents, not only gave up supporting the weakest points of the argument in the Sixth Meditation, but tried everything to avoid or soften the "scandal" by admitting that its presumed demonstration does not demonstrate anything or by suggesting that it demonstrates a result different from the one Descartes assigns to it. In this way they confirmed by anticipation what Kant will refer to as its "doubtful and *unprovable*" character.

From 1647 onward Regius seems to be the first to abandon the Cartesian argument in order to substitute for it the authority of the Scriptures pure and simple: "*Verum, etiam hoc dubim tollit divina in Sacris revelatio, qua indubitatum est, Deum coelum et terram et omnia, quae iis continentur, creasse, et etiamnum conservare.*—Nevertheless, the divine revelation of Scripture removes even this doubt, and shows it to be indubitable that God created heaven and earth and everything in them, and keeps them in existence even now."[39] In 1666, Cordemoy withdraws from the same position: "I see that the argument of the soul is indubitable and that to this point there is nothing that assures me of my body"; in fact, "it is hence possible that I think having a body without really having anything extended, but it cannot be that I think without really having any thought." Although the discussion passes surreptitiously from bod*ies* to *my* body, in order to make sure of it, Cordemoy also falls back on faith: "I will thus say in the future that I have a soul because that is evident to me by the natural light and because faith assures me of it. As to the body, I will say that I have one, because although that is not obvious to me by natural light, faith is sufficient to

---

39. AT VIII-2: 344, *Explicatio Mentis Humanae, sive Animae rationalis, ubi explicatur quid sit, et quid esse possit,* IX. "An Account of the Human Mind, or Rational Soul, Which Explains What It Is and What It Can Be," CSM I: 295.

keep me from doubting it."[40] Yet it is really Malebranche, who in 1678 in his Elucidation Six, which he adds to the second edition of the *Search for Truth*, decidedly formulates the position that corresponds even better than that of Descartes to what Kant calls "problematic idealism." It is really he who definitively challenges the Cartesian proof for the existence of material things on the basis of strict Cartesian principles (and in terms that are almost identical to those of Kant): "But although Descartes has given the strongest proofs that reason alone can muster for the existence of bodies . . . still we can say that *the existence of matter is not yet perfectly demonstrated, i.e., with geometric rigor.* For in philosophical matters, we must not believe anything till evidence obliges us to do so. . . . Thus, when we perceive bodies, let us judge only that we perceive them and that these perceptible or intelligible bodies actually exist; but why should we judge positively that there is an external material world like the intelligible world we perceive?"[41] In other words, inasmuch as it is not doubtful that we have ideas of bodies, sensory ideas received passively and intelligible ideas constituted by extension (of the simple material natures, as Descartes himself had said), all the more so does it not obviously follow that we have the least knowledge of a

40. Géraud de Cordemoy, *Six discours sur la distinction et l'union de l'âme et du corps*, chap. VI, in *Œuvres philosophiques*, ed. Pierre Clair and François Girbal (Paris: PUF, 1968), 154–55. The slippage from bod*ies* in the plural to *mine* anticipates in its very confusion two questions that are clearly distinguished in the Sixth Meditation, that is, they preview the essential element of Descartes' real line of argument. We will see this below, chap. II, §7.

41. Nicolas Malebranche, *Recherche de la vérité*, Éclaircissement VI, *Œuvres complètes*, ed. G. Rodis-Lewis, vol. III (Paris: Vrin, 1964), 60, trans. Thomas M. Lennon as *The Search after Truth* (Cambridge: Cambridge University Press, 1997), 572; emphasis added, trans. lightly modified. Similarly: "This reasoning is perhaps sound enough. Nevertheless, it must be agreed that it should not be taken as a necessary demonstration of the existence of bodies" (ibid., 574). And: "Now it must be noted that since only God knows His volitions (which produce all beings) by Himself, we can know only from Him whether there really is a material world external to us like the one we perceive, because the material world is neither perceptible nor intelligible by itself" (ibid., 573). Or also: "The existence of the body is arbitrary. If there are any, it is because God really wanted to create them." *Entretien sur la métaphysique et la religion*, VI, §5, ed. André Robinet, vol. XII–XIII (Paris: Vrin, 1965), 137. On this point, see Ferdinand Alquié, *Le Cartésianisme de Malebranche*, I, 2, C. (Paris: Vrin, 1974), and Philippe Desoche, "Parole divine et nature humaine: la preuve cartésienne de l'existence des corps face à la critique de Malebranche," in Kolesnik-Antoine, ed., *Union et distinction de l'âme et du corps*.

presumed matter outside of us: matter is neither external nor corporeal, thus bodies are defined no more by materiality than by the exteriority of the world. If one still absolutely wants to reach it, then it is advisable to leave the realm of reason in order to move to the authority of faith: "Surely only faith can persuade us that there really are bodies."[42]

By decidedly abandoning the proof of the Sixth Meditation, both as not very rigorous and as impossible, Malebranche overcomes the limits of Descartes' "*problematic* idealism" and already inaugurates "the *dogmatic* idealism of *Berkeley*, who declares space, together with all the things to which it is attached as an inseparable condition, to be something that is impossible in itself, and who therefore also declares things in space to be merely imaginary."[43] What's more, Berkeley's argument for establishing the impossibility of the existence of material things outside of us and thus also that of any matter whatsoever, really draws its entire force from a primarily Cartesian argument, namely, that of the encoding of sensory qualities by the simple material natures. If the differences between colors, sounds, tastes, or fragrances can, at least by right, all be reduced to extended shapes; if one admits that the world consists only in these combinations of simple natures and that the qualities that we attribute to the things are really only a matter of the subjective effect of objective features in the world on our *mens*; then "why might we not as well argue that figure and extension are not patterns or resemblances of qualities existing in Matter. . . . Is it not as reasonable to say that motion is not without the mind, since if the succession of ideas in the mind become swifter the motion, it is acknowledged, shall appear slower without any alteration in any external object"?[44] This doubling in the encounter with simple material natures in an argument initially raised against the objectivity of sensory qualities had in fact been more than sketched by Descartes himself, from the hyperbolic doubt of the First Meditation onward.[45] In this way Berkeley seems

42. Malebranche, *Search after Truth*, 574. One could almost say that Malebranche tries here to extend the Cartesian *magna propensio* of the imagination to an *impulsus* of the sort of *potentia aliqua superior* (see above, 24–25, note 32).

43. Kant, *Critique of Pure Reason*, B 274; 326.

44. Berkeley, *Principles of Human Knowledge*, I, §14, in *The Works of George Berkeley*, ed. Alexander Campbell Fraser (Oxford: Clarendon Press, 1901, 2005), I: 162–63.

45. AT VII: 21, 3–16. See, among other texts, Regula XII, AT X: 412, 14—413, 20, and my explanations in *Sur l'ontologie grise de Descartes. Science cartésienne et savoir aristotélicien dans les "Regulae,"* §§22–24 (Paris: Vrin, 1975, 2000), 131ff. and certainly in *Sur la théologie blanche de Descartes*, §12, 231ff.

to draw the extreme, but probably inevitable, consequence of the first skepticism, which as methodical as one might wish, in the end proves itself to be definitive. Its decisive advance consists hence less in the thesis about the nonexistence of a matter outside of us than in that of its uselessness for thinking the world. The world is not outside of our mind in a matter that is moreover unthinkable, indefinable, and unprovable. Exteriority owes nothing to matter but is deployed in thought itself. Causality never leads us outside of thought, which alone thinks it and hence comprehends it entirely. Hume simply confirms this consequence: "We may observe a conjunction or a relation of cause and effect between different perceptions, but can never observe it between perceptions and objects."[46]

One must thus agree with Kant and share in his "scandal": Not only does the proof of the Sixth Meditation not lead to any rigorous result when one analyzes it as such and from a strictly Cartesian point of view, but its failure was confirmed by the majority of those who knew of it, all the way to Kant. Thus this condemnation actually could make Kant appear naive about history—the last one to be scandalized by a failure that the whole world had noticed and found solace in for a long time.

## §6. A Critique of Kant's Critique

Must one for all that take the question to be closed, the issue to be judged? We could obviously do so if in addition to condemning the insufficiency of Descartes' demonstration Kant had himself provided the missing proof, in other words, if he had positively proven "the existence of things outside of us." Yet Kant's thesis on this point raises more difficulties than it solves.

Let us go back to the celebrated argument regarding "The Refutation of Idealism." Kant rightly notes that Descartes' problematic idealism assumes that the knowledge the ego has of itself in thinking itself brings it an unconditioned certainty, in such a way that the mind would be known before and more surely than the body. But the opposite is true, for "even our *inner* experience, undoubted by Descartes, is pos-

---

46. Hume, *A Treatise of Human Nature*, Book I, Part IV, Section 2, 212. The difference is maybe not as great in Arthur Collier, *Clavis Universalis or a New Inquiry after Truth, Being a Demonstration of the Non-Existence or Impossibility of an External World* (London: Robert Gosling, 1713), reedited by Ethel Bowman (Chicago: Open Court, 1909). See Herman J. de Vleeschauwer, "Les antinomies kantiennes et la *Clavis universalis* d'Arthur Collier," *Mind* 47 (1938): 303–20.

sible only under the presupposition of *outer* experience." How would
one prove this? By positing that my existence as ego can be established
only by reaching "something *persistent (Beharrliches)* in perception";
yet my representations, which are continually changing, cannot assure
me of such a permanence; one must hence refer to the internally moving
experience of the ego as "something persistent that is distinct even from
them [the representations]."[47] Yet in this way the difference between internal and external experience collapses, because the internal experience
implies the external permanence of objects outside of itself in order to
get its bearings within time. In other words, the internal results from the
external: "inner experience itself is consequently only mediate and possible only through outer experience"; or "inner experience in general is
possible only through outer experience in general."[48] And as external
experience puts external objects—phenomena outside of us—into play,
the internal experience itself presupposes therefore directly the existence
of material things.

Before discussing the Kantian argument itself, one could pose a
preliminary question: Did Descartes really need the external sense for
reaching permanence for the ego?[49] At the very least, one must acknowledge that Descartes maintains the opposite: in fact, he claims that the
ego accomplishes its permanence in time—the *"minimum quid . . . quod
certum sit et inconcussum*—one thing, however slight, that is certain
and unshakeable" (AT VII: 24, 12–13; CSM II: 16)—without leaving
its internal experience, so that this *"pronutiatum Ego sum, ego existo,
quoties a me profertur, vel mente concipitur, necessario esse verum*—
proposition, *I am, I exist*, is necessarily true whenever it is put forward
by me or conceived in my mind" (25, 11–13; CSM II: 17). It is thus really
*every time* that I (alone) think myself that I am (exist), and even *as long*
as I think: *"Ego sum, ego existo; certum est. Quandiu autem? Nempe
quandiu cogito.*—I am, I exist—that is certain. But for how long? For
as long as I am thinking" (27, 9–10; CSM II: 18). This repetition of
thought by itself is enough, at least for Descartes, to assure him a kind
of permanence and a first permanence: *"ut ita tandem praecise rema-*

47. Kant, *Critique of Pure Reason*, B 275; 326–27.

48. Ibid., B 277 and 278–79; 328.

49. Besides, this is exactly what Heidegger reproaches him for. On this point
and on the temporal permanence of the Cartesian ego, see my analysis in *Sur le
prisme métaphysique de Descartes. Constitution et limites de l'onto-théo-logie
cartésienne*, §14 (Paris: PUF, 1986), 180–202, trans. by Jeffrey L. Kosky as *On
Descartes' Metaphysical Prism: The Constitution and Limits of Onto-theo-logy
in Cartesian Thought* (Chicago: University of Chicago Press, 1999), 169–93.

*neat illud tantum quod certum est et inconcussum*—what is left at the end may be exactly and only what is certain and unshakeable."[50] Time as an internal sense or, more exactly for Descartes, as duration demands nothing of the external experience of the things of the world in order to reach its own internal permanence; it is enough for the ego to repeat the perceptions of its *cogitatio*. The present of permanence is based on repetition (and that is why the *mens* must think without cease, whether it is conscious or not). One should not object here that thoughts are performed within change and that they can therefore not reach permanence; for Kant himself recognizes that one can think a permanence with an act that is itself changing: "The representation of something *persisting* in existence is not the same as a *persisting representation*; for that can be quite variable and changeable, as all our representations are, even the representations of matter, while still being related to something permanent, which must therefore be a thing distinct from all my representations and external."[51] This judicious distinction actually validates Descartes' argument: the ego can reach something permanent and irreducible to its representations (*cogitationes*, achievements); they are certainly always changing, without, however, leaving experience or the internal sense.

Yet another objection arises from this, which this time works directly against Kant. Can he really assume without contradicting himself, on the one hand, in the "Refutation of Idealism" that "inner experience in general is possible only through outer experience in general" and, on the other hand, in "The Transcendental Aesthetic" that "time is an *a priori* condition of any phenomenon in general, and indeed the immediate condition of the inner phenomena (of our souls), and thereby also the mediate condition of external phenomena"?[52] Does time condition

50. AT VII: 25, 22–24; CSM II: 17. And if the external and material object (the piece of wax) can itself also *remanere* (30, 19, and 25), it owes it first of all to the permanence of thought. Kant *inverts* the connection that Descartes establishes between thought and external object by way of permanence. He thus does not criticize Descartes' position, but maybe those of Locke or Hume.

51. Kant, *Critique of Pure Reason*, B xli; 122. (The [French] translation relates this passage from the preface to the second edition of the "Refutation," very relevantly because Kant himself demands this.) But why add here "and external" as if the distinction between thought and object of thought would imply its exteriority of the world by obligation? In fact, in the "Refutation," Kant speaks more prudently and only of "something persistent that is distinct even from them [the representations]" (B 275; 327), without adding recklessly that it must for all that become external, mundane, and outside of me.

52. Ibid., B 278–79; 328 and A 34/B 51; 181, trans. modified.

the external experience of phenomena via internal experience or the reverse? That is to say, does the internal authority (experience or sense) condition the external authority (experience and sense) or is it the opposite? In order to relieve the difficulty one could certainly distinguish two types of opposition to the point of separating them so much that the distinction between the interiority and the exteriority of experience would have nothing in common with that of the internal sense (time) and the external sense (space); but this side step would become very problematic as soon as one recognizes that time also determines space in such a way that it would instead be experienced without this latter rather than the opposite. Kant's critique of Descartes threatens thus less Descartes' argument than Kant's coherence—in order to refute Descartes' presumed idealism, Kant would thus contradict himself by subordinating the internal sense to the external one and time to space.

A final difficulty remains. For even if one admits the connection that Kant maintains and that Descartes contests—namely, that the internal experience of the permanence of the *I* implies first the external experience of external and material things—what could one legitimately conclude from this? One can infer the existence of external things from it only if the existence of the *I* itself had to be absolutely established on the same model as that of external objects. Yet what *I* is at stake here? Obviously, "the mere, but *empirically* determined, consciousness,"[53] that is, the empirical *me*. (Anyway, how could it be otherwise in a section devoted to the "Postulate of *empirical* thought in general"?) It is thus a matter of experiencing an empirical *me* via an internal experience without the option of continuity with external experience. Yet what would such a continuity mean? How could this *me*, even if it is empirical (without even speaking of the transcendental *I*, which "is no more an intuition than it is a concept of any object; rather, it is the mere form of consciousness, which accompanies both sorts of representations"),[54] share even a mode of being (the same existence) with an object, when by definition it is not in the mode of objects and, above all, it absolutely *should* not be? What existence could objects of the world and the *I* share, at least if this *I thinks*? By what right would one presuppose here (and even more in the case of God) such a univocity of existence that it would always have to be understood in the same sense (that is, the position outside of thought) regardless of what sort of being is at stake, hence eliminating the differences at least of essence between the *I* and

53. Ibid., B 276; 327.
54. Ibid., A 382; 432.

the phenomena of the world? In order to avoid the difficulty, should one say that external experience constitutes only the indispensable comple- ment of internal experience, because the *I think* can be known as a really existing object only if appealing to empirical intuition? Yet, ac- cording to this hypothesis, does not what one names *external* experi- ence become only an obligatory prolonging of *internal* experience itself, from which it can no longer be distinguished? Or, what amounts to the same thing, internal experience would disappear and would be assimi- lated to an external experience, so that the external would be no more external than the internal would be internal. In short, by assuming liter- ally that "outer experience is really immediate,"[55] does Kant not repeat the situation of solipsism, because he includes its presumed exteriority in the *ipse* itself?

It is here that a "very grave objection" (*schwerwiegender Einwand*) formulated by Husserl is applicable. He asks: "When I, the meditating I, reduce myself to my absolute transcendental ego by phenomenological epoché do I not become *solus ipse*; and do I not remain that, as long as I carry on a consistent self-explication under the name phenomenology? Should not a phenomenology that proposed to solve the problems of Objective being, and to present itself actually as philosophy, be branded therefore as transcendental solipsism?"[56] In fact, if "the transcendental reduction restricts me to the stream of my pure conscious processes" and specifically to them alone, does it not accomplish precisely a per- fect solipsism, where the external can and must be reduced to the in- ternal, the transcendent to the immanent? This objection applies also, and in Husserl's mind maybe first of all, to Kant. Yet, one will respond, did Husserl not inherit his transcendental idealism directly from Kant's transcendental *I*? Does he not expose himself thus to the objection he raises against Kant? Certainly, but with an almost fundamental differ- ence: the Husserlian ego has a property available that the Kantian *I* lacks entirely, namely, intentionality: "We must, after all, obtain for our- selves insight into the explicit and implicit intentionality wherein the al- ter ego becomes evinced and verified in the realm of our transcendental ego; we must discover in what intentionalities, syntheses, motivations, the sense 'other ego' becomes fashioned in me and, under the title, har- monious (*einstimmig*) experience of someone else, becomes verified as

55. Ibid., B 276; 327 ("daß äußere Erfahrung eigentlich unmittelbar sei"), a formulation confirmed by the note: "*Immediate* consciousness of the existence of outer things is not presupposed but proved in the preceding theorem." Ibid.

56. Husserl, *Cartesian Meditations*, §42, Hua I: 121; 89.

existing (*als seiend*) and even as itself there in its own manner (*als selbst da*)."[57] At least in principle, intentionality makes it possible to explain how the object must be one with the consciousness that I have of it without all the same reducing this noematic constitution to its noesis. Even more, intentionality will characterize not only the aim of my own ego, but also, by analogy, that of an alter ego. Doubtlessly this analogy is quickly shown to be problematic and full of new aporiae; yet at least one can think it and use it. At least it decidedly rules out the obstacle of solipsism, even if it opens more onto an inter-*objectivity* than onto an authentic intersubjectivity. By contrast, Kant remains riveted to the objectness and unicity of the transcendental synthesis: the unicity of the *I*, equal for all possible empirical *me*, objectivity of the phenomenon that is always and only constituted as object. Consequently, Husserl's objection about solipsism is at bottom directed against Kant.

Therefore also, if the objection that Kant raises against Descartes suffers from internal inconsistencies and from his ignorance of intentionality, must one dismiss the plaintiffs and absolve the accused of any "scandal"? Actually, one can at the very least wonder about the stakes of the scandal. According to the accusation, the offense consists in the demonstration of the existence of material things (called bod*ies*) and the scandal in the insufficiency of the proof. One must thus figure out whether the aim of the Sixth Meditation consisted (or consisted *first of all*) in demonstrating the existence of external bodies and of material things. Now, as we have seen from the outset, this question, even if it plays an indisputable role in the Sixth Meditation, neither occupies its entire stage nor constitutes its central plot. For, from the very first lines and before wondering about the problematic existence of material things (which might remain problematic), Descartes had affirmed one existence that he did not have to demonstrate—not the existence of external things but rather that of his own living body: "*[Imaginatio] nihil aliud esse apparet quam quaedam applicatio facultatis cognoscitivae ad corpus ipsi intime praesens, ac proinde* existens.—[This imagination] seems to be nothing else but an application of the cognitive faculty to a *body which is intimately present to it*, and which therefore *exists*" (VII: 72, 1–3 = IX-1: 57; CSM II: 50). This is actually not an existence that has been demonstrated, because it has no need for it, not referring to external bodies, but showing itself to even an internal body, because close to thought itself. This existence therefore clearly concerns *not* the first question defined by the title of the Sixth Meditation (to show with

57. Ibid., 122; 90.

certainty the existence of material things), but the second (to define the distinction between mind and body proper). In other words, this posited and not demonstrated existence of a living and not an external body finally concerns thinking the *union* of the union and the distinction of the mind and my body. Why must it be thought *finally*? Why should one not have begun by thinking this undiscussed existence rather than burdening oneself by demonstrating first a different disputable existence (that of external bodies as material things)? Because, for Descartes, the aporia of the existence of bodies probably leads the order of reasoning toward the evidence of the existence of the union, that is to say, toward my body that is not material but flesh. In other words, because the final question and the essential conclusion of the Sixth Meditation concern not the (problematic) existence of external bodies, but, via its discussion, the certainty of my flesh and of my *thinking* flesh.

# 2

**Bodies and My Flesh**

*§7. A New Distinction*

It is in this way that we arrive at the final aporia of the
Sixth Meditation, at least according to the interpretation
that the dominant post-Cartesian tradition developed:
the existence of material things, more exactly that of the
materiality and the exteriority of bodies, remains problematic. Yet, although the standard commentary tends
to forget it, we also know that this is only the conclusion of the first part of the Sixth Meditation and that this
presumed aporia in either case concerns only one of *two*
questions brought together in the title of the final meditation: there is another one, the distinction between mind
and body, which together with the first thus brings about
four difficulties.[1] In contrast to what the standard readings lead us to think, this text does not treat the existence
of material things or at least *not only* that, because as I
have already stressed, this question *de rerum materialium*

---

1. Namely (see above, chap. 1, §2, 17) the following: (a) the
equivocity of the concept of *body*, (b) the order between existence of the world and the status of the relationship between my
body and mind, (c) the distinction or the union of the union and
the distinction and, finally, (d) the certainty of the proof of the
existence of material things. I have tackled only the final one,
and that only in anticipation (see below, §11, 71–78).

*existentia* [of the existence of material things] forms only the first stake, preceding another one on the *realis mentis a corpore distinctione* [real distinction between mind and body]. Does the one really precede the other? Is that so certain?

First, it so happens that Descartes turns this distinction into the result and the sole conclusion of the preceding meditations, flatly passing over the question of the existence of material things in silence: thus *"idcirco omnia quae de Deo et de veritate in tertia, quarta et quinta Meditatione scripsi, conferunt ad conclusionem de mali* mentis *a* corpore *distinctione, quam demum in sexta Meditatione perfeci*—And this is why everything I wrote on the subject of God and truth in the Third, Fourth and Fifth Meditations contributes to the conclusion that there is a *real* distinction *between the mind and the body*, which I finally established in the Sixth Meditation."[2] It is as if the existence of material things could simply be either skipped over, so to say, or passed over in silence as a consequence.

Second, the first paragraph of the Sixth Meditation, which sets forth the problem as a whole, very explicitly announces that the existence of at least one body *precedes* the demonstration of the existence of (other) corporeal things: one existence, that of material things (*"an res materiales existant,"* VII: 71, 13–14), certainly turns out to be rather problematic, but a *different* existence is in the end discovered to be already assumed beyond discussion, that of my own body "intimately present to it [to my faculty of knowing], and which therefore exists—*ad corpus ipsi intime praesens, ac proinde existens,"* IX-1: 57 = VII: 72, 2–3; CSM II: 50). A sufficiently clear argument backs up this reasoning: *"Atque facile intelligo, si* corpus *aliquod existat* cui mens sit ita conjuncta *ut ad illud veluti inspiciendum pro arbitrio se applicet, fieri posse ut per hoc ipsum* res corporeas *imaginer.*—And I can easily understand that, if there does exist some body to which the mind is so joined that it can apply itself to contemplate it, as it were, whenever it pleases, then it may possibly be this very body that enables me to imagine corporeal things" (73, 10–13 = IX-1: 58; CSM II: 51). One should not confuse the body to which the mind is applied (precisely for imagining) with the corporeal bodies it thus manages to imagine: not only is the first body

2. AT VII: 226, 23–26; CSM II: 159. See the same unique conclusion attributed to the final Meditation shortly afterward: *"Nam in eadem sexta Meditatione, in qua egi de distinctione mentis a corpore, simul etiam probavi substantialiter illi esse unitam*—For in the Sixth Meditation, where I dealt with the distinction between the mind and the body, I also proved at the same time that the mind is substantially united with the body" (227, 25—228, 3; CSM II: 160).

mine, but it enables me to think bodies that are not mine (via the modality of the *cogitatio* that constitutes the imagination). And one should also not confuse their two connections to existence. In this case, the body that the imagination requires (to which it "applies" itself) actually attests to the existence of this body ("*ac proinde existens*—which therefore exists").[3] There is thus at least *one* body whose existence is not in question: mine, more exactly the one that turns out to be required by the exercise of one of the modes of thought, the imagination. In fact, it requires a certain "*applicatio . . . ad corpus ipsi intime praesens*" (ibid.); now, the existence of my thought having been established in a more certain manner, all that involves these modes (here the imagination) is also established; thus what the imagination involves exists.

Yet what is surprising here has to do with the fact that imaginative thought involves something that Descartes still calls a *body*. The imagination intervenes here because the essence of corporeal things (the *objectum purae Matheseos*, the simply material natures reestablished in the Fifth Meditation) requires it. In fact, because in contrast to the purely intellectual (*intellectus*) mode of thought, it requires something

---

3. VII: 72, 3 = IX-1: 57; CSM II: 50. In this case, how should one understand "*si corpus aliquod existat*—if there does exist some body" (73, 11; CSM II: 51) and "*siquidem corpus existat*—if the body exists" (73, 21; 51)? Is it a mere assumption of the same simple probability of existence of bodies that the imagination attains (by application to my body)? But if the imagination remains only probable (thus if the body that it requires did not exist), it is not clear what the force of the argument invoked here would be. One must hence understand it in this way: *on the condition and provided that* there is a body (mine, to which the imaginative modality of the *cogitatio* applies itself) as an *epistemological* condition for the knowledge of other bodies, it becomes intelligible and even probable that material things also exist; but this remains a simple probability, because although distinct, the idea that the imagination gives me of the corporeal nature (extension) does not permit me to construct a restrictive argument. The existence of my body is thus certain, as a necessary but not sufficient epistemological condition for conceiving the existence (which is still doubtful and only probable) of material things. This existence in advance of my body (as an epistemological request of a mode of the *cogitatio*), when it is at least glimpsed, still remains most often underestimated: "The imagination *would* thus first engage the presence of a *particular* body," admits Rodis-Lewis in *L'Œuvre de Descartes* (Paris: Vrin, 1971), 331. Why the conditional and why not specify this *particularity* (namely mine)? Or even Williams: "Its existence [i.e., that of the imagination] suggests that this thinking thing *may also have* a body" (*Descartes: The Project of Pure Enquiry*, 217); now, Descartes says that he really does imagine and thus with a body that really and actually exists, but that the existence of material things remains only probable.

"else—*praeterea*,"[4] an application to something like a nonintellectual support, that support finds itself invested with the *cogitatio*'s existence in general. Although this other thing is called a body, it hence exists as *thought* and to the benefit of its immaterial extra-territoriality. Thus, a *corporeal* existence precedes the demonstration of the existence of "material things," which are all the same also called "*res corporeae*— corporeal things" (VII: 80, 3 = IX-1: 63; CSM II: 55). This paradox, which very clearly opens the Sixth Meditation, cannot be avoided, because it lays down the terms for the Meditation and shows within it at least two of the four difficulties that had been pinpointed from the outset. First, the term body benefits (or suffers) from a fundamental ambiguity for which this elucidation forms a condition for any comprehending of the teaching as a whole. Then, it is possible that the order of reasoning would make the (problematic) demonstration of the existence of "material things" that *precedes* it (VII: 72, 4—80, 10) rely on the account of the *corpus existens* (72, 3) implied by (imaginative) thought whose truth *follows* from it ("*aliquid in eo . . . veritatis*"; 80, 31). In this case, which is maybe unique in the *Meditations*, the rationale for grounding would come after what it grounds.[5]

This distinction between, on the one hand, a body that exists and is mine and, on the other hand, the bodies of still doubtful existence that are different from me, is not limited to an allusion. It structures the entire text, which relies on this radical ambiguity [*équivocité*] of the concept of body. At stake is not the distinction between the body in general as extended and the mind in general as thought (that was the quarrel of the first two Meditations), but the distinction between two senses of the concept of body. Such a distinction of bodies is imposed by the evidence that "*habeam corpus, quod mihi valde arcte conjunctum est*—I have a body that is very closely joined to me" (AT VII: 78,

4. VII: 71, 20 = IX-1: 57. See: "*praeter illam naturam corpoream*—many other things besides the corporeal nature" (74, 1 = IX-1: 58; CSM II: 51; trans. modified). Certainly, at stake here is not a gap between imagination and intellection, but the gap between imagination and sensation; yet one that serves to bring out the singular role of my body vis-à-vis other bodies.

5. Spinoza probably had a premonition of this: "*Hujus autem differentiae* [i.e., between seeing and sensing an external body and suffering, sensing hunger or thirst] *causam clare video me non posse percipere, nisi prius intelligam, me uni parti materiae arcte esse unitum et aliis non item.*—But I clearly see that I cannot perceive the cause of this difference unless I *first* understand that I am closely united to one part of matter, and not so to other parts." *Principia philosophiae* I, §21, trans. Samuel Shirley as *The Principles of Cartesian Philosophy and Metaphysical Thoughts* (Indianapolis: Hackett, 1998), 43–44.

14–15 = IX-1: 62; CSM II: 54; trans. modified). At stake is a nonpolitical but all the more fundamental version of *habeas corpus*: "*habeam corpus*—I have a body" (VII: 80, 28 = IX-1: 64; CSM II: 56), and my body, "*meum corpus*" (VII: 81, 24; CSM II: 56), which is absolutely real and effective. This body there, "*hoc corpus*," "*corpus illud*" (74, 20; 75, 30), is not only mine [*le mien*], belongs to me [*à moi*], but it is also myself [*moi*]: "*meum corpus sive potius me totu[s]*—my body, or rather my whole self" (81, 24; CSM II: 56), because I *sense* in and through it, *corpus sentiens* (according to a formulation of Regula XII, AT X: 412, 21; CSM I: 40, which here receives its meaning). Its union with my mind (as my *mens*) depends on the fact that without it this mind would not develop its entire *cogitatio*. These very radical properties hence modify the very concept of the body: here it is a case no longer of one of those bodies (in the plural) that make up the many things of the world separate from me, but of this body that is mine, to the point where I am it and it is me—in other words, of "*meum corpus sive potius me totum*—my body, or rather my whole self" (81, 24; CSM II: 56). Faced with this presence of the ego in person as thinking *corporeally*, or more exactly as thinking in body and flesh, which, so to speak, makes invisible thought visible in a flesh, *corpus sentiens* joining the visible and the invisible (in quasi sacramental fashion, the eucharistic allusion imposing itself here), all the other bodies merit the name only with the reservation of an essential ambiguity: that reservation is overcome only by "*reliqua corpora*—all the other bodies."[6] They have the title of body only in almost metaphorical fashion, instead bearing that of "other . . . bodies which surround—*circumjacentia corpora*" (IX-1: 65 = VII: 81, 26–27; CSM II: 56) my own body. They are added within space to my own body, which itself does not exactly fall under the jurisdiction of their range. Thus the distinction between the *mens* and the body (as in the second part of the title of the Sixth Meditation) opens onto a more essential difference between, on one side, the bodies of the material world, and, on the other, my body of flesh. And this difference of localization (or rather this difference in mode of being, precisely because only physical bodies can be located within extension without qualification) is dou-

---

6. VII: 75, 4 and 76, 3 = IX-1: 59; CSM II: 52. See: "*alia multa corpora*" (VII: 74, 20–21) or "*alia ulla [corpora]*" (76, 1). Nevertheless, certain instances of "*aliquod corpus*" (for example, 73, 11, 18, 28) remain undecided. Indisputably, "*corpus existere . . . probabiliter*" (73, 23–24) designates a material thing; and my body seems rather explained as an extended body among others in 85, 29 and 86, 4.

bled by a difference in the manner of knowing them: in fact, while the
existence of bodies must still be proven, that of my body of flesh (*"quod
habeam corpus*—that I have a body") is already and straightforwardly
imposed as a certainty: "*Nec proinde dubitare debeo, quin aliquid in
eo sit veritatis.*—So I should not doubt that there is some truth in this"
(VII: 80, 28 and 30–31 = IX-1: 64; CSM II: 56).

There is no lack of texts that very clearly indicate this double difference, one that is as much epistemological as ontic. "*First of all then,*
I perceived by my senses that I had a head, hands, feet, and other limbs
making up the body which I regarded as part of myself, or perhaps even
as my whole self. I also perceived by my senses that this body was situated among many other bodies . . .—Primo *itaque sensi me habere caput,
manus, pedes et membra caetera ex quibus constat illud corpus, quod
tanquam mei partem, vel forte etiam tanquam me totum spectabam; sensique hoc corpus inter alia multa corpora versari . . .*" (IX-1: 59 = VII:
74, 17–21; CSM II: 51–52). Or: "*Praeterea etiam doceor a natura varia
circa meum corpus alia corpora existere*—I am also taught by nature
that various other bodies exist in the vicinity of my body" (VII: 81, 15–
17 = IX-1: 64; CSM II: 56). And also: "*plane certum est meum corpus,
sive potius me totum . . . a circumjacentibus corporibus affici posse*—
makes it quite certain that my body, or rather my whole self . . . can be
affected by various beneficial or harmful bodies which surround it" (VII:
81, 24–27 = IX-1: 65; CSM II: 56). Descartes doubtlessly does not oppose the two terms literally according to a clear and tidy nomenclature
(for example, by saying "flesh" and "body"), and he limits himself to distinguishing two meanings of *corpus*, moreover not without ambiguity.[7]
Besides, this lexical lack of distinction will obligate him to explain more
clearly at a later point in what and to what extent "this word 'body' is
very ambiguous."[8] For the moment, let us hold on to the essential: just

7. See also: "*corpus illud, quod speciali quodam jure meum appellabam,
magis ad me pertinere quam alia ulla arbitrabar: neque enim ab illo poteram
unquam sejungi, ut a reliquis*—As for the body which by some special right I
called 'mine,' my belief that this body, more than any other, belonged to me had
some justification" (VII: 75, 30–76, 3; CSM II: 52). The French translation removes the ambiguity: "It was not without some justification that I believed that
this body (which by a certain special right I called mine) belonged to me more
properly than any other. For in fact I could never be separated from it as from
other bodies" (IX-1: 60).

8. To Mesland, 9 February 1645, AT IV: 166, 2–3; CSMK: 242 (see below,
chap. IV, §18, 130–38). Géraldine Caps also notices this: "The amphibological
term of the body designates either the materiality of the body or the proper
human body, united to a soul to whose influence it can be subject." *Les 'méde-*

as the question about the existence of material things is partially linked to that about the distinction of mind and body, so this distinction itself (and the union that it conditions) assumes the more essential distinction between bodies that are purely and solely extended and *my* body that not only belongs to *me* but is *myself*. Without a clear appreciation of this more essential difference (but one generally ignored in the standard interpretations), the reply to the four questions remains impossible.

### §8. Arcte, *"very closely"*

Of these two opposing terms, *"meum corpus,* my body" certainly remains the more problematic. Two difficulties arise. First, its appropriation remains enigmatic: one gets the sense that it is not a matter of simply attributing a bit of extension to the *mens,* inasmuch as the distinction of thinking and extended substances makes them by right incommensurable (besides, not even incom*mensurable,* because measure, *mensura* or *dimensio,* strictly speaking concerns only extension). And even if one could admit this attribution arbitrarily, it is unclear how the fact that a body belongs to me (which falls under the category of the *habitus*) could modify its essence (which falls under the category of substance)[9]—of course, unless one understands such an appropriation by the ego in a radical, yet to be determined sense. This doubled enigma leads to another difficulty: what makes *meum corpus* something other than an always variable and provisionally determined bit of extension depends on the fact that it is united to the ego understood as *mens.* The union to the *mens* would offer the only principle of unity for this body, which becomes mine (*meum corpus*) only because I have it (*habeam corpus*). By admitting this paradox one better understands why there is no contradiction in one of the difficulties listed above: the distinction between mind and body in general is really understood *thanks to* and not despite the union of *a* body, namely mine (*meum corpus*), with this *mens,* in distinction from all the others (*alia corpora, reliqua, circumjacentia*), which are devoid of unity because without union. The distinction sepa-

---

cins cartésiens': *Héritage et diffusion de la représentation mécaniste du corps humain (1646–1696)* (Hildesheim: Olms, 2010), 76. It would be better to say: "Either the material bodies of the world or *my* body, itself also material, but which can certainly be subject to the influence of my mind, but above all *makes* my mind *subject.*"

9. See: *"mentem corpori realiter et substantialiter esse unitam, non per situm aut dispositionem*—that the mind is united in a real and substantial manner to the body" (To Regius, January 1642, III: 493, 4–5; CSMK: 206).

rates the mind (*mens*) that senses and imagines, hence comprises *meum corpus*, on the one hand, from the bodies that are extended and hence without stable unity on the other hand. The distinction between extension and thought thus is played out over the distinction of union (which unifies *meum corpus*) and the moving dispersal of strictly and purely extended bodies. In short, the unity of the body as my body (*corpus meum*) depends on its union with the *mens*, and it is thus distinguished all the better from all the bodies that remain nonunified. The union and the distinction thus do not bear on the same two terms, but marshal three of them: thought and my body (which form the union) are distinguished from other bodies (moreover without stable unity).

In order to point out the union and the terms of the union, Descartes uses the adverb "*arcte*—closely" constantly as a clue. Thus "*habeam corpus, quod mihi valde arcte conjunctum est*—I have a body . . . that is very closely joined to me" (VII: 78, 14–15 = IX-1: 62; CSM II: 54; trans. modified). And: "*me non tantum adesse meo corpori . . . sed illi* arctissime *esse conjunctum et quasi permixtum, adeo ut unum quid cum illo componam*—I am not merely present in my body . . . but am *very closely* joined and, as it were, intermingled with it, so that I and the body form a unit" (VII: 81, 2–5 = IX-1: 64; CSM II: 56). Or: "*eandem [i.e., mens] nihilominus tam* arcte *illi [i.e., corpus] esse conjunctam, ut unum quid cum ipsa componat*—but [the mind] is shown, notwithstanding, to be *so closely* joined to it [i.e., the body] that the mind and the body make up a kind of unit" (VII: 15, 22–24 = IX-1: 11–12; CSM II: 11). This adverb appears indirectly from 1637 onward in Courcelles' Latin translation of a formulation comparable to the French original: "it is not enough that it [i.e., a reasonable soul] is lodged in a human body . . . but it must be more closely joined and united with the body—*sed requiri ut cum ipso* arctius *jungatur uniaturque*" (VI: 59, 12–16 = 573; CSM I: 141). Responding to one of Arnauld's objections, not only does Descartes take up the same formulation ("*arctam illam mentis cum corpore conjunctionem*—that the mind is closely conjoined to the body"), but he guarantees it with experience ("*quam sensibus assidue experimur*—which we experience constantly through our senses," VII: 228, 27–28; CSM II: 160). This is not negligible because in the Replies experience has its royal function, so to speak, by guaranteeing another inexplicable and yet indubitable fact of reason, namely, freedom.[10] As to the *Principia*, it

---

10. Thus against Hobbes: "*quod omnes* experimur *in nobis*—what we all *experience* within ourselves" (VII: 191, 6; CSM II: 134 = weakened [in French] by "what we sense every day in ourselves," IX-1: 148) and against Gassendi:

makes systematic use of it: "arcta *et intima mentis nostrae cum corpore unio*—from the close and intimate union of our mind with the body" (I, §48; CSM I: 209) defines a "*mens nostra* . . . arcte *corpori* . . . *alligata*—mind . . . so closely tied to the body" (I, §71; CSM I: 218) or, in turn, a "*menti nostrae corpus quoddam* magis arcte, *quam reliqua alia corpora, conjunctum*—particular body . . . more closely conjoined with our mind than any other body" (II, §2; CSM I: 224).[11] Thus, "*arcte, very closely*" here plays the role of a precise and univocal marker for identifying "*corpus illud, quod speciali quodam jure meum appellabam*—the body which by some special right I called 'mine'" (VII: 75, 30f. = IX-1: 60; CSM II: 52), this body of mine that is me myself, among extension and the provisional, changing, and indefinite bodies that accumulate, appear, and unravel there.

One must still comprehend in what this "*unio ac quasi permistio*—union and as it were intermingling" (VII: 437, 6–7; CSM II: 294)

---

"*Talia enim sunt ut ipsa quilibet apud se debeat experiri, potius quam rationibus persuaderi.* . . . *Ne sis igitur libera* [i.e., *caro*, the flesh, Gassendi], *si non lubet; ego certe mea libertate gaudebo, cum et illam apud me experiar, et a te nulla ratione, sed nudis tantum negationibus, impugnetur.*—These are the sorts of things that each of us ought to know by experience in his own case, rather than being convinced of them by rational argument; . . . You may be unfree, if you wish; but I am certainly very pleased with my freedom since I experience it within myself. What is more, you have produced no arguments to attack it but merely bald denials" (VII: 377, 19–25; CSM II: 259). [He makes] the same remark to Burman, who had asked how the soul can be affected by the body: "*Hoc explicatu difficillimum; sed sufficit hic* experientia, *quae hic adeo clara est, ut negari nullo modo possit, ut illud in passionibus etc. apparet.*—This is very difficult to explain; but here our *experience* is sufficient, since it is so clear on this point that it just cannot be gainsaid. This is evident in the case of the passions, and so on" (§44, V: 163, 22–24; CSMK: 346). See *Principles of Philosophy* I, §48.

11. The title of the same II, §2 remains more moderate and suppresses the *magis*: "*corpus humanum menti esse arcte conjunctum*—the human body is closely conjoined with the mind" (CSM I: 224). See also *Principles* I, §60: "*Ac etiamsi supponamus, Deum alicui tali substantiae cogitanti substantiam aliquam corpoream tam arcte conjunxisse, ut arctius jungi non possint, et ita ex illis duabus unum quid conflavisse, manent nihilominus realiter distinctae.*— And even if we suppose that God has joined some corporeal substance to such a thinking substance so *closely* that they cannot be more *closely* conjoined, thus compounding them into a unity, they nonetheless remain really distinct" (CSM I: 213). Or: To Regius, July 1645: "*Nunc autem econtra, considerando mentem et corpus in eodem homine arcte uniri, vis illam tantum esse* modum corporis—but then, when you observe that the mind and the body are *closely* united in the same man, you take the former to be only a *mode of the body*" (IV: 250, 12–15; CSMK: 255).

consists or, more exactly, what allows Descartes to consider it so close that in it the *mens* and *this* body could be found merged into one (and thus distinguished from "all the other bodies"). The text proposes a precise answer to this question: "*Docet etiam natura, per istos sensus doloris, famis, sitis, etc., me non tantum adesse meo corpori ut nauta adest navigio, sed illi arctissime esse conjunctum et quasi permixtum, adeo ut unum quid cum illo componam.*—Nature also teaches me, by these sensations of pain, hunger, thirst and so on, that I am not merely present in my body as a sailor is present in a ship, but that I am very closely joined and, as it were, intermingled with it, so that I and the body form a unit" (VII: 81, 1–5 = IX-1: 64; CSM II: 56). This is not an accidental or chance metaphor. Moreover, the *Discourse on Method* had already refused in the same terms that the *mens* "would be lodged in the human body like a pilot in his ship," insisting to the contrary that "it must be more closely joined and united with the body" (VI: 59, 8–16; CSM I: 141). Actually, this is a theme that Descartes gets—probably through the intermediary of Conimbres[12]—from the medievals and that opposes Plato and Aristotle to each other. Plato calls the one who contemplates οὐσία "the mind which governs the soul"; to which Aristotle responds by wondering about the mode of the link between soul and body: "It is not clear whether the soul may not be the actuality of its body in the sense in which the sailor is the actuality of the ship."[13] Thomas Aquinas comments on this exact position: "We thus do not say that the soul is the form of the body in the same way as the sailor is in his ship."[14] The intention of the argument leaves no room for doubt: In

12. *Commentaria in tres libros de Anima*, II, 1, q. 6, a. 2; cited by Étienne Gilson, *Index scolastico-cartésien* (Paris: Vrin, 1913/1979), 302.

13. Respectively, Plato, *Phaedrus* 247c6f., and Aristotle, *On the Soul* II.1, 413a8–9, ed. Jonathan Barnes in *The Complete Works of Aristotle* (Princeton: Princeton University Press, 1984), 657. The image of the pilot in his boat is not literally found in Plato's text, who all the same invokes the tradition (see Augustin Mansion, "L'immortalité de l'âme et l'intellect d'après Aristote," *Revue philosophique de Louvain* 51 ([1953]: 444–72).

14. Thomas Aquinas, *Contra Gentes* I.26: "*Non enim similiter dicimus esse formam in corpore et nautam in navi.*" We follow here the precise insights gathered by Delphine Kolesnik-Antoine, ed., *Union et distinction de l'âme et du corps*, and *L'Homme cartésien: La 'force qu'a l'âme de mouvoir le corps.' Descartes, Malebranche* (Rennes: Presses universitaires de Rennes, 2009), 137ff.; or also by Alexandrine Schniewind, "L'âme est-elle comme un marin dans son navire?," in Alexandrine Schniewind and Christophe Erismann, eds., *Compléments de substance. Études sur les propriétés accidentelles offerts à Alain de Libera* (Paris: Vrin, 2008).

contrast to the sailor, who remains a passenger in his boat, thus a (rational) accident of its (material) substance, which he can potentially leave when arriving at port or by throwing himself into the water during a shipwreck, the soul as the ἐντελέχεια of the body cannot be separated from it or even really be distinguished from it. In fact, Descartes takes up the Aristotelian position here again, the one Thomas Aquinas put forward against Plato's opinion: "Accordingly, Plato and his school held that the intellectual soul is united to the body not as form to matter, but only as mover to movable, for he said that the soul is in the body as a sailor in a boat. In this way the union of soul and body would only be by virtual contact."[15] As an Aristotelian who is resolutely opposed to an accidental union, hence also to a provisional union of the mind to *its* body, Descartes thus vindicates a human unity as radical as the one that the act and ἐντελέχεια assure.

It is even possible that Descartes pushes the argument further with a more precise point. For we can discern a different distinction here: Is it a pilot or a sailor in his ship? Descartes actually speaks in the *Discourse*

15. Thomas Aquinas: "*Plato igitur posuit, et ejus sequaces, quod anima intellectualis non unitur corpori sicut forma materiae, sed solum sicut motor mobili, dicens animam esse in corpore sicut nauta est in navi; et sic unio animae et corporis non esset nisi per contactum virtutis*—Accordingly, Plato and his school held that the intellectual soul is united to the body not as form to matter, but only as mover to movable, for he said that the soul is in the body as a sailor in a boat. In this way the union of soul and body would be by only virtual contact" (*Contra Gentes* II.57; 138). See: "*Plato posuit, ut Gregorius Nyssenus narrat, quod anima est in corpore sicut motor in mobili, ut nauta in navi, et non sicut forma in materia, unde dicebat quod homo non est aliquid ex anima et corpore, sed quod homo est anima utens corpore*—Plato asserted, as Gregory of Nyssa relates, that the soul is in the body as the motive force in something that moves, as a sailor in a ship, and not as form in matter; hence he said that man is not something [made of] soul and body but that man is a soul making use of a body" (*In Sententiarum libros*, II, d. 1, q. 2, a. 4, ad 3m); see also: "*cujus erroris occasio fuit quod animam corpori uniri posuerunt quasi accidentaliter, sicut nautam in navi, vel hominem indumento, ut de Platone Gregorius Nyssenus*— The occasion of which error was that they asserted that the soul is united to the body accidentally, as it were, like a sailor in a ship or a man in a garment, as Gregory of Nyssa [stated] about Plato" (*In Sententiarum libros*, II, d. 17, q. 2, a. 2 resp.; see *De unitate intellectus*, I, §5). In fact, the citation comes not from Gregory of Nyssa but from Nemesius of Emesa, *De natura hominis*, III, trans. R. W. Sharples and P. J. van der Eijk as *Nemesius on the Nature of Man* (Liverpool: Liverpool University Press, 2008), who, besides, does not use the formulation very literally. See Alain De Libera's note in his edition of *L'Unité de l'intellect contre les averroïstes* (Paris: GF-Flammarion, 1994), 208.

of a "pilot," and although in the Sixth Meditation he evokes only a "sailor—*nauta*" (VII: 81, 2, 8), de Luynes' translation judiciously (so it seems) chooses to render it twice by "pilot" instead of the "sailor" one would expect (IX-1: 64). This hesitation does not appear accidental here; it reflects the precise distinction Plotinus had introduced: "But it is also said that the soul is in the body as the pilot (κυβερνήτης) is in the ship; this is a good comparison as far as the soul's ability to be separate from the body goes, but would not supply very satisfactorily the manner of its presence, which is what we ourselves are investigating [i.e., the union]. For the sailor as a voyager (*nauta*, πλωτήρ) would be present incidentally in the ship, but how would he be present as a pilot (κυβερνήτης)? Nor is he in the whole of the ship, as the soul is in the [entire] body."[16] This is not a meaningless difference: The sailor is simply part of the crew, which includes indiscriminately the deckhands who operate the boat and know it, but also the workers, the employees, and passengers who travel without really knowing it or belonging to it. In contrast, the pilot, the skipper, knows the boat, possibly owns it, guides it, feels it vibrating and working, even senses it *living*, as one says, as if it were an extension of his own body into the limbs and the masts of the vessel. "The pilot knows the quality of the rudder better than the carpenter who made it," commented Mersenne.[17] In short, the pilot belongs to the ship and is—almost—one with it. Plotinus even evokes the hypothesis of an "animated rudder."[18] If thus the mind is found

16. Plotinus, *Enneads* IV: 3, 21, lg. 9–10, trans. A. H. Armstrong in Loeb Classical Library (Cambridge: Harvard University Press, 1984), 101. See Alexander of Aphrodisias, *Commentary on the Treatise of the Soul*, XIV: 3–6, trans. Athanasios P. Fotinis as *The De Anima of Alexander of Aphrodisias: A Translation and Commentary* (Washington, DC: University of America Press, 1980). The privilege of a pilot (κυβερνήτης) in contrast to a member of the crew in general or even of a simple passenger on board (*nauta*, πλωτήρ) comes from Aristotle, but from a very different context (*Politics* III, 4, 1276b20ff. and III, 6, 1279a3ff.). A relay might have been found in Isidore of Seville: "*Quod omnis gubernator nauta esse potest, omnis nauta gubernator esse non possit*—The difference between *gubernator* (helmsman) and *nauta* (sailor) is that every helmsman can be a sailor, but every sailor cannot be a helmsman." *De Differentiis Verborum* I, §276, PL 83, col. 38, trans. Priscilla Throop as *Isidore of Seville's Synonyms and Differences* (Charlotte, VT: Medieval MS, 2012), 137. The two terms are distinguished by two entries in the *Etymologiarum lib.*, XIX, §4: "*Gubernio, qui est gubernator*" and 5: "*Nauta a nave dictus per derivativum*" (PL 82, col. 663).

17. Mersenne, *Questions harmoniques* (1634), q. 2, in *Questions inouïes, etc.*, ed. A. Pessel (Paris: Fayard, 1985), 157.

18. Plotinus, *Enneads* IV: 3, 21, lg. 12. [Armstrong translates "ensouled" rudder (101).]

more closely united to the body than even the pilot (and not just the simple sailor) to his ship, one must conclude that even the most extreme maritime synergy of which true seafarers boast is not sufficient for the Cartesian conception of the union. It asks much more—a union going all the way to a perfectly homogenous (*"unum quid"* 81, 4) mixture (*"permixtione mentis cum corpore*—intermingling of the mind with the body," VII: 81, 13; CSM II: 56).

Yet, this unambiguous decision just highlights the major difficulty more visibly: Having refused the link between act and power,[19] what concept can Descartes use to argue in favor of such a strict conception of union? For the philosopher must think by concepts and cannot, like the poet, only evoke by figures, as Claudel did: "We are not in it [i.e., the body] as a rider on his horse or as a sailor in his boat, but as a laborer in his labor or as a torch in its light. We are the ones who make it; it is our expression like a word; it is the form that we give to the outside, the reality of our presence, our manner of responding to the call of God and of providing him with a likeness."[20] This opens the floor on which the debate will be pursued: By what right and by what concepts can Descartes claim to maintain and to take up the radical union of the human—mind and body—that he chooses to inherit from Aristotle, while refusing the Aristotelian doctrine that would supremely ensure it? In contrast, those contemporary philosophers who maintain the union without also renouncing Aristotle's conceptual argument are not affected by the same deficiency. When Charron decries that "philosophers prevented from saying it [i.e., the nature and kind of existence of the soul in the body] and from really joining and uniting the soul with the body, make it abide and reside in the body like a master in his house, a pilot in his ship, the coachman in his coach," he is still able to invoke the threefold Aristotelian division of the soul and make it the form of the body in all seriousness.[21] When Scipion Dupleix stigmatizes the "error . . . of Plato, Philoponus, Themistius, Averroës, and others who have held that the soul is not at all the true

19. See: *"Quis enim intelligit haec verba [actus in potentia]?"* (Regula XII, AT X: 426, 20–21). And see my commentary in *Descartes: Règles utiles et claires*, 248ff., and in *Sur l'ontologie grise de Descartes*, §24, 146ff.

20. Paul Claudel, *Positions et propositions* (Paris: Gallimard, 1942), II: 174.

21. Pierre Charron, *De la Sagesse* (1600), I.7, here using the 1604 edition, ed. B. de Negroni (Paris: Fayard, 1986), 95. See the clarification by Geneviève Rodis-Lewis, "Descartes et Charron," *Bulletin cartésien*, XXI, *Archives de philosophie* (1994) (reprinted in *Le Développement de la pensée de Descartes* (Paris: Vrin, 1997), chap. V.

shaping form of the human, but only assisting it, like the intelligences in the heavens or the pilot in his ship,"[22] he assumes the strict thesis of the shaping form [*forme informante*]. And Senault admits even more clearly that "profane philosophy" thinks the union of the soul and the body only "as a pilot who guides his vessel" and that it can be corrected with the resources of "Christian philosophy."[23] But in contrast [to these thinkers] this deficiency directly concerns Descartes, who upholds the union in Aristotelian fashion, but abandons its Aristotelian principle.

Even so, the same passage that vindicates the union without justifying it via the ἐντελέχεια nevertheless proposes the indication of a solution: if I am my body, *meum corpus*, this is because nature teaches me this. Nature, that is to say, "*complexionem eorum omnium quae mihi a Deo sunt tributa*—the complexity or the totality of things bestowed on me by God" (AT VII: 80, 25–26 = IX-1: 64; CSM II: 56; trans. modified), assures me of my corporeality, albeit without making me conceive it, through a *fact* of experience, which takes the place of argument: "these sensations of pain, hunger, thirst and so on" (*"per istos sensus doloris, famis, sitis, etc.*," 81, 1–2; CSM II: 56).[24] One must beware of an easy misunderstanding: Descartes does not say that I know my corporeality because I have sensations in general or even because I experience sensations passively; he specifies that I know my corporeality because it makes me suffer. Suffering from pain, and even more specifically from a pain that comes first of all not from the exterior (the actions of other, simply extended, bodies), but so to say from the interior; for I suffer

22. Scipion Dupleix, *La Métaphysique ou science surnaturelle* (1600), V: 9, ed. Roger Ariew (Paris: Fayard, 1992), 357 (I am correcting the inaccurate *rocher* to *cocher*). Jean de Silhon uses a more brutal metaphor: "Those who believe that it [i.e., the rational soul] is in the body not as a form, but as a convict or a prisoner in the stocks, don't think at all that it would suffer any violence by being detached." *Les deux Vérités de Silhon: L'une de Dieu et de sa providence, l'autre de l'immortalité de l'âme* (1626), ed. Jean-Robert Armogathe (Paris: Fayard, 1991), 180.

23. Jean-François Senault, *De l'usage des passions* (1641), ed. Christiane Frémont (Paris: Fayard, 1987), 48.

24. See *Principles of Philosophy* I, §48: "*Sed et alia quaedam in nobis experimur, quae . . . ab arcta et intima mentis nostrae cum corpore unione proficiscuntur: nempe appetitus famis, sitis, etc.*—we also experience within ourselves certain other things . . . [which] arise . . . from the close and intimate union of our mind with the body. This list includes, first, appetites, like hunger and thirst" (CSM I: 209); IV, §190: "*appetituum naturalium, ut famis, sitis, etc.*—natural appetites like hunger and thirst" (CSM I: 280).

from a lack: the lack of food, of water, or similar lacks. I suffer from
what is missing in *me*; thus, I have a body because I sense that it hurts.
Or, rather, I sense myself unwell within it, when I suffer from this lack
of food or of drink: "*quod habeam corpus, cui male est cum* dolorem
sentio, *quod cibo vel potu* indiger, *cum famem aut sitim* patior—that I
have a body, and that when I *feel pain* there is something wrong with
the body, and that when I am hungry or thirsty the body *needs* food or
drink" (VII: 80, 28–30; CSM II: 56). I suffer because what I experience
as my body is felt as a lack; it makes me feel this lack. I am one with my
body, because not only do I suffer *for* it (as maybe the pilot suffers for
and with his ship in a storm), but I suffer *in* and *as* it. Or rather, I suffer
inasmuch as I somatize (if not to say "corporize"), as I suffer *myself* and
suffer *from myself* inasmuch as I am incarnated in my flesh, alone capable of suffering. Pure intellection does not suffer, thus my *mens* must
take on body (be incarnated, somatize) in a flesh in order to suffer and
to suffer *itself*. The passivity of the sensory experience of other bodies
that surround me in pure and simple extension (mentioned immediately
after this passage in 81, 15–27; 56) becomes possible only on the basis
of the more original passivity of this suffering *of self* [*de soi*], of the
experience of the self *as suffering*. Suffering makes up the privilege of
the soul, that is to say, of that by which the flesh is distinguished from
extension and from "other bodies": "I do not explain the feeling of pain
without reference to the soul. For in my view pain exists only in the
understanding. What I do explain is all the external movements which
accompany this feeling in us; in animals it is these movements alone
which occur, and not pain in the strict sense."[25] This is so far only an
indication, but here at least Descartes gives no other sign that would put
us on the path of an argument justifying his claim of a radical unity of
the union. Yet this simple indication should not be underestimated, for
it contains *in nuce* Descartes' ultimate essential discovery: the possibility and the conditions of a passive *cogitatio*. In a sense from now on I
will do nothing else than follow this path as far as possible. It may lead
us to port.

## §9. Meum corpus: *The Husserlian Moment*

My reading of the Sixth Meditation has led us radically to distinguish
physical bodies in general, which I experience as other, as surrounding me, as objects in my range (*alia corpora*), from my body (*meum*

25. To Mersenne, 11 June 1640, AT III: 85, 3–8; CSMK: 148.

*corpus*), which I know by experiencing it and by experiencing myself in lack (hunger, thirst, etc.). What status should we acknowledge for this distinction? Does it play a real theoretical role or is it only a marginal note? Or does Descartes innovate instead, and if this is the case, did his innovation receive any attention, was it taken up and theorized? This really was the case, provided one reads Husserl's *Cartesian Meditations* as an exact commentary on the *Meditations on First Philosophy*. This commentary remains very close to the Cartesian text, well beyond what Husserl himself admits. He declares, a bit imprudently, that he is unable to accept anything that comes after the Second Meditation, and from paragraph 10 onward, he thinks himself committed to denouncing the premises of an obviously lamentable Cartesian turn toward an "absurd transcendental realism."[26] Actually, after reviving the *ego cogito* in accordance with the main theme of intentionality (which occupies the first through fourth Cartesian Meditations) in grand phenomenological style, Husserl will rediscover, probably without being fully conscious of it, considering how much he continues to depend on the neo-Kantian reading of Descartes (Natorp and Cassirer), the Cartesian question of the external world, of its constitution and of its existence through the aporia (assumed to be Cartesian according to Kant) of "solipsism" and the resolution of the "problem of the objective world," of its constitution and its existence.[27] Whatever appreciation one might have for this "solution," it leads him to accomplish a theoretical breakthrough in the famous Fifth Cartesian Meditation, which is still epoch-making today: the construction of an intersubjective phenomenology. Now, within this framework Husserl takes up again radically the definition of the *ego cogito* no longer only or even first of all according to the guideline of intentionality, but starting from the consideration of its inscription in the world. The world, hence the world of physical bodies (*Körper*), among which the physical bodies of other humans are found, whatever their as yet undecided status, must be able to be reduced in order to take on the status of intentional object. What happens if I reduce this world of physical bodies, including those of other people and obviously this time including mine, at least the one I seem to have in the midst of those that surround me? It is enough to try this in order to perceive a paradox: "If I literally reduce other men, I literally get bodies (physical bodies, *Körper*); if I reduce *myself* as a man, I get my flesh (*Leib*) and my soul,

26. Husserl, *Cartesianische Meditationen*, §10, *Hua* I: 63; *Cartesian Meditations*, 24.

27. Ibid., §42, 121; 89.

or myself as a psychophysical unity—in the latter, my personal I, who operates in this flesh (*Leib*) and '*by means of it*' in the '*external world*' (*Außenwelt*), who *suffers* (*leidet*) this world."[28] I certainly find myself among extended beings, as a physical body among others, but "in this Nature and this world, my body (*Körper*) is the only body that is or can be constituted originally as flesh (*Leib*) (a functioning organ)."[29] From this decisive experience, we can retain a lot, especially for understanding Descartes' argument, which links *meum corpus* to pain and opposes it to the *alia corpora*.

How are the bodies (*Körper*) distinguished from my flesh (*Leib*) for Husserl? In that my flesh as *corpus sentiens* (X: 412, 21) senses the bodies (their surface, their form, their color, the possible odors, their sounds or their tastes)—accordingly the ego begins by sensing the piece of wax—while the sensed bodies themselves do not sense anything, no more my flesh than the other bodies or themselves. There is more: my flesh can feel bodies only by sensing, that is to say by indissolubly sensing these bodies *and itself* as affected by their sensory properties; in such a way that my flesh senses only by *sensing itself* at the same time: if I sense a hard object, I sense myself sensing it and possibly sense myself bruised by it. Or I sense my fingers by my opposable thumb, I sense my fingers that my thumb senses but also my thumb sensing itself, and in the same way I have a double sensation in each of my opposite fingers. To the point that medical anesthesia not only causes the sensation of surrounding bodies to disappear, but also truly the flesh sensing *itself*

28. Ibid., §44, 128; 97 (emphasis added on final word, other emphases in original; trans. modified). For an analysis of touching and the flesh in Husserl, see Didier Franck, *Chair et Corps: Sur la phénoménologie de Husserl* (Paris: PUF, 1981), trans. Scott Davidson and Joseph Rivera as *Flesh and Body: On the Phenomenology of Husserl* (London: Bloomsbury Academic, 2014), and Jean-Luc Marion, *De Surcroît: Études sur les phénomènes saturés* (Paris: PUF, 2001/2010), IV, §2, 105ff., trans. Robyn Horner and Vincent Carraud as *In Excess: Studies of Saturated Phenomena* (New York: Fordham University Press, 2002), 87–91. I do not here deal with another point of convergence between Husserl (and contemporary phenomenology) and Descartes, the interpretation of the existence of the *ego cogito* starting from thought as (self-)affection. This point has already been called to mind in *Questions cartésiennes* (Paris: PUF, 1991), chap. V, trans. as *Cartesian Questions: Method and Metaphysics* (Chicago: University of Chicago Press, 1999). We will return to it below, chap. VI, 217ff.

29. Husserl, *Cartesianische Meditationen*, §50, Hua I: 140; *Cartesian Meditations*, 110, trans. modified. [The English translation translates both *Körper* and *Leib* as "animate organism" when it refers to the human body.]

(which is precisely the desired goal). Accordingly I experience (I experience *myself* in and as) my flesh only by passively undergoing a double (or even quadruple) sensing, which can turn into pain. Thus one really must say *my* flesh and *my* body. It is not enough to add "my" to the word "body" or to turn it into a "proper body" [*corps propre*] in order to reach my flesh as if by addition; for with my flesh that feels (*itself*), it is simply no longer a matter of an extended body, neither of one body among others nor of one of these bodies that I sense. Rather, at stake is what Husserl perfectly identifies under the title of "myself as psychophysical unity, my personal *I* within it": I am flesh inasmuch as the psychosomatic unity makes me lose, so to say, my body in order to become flesh, that is, an *ego cogito* who thinks by sensing (*sentiens*, VII: 28, 22 and 34, 21), by suffering, and thinks itself always in this way, because it could neither sense without sensing *itself* nor *suffer without (sensing)* itself *suffering*. The unity or rather the union turns me into a flesh who thinks and who thinks itself according to a new mode of thought, a passive one, namely, that of sensing [*le sentir*]. Without literally making the distinction between body and flesh so brilliantly introduced by Husserl, Descartes nevertheless anticipates it (although in a sense he masks it under the less visible distinction, still sufficiently clear to a good reader, between *alia corpora* and *meum corpus*), and the Sixth Meditation cannot be understood in any other way except through it. Husserl hence emerges as the best, albeit here involuntary, reader of Descartes because he first of all remains his heir, on this point as on so many others.[30]

Yet there is more by way of encounter. As we have seen, Husserl indicates that "my personal *I* . . . acts in this flesh (*Leib*) and *via its mediation* (*mittelst*) in the *external world* (*Außenwelt*)." Now, Descartes himself also passes from the certainty of the flesh experienced in the union and *through its mediation* (in this instance, first of all via

---

30. All the same, if he had not followed his scholarly disdain, he could have been inspired by an almost phenomenological distinction made before its time by Isidore of Seville: "*Quod in omni carne corpus est, non in omni corpore caro. Caro enim proprie ossa et sanguis est, quod tamen et corpus est. Corpus autem et lapis et lignum est, quod tamen car non est. Dictum autem est corpus a corruptione, et caro a carendo vel a cadendo*—The difference between *corpus* (body) and *caro* (flesh) is that all flesh has a body, but not every body has flesh. Flesh is properly bones and blood, which is also a body. But a body can also be a stone or a tree, which is not flesh. Body is named *corpus* from *corruptio* (corruption) and flesh is named *caro* from *carendo* (lacking) or *cadendo* (falling)." *De differentiis verborum*, I, §152 [actually 116], PL 83, col. 24; *Synonyms and Differences*, 108.

the imagination) to the question of the external world. In fact, when he introduces the essential difference between bodies (whose existence one must demonstrate) and my flesh (whose existence is experienced without demonstration, although its unity with my mind still has to be thought through), Descartes does not so much add a second task to the program of the Sixth Meditation as attempt to resolve the first question by responding to the latter. One text states this very clearly three times.

First comes the observation that what is sensory in the body remains irreducible to the simple material natures: "*Soleo vero alia multa imaginari, praeter illam naturam corpoream, quae est purae Matheseos objectum, ut colores, sonos, sapores, dolorem et similia, sed nulla tam distincte.*—But besides that corporeal nature which is the subject-matter of pure mathematics [geometry, in French text], there is much else that I habitually imagine, such as colours, sounds, tastes, pain and so on— though not distinctly" (VII: 74, 1–4 = IX-1: 58; CSM II: 51). Besides the false translation of *Mathesis* by geometry, one notices that not only the sensory qualities of things are at stake, but their effect of pain on the flesh, in other words, it is about the world such as it comes from the exterior through its qualities acting on my passible, possibly suffering, flesh. This exteriority that is passively experienced and suffered goes in diversity and activity beyond what the *Mathesis [universalis]* could ever make known to me: extended and moving shapes that I can construct mathematically and apart from representation. Descartes hence anticipates Husserl's distinction: just as the intentional object is known by a constitution that does not affect me, so the flesh is exposed to the world by an affective passivity.

Second, the same text raises the problem of the mode of knowledge for these *alia multa*, a knowledge that has become problematic from the moment that I no longer apprehend them with the clarity and the distinction that bodies allow as the object of *Mathesis*, but instead by sensation: "*et quia haec percipio melius sensu, a quo videntur ope memoriae ad imaginationem pervenisse, ut commodius de ipsis agam, eadem opera etiam de sensu est agendum*—Now I perceive these things much better by means of the senses, which is how, with the assistance of memory, they appear to have reached the imagination. So in order to deal with them more fully, I must pay equal attention to the senses" (VII: 74, 4–7 = IX-1: 58–59; CSM II: 51). One must thus inquire after the specific aspects of this sensation or more exactly of this mode of the *res cogitans* or of the ego that "*sensum appello*—I call sensory" (VII: 74, 8; 51), of the "*corpus sentiens*" (X: 412, 21). This still exactly corresponds to Husserl's formulation: "Among the bodies (*Körper*) belonging to this 'Nature' and included in my peculiar ownness, I then find *my flesh* (*meinen Leib*) as uniquely singled out—namely, as the only one of them that is not just a body but precisely a *flesh*: the sole Object within my abstract world-stratum to which, in accordance with experience, I ascribe fields of sensation (*Empfindungsfelder*)."[31] The flesh alone opens on a field of sensation, hence of experience of the world, because it alone *opens itself* by its receptivity that is precisely fleshly.

Finally, the consideration of what is not limited in my *cogitatio* to mathematical extension (soon called "intelligible") not only opens a new field of experience (the flesh), but also and in consequence of this opening allows access to the existence of that to which it is opposed, namely, the bodies of extension: "*videndumque an ex iis quae isto cogitandi modo, quem sensum appello, percipiuntur, certum aliquod argumentum pro rerum corporearum existentia habere possim*—and see whether the things which are perceived by means of that mode of thinking which I call 'sensory perception' provide me with any sure argument for the existence of corporeal things" (VII: 74, 7–10 = IX-1: 59; CSM II: 51). This is an astonishing reversal of the order of reasoning: not only do the extended bodies not encompass my own body, my not only extended union, in short my flesh, on account of the gap between what alone feels (the flesh) and what does not sense itself but makes itself sensed for and by what senses (my flesh); not only does the existence of the first [these bodies] depend on an argument drawn from the capacity of the sensibility (the imagination) of the second [my body]; but above all the first demonstration of the Sixth Meditation would rely on the second inquiry devoted to the unity of the fleshly ego (to its incarnation)[32] via a remarkable prolepsis that is maybe unique in the entire order of reasoning. This finds an echo in the paradox Husserl repeats: "Restricting ourselves to the ultimate transcendental ego and the universe of what is constituted in him, we can say that a division of his whole transcendental field of experience belongs to him immediately, namely the division into the sphere of *his* ownness . . . and the sphere of what is 'other.'"[33] In other

31. Husserl, *Cartesianische Meditationen*, §44, Hua I: 128; *Cartesian Meditations*, 97, trans. modified.

32. Ferdinand Alquié says in a note: "Here the body seems to appear next to the subject, it manifests a true incarnation of the mind." *Descartes: Œuvres philosophiques*, vol. II (Paris: Hatier, 1967), 492. Marleen Rozemond *almost* sees this point in *Descartes' Dualism*, ed. Gordon P. Baker and Katherine J. Morris (New York: Routledge, 1996), 190ff. and 201ff.

33. Husserl, *Cartesianische Meditationen*, §45, Hua I: 131; *Cartesian Meditations*, 100.

words, "I, the reduced 'human Ego' ('psychophysical' Ego [flesh]), am constituted, accordingly, as a member of the 'world' with a multiplicity of 'objects outside me' (*Außer-mir*). But I myself constitute all this in my 'psyche' and bear it intentionally within me."[34] Even and especially the external world is opened up only to my flesh and not directly as the extension of the *Mathesis [universalis]* of bodies either opposite my body, which does not think anything, or opposite my understanding, which does not sense anything.

Yet there is something even more remarkable: it is necessary and finally becomes possible to redefine the signification of the external things. Certainly the gap between the sensory and the "*objectum purae Matheseos*" had already been subject to discussion in the *Meditations* (VII: 71, 8–9, 15) as in the *Regulae* (X: 377, 11, 17, 22; 378, 1–2, 8–9; etc.); but in these schemes, the two terms held the conventional place: the sensory (the future secondary qualities) occupied the interior (the subjectivity of "ideas or feelings"), while the "objects," constituted according to simple material natures (extension, shape, and movement), occupied the exterior as "a certain movement or very rapid and lively action, which passes to our eyes."[35] Now, all of a sudden and completely contrary, the roles are reversed in the Sixth Meditation: when we imagine and sense "*alia multa . . .* praeter *illam naturam corpoream, quae est purae Matheseos objectum*—besides that corporeal nature which is the subject-matter of pure mathematics [geometry], *there is much else*" (VII: 74, 1–2 = IX-1: 58; CSM II: 51). Much else—what sort of thing? Obviously that which comes to be added as sensory to the simple material natures as from the exterior, "*foris*—outside."[36] In short, sensations mark the transcendence (the exterior) in opposition to the simple material natures, which remain immanent (interior) to the mind. One must understand the "*sensuum* externorum *judicia*—judgments based on the *external* senses" (VII: 76, 27 = IX-1: 61; CSM II: 53, trans.

34. Husserl, ibid., §44, 129; 99.

35. *Optics* I, AT VI: 84, 15–18; CSM I: 153 (concerning the physical process of light).

36. "foris *vero*, praeter *corporum extensionem, et figuras, et motus, sentiebam* etiam *in illis duritiem, et calorem, aliasque tactiles qualitates*—And outside me, besides the extension, shapes and movements of bodies, I also had sensations of hardness and heat, and of the other tactile qualities" (AT VII: 74, 27—75, 2; AT IX-1: 59; CSM II: 52). *Foris* is here a hapax of the *Meditations*; see Katsuzo Murakami, Meguru Sasaki, Tetsuichi Nishimura, *Concordance to Descartes' "Meditationes de Prima Philosophia"* (Hildesheim: Olms-Wiedmann, 1995), 339.

modified) literally. And that is precisely why Descartes could claim to find in the *sensus*, and exactly not in the *"purae Matheseos objectum*," a possible *argumentum* for the existence of corporeal things (VII: 74, 9). Therefore, everything proceeds as if the knowledge of the existence of material things did not fall under the same modality of the *res cogitans* as that used for knowing its essence. Their essence, because it refers back only to the simple material natures (innate, immanent, interior), can be known by the understanding aided by the imagination, although their existence, which refers to the "outside" of the flesh, can be known (if it can be known at all) only through sensation (or *sensus*).[37] Exteriority is hence opened only to the most intimate, *meum corpus*: "*nam quid dolore intimius*—what is more intimate than pain?" (VII: 77, 1; CSM II: 53; trans. modified).[38]

### §10. In/commoda: *The Heideggerian Moment*

Yet what concepts authorize Descartes to reverse the arrangement of interior and exterior, of "feelings" and "objects," in this way? The reason probably lies in the fact that the modes of being and of manifestation of the material bodies themselves are modified. Let us note that Descartes does not stop defining material things and their ideas as what comes to the ego: "*absque ullo meo consensu mihi advenire*—these ideas came to me quite without my consent" (VII: 75, 10–11; CSM II: 52), "*a rebus extra me positis mihi advenire*—comes from things located outside of me" (77, 12–13; CSM II: 53), "*variae istae sensuum perceptiones*

---

37. See: "*Non enim rerum materialium existentiam ex eo probavi, quod earum ideae sint in nobis, sed ex eo, quod nobis sit* adveniant, *ut simus conscii, non a nobis fieri, sed aliunde* advenire—I proved the existence of material things not from the fact that we have ideas of them but from the fact that these ideas *come* to us in such a way as to make us aware that they are not produced by ourselves but *come* from elsewhere." To Hyperaspistes, August 1641, AT III: 428, 30—429, 2; CSMK: 193. See *aliunde* at VII: 75, 21; 80, 3 at 86, 15 (neither the *cogitatio* nor the idea of God come *aliunde*, according to VII: 2, 27 and 38, 3).

38. One can here think of the externality of the flesh (albeit incorrectly named here a *body*) according to Emmanuel Levinas: "This is what makes the body the very advent of consciousness. It is nowise a thing—not only because a soul inhabits it, but because its being belongs to the order of events and not to that of substantives. . . . it is the irruption in anonymous being of localization itself. . . . To take it as an event is to say that it is not an instrument, symbol or symptom of position, but is position itself, that in it is effected the very transformation of an event into a being." *Existence and Existents*, trans. Alphonso Lingis (Pittsburgh: Duquesne University Press, 2001), 69–70.

*adveniunt*—various sensory perceptions come" (81, 20–21; CSM II: 56, trans. modified).[39] In contrast, the *res materiales*, as objects, do not come and can never come, because they subsist permanently as or in the substances.[40] Where therefore should one situate the coming as such? A text in the Sixth Set of Replies gives an indication already by distinguishing between three types of *sensus*. The first concerns only extension, because it is a matter of the immediate action of external objects on the organic body. The third concerns only thought, because it is a matter of judgments that bear on external things. The second type is left over, which "*continet id omne quod immediate resultat in mente ex eo quod organo corporeo sic affecto unita sit*—comprises all the immediate effects produced in the mind as a result of its being united with a bodily organ which is affected in this way."[41] The sensory *as such* hence exists only in the union, in other words in the reception affecting my flesh. It is here exactly designated as the whole formed by the affected body (*affectus*) to which my *mens* is united, as what follows "*ex unione ac quasi permistione mentis cum corpore*—the union and as it were the intermingling of mind and body" (VII: 437, 6–7 = IX-1: 236; CSM II: 294). For all that, one ambiguity remains: the affection of the flesh brings about two different kinds of "perceptions" that are quite different: on the

39. See the Third Meditation: "*sive velim, sive nolim,* sentio *calorem, et ideo puto sensum illum, sive ideam caloris,* a re a me diversa, *nempe ab ignis cui assideo calore,* mihi advenire—now, for example, I *feel* the heat whether I want to or not, and this is why I think that this sensation or idea of heat *comes to me from something other than myself,* namely the heat of the fire by which I am sitting" (VII: 38, 17–20; CSM II: 26; which connects exteriority and sensibility to the event in remarkable fashion). Similarly "*neque . . . illam sensibus hausi, nec unquam non expectanti mihi advenit*—it has never come to me unexpectedly, as usually happens with the ideas of things that are perceivable by the senses" (VII: 51, 7–8; CSM II: 35). And (although the hypothesis is here skirted): "*mihi forte a rebus externis per organa sensuum istam trianguli ideam advenisse*—the idea of the triangle may have come to me from external things by means of the sense organs" (64, 25–27; CSM II: 45).

40. Thus "*aliqua substantia cui insint*—some substance for them to inhere in" (79, 1; CSM II: 54–55); "*manifestum est has, siquidem existant, inesse debere corporeae sive extensae, non autem intelligenti*—it is clear that these other faculties, if they exist, must be in a corporeal or extended substance and not an intellectual one" (79, 2–4; CSM II: 55); "*superest ut sit in aliqua substantia a me diversa*—the only alternative is that it is in another substance distinct from me" (79, 15 and 18–19; CSM II: 55).

41. AT VII: 437, 2–4 = IX-1: 236; CSM II: 294. The translation here is missing what is essential, namely, affection, which is more radical than disposition or movement.

one hand "*perceptiones doloris, titillationis, sitis, famis*—perceptions of pain, pleasure, thirst, hunger," that is, sensation that cannot be objectified and that can be related only to me, but never directly to objects; and on the other hand "*perceptiones . . . colorum, soni, saporis, odoris, caloris, frigoris, & similium*—colours, sound, taste, smell, heat, cold, and the like" (VII: 437, 4–5 = IX-1: 236; CSM II: 294), which concern me or can be related to me as I sense them, but can also be related to the things, at least according to common consciousness (the one that experiences the piece of wax as sensory). How can this distinction between sense for my flesh and sense for the objects be made?

One can probably think here by anticipation (below, chapter 6) of the theme that §22 of the *Passions of the Soul* puts into place: "All the perceptions . . . come to the soul by means of the nerves. They differ from one another in so far as we refer some to *external* objects which strike our *senses*, others to our body or to certain of its parts, and still others to our soul" (XI: 345, 18–23; CSM I: 336–37). Yet such a distribution assumes that one already knows how to make the distinction between the two in order then to divide them up again, which is not yet our case: one must thus look for a solution elsewhere. I would suggest considering a different text, also treating the errors of youth, thus of sensation: "In our early childhood the mind was so closely tied to the body that it had no leisure for any thoughts except those by means of which it had *some impressions* of what was happening to the body. It did not yet consider whether these impressions were caused by anything outside itself, but merely felt pain when something harmful was happening to the body and felt pleasure when something beneficial occurred. And when nothing very *beneficial* or *harmful* was happening to the body, the mind had various sensations corresponding to the different areas where, and ways in which, the body was being stimulated, namely what we call the sensations of tastes, smells, sounds, heat, cold, light, colours, and so on—*mens nostra tam* arcte *corpori erat alligata, ut non aliis cogitationibus vacaret, quam iis solis, per quas ea* sentiebat quae corpus afficiebant: *necdum ipsas ad quidquam extra se positum referebat, sed tantum ubi* quid corpori incommodum *occurrebat, sentiebat dolorem; ubi* quid commodum, *sentiebat voluptatem; et ubi* sine magno commodo vel incommodo *corpus afficiebatur, . . . habebat diversos quosdam sensus, illos scilicet quos vocamus sensus saporum, odorum, sonorum, caloris, figoris, luminis, colorum et similium.*"[42] The first

---

42. *Principles of Philosophy* I, §71, IX-2: 58 = VIII-1: 35, 6–18; CSM I: 218–19, trans. modified.

perception (*cogitatio*) that comes to me and affects my flesh (the union) is first related to it as pain or as pleasure (as hunger or thirst) well before it can be assigned to things as sensible qualities (soon called secondary), according to the sole criterion of convenience or inconvenience. As long as that which affects me (for example the heat of the fire) causes me inconvenience at first, I allocate it to my flesh as pain; if this same affection causes me first convenience (for example the light of the same fire), I allocate it to my flesh as pleasure. Accordingly, the more the affection falls under what is useful or harmful, handy or impractical, the more it is related to my flesh. Yet to the extent that the convenience or inconvenience fades (thus paradoxically the *more* I put up with the affection and its excess), the more I can refer the thought (and its possible cause) to something other than only my flesh. In other words, the first relation that I maintain with what affects me falls under convenient or inconvenient use and not knowledge. I move on to an (even rough) theoretical connection only when bracketing my interest, my use, my worry, and my concern and only to that exact extent. Besides, the doubt of the First Meditation does not become purely theoretical until my mind is freed "of all worries—*curis omnibus*" (IX-1: 13 = VII: 17, 13f.; CSM II: 12). The affection of the flesh by the first exteriority thus does not play out in terms of knowledge (one that would be clear and distinct, according to the simple material natures), but in terms of use, according to what is agreeable/disagreeable or convenient/inconvenient about the things of the world for the life of my flesh ("*commodum ad usum vitae*—this is convenient for practical purposes").[43] And in turn the theoretical con-

43. *Principles of Philosophy* III, §29, AT VIII-1: 91, 11; CSM I: 252. See: "thus we make ourselves, as it were, lords and masters of nature. This is desirable not only for the invention of innumerable devices which would facilitate our enjoyment of the fruits of the earth and all the goods we find there, but also, and most importantly, for the *maintenance of health*, which is undoubtedly the chief good and the foundation of all the other goods in this life" (*Discourse on Method*, VI: 62, 7–15; CSM I: 142–43). This doctrine of the *in/commoda* is found in a number of texts. (a) "*Nec mirandum est, in brutorum cerebro esse satis multas diversas dispositiones, cum videmus illa tot modis moveri: oriuntur enim omnes illorum motus a duobus tantum elementis* commodis *naturae vel* incommodis, *idque vel singulis partibus vel toti, adeo ut, cum sensus exhibent aliquid* commodum *toti, protinus ea motio, quae efficit sensum, efficiat etiam motus omnes in aliis membris ad fruendum istis* commoditatibus; *si exhibent aliquid* commodum *uni parti tantum et alteri* incommodum, *motio illa quae sentitur determinet spiritus animales ad efficendos omnes motus possibiles in una parte, per quos fruatur isto* commodo, *et in alia, per quos fugiat istud* incommodum—It is not strange that there should be sufficiently various dispositions in

nection to the things appears only to the extent that this connection of use disappears.

Can this distinction, to which the Cartesian texts bear witness, be rigorously thematized? That is certainly possible, at least if one agrees to consider a terminology that Heidegger paradoxically elaborated *against* Descartes in *Being and Time*. It concerns conceiving that a being first of all discloses itself not as an object adapted to theoretical consciousness, that is, as present-at-hand (*vorhanden*), because it would subsist identical to itself, but as a tool, more exactly as common stuff (*usuel*, *Zeug*), a thing that can serve a use in some way or other (by destination or by fabrication, it matters little), a being ready-to-hand (*zuhanden*). What distinguishes these two modes of appearing relies precisely on the abstraction that permits us to reduce the being to what subsists in it (at least once) as its presumed essential properties and to what "remains— *remanet*" in it: substantial presence of the substrate, in Cartesian terms the material substance with its principal attribute (*extensio*) modeled according to shape and movement. Thus the sensible qualities (the future supposed "secondary qualities") disappear or rather find themselves placed at a distance from theoretical consideration. More essentially,

---

the brain of animals, since we see that they are moved in so many ways: for all of their motions arise from two sorts of elements, either pleasing to their nature or unpleasing, that is, pleasing to individual parts or to the whole, so that when the senses display something that is pleasing to the whole, that motion which affects the sense also affects all the motions in other parts of the body so that they may enjoy what is pleasing to them; if the senses display something that is pleasing to only one part and not pleasing to another, the motion that is felt determines the animal spirits to bring about in one part all possible motions by which it may enjoy what is pleasing to it and in other parts it determines the animal spirits by which that part may avoid what is unpleasing." *Prima cogitationes circa generationem animalium*, AT XI: 519, 7–20, according to *Écrits physiologiques et médicaux*, ed. Vincent Aucante (Paris, 2000), 88. (b) "two sorts of movements almost always follow every [sensory] action, namely external movements that serve in the pursuit of desirable things and the avoidance of injurious ones; and internal movements that commonly designate *passions*." *Traité de l'homme*, AT IX: 193, 22–27, trans. Thomas Steele Hall as *Treatise of Man* (Cambridge: Harvard University Press, 1972), 106. (c) "objects which stimulate the senses do not excite different passions in us because of differences in the objects, but only because of the various ways in which they may *harm or benefit* us, or in general have importance for us" (*Passions of the Soul*, §52, AT XI: 372, 12–17; CSM I: 371). See: "The other passions [i.e., admiration] may serve to take note of things which appear *good or evil*" (§75, XI: 384, 19–21; CSM I: 355; and §§74, 85, 111, 137, 138, 141, 207, 208, etc.).

the affections according to which utility is put into play disappear: usefulness and uselessness, conveniences and inconveniences. According to the analysis in *Being and Time*, Descartes would have been the first to reduce the thing to subsistence available to permanence (*Vorhandenheit*), eliminating with the sensible qualities and their *in/commoda* what is primordially ordinary within them (*Zuhandenheit*). This diagnosis of a "constant abiding" (*ständiger Verbleib*)[44] corresponds exactly to the treatment of material things in the first five Meditations, where it is precisely a matter of certain knowledge about permanence (*"remanet cera*—the wax remains")[45] reduced to nothing other than extension and its modes (*"remotis iis quae ad ceram non pertinent, videamus quid supersit: nempe nihil aliud quam extensum quid, flexibile, mutabile*— take away everything which does not belong to the wax, and see what is left: merely something extended, flexible and changeable," VII: 31, 1–3; CSM II: 20).

Yet, this same diagnosis is not at all suitable for what the Sixth Meditation intends when it looks at something *"praeter illam naturam corpoream, quae est purae Matheseos objectum*—besides that corporeal nature which is the subject-matter of geometry" (74, 1–2 = IX-1: 58; CSM II: 51; trans. modified). As is often the case, Heidegger sees perfectly, but only partly correctly, dependent as he remains on the neo-Kantian (and Husserlian) interpretation of Descartes conceived as a thinker exclusively occupied with the objectness of being [*de l'étant*].[46] If he had taken the measure of the innovation of this new and final point of view about corporeal things, Heidegger would most probably have developed further an indication that concludes his critical analysis in the form of a remorse or at least a scruple: "These qualities, which are themselves reducible, would provide the footing for such specific qualities as 'beautiful,' 'ugly,' 'in keeping,' 'not in keeping,' 'useful,' 'use-

---

44. Martin Heidegger, *Sein und Zeit*, §19 (Tübingen: Max Niemeyer Verlag, 1927/1963), 92, trans. John Macquarrie and Edward Robinson as *Being and Time* (New York: HarperPerennial, 2008), 125.

45. Second Meditation, VII: 30, 19–25; CSM II: 20; see *Principles* II, §4: "*ipsa [materia corporea] integra* remanente—the matter itself *remains* intact" (VIII-1: 42, 20–21; CSM I: 224).

46. See *Being and Time*, §§15–16 (for the contrast between *vorhanden* and *zuhanden*) and §§19–21 (for the interpretation of the *res extensa*, in fact of the *"purae Matheseos objectum"* as strictly *vorhanden*). On this point, see my analysis in *Reduction and Givenness: Investigations of Husserl, Heidegger, and Phenomenology*, trans. Thomas A. Carlson (Evanston, IL: Northwestern University Press, 1998), chapter 3, §4, 88–92.

less' (*passend, unpassend, brauchbar, unbrauchbar*). . . . But with this stratification, we really (*doch*) do come to those entities which we have characterized ontologically as equipment ready-to-hand (*das zuhandene Zeug*). The Cartesian analysis of the 'world' would thus enable us for the first time to build up securely the structure of what is proximally ready-to-hand (*zunächst Zuhandenen*); all it takes to round out the thing of nature until it becomes a full-fledged thing of use (*Gebrauchsding*), and this is easily done."[47] An extraordinary concession, where Heidegger himself recognizes Descartes' *in/commoda* as features of *Zuhandenheit* and thus admits that Descartes could well have thought them; he is missing only the additional recognition that the Sixth Meditation had literally thought and described it.[48]

47. Heidegger, *Sein und Zeit*, §21, 99, *Being and Time*, 131–32; trans. lightly modified. Emmanuel Martineau's translation tones down Heidegger's approval of Descartes by adding: "*It certainly seems . . . that the Cartesian analysis*," *Être et Temps* (Paris: Authentica, 1985), 90. This softening, which has no basis in the original, is even more nonsensical inasmuch as Heidegger's final reservation has to do with a completely different point: knowing whether Descartes maintains the anteriority of *Vorhandenheit* (of the *objectum purae Matheseos*) over the qualities that come only by complementing and correcting it belatedly. Yet this point could be disputed, because (a) for Descartes the *in/commoda* without doubt arrive first and before extension and (b) for Heidegger also the question of priority remains in a sense undecided (*Sein und Zeit*, §15, 71, lines 35ff.).

48. Another phenomenologist, Jan Patočka, has correctly suspected the irreducibility of this nontheoretical mode of access to the world (besides, he quotes the Sixth Meditation, AT VII: 82, 25—83, 2), but assumes that Descartes underestimates it and subordinates it to the theoretical access to the same objects: "The real distinction between soul and body being a superior truth that he [i.e., Descartes] had erected into sole absolute, it was only left for him to take this other [i.e., the union], to which he believed himself obligated to resort, to be some truth, no more than a part of truth." In other words, the relation to the *in/commoda* would remain an attitude that is limited and referring to the same objects as theoretical knowledge: "The composite of soul and body (that is to say, the personal, subjective body) decides only from the fact of the presence of the corporeal whole here and now, from the action that it exercises on me, and from the profit or the biological prejudice that follows. And even this is true only in an ordinary and general fashion. . . . The body proper has 'some' acquaintance, 'some' knowledge of a vaguely biocentric character that relates it entirely to itself, it constitutes, starting from the things that touch my interest, a personal perspective, but does not have the right to bear judgments on the essence of things." "Fenomenologia vlastiho tela" [1967–1968], in *Prirozeny svets a pohyb lidské existence*, vol. II (Prague: Oikumene, 1980); trans. [into French] Erika Abrams, "La phénoménologie du corps propre," in *Le Monde naturel et le Mouvement de l'existence humaine* (Dordrecht: Kluwer Academic

We can henceforth confirm it by going back to the Cartesian texts, which free up an equivalent of *Zuhandenheit* as the mode of being specific to the sensory in order to oppose it explicitly to the mode of being of *Vorhandenheit* that is characteristic of extension. The formulations in the Sixth Meditation leave no doubt: "*sensique hoc corpus [i.e., illud corpus, quod . . . tanquam me totum spectabam] inter alia multa corpora versari, a quibus variis* commodis *vel* incommodis *affici potest*—I also perceived by my senses that this body was situated among many other bodies, which could affect it in various favourable or unfavourable ways" (VII: 74, 20–22 = IX-1: 58; CSM II: 52); and "*meum corpus, sive potius me totum . . . variis* commodis *et* incommodis *a circumjacentibus corporibus affici posse*—my body, or rather my whole self, in so far as I am a combination of body and mind, can be affected by the various *beneficial* or *harmful* bodies that surround it" (81, 24–27 = IX-1: 65; CSM II: 56). These "sense perceptions—*sensuum perceptiones*" have the function to help me *know* not the bodies of the world in their essences but what are the ones whose existence provokes benefit or harm in my flesh: "*ad menti significandum quaenam composito, cujus pars [i.e., mens] est,* commoda *sint vel* incommoda—is simply to inform the mind of what is *beneficial* and *harmful*" (VII: 83, 17–24 = IX-1: 66; CSM II: 57). For it is valid as a general rule that "*omnes sensus circa ea . . . ad corporis* commodum *spectant*—in matters regarding the *well-being* of the body, all my senses report the truth much more frequently than not" (VII: 89, 11–12 = IX-1: 71; CSM II: 61).[49] The return to the sensory and

---

Publishers, 1988), 153–54. Even taking into account potential vagueness of the French version, it is quite visible that Descartes does not subordinate one kind of knowledge to another (the sensory included in and corrected by the intellectual), but distinguishes two irreducible relationships to the things of the world. Consequently, the supposed "metaphysical accident (*metafyzickou nahodou*)" (ibid., 151) of the union offers only an *artifact*, resulting from an original misunderstanding of the flesh in a Cartesian sense.

49. See (besides *Principles of Philosophy* I, §71, examined above, 63–64), other similar formulations: "*circa meum corpus alia corpora existere, ex quibus nonnulla mihi prosquenda sunt, alia fugienda*—various other bodies exist in the vicinity of my body, and that some of these are to be sought out and others avoided" (VII: 81, 15–17; CSM II: 56); "*quaedam ex illis perceptionibus mihi gratae sint, allae ingratae*—some of the perceptions are agreeable to me while others are disagreeable" (81, 23–24; 56); "*cum sciam omnes sensus circa ea, quae ad corporis commodum spectant, multo frequentius verum indicare quam falsum*—For I know that in matters regarding the well-being of the body, all my senses report the truth much more frequently than not" (89, 11–13; 61); "*ipsa quae tanquam persequenda vel fugienda mihi . . . exhibentur*—nature presents

to my flesh thus implies the reestablishment of the concerns suspended by the First Meditation, in order to allow a merely theoretical doubt, hence the primacy of handiness (*Zuhandenheit*) over the available permanence (*Vorhandenheit*) established by the Second Meditation.

A new mode of phenomenality follows immediately in regard to this new mode of being for sensible things. As long as what is at issue is knowing the essence of material things (as *vorhanden*), the *sensus* offers only a confused and obscure perception in opposition to the clear and distinct perception of "*solius mentis inspectio*—purely mental scrutiny" (VII: 31, 25; CSM II: 21). From now on, especially in the Sixth Meditation, the *sensus* perceives sensory things (colors, sounds, tastes, pain, etc.) "*melius*—much better" (VII: 74, 4 = IX-1: 59; CSM II: 51). How should we understand this reversal? First, because these sensible things are apprehended by the *sensus* only for their use "*ut* commodius *de ipsis agam*—more conveniently" (74, 6 = IX-1: 59; [not in CSM]), that is to say, as *zuhanden* and no longer as *vorhanden*. In fact, the clarity and distinctness are not attributed to the same perceptions, depending on whether it is a matter of knowing the essence or of dealing with existence: in the first case the ideas constructed according to the simple material natures are clear and distinct, in the other case the perceptions of the useful and harmful are alone suitable "*ad menti significandum quaenam . . . commoda sint vel incommoda, et eatenus sunt* satis clarae et distinctae—to this extent they are *sufficiently* clear and distinct" (VII: 83, 17–18 = IX-1: 66; CSM II: 57). Not only *sufficiently*, but as another passage does not hesitate to add: "multo magis *vividae et expressae, et suo etiam modo* magis distinctae—*much more* lively and vivid and even, in their own way, *more distinct*" (VII: 75, 15–16 = IX-1: 60;

---

to me as objects I should seek out or avoid" (83, 26–28; 58). This point is approached but not thematized by John Cottingham: "Sensory ideas are indeed about something: they convey information about the internal states of our bodies and the relationship between our bodies and the environment . . . the sensory grasp is adequate *for survival purposes.*" "Intentionality or Phenomenology: Descartes and the Objects of Thought," in Tim Crane and Sarah Patterson, eds., *History of the Mind-Body Problem* (New York: Routledge, 2000), 140. Also by Gordon P. Baker and Katherine J. Morris: "The objects of the internal senses are essentially connected with the organism's bodily *wellfare* or *illfare*. The person's own body is not simply logical and epistemologically special, but *prudentially* (and as we will see, perhaps *morally*)." What is missing here is the concept of the flesh, replaced by an arbitrary recourse to God: "God gave them [i.e., the sensations] to us for a different purpose, namely to make us vividly aware of things that are beneficial or harmful to us." Gordon P. Baker, *Descartes' Dualism* (London/New York: Routledge, 1996), 135f., 178; emphasis added.

CSM II: 52). This is no doubt surprising: what mode of clarity and distinctness is at stake here if not that of the ideas of simple natures? It is precisely a matter of this other mode, which can best indicate the utility or the harmfulness of things *inasmuch as* they are handy (*zuhanden*), like first of all the pain my flesh feels or, more exactly, my flesh feeling itself in experiencing the constraint that the sensory ideas coming to it as events impose on it, sometimes just like a pain. The mode of the *cogitatio* of the *sensus* is actually distinguished from others (those of the *res dubitans, intelligens, volens, imaginans*—the doubting, knowing, willing, imagining thing) first and above all by its passivity, thus by the experience of constraint.[50]

Thus there is nothing more logical for the flesh (the *cogitatio* in the mode of the *sensus*) than to be characterized by pain. For pain benefits from an astonishing privilege; Descartes actually mentions it the most often alone,[51] after the sensible qualities of things,[52] or without them,[53] or as one of the affections of the flesh,[54] in opposition to other modes of the *cogitatio*.[55] Yet this privilege has its own proper character, that of absolute interiority: "*Nam quid dolore intimius esse potest?*—For what can be more internal than pain?" (VII: 71, 1 = IX-1: 61; CSM II: 53). In fact, while I can always flee pleasure (even if this seems *moraliter* rather difficult), I cannot flee pain, *my* pain—for if I had been able to do so, I precisely would no longer experience it; hence if I still feel it despite everything, I feel it despite myself, because it cannot be separated from me, nor I from it. Colloquial language says it very well: "I feel my pain, I feel myself sick. [*J'ai senti ma douleur, je me sens mal.*]" This constraint proves neither that I sense an object in the world

50. Gueroult certainly "notices a fact in me: the fact of constraint. . . . The role of this fourth element is therefore of primary importance. Because of it, the productive faculty of sensible ideas is definitely rejected outside of me." That's certainly true, but how should one explain that this same "constraint" is exercised? Because it is a matter of "the constraint experienced in sensation," thus of "sensation with respect to the existing body," one must go all the way to proceed to the conclusion that I can receive and feel this existence only in my *flesh*, hence that I must feel myself first as my *flesh*. *Descartes' Philosophy*, II: 62, 77, 80; trans. lightly modified. This does not happen.

51. More rarely pain appears in parallel with pleasure: AT VII: 74, 23–24; 76, 4–5; 82, 26–27; CSM II: 52, 57.

52. VII: 74, 3; 80, 14; 83, 10; CSM II: 51, 55, 57.

53. VII: 76, 7 and 15; 77, 3 and 7; 80, 29; CSM II: 52, 53, 56.

54. VII: 81, 1 and 11; 83, 8; CSM II: 56, 57.

55. VII: 81, 7; 87, 10 and 17; 88, 4 and 26; 89, 1; CSM II: 56, 60, 61.

nor that I have trouble [*mal*] feeling myself, but that I am *in myself and as myself* confronted by an intimate, irreducible external influence. In this way pain owes its primacy over all the other senses of the *sensus* to the maximum constraint which it imposes on the part of something handy (*zuhanden*) that is decidedly uncomfortable. This constraint does not teach me anything about the essence of the extended body, but shows nevertheless definitively its external existence *in myself and myself more than myself.*[56] From now on, pain, as the ultimate or first figure of the *cogitatio* in the mode of the *sensus*, within it the absolute symptom of my flesh, fully shows itself to be the experience of exteriority, thus, as Descartes had announced from the outset, "*cestum aliquod argumentum pro rerum corporearum existentia*—sure argument for the existence of corporeal things" (VII: 74, 9–10; CSM II: 51). This would still have to be shown.

## §11. A Revision of the Existence of Material Things

In this way, I hope to have shown that the Sixth Meditation really manages to prove what it promises, at least on the condition of identifying correctly what it wants to prove. Contrary to what Kant reproaches it with, first of all it neither solely nor finally wants to prove the existence of the external world. In fact, one must read it as such, without stopping dead at the conclusion ("*Ac proinde res corporeae existunt*—It

---

56. Here it is impossible not to think of Levinas (see above, §9, 61, note 38): "physical suffering in all its degrees entails the impossibility of detaching oneself from the instant of existence. It is the very irremissibility of being. The content of suffering merges with the impossibility of detaching oneself from suffering. And this is not to define suffering by suffering, but to insist on the sui generis implication that constitutes its essence. In suffering there is an absence of all refuge. It is the fact of being directly exposed to being. It is made up of the impossibility of fleeing or retreating. The whole acuity of suffering lies in this impossibility of retreat." *Time and the Other*, trans. Richard A. Cohen (Pittsburgh: Duquesne University Press, 1987), 69; see also 78, 80, etc. Patočka similarly says: It is here a matter of the "principle of *need*. The body finds itself in the state of need, not in a contingent manner but essentially. The body requires care at all moments." *Introduction à la phénoménologie*, trans. Erika Abrams (Grenoble: Millon, 1992), 189. See the analyses by Emilie Tardivel, *La liberté au principe. Essai sur la philosophie de Patočka* (Paris: Vrin, 2011), especially chapter 4. One should also be surprised, among other failed encounters, that Wittgenstein's reflections and his abundant tradition have lent no attention, to my knowing, to their Cartesian origin.

follows that corporeal things exist," VII: 80, 4; CSM II: 55) of its first
part (*"De rerum materialium existentia*—Of the existence of material
things," 71, 11; CSM II: 50), but as a single argument organized in two
parts, hence into two questions. First, the question of the existence of
the bodies of the subsisting world (present-at-hand, *vorhanden*), objects
and able to be objectified, whose exteriority could not at first glance be
discovered as established except by virtue of a simple *propensio* that is
epistemologically disputable and disputed. Now, it turns out that the
text continues toward a second question: the distinction of soul and
body, which in the case of the ego actually means the union of the *mens*
to a body, or more exactly, a unique body that senses the other bodies,
thus an ego as flesh. Yet my flesh can sense bodies only by apprehending
them as handy (*zuhanden*) and thereby passively experiencing the radical exteriority where it senses its pain most intimately. A first result follows from this.[57] The Sixth Meditation appears as a block, as a whole,
and as an account where the end determines the beginning: the existence of material things depends, according to the order of reasoning,
on the union of soul and body, that is to say, on my flesh, which it all the
same precedes according to the order of the subject-matter. Or rather,
one would have to admit here an exception to the univocally analytical order of the rest of the *Meditations*: the two questions, on the one
hand that of the existence of bodies (*vorhanden*), on the other hand
the experience of my ego as a flesh (*zuhanden*), actually do not precede
each other, but develop in *parallel* fashion, according to two fields that
are mutually exclusive: subsistence and the theoretical attitude in the
first case, handiness and flesh in the other. They cannot interfere with
each other, because they correspond to two radically different and even
incompatible realms of appearing. That is most probably also why their
accounts can be inverted (thus the *Principles of Philosophy* treats my
flesh at the end of the first part in order to tackle only subsequently, in
the second part, the existence of bodies, in perfect conformity with the
inverted order of the summary of the Sixth Meditation suggested by the
Synopsis). The Sixth Meditation thus relies on an essential prolepsis: it
looks ahead to the affection of my flesh in order to prove the existence
of other bodies, namely, those of the world.

The primordial role of my flesh is then confirmed by allowing a re-
interpretation of the *propensio*, therefore of validating the proof of the

57. This serves as the response to the question (b) on the order of the two
problems, the existence of material things and the connection of soul and body
(above, chapter 1, §2, 13 and 16–17).

existence of material things on the condition of its passivity.[58] The *pro-pensio* does not appear as a weak argument, as was the case for the great majority of Descartes' successors (see above, chapter 1, §§4–5), as long as one apprehends it solely as an intellectual mode of the *cogitatio*, a simple by-product of or confused substitute for the *intellectus*. Naturally, compared with a clear and distinct idea of the *intellectus*, such a *propensio* does not fulfill the requirements of demonstration, and one would have to conclude, as has largely been done, that the Sixth Meditation fails. But there is another possibility: comprehending the *propensio* starting from the flesh, which experiences the exteriority of the world under the aspect of *in/commoda*, with a pain so "intimate" that the ego would be unable not to tend toward accepting the existence of material things inasmuch as they not only act upon it, but afflict it with pain as flesh. Thus one must reinterpret the *propensio* according to the arrival of affection within it: "Nempe quicquid sentimus, *procul dubio nobis* advenit *a re aliqua, quae a mente nostra diversa est. Neque enim est in nostra potestate efficere, ut unum potius quam aliud sentiamus; sed hoc a re illa quae sensus nostros* afficit, *plane pendet*— Now, *all our sensations undoubtedly come to us* from something that is distinct from our mind. For it is not in our power to make ourselves have one sensation rather than another; this is obviously dependent on the thing that is acting on our senses." And also: "dolores *aliosque sensus nobis* ex improviso advenire; *quos mens est conscia* non a se sola proficisci, *nec ad se posse pertinere ex eo solo quod sit res cogitans, sed tantum ex eo quod alteri* cuidam rei *extensae ac mobilis adjuncta sit, quae res* humanum corpus *appellatur*—pain and other sensations *come to us quite unexpectedly.* The mind is aware that these sensations *do not come from itself alone*, and that they cannot belong to it simply in virtue of its being a thinking thing; instead, they can belong to it only in virtue of its being joined to something other than itself which is extended and moveable—namely what we call *the human body*."[59] By way

58. This serves as the response to (d) the question about the validity of the proof of the existence of material things (above, chapter 1, §2, 15 and 16–17).

59. Respectively, *Principles of Philosophy* II, §1, VIII-1: 40, 9–14 = IX-2: 63; CSM I: 223; §2, VIII-1: 41, 17–22 = IX-1: 64; CSM I: 224. See obviously I, §75, VIII-1: 38, 26–28; CSM I: 221: "Itemque *[notitia] sensuum quorundam qui* nos afficiunt, *ut doloris, colorum, saporum, etc., quamvis nondum sciamus quae sit causa, cur ita* nos afficiant—also of certain sensations which *affect us*, such as the sensations of pain, colours, tastes and so on (though we do not yet know the cause of *our being affected* in this way)." And in the Sixth Meditation: "experiebar *enim illas absque ullo meo consensu mihi* advenire—*my experience*

of the *propensio*, we do not judge from an efficient causality of bodies subsisting outside us (*vorhanden*) on our understanding, but "*sentimus, sive potius a sensu impulsi clare ac distincte percipimus*—we have sensory awareness of, or rather as a result of sensory stimulation we have a clear and distinct perception"[60] of an alterity and exteriority at first not identified. Sensing no longer means just receiving sensory information, but suffering from it via stimulation. Thus, as a logical consequence, the same sensations that find themselves henceforth in charge of exteriority may acknowledge the mode of being of events, thus of transcendences, while the essences (according to the simple natures) subsist and occupy immanence. Exteriority, which is manifested in the suffering *sensus*, is manifested there as the arrival of an event: each sensation comes to me as what arrives but once, at *this* time, because none can be repeated in identical fashion. In contrast to conceptual knowledge, which goes back to the same and must do so (to verify an operation means to repeat it in order to arrive at the same result), sensation, even above all that of the "same" thing, arrives each time as unforeseeable, irreversible, and irreducible innovation; it cannot be handed on from one ego to the other in space, no more than it can go back to the same ego in time. This implies that the *ex*teriority of the sensory thing, the exteriority that alone demonstrates its *ex*istence, is not a matter of either substantiality or permanence, which only characterize its essence. Consequently, what the exteriority of the *sensus* discovers by coming to the ego is not in the mode of permanence (*Vorhandenheit*). Yet, in this case, the argument is no longer a matter of theory; it presupposes the relationship of handiness to the world (the *cogitato* as *sensus*) and thus the phenomenological concept of *flesh*.[61]

---

was that these ideas *came to me* quite without my consent" (VII: 75, 10–11; CSM II: 52 and also 75, 20; 52); or "*in corporibus, a quibus variae istae sensuum perceptiones* adveniunt—the body to which various sensory perceptions *come*" (81, 20–21; CSM II: 56, trans. modified).

60. *Principles of Philosophy* II, §1, VIII-1: 40, 15–16 = IX-2: 62; CSM I: 223.

61. It is fitting to underline how Wilhelm Dilthey, in his study "Beiträge zur Lösung der Frage vom Ursprung unseres Glaubens an die Realität der Außenwelt und seinem Recht," in *Gesammelte Schriften*, V (Berlin: B. G. Teubner, 1890/1924), 90ff., trans. as "The Origin of Our Belief in Reality of the External World and Its Justification," in *Selected Works*, vol. II: *Understanding the Human World*, trans. Rudolf A. Makkreel and Frithjof Rodi (Princeton: Princeton University Press, 2010), 8–57, has seen perfectly that it is the resistance to the activity of the mind ("*die Hemmung der Intention*—intention being restrained"; ibid., 102) that delimits exteriority in fleshly fashion ("*leibliche Umgrenzung*—corporeal delimitation"; ibid., 105) and not the reconstitution of a causal rela-

These distinctions, provided one admits them, allow us to respond finally to the two major objections raised against the Cartesian proof of the existence of material things (incorrectly isolated from its foundation, the flesh).

First, Heidegger's objection: "The 'scandal of philosophy' is not that this proof has yet to be given, but *that such proofs are expected and attempted again and again.* Such expectations, aims, and demands arise from an ontologically inadequate way of starting with *something* of such a character that independently *of it* and 'outside' *of it* a 'world' is to be proved as present-at-hand *(vorhanden).* It is not that the proofs are inadequate, but that the kind of Being of the entity which does the proving and makes requests for proofs has *not been made definite enough.*"[62] In short, the ontological indeterminacy of beings emerges as more scandalous than the absence of proof, which scandalized Kant to the highest degree. It alone permits, in the second degree, the demand for a proof of being; thus Descartes would not have understood what was asked of him, because he no more wonders about the mode of being of mundane things than he previously questioned that of the ego who thinks them: in both cases, the *In-der-Welt-sein* (and what it takes

---

tionship between a material origin and an effect of consciousness. But what he in this way opposes to Kant he believes wrongly to be able to oppose equally to Descartes, while it is doubtlessly a matter of a variation on the very doctrine of the Sixth Meditation. Heidegger discusses his response in the *Prolegomena zur Geschichte des Zeitbegriffs,* §24a, GA 20, 294ff., reproaching him with still believing that such a reality of the external world could be demonstrated, and in a theoretical mode on top of that. In his first article, "Das Realitätsproblem in der modernen Philosophy" (1912, *Jahrbuch der Görres-Gesellschaft,* no. 25; GA 1, p. 1), he already tackles this question, citing Brunetière: "I should very much like to know which sick person or sorry jokester—and I must also say fool—it was who first got it into his head to doubt the reality of the external world and make it a question for philosophers. Does such a question even make any sense?" Cited in "The Problem of Reality in Modern Philosophy," in *Becoming Heidegger: On the Trail of His Early Occasional Writings, 1910–1927,* ed. Theodore Kisiel and Thomas Sheehan (Evanston, IL: Northwestern University Press, 2007), 20. Curiously, no one notices that this was also Descartes' position in *The Discourse on Method,* AT VI: 37, 30—38, 3; *Meditations,* VII: 15, 27—16, 3 and 351, 1–2). Thierry Gontier had a premonition of this change: "De la *regula veritatis* à l'existence des corps: figures de la véracité divine," in the appendix to *Descartes et la causa sui* (Paris: Vrin, 2005).

62. Heidegger, *Sein und Zeit,* §43, 205; *Being and Time,* 249. One also can consult Dorothea Frede, "Heidegger and the Scandal of Philosophy," in Hubert Dreyfus and Mark Wrathall, eds., *Heidegger Reexamined,* vol. 2 (New York/London: Routledge, 2002).

responsibility for, the essence of *Dasein*) shines by its absence. Can we respond here in Descartes' favor and by mobilizing his resources alone? Surely we can, because just as it has been possible to argue that Descartes has determined the mode of the being of the ego[63] perfectly, one can reasonably suggest that he has also specified the mode of being of the material *res* in general, and even in a dual sense.

First, according to its essence (as *"purae Matheseos objectum"* for the understanding aided by the imagination, following the simple material natures), the corporeal thing is in the mode of permanent subsistence (*Vorhandenheit*). But also, according to its existence (as what constrains the flesh by pain and stimulates the *propensio* for it), the material *res* comes as an event, where the point is using it and not having knowledge of it (*Zuhandenheit*). Or more exactly the strict existence of material things is known only by the use of the flesh (*meum corpus, sensus*), without ever being able to represent itself directly to the *intellectus*. The existence of material things (in contrast to their essence) is learned by use, but is never seen. Heidegger's critique of Descartes ignores the distinction that Descartes puts to work ahead of Heidegger and quite brilliantly—that between flesh (*meum corpus*) and body (*alia corpora*), between *Vorhandenheit* and *Zuhandenheit*. Accordingly, Descartes turns Heidegger's existentials upside down, by anticipation, against him and, ironically, seems a phenomenologist who does not know it or who does not allow others to know it because he hides himself—*phenomenologus larvatus prodeo*. In this way one responds to the question about the equivocity of bodies, which Descartes indeed understands sometimes as *meum corpus*, sometimes as *(alia) corpora circumjacentia*.[64]

63. For this first case, I have tried to show elsewhere that the mode of being of the ego of the *cogito* is truly found determined at the same time as subsistent (indeed the only *substantia* in the strict sense) and as outside of subsistence (in the Second Meditation, see my article "Descartes hors sujet," *Les Études philosophiques* 88.1 [2009]: 51–62, and in morality). I will not here go back to it. See *On Descartes' Metaphysical Prism*, §§13–15, 150–205.

64. It is a matter of a first response (see below, chapter 4, §§18–19) to the question about different modes of being of that which Descartes, following the former usage, confuses under the title of "bodies" (see above, chapter 2, §7, 45). Patočka comments: "Heidegger calls the fact that one had wanted to prove the real existence of being the 'scandal of philosophy'; but this is only a stunt, a spin that tries to mask by a verbal profession of realism the fact that he is completely immersed—since the possibilities are *subjectively projected*—in an indeterminate idealism; things are admittedly known, but only in relation to possibilities I undertake as a project." "Corps, possibilités, monde, champ

Second, Kant's objection, which reverses the priority (in evidence as in certainty) of the *mens* over the body by stating that "internal experience in general is only possible by external experience in general."[65] As we have seen above (chapter 1, §6), it is not certain that Kant can think coherently what he here objects to Descartes: How can the "internal" be joined with the "external" in one sole experience? What interface can play between these two experiences, if not again the unfeasible efficient causality? All the more so as neither the flesh nor intentionality occurs within the Kantian argument, even in outline. Far from being able to invoke the existence of external bodies in order to experience my body of flesh (or rather its patent *absence* among them), as Kant does it, it would be a good idea to go back to Descartes' thesis: external material bodies (which I can experience) exist only because I experience and feel them, thus because I am a flesh (an internal body).[66] In short, material bodies exist only because I am a flesh—and not the reverse. Here the *critical* phenomenologist is called Descartes, not Kant.

A final question remains: Is it a matter of distinguishing or uniting the union and the distinction in the Sixth Meditation? More simply, is the point to establish the distinction between soul and body, in accordance with what the title announces about it (*"De ... reali mentis a corpore distinctione*—Of the real distinction of mind and body," VII: 71, 11–12), or to observe and legitimize their union *"adeo ut unum quid*

---

d'apparition," *Ms. 5E/15*, in *Papiers phénoménologiques*, trans. Erika Abrams (Grenoble: Millon, 1995), 125. To what extent can one agree with this comment?

65. Kant, *Critique of Pure Reason*, B XL; 37. This is thus a matter of a response to the question regarding the question (c) about the distinction between the distinction (of minds and of extended bodies) and the union (of my soul with my body), that is to say, of my flesh (see above, chapter 1, §2, 16–17).

66. Gilson saw this problem very well, even if he was missing the Cartesian solution: "The question is whether Descartes was able to prove the existence of the external world without presupposing the union of soul and body and consequently this existence is reduced to the following question: Can Descartes allege sensations that do not presuppose the substantial union of soul and body?" (*Études sur le rôle de la pensée médiévale*, 312). The response to this pertinent question is very simple: No, Descartes could not conclude the external world (body) without passing through the union (flesh); also he *finally* passed first of all to the flesh. And Gilson was wrong not to see this, obsessed as he remains with the question of the substantial form, without noticing that the flesh obtains the same result as it does, without having the inconveniences that its generalization to other cases than that of the union of the *mens* to the body of flesh provokes, a case that is paradoxically more intelligible because it alone can be experienced.

*cum illo [i.e., meo corpore] componam*—so that I and the body form a unit" (81, 4–5; CSM II: 56)? The necessary response is that both are at stake. This reply is easily understood: there is no contradiction between the two theses, because it is a matter not of comparing two terms but of organizing three of them. First the *mens* as *res cogitans*, so far the only one active (doubt, understanding, will, imagination), then the extended bodies, finally *meum corpus*, my flesh that thinks (it is a mode of the *cogitatio*), but passively inasmuch as affected. These three terms are organized along two poles; first by a union of the *res cogitans* and the *corpus meum* that proves indestructible because it accomplishes the totality of the modalities of the *cogitatio* and achieves the unfolding of the *res cogitans*; then the distinction between this union (which thus becomes a third primitive notion) taken as such (one no longer always mentions what it unites) and the *alia corpora*. The union itself is distinguished from all the extended bodies precisely as soon as one sees it as such—as implying the flesh, which, exactly, opposes the *res cogitans* as *sentiens* to everything that, sensed and thus thought, neither senses nor thinks. The union is set apart as fleshly union of bodies as extended. Descartes stays perfectly coherent, precisely because he breaks, *here*, with the sole order of reasoning, and conducts in parallel two orders of subject-matter which, as crossed, are strictly confirmed. The true reasoning must sometimes mock the order of reasoning, at least when reason and the thing itself demand it.

One can thus doubt the all too famous "scandal of reason."[67] Thus, I will doubt it, by trying to confirm the function of the flesh (*meum corpus*) within the whole of Descartes' texts. For "this word 'body' is very ambiguous."[68]

---

67. Robert C. Richardson has done so recently in convincing fashion, managing to transfer very rightly this expression of the proof of the existence of material things to the comprehension of the modalities of the union. "The 'Scandal' of Cartesian Interactionism," *Mind* 91 (1982): 20–37.

68. To Mesland, 9 February 1645, AT IV: 166, 2–3; CSMK: 242.

**3**

## The Indubitable and the Unnoticed

*§12. Indecisiveness (1632) and Confusion (1637)*

How far does the "ambiguity" [*équivocité*] of "this word 'body'" go? When does it begin to make reflection necessary? Is it a thesis added a posteriori, after potential unforeseen difficulties have constrained the order of reasoning to admit a rupture? Or, as was the case elsewhere (for example, with the appearance of two concepts so far unused, *substantia* and *causa*, on the same page; AT VII: 40; CSM II: 28), is it a matter of introducing, externally and deceptively, a new conceptual contribution in order to defend the original enterprise that had become unfeasible as such? In short, is this a matter of repentance and an admission of failure? Assuming that one could relieve an ambiguity (which doesn't happen very often), this dual hypothesis thus appears as the simplest and the most likely. Yet, another is still possible, namely that Descartes actually always recognized the ambiguity of the word "body" and thus would never have doubted the irreducibility of *meum corpus* to the *alia corpora*, and thus he would always have maintained the existence of my flesh, even when he doubted that of the bodies of the world. How could this final hypothesis be put to the test? By verifying whether the doubt that challenges the existence of the bodies of the world and of sensory knowledge, also manages to impugn the existence and the certainty of *meum corpus* (or of its equivalents). A contrario, could one find one case (or several) where the I, the ego of the *cogito*, would doubt the existence of not only the usual bodies of the world ("the material things") but also my body of flesh?

Now it turns out that already in the incomplete and unpublished *Search for Truth*,[1] the text that begins his reflection on and through doubt in grand style, Descartes confronts this question and this distinction directly. Here, the section of this dialogue that has been preserved in French concludes abruptly by questioning two possible senses of "this word 'body'" or, more exactly, by questioning its second sense (not "the corporeal things,"[2] but the *meum corpus*, the body of flesh): "Thus I shall be uncertain not only about whether you are in the world and whether there is an earth or a sun; but also about *whether I have* eyes, ears, *a body*, and even whether I am speaking to you and you are speaking to me. In short, I will doubt everything." The Latin translation confirms these words: "*sed praeterea num habeam oculos, num aures, ecquid corpus habeam*," as does the Dutch version: "*maar ook of ik oogen, of ik ooren, en of ik* een lighaam heb," which speaks of bodies only to designate my own, as doubtful as any of the others.[3] Even so, it is not sufficient to have the intention of doubting my flesh as much as the physical bodies in order to dispose of an argument justifying this doubt, for he would have to battle a genuine difference between the two ambiguous meanings of "this word 'body'": although I can doubt

1. The writing is probably prior to April 1630, but maybe from 1633–34: I am privileging the two most recent and the most documented hypotheses, respectively that of Ettore Lojacono, in Ettore Lojacono, Erik-Jan Bos, Franco Aurelio Meschini, Francesco Saita, eds., *La Recherche de la vérité par la lumière naturelle de René Descartes* (Milan: Franco Angeli, 2002), xxix (hereafter Lojacono [2002]); see also René Descartes, *La Recherche de la vérité par la lumière naturelle. Introduction et commentaire historique et conceptual*, ed. Ettore Lojacono (Paris: PUF, 2009), 161–201 (hereafter Lojacono [2009]), and that of Vincent Carraud and Gilles Olivo in their edition of *Descartes: Étude du bon sens. La recherche de la vérité et autres écrits de jeunesse (1616–1631)*, in collaboration with Corinna Vermeulen (Paris: PUF, 2013). See also the proceedings of the day of studies devoted to *La recherche de la vérité* (Paris, 6 June 1998), edited by Claudio Buccolini and Michaël Devaux as *Nouvelles de la République de lettres* 1999.1 (Naples: Prismi Editrice Politecnica Napoli, 1999).

2. This is a French hapax in *The Search for Truth*, AT X: 505, 21; CSM II: 105.

3. AT X: 514, 10–15; CSM II: 409 (= Lojacono [2002], 13; Lojacono [2009], 92), ed. Lojacono [2002], 39–41 and 38–40.

all the objects of my representations (the physical bodies) because they remain at a distance from me, I cannot as easily break with what is not the object of my representation because it does not differ from me. How can I doubt the *corpus meum*, if it is me? Descartes actually does not produce any argument here that would be devoted to this difficulty precisely, but limits himself to juxtaposing three of them, without indicating their particular uses: the argument of madness and that of the dream—which moreover will later concern only sensory knowledge— and the argument of divine omnipotence: "In particular, how can you be certain of this when you have learned that you were created by a superior being who, being all-powerful, would have found it no more difficult to create us just as I am describing [i.e., deceived by the senses], than to create us as you think you are?"[4] Can one admit that the argument from omnipotence would have the strength to justify the doubt that is here concerned with *corpus meum*? That is debatable for at least two reasons. First, because the text of *The Search* not only does not link the argument from omnipotence to the doubt concerning my body, but expresses it long before introducing this doubt without any logical link between them. Besides, the argument from omnipotence comes from Eudoxus (the character apparently the closest to Descartes' own point of view, especially as his argument is confirmed by the canonical texts), while the doubt about my body comes from Polyander (the dialogue's third party par excellence, not its center of gravity).[5] Second, because, as we will soon see (below, §14), when the First Meditation will attempt to construct an argument for doubting my own body (*"meipsum tanquam manus non habentem, non oculos*—I shall consider myself as not having hands or eyes," AT VII: 23, 1–2; CSM II: 15) for the first time, it precisely will appeal not to divine omnipotence (reserved for questioning the simple material natures and the mathematical truths), but to the

4. *Search for Truth*, X: 512; CSM II: 408; confirmed by the Latin: "*Praesertim quoniam intellexisti te a superiori quodam Ente creatum, cui, cum comnipotens esset, tale ac dixi, quam qualem tu te esse putas, nos creare haud difficilius fuisset.*" And by the Dutch: "*Voornamelijk dewijl gy vertaan hebt dat gy van een oppertse Wesen geschapen zijt, dat almachtig sijnde, gelijkt het is, ons met geen groter zwarigheit sodanig, als ik seg, dan sodanig, als gy meent dat gy sijt, geschapen kon hebben*" (Lojacono [2002], 37 and 36).

5. [The English translators of the dialogue explain the characters as follows: "Of the three characters appearing in the dialogue, Epistemon ('Knowledgeable') represents someone well versed in classical and scholastic philosophy, and Polyander ('Everyman') the person of untutored common sense; Eudoxus (literally 'Famous,' but the Greek root also suggests one of sound judgement) is the mouthpiece for Descartes' own views" (CSM II: 399).]

hypothesis of the "evil genius—*genius aliquis malignus*" (VII: 22, 24; CSM II: 15, trans. modified [CSM uses "malicious demon"]).[6] Now, this hypothesis does not appear here and, what's more, as we know since Henri Gouhier, it has no genuine theoretical validity, but so to say a simple exhortative function of self-confirmation for the meditating ego. Strictly speaking, the doubt that Polyander on his own authority tries to extend to my body does not, here, receive any justification, at least not an explicit or fully argued one.

Yet there is a better reason for doubting the legitimacy (for Descartes *here*) of extending the doubt beyond physical bodies all the way to my body—an explicit statement by this same Polyander who has doubts about his doubt. He now reasons in this way: although I am not a physical, extended, and hence doubtful body, but a nonextended and certain thought, nevertheless I cannot deny that I have a body (although its ambiguous characteristics in opposition to the physical bodies are *here* not yet being scrutinized): "But we have reason to say that it was a happy mistake I made, since, thanks to it, I know very well that what I am, in so far as I am doubting, is *certainly not quite* what I call my body (Dutch: *niet gantschelijk het geen is, dat ik mijn lighaam noem* = Latin: *omnino illud non esse, quod meum corpus adpello*). Indeed, I do not even know whether I have a body; you have shown me that it is possible to doubt it. I might add that I *also cannot deny absolutely* that I have a body (Dutch: *Ik voeg hier by, dat ik ook niet volkomentlijk kan loghenen, dat ik een lighaam heb* = Latin: *Hisce adjungo, ne quidem absolute negare me posse, corpus me habere*). Yet even if we keep all these suppositions intact, this will not prevent me from being certain that I exist. On the contrary, these suppositions simply strengthen the certainty of my conviction that I exist and am not a body. Otherwise, if I had doubts about my body, I would also have doubts about myself, and I cannot have doubts about that. I am absolutely convinced that I exist, so convinced that it is totally impossible for me to doubt it" (CSM II: 412; trans. lightly modified).[7] From this quite ambiguous or

6. Lojacono notes correctly that it is here a matter of a "hyperbolic" argument, that is to say, an arbitrary and "metaphysical" one (according to VII: 89, 18–20 and 459, 25—460, 12; CSM II: 61 and 308), but that is precisely not the case for the argument from omnipotence, which continues to play the central role of a characteristic of God and of a quasi-definition of his essence, if only for justifying the incomprehensibility of the idea of the infinite and of the *causa sui* (see Lojacono [2009], 145).

7. I am citing from Carraud and Olivo's translation (lightly modified). The Dutch and Latin texts are cited according to Lojacono [2002], 46 and 47.

even confused reasoning, one can draw a plausible conclusion: I am inasmuch as I think, without having to be a body comparable to those I doubt, namely, physical, extended, and worldly bodies; all the same I cannot *absolutely* deny that I have a body (*heb, habere*), even though I would have no need to be a body in order to exist. How should one describe this discrepancy? *The Search for Truth* is limited to admitting that I am *not quite* (*pas tout à fait, niet gantschelijk*) this body, which at the same time I do not presuppose (as thought) and which I cannot *absolutely deny*. It thus appears quite clearly that one body at least actually does not respect the caesura between thought and extension of physical bodies, but that this body does not yet have the rightful status that would justify its exception; for although Descartes already names it *meum corpus*, he does not yet think it as a flesh. Nevertheless this hypothesis remains open, all the more so as Polyander must admit it at the end in a retraction of his preceding doubt, which thus proves to be unfounded, because I cannot actually deny *this* body absolutely. And I cannot deny it because far from only *having* it, I *am* it.

This indecisiveness is confirmed by a confusion. For example, that of a different text in which Polyander himself also tries to eliminate my body in the name of doubt: "And yet it is true that whatever it is within me that is doubting, it is not what we call our body (Latin: *nostrum corpus*). Therefore it is also true that I, in so far as I am doubting, am not that which is nourished or walks; for neither of these actions can be performed without a body. I cannot even say that I, in so far as I am doubting, am capable of perceiving by the senses (Dutch: *ik bequuaam gevoelen*; Latin: *sentire posse*). For as feet are needed for walking, so eyes are needed for seeing, and ears for hearing; yet since I have none of these organs—because I have no body—I cannot say I perceive by the senses (Dutch: *dat ik bequaam ben om te gevoelen*; Latin: *equidem me sentire dicere non possum*). Furthermore, in the past I have thought while dreaming that I perceived by the senses (Dutch: *gevoelde*; Latin: *sensisse*) many things which I did not really sense (Dutch: *die ik waarlijk niet gevoelt heb*; Latin: *revera non senseram*). And since I have decided to admit nothing here unless its truth is such that I can have no doubts about it, I cannot say that I am a sentient being (Dutch: *niet zeggen dat*

---

It is essential to note that the Latin *non omnino* must be corrected, here as elsewhere (according to the general hypothesis of the editors), in accordance with the Dutch *niet gantschelijk*, to be translated as "not quite" [*pas tout à fait*]. The difference is important, as Carraud and Olivo note: "[The Dutch] allows for the possibility that I am my body, although I am not only that, as what follows will explain."

*ik iets ben, 't welk gevoelt*'; Latin: *me esse rem sentientem . . . dicere negueo*), i.e., one that sees with its eyes and hears with its ears. For it is possible in the way just described that I believe I am perceiving by the senses, even though I have no senses."[8] The argument here remains quite sketchy: I cannot say that I sense if I do not have the organs of sensation, thus a sensing body; now, I do not have this body, thus I am neither sensing nor sensory; all the more so as the senses can deceive, so that sensing nothing true, I can say that I do not sense at all. It is so sketchy that Descartes soon reverses it completely on multiple occasions.

First, in 1641, by assigning to sensing the role of a rightful modality of the *res cogitans*, which, as such, assures the ego of its existence as much as any other modality: "*Idem denique ego sum qui* sentio, *sive qui res corporeas tanquam per sensus animadverto; videlicet jam lucem video, strepitum audio, calorem* sentio. *Falsa haec sunt, dormio enim. At certe videre videor, audire, calescere. Hoc falsum esse non potest; hoc est proprie quod in me* sentire *appelatur; atque hoc praecise sic sumptum nihil aliud est quam cogitare.*—Lastly, it is also the same 'I' who has sensory perceptions, or is aware of bodily things as it were through the senses. For example, I am now seeing light, hearing a noise, feeling heat. But I am asleep, so all this is false. Yet I certainly seem to see, to hear, and to be warmed. This cannot be false; what is called '*sensing*' is strictly just this, and in this restricted sense of the term it is simply thinking."[9] Sensing consists not in sensing something sensory that would necessarily be true (a property of an object), but simply in feeling a feeling, one that might possibly be false as designating the property of an object, but is always true as felt. Sensing at first concerns not physical bodies (the majority of the time sensation does not allow us really to know them), but the mind (*mens*) as *cogitatio*. Therefore, inasmuch as it is a mode of the *res cogitans*, sensing leads the ego back to itself, to a *self-sensing of itself* [*un se sentir soi-même*] that is more primordial than any sensing of an object.

Second, in 1650, *The Passions of the Soul* will definitely formulate this privilege of the thinking thing as sensing thing: "we may be misled regarding the perceptions which refer to certain parts of our body. But we cannot be misled in the same way regarding the passions, in that

8. AT X: 520, 41—521, 14; CSM II: 414–15, trans. lightly modified; French translation by Carraud and Olivo (lightly modified). The Dutch and Latin texts are cited after Lojacono [2002], 52 and 53.

9. Second Meditation, AT VII: 29, 11–18 = IX-1: 23; CSM II: 19, trans. lightly modified.

they are so close and so internal to our soul that it cannot possibly feel them unless they are truly as it feels them to be. Thus often when we sleep, and sometimes when we are awake, we imagine certain things so vividly that we think we see them before us, or *feel them in our body*, although they are not there at all. But even if we are asleep and dreaming, we cannot feel sad, or moved by any other passion, unless *the soul truly has* this passion *within it*."[10] The truth of sensing here depends not on a (hypothetical) doubling of sensed by the (necessary) sensing, but on the difference between the sensing of (external) objects (through perception) and the feeling of passions (without transcendent object). Sadness and joy can do without worldly objects as external causes and can be brought to bear on the passive soul with all the more power as they revert to it in a perfect immanence that no ecstasy comes to trouble or influence. This "what the soul has *in itself*" replies to the "*in me sentire*"— the passivity of thought accordingly taking the shape of sensing.

What *The Search for Truth* had not yet decided, the 1637 writings still confuse. Actually they bear witness to the two contradictory positions. On the one hand, the distinction between the bodies and thought suffers no exception: "this 'I'—that is, the soul by which I am what I am—is entirely distinct from the body" (*Discourse on Method*, AT VI: 33, 7–9; CSM I: 127) and "our soul, that is, from that part of us, distinct from the body" (46, 16–17; CSM I: 134) or "our soul is of a nature entirely independent of the body, and consequently . . . it is not bound to die with it" (59, 29–31; CSM I: 141). Yet, on the other hand, one cannot hide the fact that there is at least one body, namely mine, that really would not be able to be reduced to "all the other bodies in our environment" (62, 3; CSM I: 142), like the simple special case of "the object studied by geometers. I conceived of this as a continuous body" (36, 5–6; CSM I: 129). When one invokes doubt in order to "pretend that I had no body and that there was no world and no place for me to be in" (32, 25–27; CSM I: 127), what does "body" mean *here*—my body or one of those that the world accommodates outside of me? Can one without commentary or precaution assimilate the physical bodies of the stars to my body, and say "with *a* body . . . there being stars and an earth, and the like" (37, 28–29; CSM I: 130), as if exactly they were obviously "similar things"?

In fact, Descartes himself does not stay any longer in this indecisiveness and this ambiguous confusion, because he already puts his trust,

---

10. *Passions of the Soul*, §26, AT XI: 348, 20—349, 7; CSM I: 338, trans. modified (see below, chapter 6, §29, 217).

albeit indirectly, in my body, for which he outlines from 1637 onward two fundamental characteristics. First, in the *Discourse on Method*, he postulates the union as a condition for sensing: "After that, I described the rational soul, and showed that . . . it is not sufficient for it to be lodged in the human body like a helmsman in his ship, except perhaps to move its limbs, but that it must be more closely joined and united with the body in order to have, besides this power of movement, *feelings* and appetites like ours and so constitute a real man" (59, 8–18; CSM I: 141). Accordingly sensing, in other words thinking via feeling, implies a body that is absolutely mine, a flesh. Then, in the *Optics* (chapter 4), he attributes sensation to the mind and not to the body: "We know for certain that it is the soul which has sensory perceptions, and not the body" (109, 6–7; CSM I: 164). This paradoxical statement—sensation disappears not when one suspends extended matter in (or around) me, but when one suspends the principle of sensing in me, namely, thought— depends on two examples. One of them often returns in other places: any injury to the brain, the organ of common sense, is enough to prevent any sense. But the other example is surprising: "For when the soul is distracted by an ecstasy or deep contemplation, we see that the whole body remains without sensation, even though it has various objects touching it" (109, 7–10; CSM I: 164). This actually concerns prayer, which lifts the mind or spirit beyond its extended body and thus makes it insensible to material things, because reciprocally the power of sensing (thus the flesh) is focused on God. One could not suggest more clearly that sensing has nothing to do with matter, but that it is entirely an act of thought or even a spiritual act, thus that the *corpus sentiens* senses only because it thinks. In other words, the passivity of sensing, which implies a corporeal body, must no less be attributed to the *mens*, thus to the *res cogitans*. This comes down to stating that the ego still and always thinks when it senses passively according to the flesh. It thinks not with its body, but in its flesh, which it obviously cannot doubt.

It remains clear that the indecisiveness about the status of my body, to which the comings and goings of *The Search for Truth* bear witness, is not being cut short in 1637. The texts, so to speak, institutionalize the confusion.

## §13. The Finally Indubitable Flesh (1641)

As we have seen, this confusion was not dispelled until the Sixth Meditation (at least in Descartes' intention, if not always in his readers' comprehension). The fact remains that the definition of *meum corpus* as a third authority between the pure *mens* and the strict *extensio* attains its entire legitimacy only here, if the prior Meditations have not disqualified it in advance, for example by having it succumb to doubt, exactly like all the beings of the realm of the world, and by excluding it from the realm of consciousness (to employ Husserlian language). The *Discourse on Method* really seems to have privileged this possibility—of disqualifying straightaway the *corpus meum* as a mundane body placed into doubt along with all the other bodies—by authorizing for itself the ambiguity of "pretend[ing] that I had no body and that there was no world and no place for me to be in" (VI: 32, 25–27; CSM I: 127). But what does *body* mean here: a worldly body or my body? In 1637 Descartes alleviates the ambiguity no more than the *Principles of Philosophy I*, §7 does in 1641: "*facile quidem supponimus nullum esse Deum, nullum coelum,* nulla corpora; nosque etiam *ipsos non habere manus, nec pedes, nec denique* ullum corpus—it is easy for us to suppose that there is no God and no heaven, and that there are *no bodies, and even that* we ourselves have no hands or feet, or indeed *any body at all*" (CSM I: 194); for how can one fail to notice that here the first use of "body," *nulla corpora*, goes exclusively back to the stars, the planets, extension, and so forth, while the second, *ullum corpus*, signals toward my body, the *corpus sentiens*, that is to say, "the soul"? The ambiguity here reaches its height, all the less noticed by the dominant commentary [tradition] because it struts about with assurance, protected by its evidence, so well adapted to the scholastic or supposedly accessible expositions. Only one path remains in order to decide, if that is possible, where Descartes is conscious of this ambiguity and to what point he distinguished the respective postures of the two types of "body" in doubt: to examine how the most elaborated and most sophisticated text about this questioning of the ambiguous body proceeds, namely, the First Meditation. Or, as we will see, more exactly the repetition of the First Meditation by the Second Meditation, a repetition that is not without discrepancy.

In constructing the trial of doubt, that is to say, by reversing skeptical doubt against itself and by transforming it into a test of certainty, Descartes makes it bear on what comes to him "*vel a sensibus, vel per sensus*—either from the senses or through the senses" (VII: 18, 16; CSM II: 12). How should we understand this distinction, for which he does not introduce any modification, but which he does not really explain?[11] For want of more specific indications, one should note one

11. See To Mersenne, 24 December 1640, AT II: 267, 27—268, 3; CSMK: 164. Burman's conversation with Descartes (§1, V: 146; CSMK: 332), once

obvious point: what I receive from them the most closely (*"ab iisdem hauriantur,"* 18, 21–22), what it seems impossible to deny (*"de quibus dubitari plane non potest,"* 18, 21), consists not only in my proximity to the fire, my clothing, my hand grasping a paper, etc., but in what makes them possible and precisely assures them their proximity, namely, my body, *"totum hoc corpus meum."* It appears from my body and from it first of all that one cannot doubt, *"qua ratione posset negari?—*by what reason could it be denied?" (AT VII: 18, 25–26; CSM II: 13, trans. modified). Let us stress this point of departure. Not only does *meum corpus* not show up suddenly like an aerolite only in the Sixth Meditation, but it appears from the opening of the First Meditation onward, in such a way that the question of what we today call the flesh (*Leib*, of incarnation, *Leiblichkeit*) belongs to Descartes' most radical investigation in 1641 and forms the stake for the entire procedure of doubt: common skepticism bumps up against the impossibility of seriously challenging my own existence, although it comes from the senses and it must, in all logic, fall into the uncertainty that strikes everything they give us (or rather do not give us) to know. In other words, it basically bumps up against the difference between what comes to us through the senses and the very act of sensing, the latter as indubitable as the former are doubtful. And the act of sensing testifies to *meum corpus*. Descartes' question is thus doubled: Can one find any information derived from the senses that would resist doubt, and especially can the condition of possibility of these pieces of information, the *corpus meum*, succumb to doubt? If one fails to distinguish these two questions, the First Meditation remains unintelligible.

Descartes first confronts the most radical question, that of the in-

---

more disappointing, reduces this distinction to that of knowledge by sight (*a sensibus*) and of knowledge by hearsay, by hearing (*per sensibus*), which is contradicted by the text. Certainly, the syntagma *a sensibus* sometimes goes back to sight (VII: 39, 20), or even imagination (34, 23), but it is above all directly opposed to *ab intellectu* (51, 7). Inversely, *per sensus* can refer to several senses (seeing, hearing, touching) and nonetheless is concerned with the *res corporae* as such (29, 10–16), while sight also operates *per organa sensuum* in order to receive the *imagines* (VII: 40, 3 and 64, 26 and 30). And it is also *per sensus* that touching informs me of *corpus meum* (VII: 80, 1–5). Maybe one must rely on one of Montaigne's reminiscences without looking for too clean a distinction: "Now all knowledge makes its way into us through the senses; they are our masters . . . knowledge begins through them and is resolved into them." Michel de Montaigne, *The Complete Essays of Montaigne*, trans. Donald M. Frame (Stanford: Stanford University Press, 1948), Book II, Essay 12 ("Apology for Raymond Sebond"), 443.

dubitability of the *corpus meum*. As it is the case of my body, what is most paradigmatically my own, he tries to doubt it by seeing whether one can doubt what is one's own [*du propre*], namely, by understanding oneself as *insanus* (VII: 18, 26). He thus questions nothing less than "good sense . . . the best distributed thing in the world," which no one considers oneself to lack (VI: 1, 17f.; CSM I: 111), the *bona mens* that the First Regula presupposes (X: 360, 19; CSM I: 9) and at which the *Studium bonae mentis* had aimed from the beginning. Now, arguments can be found (contemporary scholarship has identified them well) for impugning "good sense"—primary among them the folly of those who take themselves to be kings clothed in purple when they are naked and very poor or those who imagine themselves as cucumbers with a fragile head, a body of glass, etc. This madness comes from a disturbance of the humors (here the atrabilious), thus precisely from *corpus meum*: it would therefore be possible to doubt *corpus meum* by putting one's trust in its disturbance. Yet Descartes refuses this path: the example of the *insani*, of disturbed minds, can be generalized only if the reader (and the author) deem themselves to be *amentes*, without mind. Not only would such an assimilation of everyone to some (*se transferre*) discourage those whom one would need to convince by demanding of them straightaway to allow themselves to be assimilated to the crazy, but it would accomplish a performative contradiction: the conditions of the discussion demand common rationality, which the argument employed would precisely wipe out; folly cannot discuss itself rationally. I would hence exclude myself from the argumentation; I would become *demens*, with neither *bona mens* nor *mens* at all, if I were to settle my discourse and its reception by my readers on the example of the *amentes*, who in the end could not fail to become the *insani* (VII: 19, 5–7; CSM II: 13). The long and notorious debates on the exclusion of madness, as distracting as they were and as instructive as they remain, should not be allowed to obliterate the essential point: except by himself leaving the argumentative debate, and thus philosophy, Descartes could not and should not have doubted my body, *corpus meum, directly* through the literally *insane* disqualification that the argument from folly seems to propose.

Therefore he had to try an *indirect* way for submitting the *corpus meum* to the trial of doubt. And therefore, rather than revoking it as such and in head-on fashion, he attempts to disqualify its closest determinations, its habits and customs, *usitata ista* (VII: 19, 11): As it is a matter of clothes, of fire, of papers held in the hand (18, 22–24 = 19, 11–14) that surround and indicate my body most closely, because I actually sense them (*sentio*, 19, 16), can one not doubt them at least? Yet I really sense them and I know very well that I sense them (*prudens et sciens extendo et sentio*, 19, 16), to the point where I seem not to be able to dismiss them either. From there he moves to a doubled argument: when I dream, I dream also sometimes that I am not dreaming, but that I am awake in the daily reality of the world; and anyway I do not have definite symptoms (*certis indiciis*, 19, 20) available for distinguishing these two states or indeed these symptoms have no importance, as in the case of mathematical demonstrations that remain valid in both states. Henceforth the dream becomes as believable as the waking state and the sensations remain the same in the two cases, although maybe no real object still corresponds to this. This particular argument can be accepted for it does not imply the radical performative contradiction of madness: we can in fact really consider that life is just a dream with neither the world disappearing nor our society within it. Even philosophy can continue its argumentations in this dream (or this dream of a dream), or can do so even better. Nevertheless, Descartes does not accept it or at least not without reservations: while fully admitting his astonishment without hesitation ("*obstupescam, et . . . hic ipse stupor mihi opinionem somni confirmet*—I begin to feel dazed, and this very feeling only reinforces the notion that I may be asleep"), he immediately adds "*fere*, almost" (VII: 19, 21–22 = IX-1: 15; CSM II: 13 [the term *fere* is not reproduced in the English translation]): the argument *almost* confirms that one must doubt the habits and customs of *corpus meum*, of my flesh, but not more. From where does this strange restriction derive, which the commentaries emphasize so little?

One can find several reasons and as many confirmations for it:

(a) First the fact that, whether dreaming or not, even in the dream I sense (*sentio*) in full knowledge of the cause (*prudens et sciens*) my clothes, the heat of the fire, and the sheet of paper in my hand. This sensing remains immediate and obvious, as the Second Meditation confirms, commenting on this passage in the First Meditation retrospectively: "*Idem denique ego sum qui* sentio, *sive qui res corporeas tanquam per sensus animadverto: videlicet jam lucem video, strepitum audio, calorem* sentio. *Falsa haec sunt, dormio enim. At certe videre videor, audire, calescere.* Hoc falsum esse non potest; *hoc est* proprie quod in me sentire appellatur; *atque hoc praecise six sumptum nihil aliud est quam cogitare.*—Lastly, it is also the same 'I' who *senses*, or is aware of bodily things as it were through the *senses*. For example, I am now seeing light, hearing a noise, feeling heat. But I am asleep, so all this is false. Yet I *certainly seem* to see, to hear, and to be warmed. This cannot be false; *what is called 'sensing' is strictly just this*, and in this restricted sense of the term it is simply thinking."[12] Sensing things in a dream thus is not disqualified by the nonexistence of the things sensed while dreaming; quite the opposite, it is confirmed in its certainty, provided that one take it as such, that is to say, as *reduced* (*hoc est quod proprie quod*) to the phenomenality of the phenomena actually perceived, even if they are not really things of the world. It indisputably seems to me that I see (*videre videor*) that which I see, even and especially if what I see is not seen outside of this appearing itself, which is sufficient unto itself as a first phenomenality. Thus reduced to its proper sense, sensing accordingly remains outside of doubt, really and truly out of the question.

(b) Sensing withstands doubt only because ultimately sensing is equivalent to thinking: "*hoc est proprie quod in me sentire appellatur; atque hoc praecise sic sumptum nihil aliud est quam cogitare*—what is called 'having a sensory perception' is strictly just this, and in this restricted sense of the term it is simply thinking" (VII: 29, 16–18; CSM II: 19). Actually, the passage from the First Meditation commented on here also relies on *cogitatio* for accomplishing the sensing (*sentio*): "*quae dum cogito attentius*" (19, 19): if I cogitate [*cogite*] what I sense, I understand that my sensing remains a *cogitatio*, actually indifferent to the existence or nonexistence of external objects of this sensing. And the amazement could come precisely from the consciousness of this very indifference: sensing is equivalent to thinking and thought does not depend on the object of thought, but on the very act of thinking, which phenomenalizes from itself what it thinks. Actually, the supposed putting into doubt of the habits and customs of the one who senses ("*prudens et sciens . . . sentio*," 19, 16) rests on the indubitability of the *cogitatio* that the Second Meditation will make obvious ("*Idem denique ego sum qui sentio*," 29, 11) but that was already at work in the First Meditation.

(c) The argument of the dream no more indirectly questions the *corpus meum* in its habits and customs than the argument from madness directly puts its *mens* into question, for the gap of an "almost—*fere*" always remains still to be crossed. This is what the beginning of the following paragraph clearly confirms: "Age *ergo somniemus, nec particularia ista vera* sint . . . , *nec* forte etiam *nos habere tales manus*, nec tale totum corpus—*Suppose* then that I am dreaming, and that these particulars are not true. . . . and let us think that *maybe* our hands or

12. Second Meditation, AT VII: 29, 11–18 = IX-1: 23; CSM II: 19; trans. lightly modified. This should be complemented with *The Passions of the Soul* I, §26, cited above, §12, 85, and below, chapter 6: §29, 217.

even *our entire body* are not such as we see them" (VII: 19, 23–26 =
IX-1: 15; CSM II: 13). One could not say more clearly that the doubt
about the *corpus meum* and its environment (the *particularia ista* taking
up the *usitata ista*) constitutes a takeover (indicated by the reservation
*forte etiam*, an echo of the *fere* in the preceding phrase): in order to play
the skeptical game as far as possible, Descartes decides to act *as if* the
argument from dreaming had indirectly placed the *corpus meum* (here
represented by *totum corpus* and its hands) into doubt, *as if* it made up
for the performative contradiction of the direct argument from madness
against the same and sole stakes of the debate, my flesh. The French
translation insists on the Latin *tale*, by adding that we act as if *"maybe*
our hands, or even *our entire body*, are *not such as we see them"* and
not as if they simply did not exist. For by right that has not been demonstrated, and even in order to try a hyperbolic hypothesis (*"age*—let
us suppose"), one cannot guarantee having doubted more than one has
really managed to doubt. For there is an honesty to doubt, as Kierkegaard notes: knowing one's limits.

Therefore, how and why does Descartes keep trying to doubt if his
first object, *corpus meum*, already resists it twice? Because in each attempt he follows the same tactic: if the object itself resists doubt, one
can still attack it by increasing its distance and each time lower one's
aim. The first argument (madness) attacks the *corpus meum* at its core,
the *(bona) mens*, and in its essence. The second argument (dream) already aims at it only in its practices (senses, hands, waking) and in their
existence. The third argument (code and over-encoding) concentrates
the fire on a different target, the *generalia haec* (VII: 19, 29 and 20, 8–9),
the hands, eyes, head, the body as such (*totum corpus*) starting from its
components; and the existence of these elements is this time no longer in
question, because one admits "*res quasdam non imaginarias, sed veras
existere*—these things are not imaginary but are real and exist" (19, 30–
31; CSM II: 13). With so many concessions, how could one still attempt
the removal via doubt of the sensory "*a sensibus vel per sensus*"?

Brilliant as always, Descartes will lead the *almost* doubtful terms
to which he has reduced *corpus meum* back to what his own theory
of consciousness had, since the *Regulae*, identified as the final concepts
of the constitution of material objects, the simple natures or *naturae
simplicissimae*.[13] The components of the sensory as such (what the *corpus meum* senses) actually presuppose concepts that are themselves not

13. For this interpretation of the *naturae simplicissimae*, see *Sur l'ontologie
grise de Descartes*, §§22–24, 131ff. For the interpretation of the hyperbolic

sensory and purely intelligible, absolutely true because simpler and perfectly universal (*magis simplicia et universalia vera*, 20, 11). They are
sufficient for understanding the nature of material things (*natura corporea in communi*, 19, 15–16) in its totality. These concepts are defined
as extension, figure, their quantity, their number, the place and the time
of their duration (hence also movement).[14] Descartes' argument is hence
unfolded in this way: the felt elements of the sensory (sense, hands,
waking, etc.), as deceptive as they may turn out to be, nonetheless rely
on a minimal indubitable truth, that of the concepts transcribing them
and codifying them (or rather decoding them), as mathematics does:
not only do 2 and 3 always make 5 and the square never have more
than 4 sides, whether I am awake or when I sleep but, when I visually
sense the clear but indistinct difference of colors (red, blue, and yellow,
for example), I can always note them down and make them distinct
by different features. This result—which remains in the end "something certain and indubitable—*aliquid certi atque indubitati*" (20, 27;
CSM II: 14) in the sensory, provided that it is encoded (or decoded) by
the simple natures—being achieved, the third argument will be able to
be deployed for questioning this sensory, a sensory to the second degree
because actually intellectualized by concepts. For I have an ancient and
common opinion available, that of a God who is able to do everything.
This God is the creator of the eternal truths that are as logical as they
are mathematical and has allowed me to code (and decode) the sensory
according to simple natures (according to the example of mathematics)
and to make them thereby certain and indubitable to the second degree
*for me*. But *for him*, God, this encoding could itself be found in its turn
coded (or rather over-encoded) in accordance with a *different* system of
axioms from the one I use (the simple natures) for coding and decoding
the sensible givens. From the point of view of this super-code, to which
by definition only God's omnipotence and not the finitude of my *mens*
could have access, I would deceive myself by taking as absolutely and
unconditionally true that 2 and 3 make five, that the square has 4 sides,
just as (*quemadmodum*, 21, 7, echoing the *nec dispari ratione* of the
first coding, 20, 8) a nonphilosophical mind takes to be absolutely and

---

doubt in the First Meditation according to this doctrine of the *Regulae*, I maintain the results of *Sur la théologie blanche de Descartes*, §14, 313ff.

14. VII: 20, 16–19 (taken up again in the Fifth Meditation, VII: 63, 16–21).
In other places, especially in the *Regulae* (X: 419, 19), the list is more specific:
extension, figure, movement (which allow for place), also the time and duration
concerning them as common (to material and intellectual) simple natures. See
*Cartesian Questions*, chapter 2, "What is the metaphysics within the method?"

unconditionally true that the sun is the size of an orange, that fire is hot, that ice is cold—while all these truths, coded and decoded, to the first or the second degree, are true only conditionally and relatively from the point of view either of the *Mathesis universalis* or of God's omnipotence. Thus the sensory is finally discovered to be placed in doubt: certainly not directly, but by the discovery of its transcendental conditions of possibility—it remains certain only within the limits of rationality created by the finite *mens* and becomes problematic in connection with the infinite (the omnipotence) of God.

One question, however, remains: what do we here understand by the sensory? It is obviously a matter of what the simple material natures encode and decode, namely, the *generalia haec*, the sensory hand, head, eyes in general (VII: 19, 29; 20, 8; CSM II: 13) and, indissolubly, their conditions of intelligibility, the simple natures themselves, *natura corporea in communi* (20, 15–16). In this way, in this third argument (that of hyperbolic doubt) material things, physical bodies really find themselves placed in doubt: "*nulla plane sit terra, nullum coelum, nulla res extensa, nulla figura, nulla magnitudo, nullus locus*—there is no earth, no sky, no extended thing, no shape, no size, no place" (21, 4–6; CSM II: 14). But how could one not see that *here* it is obviously no longer the same sensory as the one that the first putting into doubt envisaged? For it aimed at *hoc corpus meum* (18, 25) and then *my* hand, *my* heat, *my* eyes, etc., in other words my own body, the one that senses (itself), in short my flesh. Now, *here* and finally, doubt puts into question only the earth and the sky, the corporeal and material things that are certainly not my flesh and that, far from sensing (themselves) and affecting me, allow themselves to be coded according to the simple material natures (shape, size, place) as physical bodies in general (*res extensa*). In short, doubt, even and especially when it is hyperbolic, *puts into question only the physical bodies of the world and never my flesh*, only the *natura corporea* and never *meum corpus*. And therefore the Sixth Meditation was perfectly right to sustain support for *corpus meum* (72, 2), when the order of the subject-matter required it, because, according to the order of reasoning, its concept had never been put into doubt and it remained, like a very embattled but unconquered space, solidly certain, available for a later advance of metaphysical meditation.

## §14. A Doubtful Doubting (1641)

All the same, if the First Meditation really leads to this result—*that doubt questions only the physical bodies of the world and never my flesh*, and that the invalidity is concerned only with the possibility that "there is no earth, no sky, no extended body [thing], no shape, no size, no place—*nulla plane sit terra, nullum coelum, nulla res extensa, nulla figura, nulla magnitudo, nullus locus*" (IX-1: 16 for VII: 21, 4–6; CSM II: 14)—Descartes contradicts it from the resumption of the argumentation in the Second Meditation onward. In fact, the stages that lead to the certainty that I am and that I exist (24, 14—25, 12) are played over several times with regard to the sensory and its possible ambiguity; and Descartes confronts or even assumes this ambiguity three times. (a) He first makes the mention of the senses precede the list of simple material natures dismissed through doubt: "*nullos plane habeo sensus; corpus, figura, extensio, motus, locusque sunt chimerae*—I have no senses. Body, shape, extension, movement and place are chimeras" (24, 16–17; CSM II: 16); now it is self-evident that here these *sensus*, which precisely I have (*habeo*), are neither one with the objectness of the simple natures nor with the body of the world, but go back to my sensing body, in short to the *corpus meum*; and thus they have not been put into doubt by the final argument of the First Meditation.[15] (b) Second, he challenges the idea that God could have sent me thoughts because there is nothing that I can call mine; nothing, that is to say, nothing corporeal, but even here also in an ambiguous sense: what does "*Sed jam negavi me habere ullos sensus, ut ullum corpus*—But I have just said that I have no senses and no body" (24, 25–26; CSM II: 16) really designate? Obviously (as it is a hendiadys) the body that has senses, thus the sensing body, *meum corpus*, and in no way the bodies of the world. Yet, once more, the First Meditation in its final argument precisely doubts only the simple natures and the extended bodies they codify and not the flesh. (c) Finally Descartes wonders whether he is "*ita corpori sensibusque alligatus*—so bound up with a body and with senses" (25, 1; CSM II: 16) that he could not be without a sensing body endowed with sense, hence a *meum corpus*; yet his response, which one certainly must understand to remain negative, adds another term to the mundane and extended bodies ("*nihil plane in mundo, nullum coelum, nullam terra . . . nulla corpora*—nothing in the world, no sky, no earth, . . . no bodies") that have been obviously doubtful in the First Meditation, namely, the term "*nullas mentes*—no minds" (25, 3–4 = IX-1: 19; CSM II: 16), for which one would be hard pressed to find a place where

---

15. The translation of de Luynes makes the distinction more neatly than Descartes' Latin: "I think that I have no senses; I believe that the body, shape, extension, movement and place are only fictions of my mind" (IX-1: 19).

the argument from omnipotence ever challenged it. In this way, the demonstration that leads to my existence at least three times presupposes a doubt larger than the one that had in fact been accomplished in the First Meditation: a doubt that would also encompass the sensing body, *meum corpus*, my flesh, rather than concerning only the material things themselves and the simple natures that codify them.[16]

Although the three arguments in the First Meditation had neither included nor attempted to include my flesh in the field of doubt with the same rank as the material things and the extended bodies assumed to be habitual, in other words, to add "*nullas mentes*—no minds" (25, 3–4) to the list of doubtful bodies, this is what the Second Meditation does in blunt fashion: it cites as a result of the First Meditation ("*Sed jam negavi . . .*—I have just said," "*Sed mihi persuasi . . .*—I have convinced myself," 24, 25 and 25, 2; CSM II: 16) what it had, however, *never* demonstrated. Actually, this ambiguity is limited to taking up again what the *Discourse on Method* had already assumed: "I could pretend that I had no body and that there was no world and no place for me to be in" (VI: 32, 25–27: CSM I: 127); acting as if the body that I have had the same status as the world and the place that are not me.[17] An ambiguity that is also found again as such in the *Principles of Philosophy*, where the two senses of *corpus* are found violently opposed but not for all that thematized: "*facile quidem supponimus nullus esse Deum, nullum coelum, nulla; corpora, nosque etiam ipsos non habere manus, nec pedes, nec denique ullum* corpus—it is easy for us to suppose that there is no God and no heaven, and that there are no bodies, and even that we ourselves have no hands or feet, or indeed any body at all" (I, §7, VIII-1: 7, 2–4; CSM I: 194). How can one explain that all these texts confuse what nevertheless is so clearly distinguished in the First and Sixth Meditations? The reply to this question about the supposition of the Second Meditation ("*Suppono igitur*," VII: 24, 14) is

16. I have already drawn attention to this gap, where the Second Meditation hyperbolizes the real result of the First Meditation, in *On the Ego and on God: Further Cartesian Questions* (New York: Fordham University Press, 2007), 12–19 and 54–55.

17. Similarly: "everything else of which they may think themselves more sure—such as their having a body, there being stars and an earth, and the like" (VI: 37, 27–29; CSM I: 130); and "We need only observe that in sleep we may imagine in the same way that we have a different body and see different stars and a different earth, without there being any of these things" (VI: 38, 6–9; CSM I: 130). Even so, the body that I am is not an extension like the stars or the earth.

most probably found in the First Meditation itself, when it introduces the preceding supposition of the "evil genius" at the end (*"Supponam igitur,"* 22, 23). Following Gouhier's demonstration,[18] I admit here that it is a matter not of a rational argument (like the three preceding ones: madness, dream, God's omnipotence), but of a voluntary and indeed arbitrary decision (*"voluntate plane in contrarium versa*—turn my will in completely the opposite direction," VII: 22, 13; CSM II: 15), which forces me to doubt *as if* I had restricting reasons to do so, replacing dogmatic prejudices with skeptical "prejudices" (22, 16) and replacing reasons with obstinacy (*"obstinate . . . defixus*—stubbornly . . . persist," 23, 4). It is in the frame of this psychological exercise without theoretical validity that the existence of the ego will be acquired (the *deceptor nescio quis, summe potens, summe callidus, qui de industria me semper fallit*—deceiver of supreme power and cunning who is deliberately and constantly deceiving me," 25, 6–7; CSM II: 17). It is also within the frame of this unfounded radicalization of doubt that Descartes adds to the revocation of the extended bodies and the material things (*"putabo coelum, aërem, terram, colores, figuras, sonos, cunctaque* externa *nihil aliud esse quam ludificationes*—I shall think that the sky, the air, the earth, colours, shapes, sounds and all external things are merely the delusions of dreams," 22, 26–28; CSM II: 15) a second suspension, clearly distinguished from the first, namely in this case that of my flesh (*Leib*): *"considerabo meipsum* tanquam *manus non habentem, non oculos, non carnem, non sanguinem, non aliquem sensum*—I shall consider myself *as* not having hands or eyes, or flesh, or blood or senses" (VII: 22, 29– 23, 3 = IX-1: 18; CSM II: 15). This final sequence merits attention: one finds here again the customary formulations *non manus, non oculos, non sensus* (no hands, no eyes, no senses) in order to designate my body; but two terms also appear here, *caro* et *sanguis, flesh* and *blood,* that are not found again in the [rest of the] *Meditations.*[19] How was Descartes led to use *caro* here, literally flesh (*Leib*)? Let me risk a hypothesis: wanting to think the *meum corpus* here radically and even oppose it

18. Henri Gouhier, *La Pensée métaphysique de Descartes* (Paris: Vrin, 1962), and my clarification in *Sur la théologie blanche de Descartes,* §13, 341. See also the *fingentes* that the *Principles of Philosophy* introduces and that dominate it, I, §7, VIII-1: 7, 1; CSM I: 194.

19. *Caro* appears only here, and the only other occurrence of *sanguis* has a strictly physiological sense, not a moral one: "*hominis corpus, quatenus machinamentum quoddam est ex ossibus, nervis, musculis, venis, sanguine et pellibus*—the body of man as a kind of machine equipped with and made up of bones, nerves, muscles, veins, blood and skin" (84, 19–21; CSM II: 58).

to the pure and simple *mens*, he calls it the flesh in reference to a dichotomy displayed by two texts from the New Testament: "*Beatus es Simon Bar Iona, quia* caro *et* sanguis *non revelavit tibi, sed Pater qui est in caelis*—Blessed are you, Simon son of Jonah! For *flesh* and *blood* has not revealed this to you, but my Father in heaven" (Matt. 16:17) and "*Caro et* sanguis *regnum Dei possidere non possunt—flesh* and *blood* cannot inherit the kingdom of God" (1 Cor. 15:50, see also Gal. 1:16).[20] The opposition without either reservation or nuance between the pure *mens* and an undifferentiated sensory comes from a voluntarist (if not to say arbitrary) tactical decision, which itself becomes reinforced by the authority of a biblical recollection and results in identifying *corpus meum* with *caro et sanguis*, in order to challenge it as if it were a matter of the *corpora* of the world. The hypothesis ("*Supponam igitur . . .*") of the *genius malignus* thus prepares, in the nontheoretical appendix of the First Meditation, the hypothesis ("*Supponam igitur . . .*") of my nonexistence. Yet, just as existence comes back to me in the evidence of the *ego sum*, the capacity of sensing will come back to me together with the reported modes of the *res cogitans* (26, 6, 20; CSM II: 17–18). The two hypotheses are hence shown to be as provisional as they are little grounded in reason, even if, for the tactic of doubting, they play a role for a time.

The flesh of *corpus meum* hence finds itself put into doubt only on two conditions. First of all, this doubt occurs only in the short section limited by the two hypotheses ("*Supponam igitur . . .*"), the one that closes the First Meditation (starting at VII: 22, 2 and especially 22, 23) and the one that leads to my existence (25, 13ff.) in the Second Meditation, a section that corresponds to the reign, albeit very brief, of the evil genius. Second, this doubt contradicts the only (three) arguments advanced by the First Meditation, of which none permit extending it to *meum corpus*. One should thus not be surprised that this doubt, once

---

20. Maybe also recalling John 1:13: "*qui non* ex sanguinibus *nec ex voluntate* carnis . . . *sed ex Deo nati sunt*—who were born, not of *blood* or of the will of the *flesh* or of the will of man, but of God." Certainly the *Fifth Replies* use *caro/chair*/flesh for polemically designating the person that Gassendi plays (VII: 253, 23; 354, 12 and 23; 357, 17; 358, 1; 364, 6; 369, 1; 377, 21; 385, 13). But even there, it is not a matter of a philosophical concept, because the biblical reference remains underlying: "*mens cum carne disseruit*—discussion between mind and flesh" (V: 390, 20; CSM II: 267) goes clearly back to Saint Paul: "*Caro enim concupiscit adversus spiritum, spiritus autem adversus carnem*—For what the flesh desires is opposed to the Spirit, and what the Spirit desires is opposed to the flesh" (Gal. 5:17).

more without basis or reason, leaves the flesh of *corpus meum* intact, a place very embattled but not conquered that the Sixth Meditation will be able to reinvest all the more easily as it had never succumbed to it.[21]

## §15. Recapitulation and Confirmations of the Flesh

It becomes henceforth possible to secure the different Cartesian meanings of *corpus*/body following their occurrences in the *Meditations* and accordingly to unfold their ambiguity.

(a) Most frequently *corpus* designates the physical body of the world, defined [as] "*illud omne quod aptum est figura aliqua terminari, loco circumscribi, spatium sic replere, ut ex eo aliud omne corpus excludat*— whatever has a determinable shape and a definable location and can occupy a space in such a way as to exclude any other body" (AT VII: 26, 14–17 = IX-1: 20; CSM II: 17). Then the *res corpora, res extensa, res materialis* are also named there or rather, in implicit contrast with my flesh, *alia corpora, circumjacentia corpora*; this concerns what the simple *material* natures of the *Regulae* allow to think (henceforth the innate ideas according to the Third Meditation).

(b) In contrast, *corpus* can designate my own body, sensing as much as sensed. It appears in this way under very identifiable titles. First with the phrase *totum hoc corpus meum*[22] or "*corpus illud . . . meum*,"[23] common to the First and Sixth Meditation; they are the two extremes. The undeniable echo with the formula of the eucharistic consecration is doubled by a less obvious political resonance in the formulation

21. Maine de Biran had seen this difficulty: "Descartes' doubt, which assumes the body to be obliterated while thought remains, is absolutely contrary to the primitive fact in the way in which I am considering it [that is, the internal perception of presence or of the coexistence of sensory bodies]." *Essai sur le fondement de la psychologie*, ed. F. C. T. Moore, in *Œuvres*, vol. VII (Paris: J. Vrin, 2001), 150–51. But he had not noticed that this doubt, assumed by the Second Meditation, did not have by right any support in the First Meditation and that its hyperbole remains rhetorical, not conceptual. One must rather say that Descartes' doubt, which does *not* annihilate the *meum corpus* while the *ego cogito* subsists, already enunciates what Biran defines as the *primitive fact*.

22. Full opening formulation of the First Meditation, VII: 18, 25; CSM II: 13. See *tale totum corpus* (19, 25f.), *totumque corpus* (19, 30).

23. See "*varia circa meum corpus alia corpora existere*—various other bodies exist in the vicinity of my body" (81, 15–16; CSM II: 56) and "*meum corpus sive potius me totum*—my body, or rather my whole self" (81, 24–25; CSM II: 56); besides VII: 18, 25, compare "*hoc corpus inter alia multa*—this body . . . among many other bodies" (74, 20; CSM II: 52).

*habeam corpus.*[24] Other variants underline the *unique* [*propre*] character of the flesh: "*illud corpus, quod tanquam* mei *partem, vel forte etiam tanquam* me totum *spectabam*—the body, which I regarded as part of *myself*, or perhaps even as *my whole* self";[25] or its character of being *united* to the mind: "*corpus ipsi* [i.e., the faculty of knowing] *intime praesens*—a body which is intimately present to it."[26] Finally the *corpus* also becomes recognized as *meum*, hence as flesh, by its proximity either to the instruments of its passivity, hands, eyes, ears, head, and so forth ("*oculos, caput, manus, totumque corpus*," VII: 19, 29–30), or to the ability to sense ("*negavi me habere ullos sensus, et ullum corpus*—I have just said that I have no senses and no body").[27] These final two determinations are encountered at least once more in a sequence that is exceptional because it explicitly uses the title of *caro*, flesh: "*manus non habentem, non oculos, non carnem, non sanguinem, non aliquem sensum*—not having hands or eyes, or flesh, or blood or senses."[28]

(c) A final possibility remains: that my body of flesh would become an extended body. In this case one speaks of a corpse, precisely constituted by its members like a machine by its wheels, but which decidedly lacks the faculty of passivity, the sensing ("*vim . . . sentiendi . . . nullo pacto ad naturam corporis pertinere.*—For, according to my judgment,

24. Two occurrences: "*habeam corpus, quod mihi valde arcte conjunctum est*—I may have . . . a body that is very closely joined to me" (VII: 78, 14; CSM II: 54), "*habeam corpus, cui male est cum dolorem sentio*—I have a body, and that when I feel pain there is something wrong with the body" (80, 28–29; CSM II: 56).

25. VII: 74, 18–20; CSM II: 52. See "*corpus illud quod speciali quodam jure meum appellabam*—the body which by some special right I called 'mine'" (75, 30f.; CSM II: 52).

26. VII: 72, 2; CSM II: 50. See "*illud sensus organo [sit] praesens*—unless it was present to my sense organs" (75, 12–13; CSM II: 52), "*corpus aliquod . . . cui mens sit ita conjuncta*—there does exist some body to which the mind is so joined" (73, 11; CSM II: 51), "*meo corpori . . . arctissime esse conjunctum et quasi permixtum, adeo ut unum quid cum illo componam*—my body . . . that I am very closely joined and, as it were, intermingled with" (81, 2f. = 15, 23f.; CSM II: 56), "*quasi permixtione mentis cum corpore*—as it were, intermingling of the mind with the body" (81, 13f.; CSM II: 56), "*toti corpori tota mens unita*—the whole mind . . . united to the whole body" (86, 4–5; CSM II: 59).

27. VII: 24, 25–26; CSM II: 16. See "*Summe ita corpori sensibusque alligatus . . . ?*—Am I not so bound up with my body . . . ?" (25, 1; CSM II: 16).

28. VII: 23, 1–3; CSM II: 15. The beginning sequence of the Third Meditation dispenses with saying *meum corpus*, although it evokes its characteristics perfectly, because it uses all these linked formulations.

the power of self-movement, like the power of sensation or of thought, was quite foreign to the nature of a body" (VII: 26, 20–21 = IX-1: 20; CSM II: 17); and in this case one must designate it *"corporis no-mine*—by the name of the body."[29] In this way, we reach a first confirmation: one cannot attribute a dualism between soul and body to Descartes, precisely because he admits not two but *three* terms (besides the corpse): the physical, extended body, *"illud omne quod aptum est figura aliqua terminari*—whatever has a determinable shape" (VII: 26, 14–15 = IX-1: 20; CSM II: 17), the soul that thinks in all the fullness of the *cogitatio*, finally and above all my body, *meum corpus.*

The confusion of these three terms under debate with a simple dichotomy could in the end constitute the sole and simple origin of the long complaint against the supposed unintelligibility of the union of soul and body (a complaint that functions like a very ordinary basso continuo regardless of whatever ornament adds its variations to it). As so often, one of Gassendi's objections prefigures that of many others. He challenges in fact the *conjunctio et quasi permistio* under the pretext that such a joining and mingling assumes parts and hence "a certain proportion between the parts" (344, 5f.; CSM II: 238). Accordingly, if one must have "intimate contact" between the air and a rock, a common point is necessary, in this case a pumice stone.[30] Descartes responds to this that one must not compare the interlacing of soul and body with the mingling of two bodies (*"mentis et corporis permistionem cum permistione duorum corporum vis comparare"*): the mingling of bodies implies the mingling of their parts, in shared extension, while the interlacing (still a mingling, but of a different type) between the soul and *its* body offers a connection between one thing that has no parts and one that does have parts. This mingling and union is so intimate that finally what has parts (what there is *machine-like* in the *corpus meum*) ends by having in turn no more than that to which it is being united, namely, thought. For thought (and hence also my body that senses) understands extension precisely by *not* being extended: thought does not contain the world in extension and hence by being extended (*"extensione major*

---

29. VII: 26, 5 (= IX-1: 20); CSM II: 17; trans. modified; one will also speak of *"machinamentum quoddam* [a kind of machine] (84, 20; 85, 5; CSM II: 58); of *compages* [structure] (27, 18–19; CSM II: 18) and of *automata* (32, 10; CSM II: 21).

30. VII: 343, 21—344, 18; CSM II: 238. The formulation of 343, 22 cites approximately the Sixth Meditation, 81, 3–4.

*orbe terrarum"*), but contains it in thought and by thinking it.[31] Gassendi is here the one who remains the most intellectualist, conceiving of no other union than what is understood according to and within extension. Descartes is here the one who leaves himself exposed to apprehending the tight union of mind with body in conformity with what we continue really to *experience* constantly *through the senses* (*"arctam illam mentis cum corpore conjunctionem, quam* sensibus *assidue* experimur*—the fact that the mind is closely conjoined with the body, which we *experience* constantly through our *senses,*" 228, 27f.; CSM II: 160). There is an experience of thought *through the body*, obviously on the condition that it would really be *mine*, that is to say flesh, thus that it could sense (itself) and thus think in the mode of passivity. Yet this experience cannot be described either in the mode of objectivity or in that of extension. Not everyone does so, or when they do so they do not all understand it.

An objection that is very often addressed to Descartes or at least to his so-called "official" interpretation (that is to say, without any textual basis)[32] could here become more intelligible and its misinterpretation more interesting. The error, apparently of Cartesian origin, would consist in confusing the sensations with the knowledge of objects; but really "sensations do not have dimensions, shapes, positions, temperatures, colors or sounds," such that "having sensations is not in itself describing, not any more than these bricks are a house or these letters a word." Actually our sensations are inaccessible and incommunicable to the other not because an iron curtain hides them from him, but because I myself cannot observe them, see them, and know them and because "the notion of the sensory object is absurd," in other words, "'the sensory

---

31. Fifth Set of Replies, n. 4–5, VII: 388, 13—390, 14; CSM II: 266. Could this discussion have served as the point of departure for Pascal ("thinking reed")? *Pensées* [Lafuma edition], §123, trans. A. J. Krailsheimer (New York: Penguin Books, 1966). Regarding this extension proper to thought, see below, chapter 4, §19.

32. Gilbert Ryle, to whom I refer here, admits straightaway, without noticing the strangeness of the admission, that "it would not be true to say that the official theory [whose?] derives solely from Descartes' theories" in *The Concept of Mind* (Chicago: University of Chicago Press, 1949, 2000), 23. Thus, why attribute it to Descartes if it does not really come from him ("The official doctrine, which is for the most part identified with Descartes . . ." [ibid., 11]). Wolfgang Röd has said what needs to be said about the unsupportable approximation of this nonreading of Descartes and its pretentious ignorance in "Descartes' Mythos oder Ryles Mythos? Überlegungen zu Ryles Descartes-Kritik," *Archiv für Geschichte der Philosophie* 55.3 (1973): 310–33.

object' is a formulation devoid of sense."³³ In fact, Ryle objects to one of Descartes' distinctions and does not see that it constitutes the very inno-vation of the *Meditations*. Of course, what the flesh of the *meum corpus* experiences remains a thought that is sensed (*sensus*), which besides concerns usefulness (the *in/commoda*) and not theoretical knowledge. As to the constitution of sensory objects, it requires the codification of these *sensus* by the simple material natures that alone will permit to speak (in other words, to measure) the shapes, dimensions, positions, and so forth, in short to know physical bodies. The distinction that Ryle brandishes relies precisely on the distinction, made by Descartes, between the flesh and the bodies: it proves to be trivial, and trivial from a Cartesian point of view.

Obviously, behind this superficial polemic, one must hear a more se-rious debate, which took place between G. E. Moore and Wittgenstein. From "A Defense of Common Sense" in 1925 onward all the way to the "Proofs of the External World" in 1939,³⁴ Moore upholds against Kant (hence in the line of Kantian readings of Descartes) that there is no scandal in the absence of a proof for the existence of external things, because this proof finds itself replaced by the experience of my flesh: If I lift my two hands, if I move the one on the right by saying "Here is a hand," if I shake the one on the left saying "And here is another one," I attest that there are existing bodies, existing hands. What stands out, in fact, is not one of the bodies of the world (*corpora*, *Körper*), but my body, my sensing body, my flesh, and this displacement of the Kantian question by Moore's reply makes up the entire force of his argument. "At this very moment there is a living human body that is *my* body. This body is born at a certain instant in the past and has continued to exist since then, but not without undergoing changes. For example, it was smaller at birth and indeed for quite a while than it is at present."³⁵ Wittgenstein's rather waffling refutation of Moore in a sense only re-inforces the Cartesian framework of the distinction; if Moore's quasi-proof shifts the argument about bodies to *meum corpus*, from objects to the flesh, which cannot be contested, then one must pay the price of this

33. Ibid., 208, 214, [205], 237, and 236, respectively.

34. See George Edward Moore, *Philosophical Papers* (London: Allen & Unwin, 1959). Françoise Armengaud, *Moore et la genèse de la philosophie ana-lytique* (Paris: Klincksieck, 1985). Élise Domenach remarks precisely that this fi-nal translation does not underline the Cartesian origin of the debate sufficiently, in "Scepticisme, sens commun et langage ordinaire," *Revue de métaphysique et de morale* 51.3 (2006): 385–97.

35. Armengaud, *Moore et la genèse de la philosophie analytique*, 150.

indubitability; one must admit that the flesh, as certain as it becomes from itself and hence also from exteriority, does not for all that *know* it. The knowing that I have from my hand remains of a type completely different from that by which I know the existence of the planet Saturn: I do not *know* the existence of my hand, although I *sense* it, no more than "I am in pain" allows me to say that "I know" that I am in pain.[36] Yet one could not even speak of a grammatical mistake between the sensing and the knowing, if one had not already recognized the legitimacy of a distinction between flesh and objects, between *meum corpus* and the *alia corpora*—that is to say, if one had not admitted the essential distinction established by Descartes. Thus the objections that one thinks one can make against Descartes without cease and without progress not only have no bearing upon his real teaching but presuppose it.

## §16. The Modalities of the Cogito and the Privilege of Passivity

In this way, a third term, that of my body, is found between pure thought and material things: this result explains the fact that the occurrences of this third term, *meum corpus*, frame the entire Meditations into two groups of texts, the first two and the final one (I–II, VI). How shall one explain this constancy and, at the same time, its absence in the middle part (III–V)?

36. See Ludwig Wittgenstein: "'Doubting the existence of the external world' does not mean for example doubting the existence of a planet, which later observations proved to exist.—Or does Moore want to say that knowing that here is his hand is different in kind from knowing the existence of the planet Saturn? Otherwise it would be possible to point out the discovery of the planet Saturn to the doubters and say that its existence has been proved, and hence the existence of the external world as well." *On Certainty*, trans. Denis Paul and G. E. M. Anscombe (Oxford: Basil Blackwell, 1974), §20, 4e. Also: "The wrong use made by Moore of the proposition 'I know . . .' lies in his regarding it as an utterance as little subject to doubt as 'I am in pain.' And since from 'I know it is so' there follows 'It is so,' then the latter can't be doubted either." Ibid., §178, 25e. On this debate, see Élise Marrou, *Wittgenstein. De la certitude* (Paris: Ellipses, 2006). It is obviously in this context that one must place the discussions, as fastidious as sterile, that inquire whether Descartes attributes sensations to the body or to the soul (in fact neither to one nor to the other but to the *meum corpus*), or whether he doubts his own body or not (he doubts his *corpus*, but not *meum corpus*). Thus Baker and Morris, eds., *Descartes' Dualism*, discussed by Steven Nadler, "Descartes' Dualism?" *Philosophical Books* 38.3 (1997): 157–69; Sarah Patterson, "How Cartesian Was Descartes?" in Tim Crane and Sarah Patterson, eds., *History of the Mind-Body Problem* (New York: Routledge, 2000), 70–110.

By considering seriously the unity of the *res cogitans*, hence also the irreducible multiplicity of its modes. For the Cartesian ego, once its existence is achieved, then its essence assured, is defined by a series of modes, namely, the very ones that state what Descartes understands by *cogitatio*, and what one cannot comprehend by confining oneself to the imprecision of its translation by "thought," a translation that is all the same inevitable and well established. For it is a matter not so much of representative thought in general as of what makes it possible, the act of gathering, within the unity of a repetitive (*cogitare*, frequentative of *cogere*) apperception (*cogitare*, from *co-agere*), what can appear as certain from experience. Contrary to a dominant opinion, the *res cogitans* cogitates neither exclusively nor first of all according to the understanding.[37] Besides, how could one fail to notice that the sequence that best seems to justify such a privilege of the understanding—"*sum igitur praecise tantum res cogitans, id est, mens, sive animus, sive intellectus, sive ratio*—I am, then, in the strict sense only a thing that thinks; that is, I am a mind, or intelligence, or intellect, or a reason" (VII: 27, 13–14 = IX-1: 21; CSM II: 18)—precisely disqualifies its presumed primacy and for several reasons?

First, because in this formulation, the understanding is along with three other concepts in an equivalence sufficiently loose for marking them all with the same indeterminacy ("*voces mihi prius significationis ignotae*—words whose meaning I have been ignorant of until now," VII: 27, 15 = IX-1: 21; CSM II: 18). Then, because all these concepts become immediately dismissed because of their indeterminacy: "*Nescio, de hac re jam non disputo; de iis tantum quae mihi nota sunt, judicism ferre possum*—I do not know, and for the moment I shall not argue the point, since I can make judgements only about things which are known to me" (VII: 27, 26–28 = IX-1: 21; CSM II: 18). Doubting the categories

---

37. Among others but more than any other, for example Gueroult: "The intellect is the principal attribute among all the attributes that the thought substance possesses." *Descartes' Philosophy Interpreted According to the Order of Reasons*, trans. Roger Ariew (Minneapolis: University of Minnesota Press, 1984), I: 45, trans. lightly modified. A surprising formulation, which does not sound very Cartesian, because (a) the ego of the *res cogitans* is not a *thought* substance (a formulation that would rather designate *extended* substances) but a *thinking* substance, *substantia cogitans*; (b) the principal attribute of the *substantia cogitans* remains the *cogitatio* in general and never the understanding; (c) the understanding (*intellectus*, not "intelligence") is not an attribute, neither of the substance nor of the *cogitatio*, but one of its modes; (d) it is mentioned by itself (VII: 28, 21; 34, 19; 160, 9; etc.) without privilege in regard to the others.

of the old metaphysics also strikes them with futility. In fact, the concepts of the *mens*, the *intellectus*, and *ratio* are here being repealed in the same manner as those of the ancient definition of the human as *animal rationale*: "*Dicamne animal rationale? Non, quia postea quaerendum foret quidnam animal sit, et quid rationale, atque ita ex una quaestione in plures difficiloresque delaberer.*—Shall I say 'a rational animal'? No; for then I should have to inquire what an animals is, what rationality is, and in this way one question would lead me down the slope to other harder ones."[38] Finally and above all, because the enumeration of these imprecise and disqualified concepts is being framed and corrected by a double occurrence of the *res cogitans*: "*sum igitur praecise tantum res cogitans . . . Sum autem res vere, et vera existens; sed qualis res? Dixi, cogitans*—I am then, in the strict sense only a thing that thinks . . . But for all that I am a thing which is real and which truly exists. But what kind of a thing? As I have just said—a thinking thing" (VII: 27, 13 and 16–17 = IX-1: 21; CSM II: 18). Thus it clearly appears that the ancient concepts rely on simple approximations, semantically unstable, of the only indubitable, performable, and verifiable given—the *res cogitans* itself. Thus we must comprehend starting from it alone how and to what point it is broken down into its diverse modes, of which the understanding offers just a simple case, one that is not even privileged.

Let me cite two complex formulations that we must now make a topic of discussion. First: "*Sed quid igitur sum? Res cogitans. Quid est hoc? Nempe dubitans, intelligens, affirmans, negans, volens, nolens, imaginans quoque, et sentiens.*—But what then am I? A thing that thinks. What is that? A thing that doubts, understands, affirms, denies, is willing, is unwilling, and also imagines and has sensory perceptions." Then: "*Ego sum res cogitans, id est dubitans, affirmans, negans, pauca intelligens, multa ignorans, volens, nolens, imaginans etiam et sentiens.*—I am a thing that thinks: that is a thing that doubts, affirms, denies, understands a few things, is ignorant of many things, is willing, is unwilling, and also which imagines and has sensory perceptions."[39] These two formulations

38. VII: 25, 26–29 = IX-1: 20, which one will compare to the discussion on the simplicity of *naturae simplicissimae*, X: 418, 19—419, 5, for which these terms furnish an example a contrario.

39. VII: 28, 20–23 = IX-1: 22; CSM II: 19 and VII: 34, 18–21 = IX-1: 27, 9–12; CSM II: 24, respectively. And also in the Sixth Meditation: "*una et eadem mens est quae vult,* quae sentit, *quae intelligit*—since it is one and the same mind that wills, and understands and *has sensory perceptions*" (86, 9–10; CSM II: 59). See also: "But when we try to get to know our nature more distinctly we can

thus lead to the same list of modes, all the more irreducible to each other as each is unfolded in one of the Meditations.

(a) Doubting offers the shape and the mode of the *cogitatio* developed by the entire First Meditation: "*In tantas* dubitationes *hesterna meditatione* [the preceding one, as the second says] *conjectus sum*—so serious are the doubts into which I have been thrown by yesterday's meditation" (VII: 23, 22–23; CSM II: 16).[40]

(b) Understanding, in other words thinking in the mode of understanding, mobilizes the Second Meditation ("*ipsamet corpora . . . a solo* intellectu *percipi*—even bodies are . . . perceived . . . by the *intellect* alone," 34, 1–3; CSM II: 22) and the Third Meditation ("*dum in meipsum mentis aciem converto, non modo* intelligo *me esse rem incompletam et ab alio dependentem . . . sed simul etiam* intelligo *illum, a quo pendeo, . . . Deum esse*—when I turn my mind's eye upon myself, *I understand* that I am a thing which is incomplete and dependent on another . . . but I also *understand* at the same time that he on whom I depend has within him all those greater things . . . that he is God").[41]

(c) The will intervenes as the mode of thought set out in the Fourth Meditation, where it finds itself in charge of nothing less than the truth in judgment and the image of God in the human; besides, it benefits from a remarkable redundancy that is worthy of questioning: it reveals itself not by one but by two dichotomous terms (28, 21–22 and 34, 19),

---

see that our soul, in so far as it is a substance which is distinct from the body, is known to us merely through the fact that it thinks, that is to say, understands, wills, imagines, remembers and has sensory perceptions; for all these functions are kinds of thought." (*Description of the Human Body*; AT XI: 224, 21–28; CSM I: 314. Or: "*Cogitationis nomine, intelligo illa omnia, quae nobis consciis in nobis fiunt, quatenus eorum in nobis conscientia est. Atque ita non modo intelligere, velle, imaginari,* sed etiam sentire, *idem est hic quod cogitare*"—By the term 'thought,' I understand everything which we are aware of happening within us, in so far as we have awareness of it. Hence, 'thinking' is to be identified here not merely with understanding, willing and imagining, *but also with sensory awareness*" (*Principles of Philosophy* I, §9, VIII-1: 7, 22–23; CSM I: 195).

40. See, besides *The Search for Truth* (X: 523, 24–25), "to infer that one exists from the fact that one is doubting" (To X, November 1640 [in English translation: To Colvius, 14 November 1640], AT III: 248, 1–4; CSMK: 159.

41. VII: 51, 23–29; CSM II: 35 (see among other significant occurrences of *intelligere*, VII: 25, 14; 29, 5; 34, 5; 38, 1; 40, 18; 43, 6; 44, 30; 45, 11, 12, 26 and 30; 46, 23 and 29; 47, 16; 50, 19 and 23; 51, 27, etc.).

and even by two repeated dichotomies (*"affirmans, negans, . . . volens, nolens,"* 34, 18, 19).[42]

(d) To imagine defines clearly the mode of thought proper to the Fifth Meditation: "*Nempe distincte* imaginor *quantitatem*—I distinctly *imagine* the extension of the quantity" (63, 16; CSM II: 44).

(e) Thus it remains only to state that sensing finally determines the mode of thought appropriate to the horizon of the Sixth Meditation: Relying on the imagination put into place in preliminary fashion, sensation and the *sensus* become in fact a mode of thought or even consciousness, albeit one that is nonobjectifying: "*haec percipio melius* sensu—I perceive these things much better by means of the senses" (VII: 74, 4 = IX-1: 58); or: "cumque *ideae* sensu *perceptae essent multo magis vividae et expressae, et suo etiam modo magis distinctae, quam ullae ex iis quas ispe . . . effingebam*—And since the ideas perceived by the senses were much more lively and vivid and even, in their own way, more distinct than any of those which I deliberately formed through my meditating" (VII: 75, 14–17 = IX-1: 60; CSM II: 52). Let us conclude not only that the different modes of the *cogitatio* are developed one after the other without being confused or separated, but above all that, in order to be developed in this way, they require each time at least one of the Meditations.

For all that, the essential lies elsewhere. In fact, one can maintain that to almost any mode of the *cogitatio* corresponds a *cogitatio sui*, a possibility for the ego to assure itself of its existence in an indubitable proof of itself. A quick review confirms this. (a) One could in no way contest that the *cogitatio*'s mode of doubt allows the performance of a certainty of existence for and by the ego, not only because the Second Meditation (24, 2–10) employs it again after the First Meditation has already done so, but because the *Search for Truth* undertakes it and

42. This insistence can certainly be explained by the disjunction implied by any decision made by the will; but this does not suffice to explain either the redundancy of the two terms of the decision or even the connection between the making of the decision and the *cogitatio*. In fact, is it self-evident that wanting implies an authentic thought? Descartes' customary argument—"For we cannot will anything without knowing that we will it, nor could we know this except by means of an idea" (To Mersenne, 28 January 1641, AT III: 295, 24–27; CSMK: 172; see To Regius, May 1641, 372, 13–16; CSMK: 182 and To Hyperaspistes, August 1641, 432, 5–7; CSMK: 195)—in fact establishes only that the will implies thought, but not that it is directly a thought. The privilege accorded to the will among all the modalities of the *res cogitans* thus surprises all the more as the intrinsic cognitive character of the will remains to be established. See below, chapter 6, §28.

indisputably succeeds at it (see above, §12). (b) This point certainly cannot be disputed for the *cogitatio* as *intellectus*, such as the *"cogito"* of the Second Meditation puts to work.[43] (c) One can likewise maintain without great difficulty that the will produces, at least in the infinity of the will and in the generosity that it puts to work, an equivalent to the certain existence of the cognizing ego.[44] (d) One can finally understand why the *cogitatio*'s mode of imagination, and it alone, does not allow the performance of the certainty of existence. In fact, its function is to perceive the extension of geometry: *"Per extensionem intelligimus, illud omne quod habet longitudinem, latitudinem, et profunditatem, non inquirentes, sive sit verum corpus, sive spatium tantum; nec majori explicatione indigere videtur, cum nihil omnino facilius ab imaginatione nostra percipiuntur*—By 'extension' we mean whatever has length, breadth and depth, leaving aside the question whether it is a real body or merely a space. This notion does not, I think, need any further elucidation, for there is nothing more easily perceived by our imagination"; or, more clearly still: *"ea sola esse imaginabilia, quae in extensione, motu et figura consistunt*—the objects of the imagination are restricted to those which have extension, motion and shape."[45] Yet

43. With the reservations that are henceforth imposed on this formulation. See *On Descartes' Metaphysical Prism*, 128, and *On the Ego and on God*, 146.

44. I have attempted to establish this in *Cartesian Questions II*, chapter 5, §5, 157–60. Renouvier declared imprudently that "Descartes could not have said: I will therefore I am." In Charles Renouvier, *Manuel de philosophie moderne* (Paris: Paulin, 1842), 398, note 1. Heidegger, an excellent reader of Descartes, saw very well that quite to the contrary this was the case: "Nietzsche refers the *ego cogito* back to an *ego volo* and interprets the *velle* as willing in the sense of will to power, which he thinks as the basic character of beings. *But what if the positing of this basic character became possible only on the basis of Descartes' fundamental metaphysical position?* Then Nietzsche's critique of Descartes would be a misunderstanding of the essence of metaphysics." Martin Heidegger, *Nietzsche: der europäische Nihilismus* (1940), *GA* 48: 242, trans. Frank A. Capuzzi as *Nietzsche*, vol. IV, ed. David Farrell Krell (San Francisco: Harper & Row, 1982), 129. I owe this link to Charles Perrin's scholarship.

45. *Regula* XIV, AT X: 442, 17–21; CSM I: 59 and *Principles of Philosophy* I, §73, VIII-1: 37, 15–16; CSM I: 220. See *"Nempe distincte imaginor quantitatem, quam vulgo Philosophi appellant continuam, sive ejus quantitatis aut potius rei quantae extensionem in longum, latum et profundum.*—Quantity, for example, or 'continuous' quantity as the philosophers commonly call it, is something I distinctly imagine. That is, I distinctly imagine the extension of the quantity (or rather of the thing which is quantified) in length, breadth and depth" (Fifth Meditation, VII: 63, 16–19; CSM II: 44). This is similar to the formulation

extension imagined in this way remains that of an object, by definition opposed to the *cogitatio* that thinks it; hence imagination, appropriated to extension alone, in turn cannot think the *cogitatio* that it neverthe-less puts to work: imagination, riveted to extension, cannot imagine itself, while doubt can doubt itself, understanding can apprehend itself, will can will itself. In this way, while the other modes of the *cogitatio* can double themselves, the imagination cannot imagine the cognizing ego, because it deals only with extension, thus with bodies. This has as a result that the imagination remains limited to mathematics or more exactly to that which assures them their certainty—the transposition of difficulties to extension, which permits their modeling according to the *Mathesis universalis*. And just as the *cogitatio* cannot provide an object to the modeling in extension, so imagination cannot perform any existence through and in the act of cogitating. This is what the *Regulae* confirms, which mentions all the elements of the *cogito* to come (*"Ita unusquisque animo potest intueri, se existere, se cogitare*—Thus every-one can mentally intuit that he exists, that he is thinking")[46] without ever managing to join them together in a single argument. More gener-ally the incompatibility between imagination and *cogito* provokes (or results from) the incompatibility between philosophy and mathematics: "Experience has taught me that most minds who have the facility to un-derstand the reasoning of metaphysics are not able to understand that of algebra, and reciprocally that those who easily understand the latter are ordinarily incapable of other sorts of reasoning."[47] In any case, the

---

*triangulum imaginor* (64, 12 and 72, 6, etc.). Descartes defines in advance Kant's thesis linking the (productive) imagination to the construction of the phenom-enon in space (see my sketch "Constantes de la raison critique—Kant et Des-cartes," in *Questions cartésiennes II*, chapter 8, §5, p. 305ff.; untranslated in *On the Ego and on God*). This exception of the imagination running counter to the other modes maybe explains why the two formulations of the *res cogitans* introduce it only with two reservations: "*imaginans* quoque" (28, 22 = "which *also* imagines," IX-1: 22; CSM II: 19) and "*imaginans etiam*" (VII: 34, 20 = "*also* which imagines," IX-1: 27; CSM II: 24).

46. Regula III, X: 368, 21–22; CSM I: 14; see XII: 421, 26—422, 1 and XIII: 432, 24–27 (and my comments in *René Descartes: Regles utiles et claires*, 244, 252).

47. To Elizabeth, November 1643, IV: 46, 6–12, trans. Lisa Shapiro in *Princess Elisabeth of Bohemia and René Descartes, The Correspondence be-tween Princess Elisabeth of Bohemia and René Descartes* (Chicago: University of Chicago Press, 2007), 78. Thus also the case of Fermat: "I believe that he knows mathematics, but in philosophy I have always noticed that he reasons very badly" (To Mersenne, 4 March 1641, III: 328, 12–14; [this passage of the

conclusion becomes necessary that *this* mode of the *cogitatio*, the imagination, cannot by its very definition provoke the exercise of the *cogito*.

Henceforth, should not the same be true also of thought in the mode of sensing, because it shares with the imagination the same dependence on the body and hence extension? "I do not see any difficulty in understanding on the one hand that the faculties of imagination and sensation belong to the soul, because they are species of thoughts, and on the other hand that they belong to the soul only in so far as it is joined to the body, because they are kinds of thoughts without which one can conceive the soul in all its purity."[48] If imagination and sensation are equally linked to the body, how shall we understand the fact that the first allows no *cogito* but the second does? Because a decisive difference separates them: sensing permits also sensing *oneself* as thinking, while imagination never permits one to imagine *oneself* as thinking. Yet this difference itself is comprehended only by another opposition: while the imagination unilaterally thinks extended bodies actively (as the production of the models of extension and the parameters of measurement, but also the expenditure of attention, thus of energy required) at the price of a fatigue of the mind that limits its effort and its effect, sensing retains the double faculty of thinking the sensory and of thinking *itself*, because it thinks passively starting from a source different from itself, a source from abroad [*d'ailleurs*] (or rather from *the* elsewhere [*l'ailleurs*]), in such a way that it could not sense anything other without sensing itself affected, thus experiencing itself as *cogitatio* in action. The performance of the *cogito* can accomplish itself even with a thought linked to the body: "*Sentire? Nempe etiam hoc non sit sine corpore*—Sensing? This surely does not occur without a body" (VII: 27, 5–6; CSM II: 18, trans. lightly modified). But on one condition: this connection to the body cannot remain active, because in this case, precisely the case of the imagination, thought thinks the body only as an object in real extension or by modeling extension, hence thinks only unilaterally (in a centrifugal sense) without authorizing any return on the ego. Now this becomes the

---

letter not translated in CSMK]. But it is a matter of a general fact: "*et fere omnibus usu venit ut, si versati sint in metaphysicis, a geometricis abhorreant; si vero geometriam excoluerint, quae de prima philosophia scripsi non capiant*—and it generally happens with almost everyone else that if they are accomplished in Metaphysics they hate Geometry, while if they have mastered Geometry they do not grasp what I have written on First Philosophy." *Principia philosophiae*, Epistola dedicatoria, VIII-1: 4, 3–6; "Dedicatory Letter to Elizabeth," *Principles of Philosophy*, CSM I: 192.

48. To Gibieuf, 19 January 1641, III: 479, 10–16; CSMK: 203.

case with the *cogitatio* as sensing: here thought thinks the body, but passively, starting from its action on it; from here on the notion of bodies is doubled between extension (depicted and in movement), which acts on the sensing ego, and this passive ego as sensing.

How can the ego sense, in other words, think passively? By allowing itself to be established as flesh, under the name of *meum corpus*—no longer only as thinking ego according to the spontaneity of apperception and the diverse activities of the "entirely pure soul" (arranged according to their growing content: doubt without content, understanding with an abstract content, will with a content without limitation, imagination with a limited material content), but as thinking ego according to the receptivity toward all of what becomes present to it, not at all by the modeling that the bodies undergo, but by the aspect and the effect that they impose on its flesh. Being imposed on the ego, what is sensed renders this ego passively thinking, a *reflectively* thinking ego [*ego pensant pensif*] that thinks as flesh. Thinking passively as flesh has a precise sense and designates the privilege of the thought of the reflective ego: it can sense [*sentir*] only what it feels [*ressent*]; and thus, because it can feel [*ressentir*] only by sensing itself sensing [*se sentant sentir*] what it feels [*ressent*], it cannot sense anything without sensing *itself*. Henceforth, exactly the opposite of the centrifugal and unilateral imagination, which by definition is limited to constituting the object actively in extension without any proof in turn of the thinking self, the centripetal and reciprocal sensing cannot sense anything except by sensing *itself* first and simultaneously in itself. Thus, it cannot ever think anything passively without thinking not only that it thinks it in receiving it, but that it thinks *itself* by receiving *itself* there. In this way not only does the mode of thought of sensing not forbid (like the imagination) the certainty of the *cogito*, not only does it allow its accomplishment by doubling thought (doubt doubting itself, understanding understanding itself, will willing itself), but it implies it intrinsically by its most essential determination, that of thinking passively, that is to say of thinking while having to offer itself to affection, thus of submitting to it, from a passivity that senses [*sent*] only by feeling *itself* [*se ressentant*]. I sense, thus I sense *myself* sensing myself, thus I am and I exist. A first result proceeds from this: all sensing implies an *ego [cogito] sum*.[49]

This is confirmed by the example, or better the paradoxical counter-

49. Actually, we had already established this in the analyses of the union *arctissime* of the soul with my body (above, chapter 2, §§8–9) in the Sixth

example, of animals. Descartes admits (in 1649) that one can most prob-ably in some sense and for a time argue that they think (*"pro brutorum cogitatione militare*—for animals having thoughts"), because they sense (*"versimile . . . sentire sicut nos*—it seems likely that they have sensation like us") with organs that are similar to ours and because for us sens-ing implies thought (*"in nostro sentiendi modo cogitatio includitur*—thought is included in our mode of sensation"). Yet other arguments intervene in order not to interpret the sensation of animals as a *cogi-tatio*: the components of bodies can produce movements without any *cogitatio*, the machine can obtain better performances than thought; and above all animals do not speak. One hence must oppose thought and sensation in order to separate them: *"me loqui de cogitatione, non de vita, vel sensu*—Please note that I am speaking of thought, and not of life or sensation."[50] Does Descartes become incoherent by opposing here what he identified beforehand? Probably not, if one considers a differ-ent reflection (from 1637) on the same question: at stake is to compre-hend what sensing means for us, for humans; do we sense as animals sense? We sense in such a way that in sensing we think: *"videre . . . ut nos, hoc est sentiendo sive cogitando se videre*—do not see as we do when we are aware that we see," in other words by including the *sensus* in the *res cogitans*, as one of its modes. Now, animals could perfectly well not sense what they think, but be limited to registering impressions transmitted by the nerves to their brain, without being immediately affected by them, these impressions remaining those of "external—*externorum*" objects.[51] The question in fact has bearing neither on the thought of animals nor on their sensibility, but on the link between the two; in a sense, animals sense without thinking ("animals . . . have no thoughts"); in another they think without sensing (themselves) ("We observe in animals movements similar to those which result from our imaginations and sensations; but that does not mean that we observe imaginations and sensations in them");[52] but in all these cases they do not experience themselves in their thought, *because* they do not sense themselves in it. They lack thought *because* they lack sense. Animals

Meditation and the indubitability of the flesh in the First and Second Medita-tions (above, chapter 3, §13).

50. To Henri More, 5 February 1649, AT V: 277, 1–8 and 278, 26–27; CSMK: 365 and 366, respectively.

51. To Plempius, 3 October 1637, AT I: 413, 15—414, 5; CSMK: 61–62.

52. To Newcastle, 23 November 1646, IV: 575, 14–15; CSMK: 303, and To Gibieuf, 19 January 1642, III: 479, 17–20; CSMK: 203, respectively.

thus do not manage to think by sensing (themselves), or therefore to sense (themselves) if by chance they thought.

Even more paradoxically, this powerlessness to "think like us" is found again at the other end of our finitude, in angels. For, Descartes remarks to Regius, "*si enim Angelus corpori humano inesset, non sentiret ut nos, sed tantum perciperet motus qui causarentur ab objectis externis*—if an angel were in a human body, *he would not have sensations as we do*, but would simply perceive the motions which are caused by external objects";[53] an angel certainly would see movements in the extension of bodies, in material things, and would maybe be able to reconstitute the physiological effects, identifying which cause pain (*sensus doloris*) or pleasure, but not having his own body, a *totum hoc corpus meum*, an angel would not experience them within himself because he precisely would not have any self for sensing them, that is to say, for thinking them passively. In short, the angel, face to face with *meum corpus*, which anyway he does not have and is not, would remain at best like a pilot in his ship.

Without doubt Descartes has perceived this strange rapprochement because he describes it as an objection: "*si fas est dicere, brutorum sensus ad Dei et angelorum cognitionem magis quam humana ratiocinatio accedat*—it seems, if one dares to say it, that sensation in animals is closer to cognition in God and the angels than human reasoning is." Presumably that is why he turns this reproach immediately on his enemies, by arguing that in attributing a sensory soul to animals, they finally oppose a discursive (human) knowledge to two cognitions "*simplicissimas . . . et intuitivas, sive apprehensivas*—utterly simple and intuitive, a sheer apprehension," that of animals and the whole ensemble of angels and God.[54] Yet this reproach about the difference between discursivity and intuitiveness (for of course animals can neither decipher the movements within extension nor see external objects there as causes of sensory effects) conceals another debate and does so badly: only humans sense by thinking and think by sensing, which is what their inferiors, the animals, or their superiors, angels or God, cannot do and thus they remain like the spectators of the machine, which does not experience itself in thinking itself and sensing itself.

Yet, if thought does not take on its precise (that is to say, human) meaning of the *cogitatio* except by proceeding through the *sensus* as the *res cogitans*, what functions does *this* sensing fulfill? How far does this

53. To Regius, January 1642, III: 493, 14–17; CSMK: 206.
54. To Plempius, 3 October 1637, AT I: 415, 21–23 and 19–20; CSMK: 62.

privilege go? And, besides, what does *sense* still mean, in particular the (since Aristotle) fundamental sense, the sense of touch? For in a rather enigmatic statement, Descartes does not hesitate to admit that we can "touch with our mind"[55] even immaterial truths like our soul, thus confirming that we can *attingere cogitatione* even the existence of God.[56] What do we do when we sense, that is to say, finally touch, if we are even touching immaterial things?

The response to this question can only come from the consideration of a different question—left itself for a long time not only without response, but even without attention—the question of the mode of thought that the *cogitatio* must take in order to reach and validate the *cogito*.[57] The limits of the most widespread and even the oldest interpretations all depend on an aporia that to my eyes has been definitively stigmatized by Michel Henry's most recent reading.[58] In fact, they all conceive of the access of the *ego cogitans* to itself on the model of its access to any other *res cogitata*, that is to say, following the gulf that intentionality opens between its primordial pole and its target: in the same way as the ego reaches its object as that which confronts it, at a distance from constitution and the intentional (or quasi-intentional) target, it turns back, so to say, on itself before its gaze and apprehends itself at a distance from the target. Now, all other considerations set aside (about representation, intentionality, constitution, etc.), one sees immediately that a device would not allow the ego to reach the certainty of its existence as cognizing itself, because the gap particular to the *cogitatio*, the gap between the *ego cogitans* and the *cogitatum*, remains intact. It is simply transposed between the *ego cogitans* and the *ego (me) cogitatum*, a gap that is sufficiently large for its evidence not to fall under the suspicion that would be cast by—still in this case and as easily as between the ego and the supposed evidence of the simple material natures (or the mathematical truths)—the hypothesis of an all-powerful God. After all, why not deceive myself *still and also* when I give in to the evidence

55. To Newcastle, March or April 1648, V: 137, 29; CSMK: 331 (in the English translation the letter is entitled "To [Silhon]").

56. Third Meditation, VII: 52, 2; CSM II: 35.

57. On the different interpretations of what one names without precaution the *cogito*, I maintain the results of my previous studies, *Sur la théologie blanche de Descartes*, II, 2, §16, 370ff., *On Descartes' Metaphysical Prism*, chapter 3, §§11–15, 128–205, and *On the Ego and on God*, chapter 1, §§1–7, 3–29.

58. See Michel Henry, *The Genealogy of Psychoanalysis*, trans. Douglas Brick (Stanford: Stanford University Press, 1993), chapters 1 and 2 (and my analysis in *Cartesian Questions*, chapter 5, 96–117).

that "*hoc pronuntiatum,* Ego sum, ego existo, *quoties a me profertur,
vel mente concipitur, necessario esse verum*—this proposition, *I am, I
exist,* is necessarily true whenever it is put forward by me or conceived
in my mind,"[59] if at least I think it still as I think everything else—at an
ecstatic and intentional distance from my *cogitatio,* freeing the space
where the offensive of doubt bearing on any evidence is crushed? The
argument called that of the *cogito* could not resist hyperbolic doubt,
if it thought according to the habitual, purely epistemological, use of
the *cogitatio* that this doubt precisely functions to disqualify. Descartes
specifies that in contrast in metaphysics it is required that the *cogitatio
immediately* reaches that of which it becomes conscious: "Cogitationis
*nomine complector illud omne quod sic in nobis est, ut ejus* immediate
*conscii simus.* . . . Ideae *nomine intelligo cujuslibet cogitationis formam
illam, per cujus* immediatam *perceptionem ipsius ejusdem cogitationis
conscius sum*—Thought. I use this term to include everything that is
within us in such a way that we are *immediately* aware of it. . . . *Idea.* I
understand this term to mean the form of any given thought, *immediate*
perception of which makes me aware of the thought" (AT VII: 160, 7–
10 and 14–16 = IX-1: 124; CSM II: 113). How does one reach such an
immediacy, required for any thought, hence a fortiori for the one that
deduces the *cogito,* if the ego continues to think (itself) according to the
gap of representation, according to the ecstasis of intentionality, according to the gap of objectness?

Now, Descartes does not stop underlining that the ego's connection
to itself owes nothing to the ecstasis that allows it to be related to its
objects, but, to the contrary, is a matter of an absolute immediacy, of
a relation of self to self without solution of continuity, by which representation (and the "accompaniment" of Kantian apperception) cedes
to self-affection of the *mens* by itself. Once more, the same and now
celebrated argument intervenes: if "*videre videor, audire, calescere,*" if it
seems to me that I see, hear, warm myself, it is quite possible that I do
not in truth see any object—doubt remains always possible, because see-

59. Second Meditation, VII: 25, 11–13 = IX-1: 19; CSM II: 17. Fénelon
counts among the rare people (together with Nietzsche) who have pinpointed
this difficulty in texts that are unfairly underestimated. The *Demonstration of
the Existence of God* is one of those (especially section II, chapter 1): "Even
more, what wonder to cause nothingness to act, to cause it to believe itself true
and real and to make it say to itself, as to someone: I think, therefore I am! But
no, maybe I think without existing and I deceive myself without having left
nothingness." Fénelon, *Démonstration de l'existence de Dieu,* in *Œuvres,* ed.
Jacques Le Brun (Paris: Gallimard, 1997), II: 604.

ing implies the intentional gap from the seen, therefore offers the space for a doubt and a deception; but, to the contrary, the fact that "it seems to me—*videor*" accomplishes, as pure semblance and as pure appearance, an immediate manifestation, thus without gap with the ego, which would never be able to disappoint me and betray me: "*Hoc falsum esse non potest*—This cannot be false," "*sensu[s] sive conscientia videndi . . . est plane certa*—applied to any sense or awareness of seeing . . . then the conclusion is quite certain."[60] In the second degree, appearing itself never deceives, because it *is* mine and even me, even if what appears in the first degree deceives me, because it *is* neither mine, nor me, but the object other than me, in extension. And that which, in the appearing of a phenomenon, remains me, is called my body, *meum corpus*, which I sense and where I sense myself. Now, it turns out that Descartes explicitly defines this immediate connection of the ego to itself as a sensing, more original than the sensation of things of the world (maybe still subordinate to intentionality), even if it makes them possible. The previous sequence anyway continues as follows: "*hoc est proprie quod in me sentire appellatur*—what is called 'sensing' is strictly just this"; specifying immediately that it is a matter therefore of the primordial shape of thought itself: "*atque hoc praecise sic sumptum nihil aliud est quam cogitare*—and in this restricted sense of the term it is simply thinking."[61] The *cogitatio*, when it phenomenalizes itself primordially as *cogitatio* of the self, appears and practices itself thus under the modality of the "sensing." Testimonies for this are not lacking. Thus: "*videre plane ut nos, hoc est* sentiendo sive cogitando *se videre*—see just as we do, i.e., *being aware or thinking* that they see" or also: "*[nostram] mentem, quae*

---

60. Respectively, Second Meditation, VII: 29, 14–16; CSM II: 19, and *Principles of Philosophy* §9, VIII-1: 7, 30—8, 2; CSM I: 195. See also: "*negatis unumquemque, ex eo quod cogitet, recte posse, concludere se existere: vultis enim Scepticum inde tantum concludere,* sibi videri *existere, tanquam si quis ratione utens, quantumvis sit Scepticus,* sibi videri *possit existere, quin simul intelligat se revera existere, quandoquidem id sibi videtur. Atque ita negatis propositionem qua nulla unquam evidentior in ulla scientia esse potest*—you deny that *anyone can correctly conclude from the fact that he is thinking that he exists;* thus you desire a skeptic to conclude from this rather that he *has the feeling of seeming* to exist, as if someone, as skeptical as can be, can *have the feeling of seeming* to exist without comprehending at the same time that he truly exists, because it seems so to him. And thus you deny a proposition that is more evident than any other that can be found in any science." To Voetius, VIII-2: 165, 11—166, 7; untranslated in CSMK.

61. Second Meditation, VII: 29, 16–18 = IX-1: 23; CSM II: 19; trans. lightly modified.

*sola* sentit sive cogitat *se videre aut ambulare*—since it relates to the mind, which alone has the *sensation or thought* that it is seeing or walking"; and also: "Yet this knowledge [i.e., I think, therefore I am] . . . is something your mind sees, feels and handles."[62] This sensing certainly is not confused with the sensation of things of the world, because it is a matter of an idea "*quae me ipsum mihi exhibet*—which gives me a representation of myself"; and the *res cogitans* would not be "also sensing—*et sentiens*,"[63] a mode of thought among the others, if it was not first characterized by the immediacy of a more original sensing where it phenomenalizes itself for itself in the mode of auto-affection.

I will thus conclude that the modality of the *res cogitans* as *sentiens* illustrates the interpretation of the *cogito* in accordance with the auto-affection of thought. From this follows a second result: not only does all sensing imply an *ego [cogito] sum*, but any performance of the *ego [cogito] sum* implies a primordial sensing, thus the *meum corpus* as ultimate shape of the ego.

62. To Plempius, 3 October 1637, AT I: 413, 15–16; CSMK: 61; *Principles of Philosophy* I, §9, VIII-1: 8, 1–2; CSM I: 195; and To Newcastle [?], V: 138, 3–6; CSMK: 331, respectively.

63. Respectively, VII: 42, 29–30 and 28, 22 = IX-1: 34, 20–21; CSM II: 29 and 19; trans. modified.

# 4

## The Third Primitive Notion

### §17. *From Simple Natures to Primitive Notions*

If the Cartesian use of the *meum corpus* truly thematizes the phenomenon of the flesh, or more exactly of *my* flesh (chapter I), and if this phenomenon owes it to the auto-affection within it to sense itself, more exactly to experience an original sensing of the self to the point of opening for the ego a privileged access to the *cogito* (chapter II) and in that way to be exempt from the hypothesis of hyperbolic doubt (chapter III), how can we henceforth fail to admit for it the status of a principle within the whole of Cartesian metaphysics? Yet how can we add a new principle to those already competing with each other within the shared and limited interpretation of this metaphysics—in other words, within the most common interpretation, which, for the majority of cases, understands the Cartesian path as if it included neither the second part of the Sixth Meditation nor the least definitive morality? Furthermore, does not the difficulty of reconciling the two contenders for the function of first principle, namely, the ego insofar as it thinks (itself) and the *causa sui* God, thus of articulating between them the two figures of the onto-theo-logical constitution of Cartesian metaphysics (the onto-theo-logy of the *cogitatio*, the onto-theo-logy of the *causa*), already compromise any attempt to introduce a third first principle, in this case the *meum corpus*? Far from underestimating or especially from concealing this difficulty, Descartes instead confronts it by radicalizing it: he cuts deeper than the duality of the ontic principles (the ego and the *causa sui*) by going back all the way to the "primitive notions" and the "simple notions" that make them epistemologically thinkable.[1] In other words, the innovation required by the privilege of *meum corpus* not only leads to revising the metaphysical position of the *Meditations* in 1641, but to going back to the *naturae simplicissimae*, to the (very) simple natures established by the *Regulae* in 1627. It is a matter not of adaptation or evolution, but of revision, which at least tacitly implies a retraction. Without this retraction Descartes cannot accomplish the new beginning he is risking: to set up the ego not only as the principle of any science of objects (in the *Regulae*), not only as the ontic and final principle of a metaphysics of the infinite (in the *Meditations*), but as a *cogitatio* unfolding all its possible modes up to passive thought, thus all the way to the *meum corpus* taking flesh.

His first response to Elizabeth allows no ambiguity to hover over the radical nature of this third beginning of the ego, or over the equally radical revision of the scheme of the *Regulae*. First, the new list of the "primitive notions": there is no ambiguity about what step to take, because it is a matter of passing from one fact to the other between "two facts about the human soul on which depend all the knowledge that we can have of its nature. The first is that it thinks, the second is that, being united to the body, it can act and be acted upon along with it" (III: 664, 23–27; CSMK: 217–18). The *Regulae* itself also observes that in knowledge "*duo tantum spectanda sunt, nos scilicet qui cognoscimus, et res ipsae cognoscendae*—only two factors need to be considered: ourselves, the knowing subjects, and the things which are the objects of knowledge" (X: 411, 3–4; CSM I: 39). But here it is precisely just a matter of knowing and of knowing only one thing other than oneself actively, that is to say, by (re)constituting the thing as an object. The duality that has to be envisioned therefore remained entirely in the field that in 1643 concerns only the first "thing," namely, the (active) exercise of thought (of the object), and is still perfectly unaware that this thought itself remains "united to a body," by which it can not only act but also "be acted upon" [*pâtir*]. Descartes passes from such a solely epistemic, active, external, and unilateral duality to a duality that henceforth

1. To Elizabeth, 21 May 1643, III: 665, 10 and 666, 26; CSMK: 218 and 219, respectively.

would be *internal* to the *cogitato*, reciprocal, passive, or more essentially pathic, where the thing instead acts on the ego. From there the actually dual list of the *res simplicissimae* becomes a triple one. In fact, it remained dual in 1627, despite its three rubrics, because the common simple natures (existence, unity, duration, and similar ones) (X: 419, 12) would cover everything that the *metaphysica generalis* takes as its object—the determinations of any being in general. The undetermined universality of these concepts accordingly makes them perfectly neutral without introducing the least real third term; and this is why the first five Meditations could take them up again metaphysically without putting into question the epistemic scheme of the *Regulae* (albeit surpassing it via a more radical grounding).[2] Two real rubrics of *naturae simplicissimae* thus remain. On the one hand those that, without ever having recourse to the least *idea corporea*, or to "the aid of any corporeal image—*absque ullius imaginis corporeae adjumento*," allow one to represent to oneself "*quid sit cognitio, quid dubium, quid ignorantia, item quid sit* voluntatis actio, *quam volitionem liceat appellare, et similia*—what knowledge or doubt or ignorance is, or the *action of the will*, which may be called 'volition,' and the like" (X: 419, 10–15; CSM I: 44). One should notice here the insistence on activity, thus on the will, and the absence of sensation, thus of the least passivity: it is thus only a matter of "*nos qui cognoscimus*—what we know," in the unilateral epistemic relationship. On the other hand, the *Regulae* mentions the *naturae simplicissimae* [simple natures] that, like "*figura, extensio, motus*, etc.—shape, extension and motion," are sufficient to describe purely material things, the physical bodies (X: 419, 18–20; CSM I: 45): it is there still just a matter of *res cognoscendae*, these things that are to be known as pure objects. In 1643, we find again a similar list. First "the most general" notions, being, number, and duration, which introduce no particular term. Then the couple of combined notions that define the epistemic attitude: "Then, as regards the body in particular, we have only the notion of extension, which entails the notions of shape and motion," and "as regards the soul on its own, we have only the notion of thought, which includes the perception of the intellect and the inclinations of the will," thought—let us note this—here also exclusive of the passivity of sensation (III: 665, 15–20; CSMK: 218). Yet the list of 1643 becomes radically different from that of 1627 (and of 1641) with its final addition: "Lastly, as regards the soul and the body together, we

2. On this use, see *Cartesian Questions*, chapter 3, "What Is the Method in the Metaphysics?" 43–66.

have only the notion of their union, on which depends our notion of the soul's power to move the body, and the body's power to act on the soul and cause its *sensations* and *passions*" (III: 665, 20–24; CSMK: 218). Here is thus finally a third notion, very simple and primitive, that is to say irreducible to any other, but which assures and recognizes the possibility of a passive thought of the *ego cogito*.

What scope should one grant to this new list of "primitive notions" that complete and correct those of the *naturae simplicissimae*? One should not allow oneself to be fooled by an apparent restriction—"as regards the soul and the body together, we have *only* the [primitive] notion of their union" (III: 665, 21–22; CSMK: 218)—as if the third primitive notion remained restricted to a single term improvised ad hoc, without theoretical validity comparable to the two other series. Actually the two other series also become deduced from a single notion, for there is "*only* the notion of extension" and "*only* the notion of thought" (III: 665, 16, 18; CSMK: 218). Accordingly the juxtaposed lists from the *Regulae* (and the *Meditations*) are rendered consistent: each time one notion generates the others in the way that the principal attribute of substance allows one to conceive its modes. By right, the primitive notion of union has the same rank as the other two, because starting from it one can similarly conceive of "the soul's power to move the body, and the body's power to act on the soul"—in short, conceive the passivity of thought in its passions and its feelings. Let us for a moment leave open two questions that seem as formidable as inevitable (Does the union offer the principal attribute of a third substance? What cause operates between soul and body?) in order to confirm this new list with a conclusive parallel from an exactly contemporary stage, *Principles of Philosophy* I, §8. Reflecting on our thoughts as they are gazing at things, Descartes here makes an inventory first of the usual *maxime generalia* of his *metaphysica generalis*, then of the notions concerning on the one hand intellectual things, hence thought, on the other hand material things, hence extension: it is accordingly just a matter of the list of *naturae simplicissimae* elaborated by the *Regulae* and maintained by the first five Meditations.[3] Yet, here he now adds a third authority: the "notion of the union that everyone invariably experiences in himself"[4] in the

---

3. Besides, *Principles of Philosophy* I, §47 mentions explicitly that it is a matter of "simplices *omnes notiones, ex quibus cogitationes nostrae componuntur—simple* notions which are the basic components of our thoughts" (VIII-1: 22, 23–24; CSM I: 208 and the title: "*simplices notiones*—simple notions").

4. To Elizabeth, 28 June 1643, III: 694, 1–2; CSMK: 228.

name of the same experience as in the Sixth Meditation (*experior*, VII: 71, 21): "*Sed et alia quaedam* in nobis experimur, *quae nec ad solam mentem, nec etiam ad solum corpus referri debent, quaeque . . .* ab arcta et intima *mentis nostrae cum corpore* unione *proficiscuntur*—But we also *experience within ourselves* certain other things which must not be referred either to the mind alone or to the body alone. These arise . . . *from the close and intimate union* of our mind with the body" (VIII-1: 23, 12–17 = IX-2: 45; CSM I: 209).[5] This obvious allusion to *meum corpus . . . arctissime conjunctum et quasi permixtum* to the soul that forms *unum quid* with it refers back directly to the argument of the second part of the Sixth Meditation (VII: 81, 3–4). This is confirmed by the modes of this primitive notion, actually by the *corpus meum* where the ego experiences itself as affected, because what the Sixth Meditation already identifies, albeit in a different order, is also at stake in §48 of the *Principles of Philosophy* I: (a) *sensus omnes,* and first of all pain and pleasure;[6] (b) then light and colors, odors and tastes, heat and hardness and the other qualities of touch (VIII-1: 23, 21–23 = VII: 74, 3; 75, 2; 81, 18–19; CSM II: 51, 52, 56); (c) hunger and thirst (VIII-1: 23, 17 = VII: 81, 1, 10, 11; CSM II: 56). (d) Finally joy, sadness, anger and love, already mentioned in 1641, with the significant exception of love, as we know.[7] What is a significant difference especially is that at this moment it is a matter only of the *appetitus* and the *affectus* and not yet of the *commotiones, sive animi pathemata*:[8] the path that leads the affections of passive thought to the passions of the soul is thus not yet opened in 1641, although it becomes obvious in 1643 and 1644. One must thus conclude that the *meum corpus*, in other words, the flesh,

5. VII: 75, 10; 81, 2–5; 87, 25; or Fourth Replies, VII: 228, 28, etc. See *Discourse on Method*, VI: 59, 13, and the texts cited above, chapter 2, §8, 47ff.

6. VIII-1: 23, 21 = VII: 71, 23 and 74, 3; 77, 1, 3 and 6; 80, 29; 81, 1; 83, 8, etc. then 74, 24; 82, 27. On the *Principles of Philosophy*, see also Gianfranco Cantelli's analysis "La terza notione primitiva e l'analisi dei sensi esterni e interni svolta nei *Pr.* IV, §188–189," in Armogathe and Belgioioso, eds., *Descartes. Principia Philosophiae (1644–1994).*

7. VIII-1: 23, 9–10; CSM I: 208 and VII: 74, 26–27; CSM II: 52, respectively. Love nevertheless appears at least once among the primitive notions for the count of the *cogitatio*: "*Ita amor, odium, affirmatio, dubitatio, etc. sunt veri modi in mente*—Thus love, hatred, affirmation, doubt, and so on are true modes in the mind" (To X, 1645 or 1646, IV: 349, 8–9; CSMK: 280). One must thus correct, at least marginally, my initial comment in *The Erotic Phenomenon*, trans. Stephen E. Lewis (Chicago: University of Chicago Press, 2007), 7–8.

8. VII: 76, 3; 74, 25; CSM II: 52 and VIII-1: 23, 17–18; CSM I: 209, respectively.

really constitutes, if not a first principle, at the very least one of the primitive notions, or *naturae simplicissimae*, whose intelligibility cannot be deduced from any other notion and which alone makes other notions intelligible.[9]

Consequently, the union is primitive. This means first of all that the union of soul and body certainly should not be understood as a composition that would result, on second appeal and *secunda battuta*, from the compromise or the addition of two other primitive notions. The union comes before soul and body, or at least *from elsewhere*. One must think the union starting from itself and itself alone, never starting from the soul and/or the body, hence also not starting from notions that would be primitive in some other sense, which would permit one to think soul and body starting from each of them. The union of soul and body must be thought starting from the union itself and *only* from the union. "I observe next that all human knowledge consists solely in clearly distinguishing these notions and attaching each of them only to the things to which it pertains. . . . for since they are primitive notions, each of them can be understood only through itself" (III: 665, 25—666, 6; CSMK: 218). This requirement is not self-evident and imposes a paradox, so much do we remain inclined to the natural attitude that desires that the union would *result* from what it unites and, obviously, from what seems to us self-evident, namely, the extension of bodies: "The use of our senses has made the notions of extension, of shapes and of motions much more familiar to us than the others; and the main cause of our errors is that we commonly want to use these notions to explain matters to which they do not pertain" (666, 6–11; CSMK: 218). What Descartes stigmatizes here is deployed today, both triumphantly and naively, under the heading of the *naturalization* of thought: to think thought starting from another primitive notion than his; not only thinking thought starting from extension (as any reductionism does), but thinking the union of soul and body starting from extension alone (naturalization), in a simple inversion reacting to idealism, which stubbornly thinks this union starting from thought alone. Descartes can

9. *The Principles of Philosophy* I, §75 marks at the same time this dignity by including the *sensus* that affects us among the "*notiones, quas ipsimet in nobis habemus*—notions that we have within us" and a certain embarrassment in adding them to a list that juxtaposes at the same time the other *naturae simplicissimae* (extension and *cogitatio*) and the two contenders for the title of "first principle," "*nos existere . . . et* simul etiam, *et esse Deum et nos ab illo pendere*—we exist . . . and *simultaneously* . . . that there is a God and that we depend on him" (VIII-1: 38, 14–15 and 17–18; CSM I: 221).

merely oppose a difficulty to these two easy options: to think the union starting from itself, that is to say, starting from the experience (possibly incomprehensible, according to the precise meaning of the term) of what we sense in ourselves, of that which "*in nobis experimur*—we experience in ourselves" (VIII-1: 23, 13; CSM I: 209).

Yet what do we experience in ourselves? The immediacy of experience does not have a good epistemological reputation, so much do we suspect it of confusion and illusion. Obviously Descartes has doubts about it and at first limits himself to defining it negatively. But, as we will see, this negative definition says quite a bit and does not lack force. To experience the union within ourselves starting from itself requires at least that we not claim to comprehend it starting from another authority (or primitive notion) than itself, "as when we try to use our imagination to conceive the nature of the soul, or we try to conceive the way in which the soul moves the body by conceiving the way in which one body is moved by another" (III: 666, 12–15; CSMK: 218). In other words, we know at least and on principle that the union of soul and body does not obey the rules of the interaction of bodies among themselves. In still other words, the entire debate of occasionalism about the type of physical or quasi-physical causality that would allow the soul (assimilated with no good sense to the pineal gland) to move or be moved by the body (assimilated with no good sense to the inanimate physical body) makes no sense, has no pertinence and no standing: it unfolds in a theoretical non-place, nonsensical and absurd. A recent critic has underlined this very well. Daniel Garber remarks in fact that "from Descartes' point of view there just *is* no problem reconciling interactionism [i.e. of the soul with the body] with the laws of nature" because "denying that the conservation laws [i.e. of movement] must hold for animate bodies [i.e. the *meum corpus*]," "he left open the possibility that the activity of minds is not constrained by the laws of nature that hold for bodies." Against Leibniz (and surely Malebranche, as most probably also Spinoza), Descartes does not hesitate to admit the irreducibility of the *meum corpus* to the two other primitive notions, and first of all to extension, so far as "to deny the universality of physical law and to deny that animate bodies are constrained by the same laws that govern the purely material world."[10] The material world, at least that of objects

10. Daniel Garber, *Descartes Embodied: Reading Cartesian Philosophy through Cartesian Science* (Cambridge: Cambridge University Press, 2001), 150, 152. The Cartesian program would accordingly "exempt animate bodies from the laws that govern inanimate bodies in motion in a coherent and nonarbitrary

constructed according to the primitive notion of extension, but maybe also that of minds recognized according to the primitive notion of the purely active *cogitatio*, thus does not concern that of the union. But then what world would remain open to the union?

Descartes suggests a hypothesis that is exactly opposite to the one that leads to the aporia of occasionalism by applying the laws of inter-action between bodies to the union of soul and body—namely, that the mode of action appropriate to the union obeys the same rules as those that allow God or angels to act on material things in the created world. In other words, the most appropriate model for thinking the action (or the passion) of the soul toward material bodies, the action that precisely defines *meum corpus*, should be borrowed not from the material world of inanimate bodies (whose interaction remains already problematic in itself, if not incomprehensible), but from the most radically immaterial world, the world outside the world. The audacity of such a recourse to a divine and angelic model is all the more surprising as Descartes most frequently rejects the least univocity between God and finite beings: not only is substance "*non convenit Deo et illis [i.e., rebus] univoce*—not fitting for God and things univocally,"[11] but also the eternal truths, as they are all equally a matter of creation. In the case of the action of the union, however, one must make an exception to this rejection of uni-vocity. Taking up one of Henri More's suggestions, Descartes ends up using the model of divine action (one obviously admits that God acts on bodies, although he remains plainly incorporeal) for thinking the union in his correspondence with More, who asks him in every possible way how (*quomodo*)[12] our mind acts on our body and the other bodies: "*Ita etiam eum non dedecet aliquid simile de allis substantiis incorporeis judicare. Et quamvis existimem nullam agendi modum Deo et creaturis* univoce *convenire, fateor tamen, me nullam in mente mea ideam re-perire, quae repraesentet modum quo Deus vel Angelus materiam potest*

---

way and . . . allow mind to affect the behavior of body" (ibid., 167). I would add: and it does so reciprocally, allowing the mind to find itself affected by its *meum corpus*. One could also say that "such bodies stand, as it were, outside the world of purely mechanical nature" (ibid., 165), on the condition of under-standing that it is only in this way that they become exposed to the real world (obviously in a non-Nietzschean sense).

11. *Principles of Philosophy* I, §51, VIII-1: 24, 27; CSM I: 210. [CSM translate: "there is no distinctly intelligible meaning of the term which is com-mon to God and his creatures."]

12. H. More to Descartes, 5 March 1649, V: 313–14; not translated in CSMK.

*movere, diversam ab ea quae mihi exhibet modum, quo* ego *per meam cogitationem* corpus meum *movere me posse mihi conscius sum.*—So it is no more of a disgrace for him to think much the same of other incorporeal substances. Of course I do not think that any mode of action belongs *univocally* to God and his creatures, but I must confess that the only idea I can find in my mind to represent the way in which God or an angel can move matter is the one which shows me the way in which I am conscious *I* can move *my own body* by my own thought."[13] Thus, far from the physical world of material things providing the model of the union (and the interaction) of soul and body, one must rather in a completely opposite fashion and for once without reluctance in regard to univocity find it in the action of immaterial agents on the physical bodies of material things.[14] Thus one should not conceive of the union

---

13. To H. More, 15 April 1649, V: 347, 14–22; CSMK: 375. The first thesis will be taken up again and explicated in detail in other places: "*Vis autem movens potest esse ipsius Dei conservantis tantumden translationis in materia, quantum a primo creationis momento in ea posuit;* vel etiam substantiae creatae, ut mentis nostrae, *vel cujusvis alterius rei, cui vim dederit corpus movendi*— The moving force can be, however, from God himself the preserver just as much of the translation in matter that he placed in them from the first moment of creation; *as also of created substance, such as our mind,* or of any other thing to which the body of the mover gave force" (To H. More, August 1649, V: 403, 28—404, 3; not translated in CSMK). Garber cites and comments on these texts in *Descartes Embodied.* He concludes that "[the picture one gets from the physics is one of] inert matter being shuffled around from moment to moment by an active God and, from time to time, by active incorporeal minds" (*Descartes Embodied,* 184). The only correction required is that the mind in question can be incorporeal if it is that of an angel, but that if it is that of a human, not only is it incarnated in a flesh (*meum corpus*), but it cannot exert the least action except by this incorporating flesh. Furthermore, one cannot say that the physical bodies put in motion by God constitute the flesh of God (ibid., 182–84), but only that putting physical bodies into motion happens *for me,* who alone am incarnate, via my flesh, which serves as first effect, if not first cause, of movement.

14. This belated response convinces more than the preceding recourse to the comparison of action of the soul on the body with the setting in motion of a body by its heaviness (To Elizabeth, 21 May 1643, III: 667, 4—668, 4). Descartes argues in this way: certainly the heaviness is not a real quality of the body it moves and thus does not constitute a physical explanation (of extension by extension); but it offers at least the advantage of making us conceive a body's setting in motion without its being "produced by a real contact between two surfaces" (III: 667, 24–25; CSMK: 219). In fact it offers a nonphysical explanation, "given us for the purpose of conceiving the manner in which the soul moves the body" (III: 668, 3–4; CSMK: 219), and not for the way in which one body moves another body. It is thus by right really and truly a model (a

starting from another notion than itself, and certainly not starting from the interaction of bodies in extension, also not starting from the production of a thought by another. What is valid for the two other notions is also valid for the union, "since they are primitive notions, each of them can be understood only through itself" (III: 666, 4–6; CSMK: 218). At this point in the Cartesian argument, we observe that the soul acts on its *meum corpus* or suffers from it, without for all that still conceiving the type of causality (if that term is still even suitable) that is implemented in this way. One must thus admit this fact "*quamvis* nondum *sciamus quae sit causa, car ita nos afficiant [i.e., sensus]*—although we do not *yet* know whether it is the cause, which makes the senses affect us."[15] The union becomes necessary as a fact, because it imposes nothing less than the *facticity* of the flesh, that I am because of *meum corpus*, always *already* and without having either chosen it or wanted it and possibly without ever being able to explain it. "*Quod autem mens, quae incorporea est, corpus possit impellere, nulla quidem ratiocinatio vel*

---

"comparison," To Elizabeth, 28 June 1643, III: 691, 14; CSMK: 226; see *Optics* I, VI: 83, 16–17: "that I might use two or three comparisons"); but a model that is wrong (III: 694, 10) because in the vocabulary of the School it is precisely given not as a (necessarily formal) model, but as a real determination. This is the reason why the *Essais* of the method had been disqualified. The properly physical explanation comes, for Descartes, from the mechanics of turbines: "Now I think that weightiness is no other thing than terrestrial bodies *really* being pushed against the center of the earth by subtle matter" (To Mersenne, 29 January 1641, III: 9, 25—10, 3; emphasis added; untranslated in CSMK). On this question see also To Clerselier on the Fifth Objection: "And yet, those who admit the existence of real accidents like heat, weight and so on, have no doubt that these accidents can act on the body" (IX-1: 213, 17–19; CSM II: 275); and To Hyperaspistes, August 1641, III: 424, 19—425, 3 (weightiness becomes included in the hypothesis of *accidentia realia* in general); To Arnauld, 29 July 1648, V: 222, 30—223, 13 (*gravitas lapidis*), similarly Rodis-Lewis' clarification in *L'Œuvre de Descartes*, 361ff.

15. A phrase Baillet does not translate in *Principles of Philosophy* I, §75, VIII-1: 38, 27–28, but that is confirmed by II, §40: "*Atque omnes causae particulares mutationum, quae corporibus accidunt, in hac tertia lege continentur, saltem eae quae ipsae corporeae sunt; an enim, et qualem, mentes humanae vel angelicae vim habeant corpora movendi,* non jam *inquirimus, sed ad tractationem* de homine *reservamus.*—All the particular causes of the changes which bodies undergo are covered by this third law—or at least the law covers all changes which are themselves corporeal. I am *not here* inquiring into the existence or nature of any power to move bodies which may be possessed by human minds, or the minds of angels, since I am reserving the topic for a treatise *On Man*" (VIII-1: 65, 14–19 = IX-2: 87; CSM I: 242).

*comparatio ab aliis rebus petita, sed certissima et evidentissima* experientia *quotidie nobis ostendit; haec enim una est ex rebus per se notis, quas, cum volumus per alias explicare, obscuramus.*—That the mind, which is incorporeal, can set the body in motion is something which is shown to us not by any reasoning or comparison with other matters, but by the surest and plainest everyday *experience*. It is one of those self-evident things which we only make obscure when we try to explain them in terms of other things."[16] One must admit the union as a fact that imposes itself even, or *especially*, when we do not understand it, because our lack of understanding is due to the excess of our experience over our comprehension: "*Hoc explicatu difficillimum; sed sufficit hic experientia, quae hic adeo clara est, ut negari nullo modo possit, ut illud in passionibus etc. apparet.*—This is very difficult to explain; but here our experience is sufficient, since it is so clear on this point that it just cannot be gainsaid. This is evident in the case of the passions, and so on."[17] Thus it remains a fact of reason, but a reason that is not explained

16. To Arnauld, 29 July 1648, V: 222, 15–20; CSMK: 358. The example that follows concerns the explanation of the movement of bodies by weightiness (*gravitas*), of which the human mind precisely has no clear and distinct idea. One can here recall Saint Augustine, who in comparing the union of soul and body [judges it to be] in itself incomprehensible except by using the more comprehensible hypostatic union in Christ: "*Quid ergo incredibile est, si aliqua una intellectualis anima modo quodam ineffabili et singulari pro multorum salute suscepta est? Corpus vero animae cohaerere, ut homo totus et plenus sit, natura ipsa nostra teste cognoscimus. Quod nisi usitatissimum esset, hoc profecto esset incredibilius; facilius quippe in fidem recipiendum est, etsi humanum divino, etsi mutabile incommutabili, tamen spiritum spiritui, aut ut verbis utar quae in usu habetis, incorporeum incorporeo, quam corpus incorporeo cohaere.*—Why is it incredible, then, that, in an ineffable and singular manner, the Son of God should assume one intellectual soul for the salvation of many? Moreover, we know from the testimony of our own nature that a man is whole and complete only when the body is united with a soul. This certainly would be more incredible, if it were not the commonest thing of all. For it is easier to believe in a union between spirit and spirit, or, in the language which you customarily use, between the incorporeal and incorporeal—even though the one were human, the other divine, the one mutable and the other immutable—than in a union between the corporeal and the incorporeal." *De Civitate Dei* X.29.2, trans. R. W. Dyson as *The City of God Against the Pagans* (Cambridge: Cambridge University Press, 1998), 436–37.

17. Conversation with Burman, 16 April 1648, §44, 163; CSMK: 346, see *Entretien avec Burman*, ed. Jean-Marie Beyssade (Paris: PUF, 1981), 89. Thus not only must one say that "Descartes does not theorize the union of soul and body, but remains at the observation of an anthropological lived experience" (Caps, *Les "médecins cartésiens,"* 50), but it is appropriate to raise the

by anything other than by the (thought) experiment [*expérience*] we perform on it, precisely because it is explained, as primitive notion, only by itself.

### §18. The Third Is the First

In this way, the facticity of the union takes on the status of a primitive notion. But this is a primitive notion that is less added to the two others (thought and extension) than opposed to them. It imposes itself as primitive, that is to say as irreducible to the others, not with but "without" them.[18] What's more, this institution follows from an incompatibility between them: while the distinction of the first two notions reinforces the characteristics of each of them, the third notion, that of union, turns out to be "harmful" (III: 665, 4; CSMK: 218) to the knowledge of this very distinction. Either one thinks the first two primitive notions all of a sudden in and thanks to their distinction, which makes them reciprocally clear and distinct, or one thinks a new union, anew and starting from itself, by suspending the other two notions and their distinction (as much ontic as eidetic). Thus the third primitive notion is not simply being added to the first two either by composition or by derivation (which would contradict its primitive character), but it becomes necessary only by contradicting the other two, more exactly by imposing a new beginning. Of the "two facts about the human soul on which depend the knowledge we can have of its nature," namely "that it thinks" and "being united to the body, it can act and be acted upon" (III: 664, 23–27; CSMK: 217–18), one cannot be conceived as the continuation of the other, but only as rupture and opposition, because (as we will see below, §20) this new beginning imposes a new theoretical attitude. A question is thus inevitably raised: in what sense and to what extent can the third primitive notion not only be conceived just by itself, but also have to be

---

acknowledgment of facticity, of the *fait accompli* of the union, positively. More informed readers are not deceived [about this]. Thus Pierre Guénancia: "Descartes does not respond to this difficulty, most probably because he takes it to be lifted by the very *fact* of union. The existence of a fact renders any approach trying to go back to its conditions of possibility useless." *L'Intelligence du sensible. Essai sur le dualisme cartésien* (Paris: Gallimard, 1998), 213; see also: "the fact, facticity," 298. Or Denis Kambouchner: "The same passions that make us sense our animal condition constitute at the same time, absolutely, *the first factum of our humanity.*" *Descartes et la philosophie morale* (Paris: Hermann, 2008), 112.

18. To Elizabeth, 21 May 1643, III: 666, 22; CSMK: 218.

conceived as the first of three, thus as a new beginning, in contrast to that of the distinction of the first two?[19]

Descartes often names it a union, without even specifying what it unites (soul and body): he omits it because these two terms are self-evident, but maybe also so as not to maintain the deceptive appearance that it would result from and would consist in the union of two components, of which it would offer a derived blend. For if the union really links up two substances, not only does it not itself consist in a new substance (as we will see below, §20), but it establishes absolutely new rules for uniting their principal attributes, thought and extension. These new rules provoke several paradoxes, which one must unfold and describe with all the more care as they mark the irreducibility of the third primitive notion and, most probably, its *final* priority over the two others.

The first of these paradoxes (we have already seen it above, §9) has to do with the ambiguity of the concept of body: "First of all, I consider what exactly is the body of a man, and I find that this word 'body' is very ambiguous." The ambiguity of the word derives here from the irreducibility of its complement: *body* becomes ambiguous because *man* requalifies it in opposition to its meaning as a pure and simple physical body. In the sense of "a body in general," the body is defined by extension, thus by matter formed into shape, but above all measured in a finite quantity, however large it might be: "a part of the quantity of which the universe is composed." What forms its unity is thus summarized in its quantity, and it is made or unmade according to these quantitative variations. But another meaning of body can be found, where the term, as applied to the body *of a man*, no longer means "a determinate part of matter, or one that has a determinate size," but "simply the whole of matter which is united with the soul of that man." Once the body

19. This is a new beginning, because it is a matter only of a *fact* experienced by the union, not without a connection with the experienced fact of the will: "our volitions, for we *experience* them as proceeding directly from our soul and as seeming to depend on it alone" (*Passions of the Soul*, §17, AT XI: 342, 14–17; CSM I: 335; emphasis added); or the experienced fact of our freedom: "You are right to say that we are as sure of our free will as of any other primary notion; for this is certainly one of them" (To Mersenne, December 1640, III: 259, 9–11; CSMK: 161). The union and freedom are necessary from the fact of experience, despite their incomprehensibility (see *On Descartes' Metaphysical Prism*, chapter 3, §15, 204, note 85). Can one *in a sense* include the will in the third primitive notion? That would not be absurd, if one considers that the question of freedom remains as unintelligible (confronted with divine omnipotence and omniscience that make determinism almost inevitable) as the union (which besides would seem the most exposed to this determinism).

is determined by adding a name to it, it does not base its unity on the measure of extension, a unity that is always provisional because susceptible to variation according to its quantity, but on the union. What unifies the body of a man consists in the union of a potentially variable portion of extension with an invariant, namely, thought in act. Identity cannot be measured (in terms of quantity), but according to the union of a part of extension with what remains beyond extension and variation, namely, the thought of an ego. This ego unifies everything that in extension can remain united to it: "even though that matter changes, and its quantity increases or decreases, we still believe that it is the same body, *idem numero*, numerically the same body, so long as it remains joined and substantially united with the same soul." The body remains unified in itself insofar as it can organize itself in order to remain united to the soul, "as long as it has in itself all the dispositions required to preserve that union."[20] The unity of the body depends on its organization, which Descartes names especially its disposition: "For the body is a unity which is in a sense indivisible because of the arrangement of its organs, these being so related to one another that the removal of any one of them renders the whole body defective."[21] This disposition allows a region of extension to become *received* by thought, in the sense in which a transmission of signals by a transmitter is received by a recipient, then restored and amplified. Thus, according to the disposition of organs, the body sees its signals received in the soul, and this reception that alone testifies to the union results from an original unity of the act of the *cogitatio*. Accordingly, the difference between "a body in general" and "the body of a man" depends on a principle of unification: either the quantity of extension, whose (provisional) permanence defines the unity by a measure, or the union on the authority of the *cogitatio*, the "soul" whose action (which does not cease, because the soul always thinks) maintains the unity even within the variations of the part of extension

20. To Mesland, 9 February 1645, IV: 166, 1–22; CSMK: 244–43. See: "*corp[us] haben[s] omnes dispositiones requisitas ad animam recipiendam, et sine quibus non est proprie humanum corpus*—if the body has all the dispositions required to receive a soul, which it must have to be strictly a human body" (To Regius, mid-December 1641, III: 460, 27—461, 2; CSMK: 200). From this derives the new definition of death, no longer as a flaw of the soul (which would disappear), but as a flaw of the body, whose "disposition" fails.

21. *Passions of the Soul*, §30, XI: 351, 8–12; CSM I: 339 (an indivisibility that certainly must be compared with the letter To Mesland, 9 February 1645, IV: 167, 13; CSMK: 243); see "disposition of organs" (*Passions of the Soul*, §211, XI: 486, 14; CSM I: 403).

that remains united to it, provided and as long as it remains united to it. The body becomes human not by virtue of the extent of its quantity, but owing to its union to the *cogitatio*, which itself is not measured (because it alone measures the rest). It maintains the unity of what, in this correctly laid out position of extension, henceforth merits the title of this body *of a man* and all the same will not cease to vary in quantity. In this way one understands retrospectively the extraordinary difference between the *alia corpora* and the *meum corpus* that introduces, without precaution or preparation, all of a sudden, the second part of the Sixth Meditation (see above, §16).

We still have to explain how the "soul" can thus unify a part of extension and turn it into "the body *of a man*." One could here appeal to an argument that Kant will formulate, but that Descartes to my knowledge never displays as such: the unity of the "body of a man," the unity that assures him his union to the soul, proceeds from the authority that the *cogitatio* exercises and that the principle of unity, defining the *cogitatio* itself, unfolds, namely, the originally synthetic unity of apperception. In fact, the ego thinks only by unifying what it thinks, either by the *intuitus* or by the *deductio*, because it does not think anything without affecting itself with its own thought, thus without identifying itself with and within it under the primordial form of the *videre videor* (above, §13). The ego thinks itself only by unifying itself, thus it unifies everything it thinks.[22] And, more than any other thing, it unifies what unites itself to it when it thinks, "the body of a man."

Yet, one will object, even if one admits this anachronistic argument, if one relies on it in order to ground the union (of soul and body) on the unity of the *cogitatio*, does one not confuse what established the distinction between the *cogitatio* and the *extensio*? How should such an originally unifying apperception of thought be exercised beyond the domain of the *cogitationes*? Why could it be extended all the way to the extension of a body, even of my body? By what right could the originary apperception of the cognizing ego claim "some special right—*speciale quodam jus*" (VII: 75, 30; CSM II: 52) over a part of extension? Such a use of the principle of unity in the *cogitatio* (of apperception) in extension would suffer not only from anachronism but also from inconsistency. It is all the same quite sufficient to respond to this objection with the paradox of the third primitive notion: the union cannot contradict

---

22. Is this not the way in which one could understand the declaration in the *Passions of the Soul*, §32 (XI: 353, 4–5; CSM I: 340): "But in so far as we have only one simple thought about a given object at any one time"?

the distinction (between the two first primitive notions), because it does not refer to them and does not depend on them. For inasmuch as it is primitive, it launches a new beginning, which need not be made compatible with the other primitive notions, but shares their primordiality by exercising it without compromise or relationship. The union precedes and redefines what it unites, soul and body ("of a man"), in a new term, *meum corpus*; it need not be made compatible with the distinction between the two other primitive notions, but obeys only its own establishment. The question thus becomes far simpler: it is only a matter of understanding why, in order to think and according to its proper requirements of cognizing, the ego must be united to a portion of extension, which it accordingly unifies in a "body of man" or a *meum corpus*. In what way can extension not only be united to thought, but lend it its principle of unity?

This is probably so because thought itself demands this union to the body in order to accomplish itself as thought. The ego can first be defined as *res cogitans*, that is to say, as a thing "*dubitans, intelligens, affirmans, negans, volens, nolens, imaginans quoque, et sentiens*—that doubts, understands, affirms, denies, is willing, is unwilling, and also imagines and has sensory perceptions."[23] Yet the *cogitatio* cannot sense on its own, while it can doubt, understand, desire, and imagine on its own; for in order to think according to sensing, one must feel, and feeling presupposes the passivity of an arrival coming from the exterior. This exteriority of thought, in other words this passivity, cannot be accomplished according to the sole (active) spontaneity of apperception; it requires an authority permitting (passive) receptivity of perception, hence a body: "*Sentire? Nempe etiam hoc non sit sine corpore*—Sensing? This surely does not occur without a body" (VII: 27, 5–6; CSM II: 18, trans. lightly modified). Body must obviously here be understood as the body of a man, that is to say, as the body of the union: "But pleasures are of two kinds: those that belong to the mind alone, and those that belong to the whole human being, that is to say, to the mind in so far as it is united with the body."[24] Yet what is particular to the body of a man, to the body of the union, in short to *meum corpus*, does not lie in the addition of a particle of extension to thought. (How could two heterogeneous entities become contiguous in this way through adding them together?) Actually, if the body of a man is distinguished from extension by its principle of unity, it is also distinguished from pure thought

---

23. AT VII: 28, 20–22; CSM II: 19; see 34, 18–21; CSM II: 24 and above, §16.
24. To Elizabeth, 1 September 1645, IV: 284, 6–9; CSMK: 263.

inasmuch as it alone can render the *res cogitans* no longer only active, but passive, subject to affection; and the mind can be called corporeal to the precise extent that it affects the body of the union: "*si enim per corporeum intelligatur id omne quod potest aliquo modo corpus afficere, mens etiam eo sensu corporea erit dicenda*—If 'corporeal' is taken to mean anything which can in any way affect a body, then the mind too must be called corporeal in this sense."[25] And if the mind becomes corporeal by affecting the body, it becomes so a fortiori even more, and first and foremost, by letting itself be affected by the body of the union. In this way it becomes mind exposed to passivities, to passions: "our soul would have no reason to wish to remain joined to its body for even one minute if it could not feel them [i.e., the passions]."[26] The mind senses only through the body, which is the sole authority of passivity. To feel "*affectus . . . , sive animi pathemata*—emotions or passions of the soul" means to think with "*confusae quaedam cogitationes, quas mens non habeat a se sola, sed ab eo quod a corpore, cui intime conjuncta est, aliquid patiatur*—confused thoughts, which the mind does derive from itself alone but experiences as a result of something happening to the body with which it is closely conjoined."[27] The passions of the soul

25. To Hyperaspistes, August 1641, which continues: "*Sed si per* corporeum *intelligatur id quod componitur ex ea substantia quae vocatur corpus, nec mens, nec etiam ista accidentia, quae supponuntur esse realiter a corpore distincta, corporea dici debent; atque hoc tantum sensu negari solet mentem esse corpoream*— but if 'corporeal' is taken to mean whatever is made up of the substance called body, then the mind cannot be said to be corporeal, but neither can those accidents which are supposed to be really distinct from body. It is only in this latter sense that the mind is commonly said not to be corporeal" (III: 424, 26—425, 3; CSMK: 190). See also To Arnauld, 29 July 1648: "*Si enim per corporeum intelligamus id quod pertinet ad corpus, quamvis sit alterius naturae, mens etiam corporea dici potest, quatenus est apta corpori uniri; sin vero per corporeum intelligimus id quod participat de natura corporis, non magis ista gravitas, quam mens humana corporea est*—For if we count as corporeal whatever belongs to a body, even though not of the same nature as body, then even the mind can be called corporeal, in so far as it is made to be united to the body; on the other hand, if we regard as corporeal only what has the nature of body, then this heaviness is no more corporeal than the human mind is" (V: 223, 7–13; CSMK: 358).

26. To Chanut, 1 November 1646, IV: 538, 9–11; CSMK: 300.

27. *Principles of Philosophy* IV, §190, VIII-1: 317, 23–27 = IX-2: 312; CSM I: 281. See: "this rational love is commonly accompanied by the other kind of love, which can be called sensual or sensuous. This (as I said briefly of all passions, appetites, and sensations on page 461 of the French edition of my *Principles*) is nothing but a confused thought, aroused in the soul by some motion of the nerves" (To Chanut, 1 February 1647, IV: 602, 22—603, 1; CSMK: 306).

indicate first the whole of all the forms of passivity, which happen to it only when and to the extent to which it becomes body in *meum corpus* and in that way becomes, for the first time, capable of passivity, thus qualified to think in the mode of sensing. The ego effectively unfolds its *modus cogitandi* of sensing only by passing from the simple distinction (where the body remains a thinkable extension) to the union (where the *meum corpus* becomes an extension willing to allow passive thought, a thought via reception). The *res cogitans* assumes its final mode of thought, namely, sensation as a finally passive thought, only by taking flesh in the *meum corpus*. In this way the union displays the possibilities of the *res cogitans* more completely (in the Sixth Meditation) than the distinction allowed it to do (in the first five Meditations). It consequently has ultimately priority over the two other primitive notions.

An objection remains all the same possible: if the confused thought that comes via *meum corpus* makes me think despite myself ("*absque ullo meo consensu*—without my consent," VII: 75, 10–11; CSM II: 52), thus if "it is not in our power to make ourselves have one sensation rather than another—*ut unum potius quam aliud sentiamus*,"[28] then one understands certainly well that the first passive affection of the soul consists in a pain: "*mentis nostrae corpus quoddam magis arcte, quam reliqua alia corpora, conjunctum esse, concludi potest, ex eo quod perspicue advertamus* dolores *aliosque sensus nobis ex improviso advenire*—the conclusion that there is a particular body that is more closely conjoined with our mind than any other body follows from our clear awareness that *pain* and other sensations come to us unexpectedly."[29] The union would thus have to make manifest its priority as first primitive notion by the primacy of pain over any other affect. Yet, quite to the contrary, Descartes postulates that "the first passion is joy." Must one choose between joy and pain?[30] Maybe not. First, because pain is opposed to pleasure, both being feelings that relate within the soul to the body, while joy is opposed to sadness, both falling under passions in the soul but connected to the soul; it is thus not a matter of rival or exclusive terms. But especially because, just like pain, joy owes its priority to the absolutely intimate connection to *meum corpus*. In fact, pain makes me experience the union in the fact that my flesh is being

The Institut's copy of Clerselier's edition of the *Letters*, ed. Claude Clerselier (Paris, 1666), ed. Jean-Robert Armogathe and Giulia Belgioioso (Lecce: Conte, 2005), I: 108, precisely goes back to *Principles of Philosophy* IV, §§189–90.

28. *Principles of Philosophy* II, §1, VIII-1: 40, 11–12 = IX-2: 63; CSM I: 223.
29. Ibid., §2, VIII-1: 41, 14–17 = IX-2: 64; CSM I: 224.
30. To Chanut, 1 February 1647, IV: 604, 31; CSMK: 307.

affected by the resistance of an external extended body that it cannot divert or avoid, or, more intimately still, affected by itself inasmuch as it experiences a physiological lack (hunger and thirst) and, experiencing them, experiences *itself* all the more itself; pain makes the soul experience itself by the relay of the passivity of its flesh. But joy is very similar; it is defined as "a pleasant emotion which the soul has when it enjoys a good which impressions in the brain represent to it as its own."[31] What good does primitive joy then enjoy in order to merit the title of "first passion" (IV: 604, 31; CSMK: 307)? It is a matter not of a priority in the logical deduction of the passions (in which case wonder would come first), but of a priority in the chronology, which follows from history, not that of "my mind," but that of the *meum corpus,* that of the ego's taking flesh: "it is not credible that the soul was put into the body at a time when the body was not in a good condition; and a good condition of the body naturally gives us joy."[32] In other words, the union links thought not to extension in general, but to a very particular part of extension—susceptible to allowing it to think passively and to find itself affected, that is to say, having "in itself all the dispositions required to preserve that union."[33] The disposition means that the body must add to the simple position in extension (the always changing form, because it is susceptible of movement) an organization whose quantitative variations in space would all the same not forbid its organic functioning at least for a time (until death); only on this condition, the *dis*-position, does the body "in general" become "the body of a man," in this case *meum corpus.* Thus joy takes its priority from the first taking of the flesh, or more exactly from the primordial character of this taking of flesh. The cause of joy accordingly makes possible other passivities, by assuring them the primordial passivity of *meum corpus*; in particular, pain, which is born (in hunger) from the fact that "food happened to be lacking,"[34] presupposes the cause of joy, the taking of the flesh, hence comes paradoxically from a more primordial joy. There is thus no contradiction between the symptomatic privilege of pain and the priority of joy in the description of *meum corpus* and the union it enables.

The third primitive notion thus emerges really, in a radical sense, as the first—first accomplishment of all the modes of the *res cogitans*, first among all the passions in the chronology of the taking of flesh.

31. *Passions of the Soul*, §91, XI: 396, 21–24; CSM I: 360.
32. To Chanut, 1 February 1647, IV: 604, 31—605, 4; CSMK: 107.
33. To Mesland, 9 February 1645, IV: 166, 21–22; CSMK: 243.
34. To Chanut, 1 February 1647, IV: 605, 13; CSMK: 309.

## §19. The Ontic Paradoxes

The third notion thus claims its primitive character—owing its evidence to nothing other than itself—to the point of restructuring the classification of all the *naturae simplicissimae* and of ultimately imposing itself as the first among them. This strange postulation, whose ultimate implications for the whole Cartesian enterprise one would have to measure (below, §21), already explains and extends itself in several paradoxes. Descartes assumes them very explicitly on the basis of the primordial paradox, that of the ambiguity of the concept of body and of the irreducibility of the *meum corpus* that provokes it (above, §18), vis-à-vis the interlocutors who see in them, at least at first and like a number of modern readers, only incoherence or even doctrinal improvisations undertaken ad hoc in order to alleviate theoretical aporiae. One must thus instead examine them and give them their due, because they will allow us to appreciate more fully the radical nature of the final Cartesian establishment. The first two among them present an ontic character because they modify two beings, soul and body; they modify them or rather invert them, because they take up soul and body no longer starting from themselves, as the first primitive notions do, but starting from the third, from the union, taken henceforth as the first of the three. In this way paradoxes spring up because the terms of the debate are, for the first time, effectively being described starting from the union, which is henceforth primordial.

A first paradox is constructed from one of Gassendi's objections in 1641 to a response on 28 June 1643 to Elizabeth, where Descartes attributes "this matter and extension to the soul" (III: 694, 19–20; CSMK: 228). Gassendi's characteristically quite weak objection is against the distinction of the first two primitive notions, the thinking and nonextended thing, the extended and nonthinking body: Gassendi wonders how an "unextended subject" could accommodate the idea of an extended body, which idea would itself necessarily be extended. Also, defining the thinking thing as nonextended does not reach anything clear and distinct, but only supplies a purely negative definition (just as stating that Bucephalus is not a fly is not enough to define what it is). Descartes responds in two phases. First by recalling the evidence (first of all for Aristotle) that the mind perceives without material species, but by pure intellection of things that are as much incorporeal as they are corporeal (*"nullam speciem corpoream in mente recipi, sed puram intellectionem tam rei corporea quam incorporeae*—the mind does not receive any corporeal semblance; the pure understanding both of corporeal and incorporeal things occurs without any corporeal semblance"). Then, in specifying that the mind, not perceiving extension by a species that is itself extended, has no need to be extended in order to unite itself with the totality of the body. It is enough for it to think in order to manage to do so, which is what really defines it ("*Etsi enim mens sit unita toti corpori, non inde sequitur ipsam esse extensam per corpus, quia non est de ratione ipsius, ut sit extensa, sed tantum ut cogitet*—Even though the mind is united to the whole body, it does not follow that it is extended throughout the body, since it is not in its nature to be extended, but only to think").[35] Even so, if the first response is self-evident, the second still remains perfunctory: In what sense is the mind united to the *whole* body and in what sense can thought not only perceive extension, but be united to it? Descartes' hesitation is marked by his recourse (already) to weightiness, supposed to be exerted on the totality of the surface of a body without itself being localized in any point of its extension: "*Nec sane jam mentem alia ratione corpori coextensam, totamque in toto, et totam in qualibet ejus parte esse intelligo*—This is exactly the way in which I now understand the mind to be coextensive with the body—the whole mind in the whole body and the whole mind in any of its parts."[36] Besides the limits of such a use of the quality of weightiness (he will anyway quickly admit that the comparison *limps*),[37] one does not yet see the specificity of the connection of *mens* to extension in the union of *meum corpus*, in contrast to the simple relationship of representation of a material thing to an immaterial idea. This seems already like Spinoza's aporia, identifying the union with the consciousness of extended modes via the thinking mode.

Descartes gets out of this aporia by going back to the ambiguity of the concept of body, in order to repeat the aporia firmly with a clear distinction between two meanings of corporeity: "*Nec refert quod accidentia illa dicantur esse corporea; si enim per* corporeum *intelligatur id omne quod potest aliquo modo corpus afficere, mens etiam eo sensu corporea erit dicenda; sed si per* corporeum *intelligatur id quod*

35. Fifth Set of Replies (to the objections to the Sixth Meditation, n.4, VII: 337–339; CSM II: 233–35), first VII: 387, 8–11; CSM II: 265, then 388, 13–389, 4; CSM II: 266, respectively.

36. Sixth Set of Replies, VII: 442, 18–20; CSM II: 298. And also To Clerselier on the Fifth Objections, IX-1: 213, 17–29. On weightiness and its Cartesian use, see above, §17, 127, note 14. Descartes certainly here cannot utilize the solution proposed by Thomas Aquinas (among others), who relies on a status of the *forma substantialis* of the soul (*Summa Theologiae* Ia, q. 76, a. 8, c).

37. To Elizabeth, 28 June 1643, III: 694, 20; CSMK: 228.

*componitur ex ea substantia quae vocatur corpus, nec mens, nec etiam*
*accidentia, quae supponuntur esse realiter a corpore distincta, corporea*
*dici debent.*—It makes no difference that these accidents are called corporeal. If 'corporeal' is taken to mean anything which can in any way
affect a body, then the mind too must be called corporeal in this sense;
but if 'corporeal' is taken to mean whatever is made up of the substance
called body, then the mind cannot be said to be corporeal, but neither
can those accidents which are supposed to be really distinct from body.
It is only in this latter sense that the mind is commonly said not to be
corporeal."[38] "Corporeal" thus can be understood either in a substantial sense (and in this case neither the *mens* nor the accidents distinct
*from the body* are corporeal), or in the sense of an ability to affect this
body in whatever way—in which case obviously the *mens* is corporeal
because it indisputably affects its body or even becomes affected by its
body. Body can thus be understood either as an (extended, material)
substance or as the affected and/or affecting flesh of the *meum corpus.*
The *mens* (or soul) can in this way become corporeal by relation, by
destination, by affection (received or exercised). Several years later, Descartes will take up this distinction again, once more in connection with
the "comparison" of weightiness, in order to conclude from it that "*si*
*enim per* corporeum *intelligamus id quod* pertinet ad corpus, *quamvis*
*sit alterius naturae, mens etiam corporea dici potest,* quatenus *est apta*
*corpori uniri; sin vero per corporeum intelligimus id quod participat*
*de natura corporis, non magis ista gravitas, quam mens humana, cor-*
*porea est*—if we count as *corporeal* whatever *belongs to a body,* even
though not of the same nature as body, then even the mind can be called
corporeal, *in so far as* it is made to be united to the body; on the other
hand, if we regard as corporeal only what has the nature of body, then
this heaviness is no more corporeal than the human mind is."[39] In other
words, corporeity is no longer defined (at least not solely) by its nature
(obviously material according to the *naturae simplicissimae* of extension, of shape, and of movement), that is to say substantially, but by the
pertinence, the reference, and the intentionality of the *mens* toward the
body, itself understood *as* body of the union, that is to say, as *meum cor-*
*pus.* What turns a portion of extension into a *meum corpus* and [causes
it to be] no longer matter depends uniquely on the soul that is united
to it and unifies it. Vice versa, what makes the soul corporeal depends

---

38. To Hyperaspistes, August 1641, III: 424, 25–425, 3; CSMK: 190 (cited
above, §18, 135, note 25).
39. To Arnauld, 29 July 1648, V: 223, 7–13; CSMK: 358.

on the fact that it can be united to a portion of extension that it makes more its own by affection (received or exercised) than it is other by nature. The union thus transforms the extension to which it is united into thought more than its nature keeps this extension in materiality. Corporeity can (and must) be understood *first* (following the privilege of the first primitive notion) starting from that which, of extension, manages to be united to the soul to the extent of its possible "disposition" in order to ensure that it will think passively. In order to allow it a passive thought, the union appends to the soul the portion of extension that its "disposition" makes capable of affecting or that it feels itself capable of affecting. The ambiguity of the *corporeal* and of the *extended*, like the passage from one sense to another, becomes ruled by the union, that is to say, by the soul *insofar* as via affection it is related to a portion available to this effect of extension.

This thesis finds its definitive formulation in 1643: "Your Highness observes that it is easier to attribute matter and extension to the soul than to attribute to it the capacity to move and be moved by the body without having such matter and extension. I beg her to feel free to attribute this matter and extension to the soul because that is simply to conceive it as united to the body."[40] Obviously the extension of thought should be conceived only as the consequence of the union and not the union as the result of the addition of the material *natura simplicissima* of extension to the intellectual *natura simplicissima* of thought: it is a matter of a third and yet first primitive notion, which begins and ends with the union, as the instance of the primordial affection of *meum corpus*. It also does not contradict the other two primitive notions, whose differences it respects and recovers by abstraction: "And once she has formed a proper conception of this and *experienced it in herself*, it will be easy for her to consider that the matter she has attributed to the thought *is not* thought itself, and that the extension of this matter is *of a different nature* from the extension of the thought, because the former has a determinate *location*, such that it thereby excludes all other bodily extension, which is not the case with the latter."[41] One would not be

40. To Elizabeth, 28 June 1643, III: 694, 15–21; CSMK: 228.
41. Ibid., 21–28. Elsewhere Descartes uses a more scholastic, but less illuminating, formulation: "*Quantum autem ad me, nullam intelligo nec in Deo nec in Angelis vel mente nostra extensionem substantiae, sed potentiae duntaxat*—For my part, in God and angels and in our mind I understand there to be no extension of substance, but only extension of power." To Henry More, 15 April 1649, V: 342, 13–15; CSMK: 372; see 343, 7–10; CSMK: 373; with this time still the admission of a univocity, 347, 16; CSMK: 375; and still to the same, August

able to say it more clearly: the extension assumed of the union is not in any way localized in an extended matter; it does not belong to its (*simplicissima?*) nature and thus has no other site than in thought itself; it is thus nonextended. The nonlocalized extension (or quasi-extension) of *meum corpus* is a matter of thought and takes quasi-place only in it—it allows it passivity. Such are the "properties of the soul that are [no longer] unknown to us" and which, against Elizabeth's fears, allow us to surpass the dualistic appearance "of the non-extendedness of the soul."[42] Such is the paradox of the extension of the soul of the union.

A second paradox matches the paradox of the extension of the soul exactly (on the occasion of the eucharistic debate with Mesland in 1645), that of the indivisibility of the body, in the sense of *meum corpus.* In fact, if "when we speak of the body of a man, we do not mean a determinate part of matter, or one that has a determinate size; we mean simply *the whole of the matter which is united with the soul* of that man,"[43] the unity of this body depends not on the variations that measure its quantity of extension, but on the unity of the soul to which it finds itself united. Once more its unity depends on its union, which depends itself on the unity of apperception of a *cogitatio*, but of a *cogitatio* henceforth passive. Although the *meum corpus* never remains identical quantitatively (*idem numero*), it still remains the same from the fact of the union: "our body, qua human body, remains always numerically the same *so long as it is united with the same soul.* In that sense, it can even be called indivisible; because if an arm or a leg of a man is amputated, we think that it is only in the first sense of 'body' that his body is divided—we do not think that a man who has lost an arm or a leg is less a man than any other. Altogether then, *provided that a body is united with the same rational soul,* we always take it as *the body of the same man,* whatever matter it may be and whatever quantity or shape it may have; and we count it as the whole and entire body, provided that it needs no additional matter in order to remain joined to this soul."[44] In other words, from the moment that the measure of the quantity of extension no lon-

---

1649, V: 403, 12–17; CSMK: 381. See Jean Luc Nancy's analyses, "L'extension de l'âme," *Poésie* 99 (2002): 77–83.

42. Elizabeth to Descartes, 5 July 1643, IV: 2, 11–12 and 14; untranslated in CSMK. One can maybe approach this extension from the "interior space of the proper body" according to Maine de Biran, *Essai sur les fondements de la psychologie*, I, II, chapter 3, in *Oeuvres*, vol. VII: 1 (Paris: J. Vrin, 2001), 143.

43. To Mesland, 9 February 1645, IV: 166, 11–16; CSMK: 243; emphasis added.

44. To Mesland, 9 February 1645, IV: 167, 10–25; CSMK: 243; emphasis added.

ger forms the principle of unity and the union is imposed in its place, the unity of the body no longer follows the rules and the characteristics of extension, but those of the soul. Via the union it depends on the very unity of the *cogitatio* (henceforth passive); the "body of a man" remains unified just as long as its organization (the "disposition" of its matter) is sufficient for ensuring to the *cogitatio* its passive function (providing it with feelings, perceptions, and passions, in short the passivities that can refer either to the things of the world or to *corpus meum*, or to the soul). As long as "the body of a man" remains organized to the benefit of the union, it remains united (to the soul) and hence unified (organic). In this sense, it remains indivisible: the properties of the *cogitatio*, in the first rank of which are found indivisibility and unity, become the properties of *meum corpus* (for a clear communication of idioms that owes no little to theology here, as much to the incarnation as to the Eucharist). One can thus confirm one of Alquié's conclusions: "Here the body [i.e., *meum corpus*] seemingly appearing from the very side of the subject [i.e., of the *mens*] reveals a true incarnation."[45]

The *Passions of the Soul* will take this paradox up again in a masterful argument. No one will deny that it would be absurd to claim "to conceive of a half or a third of a soul, or of the extension which a soul occupies." Now, the body of the passions (*meum corpus*, "the body of a man") "has no relation with extension, or to the dimensions or other properties of the matter of which the body is composed: it is related solely to the whole assemblage of the body's organs," that is to say, to the disposition of the organism permitting the *cogitatio* to think passively; in other words, *this* body must itself be interpreted according to the intellectual *naturae simplicissimae* and not the material ones, without recourse to extension, shape, or movement. Thus, to the exact extent to which "the soul is really joined to *the whole body*," the body is revealed, like the soul, to be without parts: "the body is a unity which is in a sense indivisible."[46] Should one share the surprise of some interpreters about the fact that Descartes immediately seems to temper this thesis by saying that "*humanam animam, etsi totum corpus informet, praecipuam tamen sedem suam habere in cerebro, in quo solo non modo intelligit et imaginatur, sed etiam sentit*—It must be realized

45. Ferdinand Alquié, *La Découverte métaphysique de l'homme chez Descartes* (Paris: PUF, 1950, 2011), 301. See "the incarnation of the mind" (303); "I must accept . . . my incarnation and my finitude" (316).

46. *Passions of the Soul*, §30, XI: 351, 17–18, 13–15, 5–6, and 8–9; CSM I: 339; emphasis added.

that the human soul, while informing the entire body, nevertheless has its principal seat in the brain; it is here alone that the soul not only understands and imagines but also has sensory awareness"?[47] In fact there is probably no contradiction in this claim that the soul is united to the whole body of the man and that it has its seat in the brain, precisely because the gland that is found there does not intervene as an intermediary in extension, but allows an "immediate"[48] interaction. In fact, if the soul senses (in other words, thinks passively) via the body or wills (in other words, thinks actively), it does so via the whole body serving as the network either of the nerves or of the "fibers,"[49] which cross it from top to bottom. My body remains the united body of a man as long as the disposition of its organs (in this case, the link of the pineal gland to the nervous system) makes it capable of union with the *mens*, which can in this way, among other operations, think passively. In this sense, as a body unified by the union of thought, *this* body really remains, just like thought, indivisible.

In this way the initial paradox of the radical ambiguity of the concept of body (between extension of bodies in general and the original sensing of the body of a man, *meum corpus*) changes into two other paradoxes defining two beings: first the extension (or co-extension) and the corporeity of the soul, then the indivisibility of *meum corpus*. Yet, just as these paradoxes redefine the *naturae simplicissimae*, in fact their two first rubrics (the intellectual and the material ones), these ontic determinations depend first and above all on the conditions of their knowledge: just like any *natura simplicissima*, the primitive notion of the union is defined and decided in terms of the theory of knowledge. One must hence arrive at the epistemological paradox that was already supporting and silently provoking these ontic paradoxes.

47. *Principles of Philosophy* IV, §189, VIII-1: 315, 23–26; CSM I: 279–80. Also *Passions of the Soul*, §31: "We need to recognize also that although the soul is joined to the whole body, nevertheless there is a certain part of the body where it exercises its functions more particularly than in all the others" (XI: 351, 26—352, 2; CSM I: 340). Objections are raised by Alquié, *La Découverte métaphysique*, 312, and Margaret Wilson, *Descartes* (London/Boston: Routledge, 1978), 205ff.

48. See for example, §32: "there cannot be any other place in the whole body where the soul directly exercises its functions" (AT XI: 352, 25–27; CSM I: 340); §33: "our soul should exercise its functions directly in the heart" (XI: 354, 2–3; CSM I: 341); §35: "the gland, which acts directly upon the soul and makes it see" (XI: 356, 4–6; CSM I: 342).

49. *Passions of the Soul*, §34, XI: 354 *passim* (going back to §16); CSM I: 341.

## §20. The Epistemological Paradox

One cannot, in fact, avoid a huge difficulty regarding the knowledge of the union. At least one mode of thought corresponds to each category of the *naturae simplicissimae*, all of them by definition intelligible and even perfectly intelligible. Descartes' teaching remains constant on this: thought is known precisely "by the understanding alone" (and possibly by its variations of doubt and will), launching the career of metaphysics; extension (and its variations of shape and movement) is known "much better by the understanding aided by the imagination,"[50] allowing mathematics, its models and parameters. Yet how can one know their union? Obviously neither through pure understanding, which thinks as such only the *res cogitans* (and God as *res cogitans infinita*), nor through understanding assisted by the imagination, because, when it is not a matter of a strict *res extensa*, "your imagination insistently mixes itself up with your thoughts and lessens the clarity of this knowledge by trying to clothe it with shapes."[51] Obviously also, no other mode of thought than the senses remains available; but how could one claim that they "know very clearly,"[52] when, according to a clear distinction of the *Principia*, sensation is perceived with clarity but without any distinction? The privileged example of pain provides a perception that is "indeed very clear—*clarissima quidem . . .*—but is not always distinct—*sed non semper est distincta.*"[53] It is certainly clear, because "present and accessible to the attentive mind—*menti attendenti praesens et aperta*": I cannot perceive my pain without identifying it indubitably as such and mine; its presence imposes itself as indubitably as its potential ending. Yet there is nothing distinct in it, if one understands that to mean that it would be "so sharply separated from all other perceptions that it contains within itself only what is clear—*ita sejuncta est et praecisa, ut nihil plane aliud, quam quod clarum est, in se contineat.*" In fact, the perception of pain leads almost irresistibly to import into the body or the suffering member "something they suppose to resemble the sensation of pain—*in parte dolente simile sensui doloris.*"[54] Pain (like hunger, thirst, pleasure, but also qualities of sensory objects) remains indistinct. And actually in two senses, not just in one. First, as this text just said,

50. To Elizabeth, 29 June 1643, III: 691, 22 (= 692, 1) and 25–26; CSMK: 227, trans. lightly modified.

51. To Silhon, March or April 1648, V: 138, 7–9; CSMK: 331.

52. To Elizabeth, 28 June 1643, III: 692, 3. See above, §16.

53. *Principles of Philosophy* I, §46, VIII-1: 22, 11–12; CSM I: 208.

54. Ibid., §45, 22, 3–9 and §46, 22, 14; CSM I: 207–8, respectively.

sensory perception does not distinguish what it perceives clearly from the cause or the thing that accompanies it, to which it really tends to attribute sensation, thus a mode of thought that is produced only in and for the ego alone thinking. Then, because the ego itself cannot describe the differences between its sensations in such a way as to characterize them as certain objects: I can describe neither a color nor the difference between two colors, nor between sounds, flavors, and so forth (except by classifying them into models that record them in terms of the extension imagined by the mathematicians, as proposed by Regula XII, AT X: 413, 3ff.). One must thus maintain that "the senses," that is, the mode of thought of the *sensus*, which is anyway always mentioned in final place in the definition of the *res cogitans* ("*et sentiens*—and sensing," VIII: 28, 22 and 34, 20 ff.), never allow distinct knowledge, however clear their perception might be. Thus Descartes would not have the right to appeal to them for ensuring the knowledge of the union.

Yet Descartes precisely speaks here only of knowing the union "very clearly by the senses" (III: 692, 3; CSMK: 227) without claiming to know it distinctly; he always maintains that the sensory ideas or perceptions remain "confused."[55] Then, he refers back implicitly but without ambiguity to a thesis from the second part of the Sixth Meditation (see above, §10), which underlined not only already that, concerning colors, sounds and flavors, but also for pain and so forth, "*percipio melius sensu*—I perceive these things much better by means of the senses" (VII: 74, 4 = IX-1, 58; CSM II: 51), but also and above all that this clarity of sensory perceptions goes so far as to produce *a kind of quasi-distinction*:

55. For example, To Hyperaspistes, August 1641: "*nihil magis rationi consentaneum est, quam ut putemus mentem corpori infantis recenter unitam* in solis ideis *doloris, titallationis, caloris, frigoris et similibus, quae ex ista unione et quasi permistione oriuntur,* confuse percipiendis sive sentiendis *occupari*—So if one may conjecture on such an unexplored topic, it seems most reasonable to think that a mind newly united to an infant's body is wholly occupied *in perceiving in a confused way* or feeling *the ideas* of pain, pleasure, heat, cold and other similar ideas which arise from its union and, as it were, intermingling with the body" (III: 424, 7–12; CSMK: 190). Or To Regius, January 1642: "*hoc, quod percipiamus sensus doloris, aliosque omnes, non esse puras cogitationes mentis a corpore distinctae, sed* confusas illius realiter unitae perceptiones—by saying that we perceive that sensations such as pain are not pure thoughts of a mind distinct from a body, but *confused perceptions of a mind really united to a body*" (III: 493, 11–14; CSMK: 206). Or also To Chanut, 1 February 1647: "only sensations or very confused thoughts" (IV: 605, 20–21; CSMK: 308). And To Silhon, March or April 1648: "I agree that such knowledge is somewhat obscured by the soul's mingling with the body" (V: 137, 26–27; CSMK: 331).

"*ideae sensu perceptae essent multo magis vividae et expressae,* et suo etiam modo magis distinctae, *quam ullae ex iis quas ipse prudens et sciens meditando effingebam*—the ideas perceived by the senses were much more lively and vivid *and even, in their own way, more distinct* than any of those which I deliberately formed through meditating."[56] How are we to understand *the way* in which sensory perceptions can appear as more distinct than the pure ideas of the understanding and of the imagination? The Sixth Meditation explained this by applying these ideas to *meum corpus*, not at all so as to communicate to it in this way pieces of information about the world of theoretical objects, but so as to allow it to orient itself to its advantage among the beings of usage (*in/commoda, Zuhandene*):[57] the sensory ideas are sufficiently clear and distinct only to the extent that they indicate to the composition of the union what is appropriate to it or not: "*ad menti significandum quaenam composito, cujus pars est, commoda sint vel incommoda,* et eatenus sunt satis clarae et distinctae—is simply to inform the mind of what is beneficial or harmful for the composite of which the mind is a part; and *to this extent they are sufficiently clear and distinct*" (VII: 83, 17–19 = IX-1: 67; CSM II: 57). The ideas of sensation become clear and, *in their own way*, distinct only in regard to the usefulness or harmfulness of things in regard to the union, in no way in regard to the knowledge of thought or extension. One must either think the distinction or think the union, because they cannot be thought "very distinctly and at the same time" (III: 693, 22–23; CSMK: 227; trans. modified). A break with the mode of thought is thus required in order to think the union as such by the only way remaining open, sensation—thinking by the *sensus*. How does one think by the mode of thought of the *sensus* alone? We already know—passively. But how shall one describe this passive thought?

Actually, "the notion of the union which everyone invariably experiences in himself"[58] is known only by experience, more exactly by the experience of the self in the flesh that senses itself purely and simply. Those

56. VII: 75, 14–17 = IX-1: 60; CSM II: 52. In the light of these texts one can maybe better understand a surprising declaration: "Can you doubt that our mind, when it is detached from the body, or has a glorified body which will no longer hinder it, can receive such *direct* illumination and knowledge? Why, *even in this body the senses give it such knowledge of corporeal and sensible things* . . ." To Silhon, March or April 1648, V: 137, 18–23; CSMK: 331; emphasis added.

57. In other words, "it is not the theory but the practice which is difficult" (To Elizabeth, May or June 1645, IV: 220, 21–22; CSMK: 250).

58. To Elizabeth, 28 June 1643, III: 694, 1–2; CSMK: 228.

who "use only their senses have no doubt that the soul moves the body and that the body acts on the soul. They regard both of them as a single thing, that is to say, they conceive their union" (III: 692, 4–8; CSMK: 227). At stake is a thought that does not allow itself to be distracted from the experience of the self by any object that is by definition distinct from it. Yet, in order to do this, it is not enough to reject the objects constituted within extension according to the material *naturae simplicissimae* to the benefit of those constituted in the *cogitatio* according to the intellectual *naturae simplicissimae*. One must challenge the constitution of any object in general, whether it is a matter of thought or just as much of extension, in order for the soul to think no longer as knowing but as *experiencing* either that the body moves it or that it moves the body. And this is possible only if the *mens* (which mainly operates here what one also calls the soul) renounces constituting any object whatsoever, that is to say, stops privileging the theoretical attitude—precisely the attitude that requires abstracting the mind from the senses and provokes the "*abductio mentis a sensibus*—the mind to be led away from the senses" (VII: 12, 7–8; CSM II: 9). One would henceforth have to reflect (on the objects of thought by pure understanding) *less* than to imagine (the objects of extension by the understanding helped by the imagination). This raises the question: How can one think without thinking any object? Answer: "it is *using* only the ordinary course *of life* and conversation, and *abstaining from meditation* and from the *study of the things* which exercise the imagination, that teaches us how to conceive the union of the soul and the body" (III: 692, 16–20; CSMK: 227); the term "life," customarily too vague and often an admission of failure in philosophy, becomes here a quasi-concept, at least in a negative sense, because it designates the nonobject of a thought, which, in this "usage," thinks nothing other than itself, thus thinks in experiencing *itself*. The Cartesian thesis comes down to endorsing that *thinking without object remains still thinking*, and thinking with a kind of countermethod: if one precisely must detach thought from any object, one must thus learn to relax [*relâcher*] the inevitably objectivizing attention, to pay attention to no longer paying attention in order in this way to release [*lâcher*] any hold over any object whatsoever: "I have given all the rest of my time to the *relaxation* of the senses and the repose of the mind."[59]

59. To Elizabeth, 28 June 1643, III: 693, 1–2; CSMK: 227. Other occurrences of this relaxation concern the union less directly; thus To Elizabeth, June 1645: "the distractions of study . . . might sometimes provide her with *relaxation*" (IV: 238, 1–3; CSMK: 254). Or To Elizabeth, 6 October 1645: "our mind

With this "repose," it is a matter not only or first of all of "bodily *comfort*" but of persuading the *mens* "to adopt a more *carefree* outlook" so as to practice and experience "thoughts requiring *less attention.*"[60] Now, these vague and objectless thoughts neither vaguely prove to be thoughts nor are they thoughts without a stake. Descartes has always known such thoughts, experienced without attention, but with a serious and enduring "nonchalance." *Nonchalance*, in other words the suspension of what makes me hot [*me chaut*], what could matter to me [*me chaloir*] (make me hot or cold), of what it would be important for me to know outside of me, *including here this me as purely thinking*. It is not a matter of suspending the world in order to assure me of certainty in the theory of reduced objects, but of suspending the theoretical attitude itself. These thoughts, which suspend the exercise of any thought of the object, amount to what Descartes names daydreams [*rêveries*], dreams all the more irreducible to objectivizing attention as they impose themselves during the day, without sleep, *waking* dreams,[61] bearing on nothing other than the de-realization of any definable content. In this way, "chimeras and hypogryphs are formed in the imagination of those who *daydream*, that is to say who let their fancy wander *listlessly* here and there *without external objects* diverting it and without the fancy's being directed by *reason*"; for "such are the illusions of our dreams and also the daydreams we often have when *we are awake* and our mind wanders *nonchalantly without applying itself* to anything of

---

needs much *relaxation* if it is to be able to spend usefully a few moments in the search for truth" (IV: 307, 3–5; CSMK: 268–69). See: "Listlessness is an inclination felt in all the limbs to *relax* and remain motionless" (*Passions of the Soul*, §119, XI: 416, 17–18; CSM I: 370).

60. To Elizabeth, 6 October 1645, IV: 309, 9; CSMK: 270; then To Elizabeth, June 1645, IV: 237, 25–26; CSMK: 253; and To Elizabeth, 28 June 1643, III: 693, 19; CSMK: 227; emphases added.

61. See To Balzac, 5 May 1630: "I take a walk every day among the confusion of many people, with as much liberty and repose as you can have in your country roads, and I do not think of the people that I see there other than I do of the trees that are encountered in your woods or the animals that graze there. The very noise of their troubles does not interrupt me any more than *my daydreams*, which turn them into some stream" (I: 203, 19–21; untranslated in CSMK). Thus one could speak of "the distinct idea of confusion" or "of a philosophy for which confusion exists" as does Jean Laporte, *La Rationalisme de Descartes* (Paris: PUF, 1945, 1988), 251 and 254. Or one could even evoke with Levinas "the magnitude of relaxation," *De l'évasion* (Paris: Fata Morgana, 1935, 1982), 108, trans. Bettina Bergo as *On Escape* (Stanford: Stanford University Press, 2003), 61, trans. modified.

its own accord"; "whether they are real dreams in sleep or daydreams in *waking* life when the soul *does not determine itself* to anything of its own accord, but *nonchalantly* follows the impressions that happen to be in the brain."[62] This waking without awakening brings to light the thought without object, not even the object of its own reflective thought, a thought no one cares about, a thought that is experienced more than it is thought, because it thinks of nothing.

Moreover, Descartes explains mechanically the possibility of thinking of nothing: it is enough that the spirits that act on the soul by the immediate intermediary of the gland, instead of following the movements defined by the action of the subtle matter shattered by a precise object, rather follow the traces of prior movements, traces perused sufficiently to guide their journey spontaneously or even "by chance,"[63] with no reason or cause other than habit.[64] In this way the object can blur as origin of the idea, which becomes the empty unfurling of thought without the motive of an object, pure practice of self without even the consciousness *of self*. To think of nothing does not mean not to think, it means to think without experiencing any material or intellectual object, whether of pure understanding or clothed with shape by imagination, thus experiencing a thought thinking itself in me, but without me, self-consciousness, but without my ego directing it, in short an autonomous or even automatic thought. Descartes, "lover of poetry" (VI: 7, 11–12), evokes "people who convince themselves they are *thinking of nothing* because they are observing the greenness of a wood, the colours of a flower, the flight of a bird, or something else requiring *no attention*" (IV: 220, 14–15; CSMK: 250; emphasis added). He thus finds again what Rimbaud, among other poets, will put down in several verses: "Through blue summer nights I will pass along paths, / Pricked by wheat, trampling short grass: / Dreaming, I will feel coolness underfoot, / Will let breezes bathe my bare head. // Not a word, not a thought: / Boundless love will surge through my soul, / And I will wander far away,

---

62. Respectively, *Treatise of Man*, XI: 184, 27–31; Hall, 96; *Passions of the Soul*, §21, XI: 345, 2–5; CSM I: 336, trans. lightly modified; and To Elizabeth, 6 October 1645, IV: 311, 5–8; CSMK: 270–71 [the English translations render "*nonchalamment*" as "idly"]. These two terms "relaxation" and "nonchalance" could respond to Aristotle's ἀνάπαυσις, which suspends the effort of work and of preoccupations (*Nicomachean Ethics* IV.14, 1127b33 and 1128b3; X.6, 1176b34ff.; *Politics* VIII.3, 1337a39ff., and *Rhetoric* I.11, 1370a11).

63. *Passions of the Soul*, §21, XI: 345, 1; CSM I: 336; similarly "fortuitous movement of the spirits," §26, XI: 348, 12–13; CSM I: 338.

64. See *Passions of the Soul*, §§34–39.

a vagabond / In Nature—as happily as with a woman."[65] Who can think in this way about nothing, not even about oneself, and nevertheless experience oneself thus purely as united to self, as pure interactive union of soul and body? Obviously the *meum corpus*. In *this sense*, the sense of primordial sensing as the self, Descartes has himself certainly also thought that the body thinks.

## §21. Meum corpus *and the Exception*

Yet, what does "not thinking of anything" mean? Is it simply a way of speaking, a metaphorical evocation of the indeterminacy of the knowledge of *meum corpus* by the ego of the union, which would remain, by comparison, a peripheral venture into the realm of knowledge, certainly less sure and less controllable, but still *de jure* ("*quod speciali quodam jure*—which by some special right," VII: 75, 30; CSM II: 52) a quasi-province of philosophy? The response to this question—the question of the limits of philosophy as the ego moves away from the center, the *res cogitans*, in order to venture to the furthest distance, the ego of the union as *meum corpus*—is not self-evident, so much must one precisely enter into the field of imprecision, of the indefiniteness of the limit. At least one should not underestimate the question. We will proceed by gradually juxtaposed comments.

First, one will admit that the union consists in an *experience of fact*. This means first of all, as for freedom, that one must admit it in its facticity, even and above all if we cannot comprehend it without a concept. Just as freedom, even when it is contradicted or threatened *from our finite rational point of view* by God's omnipotence, total causality, and providence, is imposed by fact and experientially on the *res cogitans*, in the same way the union of soul and body is imposed by fact and experientially on the *res cogitans*, despite the fact that it can be reduced neither to the modes of the *cogitatio* and to the sequence of reasons generating the deduction of ideas on the one hand (first primitive notion) nor to causality which models between them the measures set by the *Mathesis universalis* (according to *ordo et mensura*) on the other hand (second primitive notion). Descartes' final undertaking does not aim at explaining the union by a mechanism where thought and extension would find a common functioning, in contrast to his successors, who will rush to destroy themselves [*se rueront et se ruineront*] by imagining the mecha-

65. Arthur Rimbaud, *Rimbaud Complete*, trans. Wyatt Mason (New York: Modern Library, 2002), 11.

nisms governing by a desperate (and despairing) diplomacy the compromise of an interaction between two decidedly heterogeneous terms. This endeavor aims at describing, as far as that is possible, a fact of reason inconceivable by a construction of concepts. The primitive notion of union in this way takes up on its own behalf one of the fundamental characteristics of *naturae simplicissimae*, precisely experience. For their combinations (here those of the soul and the body in the union) "*a nobis cognosci, vel quia* experimur *quales sint, vel quia nos ipsi componimus*— are known by us either because we learn from *experience* what sort they are, or because we ourselves combine them."[66] Obviously because we do not ourselves compose the union (the opposite would be more correct), we must admit that we experience it; and because "experimur *quidquid sensu percipimus, quidquid ex aliis audimus, et generaliter quaecomque ad intellectum nostrum, vel aliunde perveniunt, vel ex sui ipsius contemplatione reflexa*—our *experience* consists of whatever we perceive by means of the senses, whatever we learn from others, and in general whatever reaches our intellect either from external sources or from its own reflexive self-contemplation,"[67] we must say that we experience via sensation (*sensu percipimus*). Now, as Descartes also specifies in 1627, "*intellectum a nullo unquam experimento decipi posse*—the intellect can never be deceived by any experience,"[68] provided it knows how to separate what it really perceives from what it believes it perceives and wrongly puts together with its real experience. In relation to the union, this argument indicates that the experience we have of it via sensation, which by definition cannot be broken down into its two terms (for the union precisely neither combines soul and body nor results from their combination, because it precedes it), thus never deceives us. Never deceiving us, the union thus has the rank of "the most certain and most obvious experience—*certissima et evidentissima experientia*."[69] We do not have to explain it, but describe it in order to use it correctly and maybe even morally.

Second, one will admit that the union, constituting a third primitive notion (and probably the first), remains *incomparable* to the other two. Incomparable, in the strict sense of the Cartesian vocabulary, means without comparison, without possible model—similar only to itself,

66. *Regulae*, Regula XII, X: 422, 24–25; CSM I: 46.

67. Ibid., X: 422, 25—423, 1; CSM I: 46–47.

68. Ibid., 423, 1–2; CSM I: 47.

69. To Arnauld, 29 July 1648, V: 222, 17–18; CSMK: 358, trans. modified. One can liken this facticity to the frequent recourse to the teaching of nature: "*Docet etiam natura*" (VII: 81, 1; see 81, 15, etc.; CSM II: 56).

without parallel, without explanatory model (except for the "comparison" with weightiness, which "limps")—and without explanatory argument: "*Quod autem mens, quae incorporea est, corpus possit impellere, nulla quidem ratiocinatio el comparatio ab aliis rebus petita, sed certissima et evidentissima experientia quotidie nobis ostendit; haec enim una est ex rebus per se notis, quas, cum volumus per alias explicare, obscuramus.*—That the mind, which is incorporeal, can set the body in motion is something which is shown to us not by any reasoning or comparison with other matters, but by the surest and plainest everyday experience. It is one of those self-evident things which we only make obscure when we try to explain them in terms of other things."[70] Once more, Descartes recovers at the end of the path a thesis from its beginning: "*Quamobrem hic de rebus nos agentes, nisi quantum ab intellectu percipiuntur, illas tantum simplices vocamus, quarum cognitio tam perspicua est et distincta, ut in plures magis distincte cognitas mente dividi non possint*—That is why we are concerned here with things only in so far as they are perceived by the intellect, we term 'simple' only those things which we know so clearly and distinctly that they cannot be divided by the mind into others which are more directly known."[71] Concerning the union, this implies that it could not and hence should not be conceived either as resorting to the first primitive notion and to the model of thought (as Leibniz will attempt it), or as being inspired by the second primitive notion on the model of causality (whether occasional or not, as Malebranche will do it), or by identifying the first two primitive notions and by assimilating the logical deduction of ideas to the causality of the modes of extension (as Spinoza will claim it), but only starting from itself. The union cannot be modeled according to extension; it should not be conceived according to the order of the *cogitatio*. For to separate it into other terms, to make it a composite result, would make it more obscure (or even would add obscurities to the two other notions) than its very fact, which is at the very least indisputably experienced. For the union, just like the sensation where we experience it, turns out to be *much* more vivid and expressive and even *in its own way* more distinct than the other two primitive notions. We still need to think this manner and this style, which form an exception to the manner and to the style of the two other primitive notions.

The union is experienced by a consciousness, but a *diminished* consciousness, because it is without memory: "*Aliud est esse conscios no-*

70. To Arnauld, 29 July 1648, V: 222, 15–20; CSMK: 358.
71. Regula XII, AT X: 418, 13–17; CSM I: 44.

*strarum cogitationum, eo tempore quo cogitamus, et aliud earum postea recordari; sic nihil in somniis cogitamus, quin eo ipso momento simus cogitationis nostrae conscii, quamvis statim ejus ut plurimum obliviscamur*—Being conscious of our thoughts at the time when we are thinking is not the same as remembering them afterwards. Thus, we do not have any thoughts in sleep without being conscious of them at the moment they occur; though commonly we forget them immediately."[72] Consciousness does not imply, in the case of sleep and maybe in other cases, the memory of that of which one has been conscious, even less the memory of having been conscious. This gap allows us to comprehend that the same can be true of the consciousness of the organic movements of the body moved by the soul; for although there is clearly a consciousness of thought in the state of union, this does not imply the consciousness of movements of the body: "*Verum autem est, nos non esse conscios illius modi, quo mens nostra spiritus animales in hos vel illos nervos immittit; iste enim modus non a mente sola, sed a mentis cum corpore unione dependet*—But it is true that we are not conscious of the manner in which our mind sends the animal spirits into particular nerves; for that depends not on the mind alone but on the union of the mind with the body" (V: 221, 30—222, 3; CSMK: 357). In other words, we are conscious of the action that produces the movement of my body *inasmuch* as it remains in the mind, as mode of the *cogitatio* of the will ("*sumus tamen conscii omnis ejus actionis* . . . quatenus . . . *est in mente*—we are conscious, however, of every action . . . *in so far as* such action is in the mind," 222, 3–5; CSMK: 357); but the detail and the "disposition" of these movements of the mind can very well never have the least consciousness ("*corporis configurationem, quam mens* potest ignorare—[the appropriate way] the body is constructed, of which the mind *may not be aware*," 222, 10–11; CSMK: 357). In the regime of union with the body, the soul (taken as *mens*, mind) certainly has "immediate"[73] consciousness of this union ("*unionem, cujus* sane *mens*

72. To Arnauld, 29 July 1648, V: 221, 26–30; CSMK: 357; in response to an objection in V: 214, 22–25.

73. Here is probably the place for giving its full import to the definition of the *cogitatio* set by the appendix of the Second Replies: "Cogitationes *nomine complector illud omne quod sic in nobis est, ut ejus immediate conscii simus. Ita omnes voluntatis, intellectus, imaginationis et sensuum operationes sunt cogitationes. Sed addidi* immediate, *ad excludenda ea quae ex iis consequuntur, ut* motus voluntarius cogitationem quidem pro principio habet, sed ipse tamen non est cogitatio—Thought. I use this term to include everything that is within us in such a way that we are *immediately* aware of it. Thus all the operations of

*conscia est*—the union . . . of which the mind is certainly conscious,"
222, 12; CSMK: 357), but not of the body of the union (except maybe
in mediated fashion). The knowledge, hence the consciousness, of the
union is never extended to a consciousness of the portion of extension
to which the *mens* finds itself united. Or, to say it by reversing the terms,
the mind, conscious of the union, also becomes conscious that the sensations that come to it from the "disposition" of its body do not come
from that of which it is conscious: "*quos [i.e., dolores] mens est conscia
non a se sola proficisci, nec ad se posse pertinere ex eo solo quod sit res
cogitans, sed tantum ex eo quod alteri cuidam rei extensae ac mobili
adjuncta sit*—The mind is aware that these sensations [of pain] do not
come from itself alone, and that they cannot belong to it simply in virtue
of its being a thinking thing; instead, they can belong to it only in virtue
of its being joined to something other than itself which is extended and
moveable."[74] The consciousness of the union thus remains a diminished
consciousness, which must admit at its margins "the existence of something sub-rational."[75]

Consequently, the union is finally defined by the facticity of an experience, comparable to no other and for a diminished consciousness.
As we have seen, it is essential for it neither to be able to let itself be
led back to the intelligibility that the two primitive notions assure it
nor to take up from them the corresponding *naturae simplicissimae*.
Accordingly, the union would mark a kind of extraterritoriality in regard to the central principles of Descartes' philosophy: not only does
it remain irreducible to the modeling and measures of extension by the
*Mathesis universalis*, but it is not inscribed in the chains of reasons of
the pure *cogitatio*. Yet how should one conceive and justify such an

---

the will, the intellect, the imagination and the senses are thoughts. I say 'immediately' so as to exclude the consequences of thoughts; a voluntary *movement*,
for example, originates in a thought but is not itself a thought" (VII: 160, 7–13;
CSM II: 113). This "voluntary movement" thus comes from thought (of the
will), but since as a movement it is conducted by the spirits and their "fibers," it
falls under the body and its organic "disposition," not under thought. The same
is true for the definition of the idea as "*cujuslibet cogitationis formam illam, per
cujus* immediatam perceptionem ipsius ejusdem cogitationis *conscius sum*—the
form of any given thought, *immediate perception of which* makes me aware *of
the thought*": it excludes images situated in corporeal imagination, enlisted in a
part of the brain ("*quatenus sunt in phantasia corporea, hoc es in parte aliqua
cerebri depictae*—in so far as these images are in the corporeal imagination, that
is, are depicted in some part of the brain"; 160, 21—161, 1; CSM II: 113).

74. *Principles of Philosophy* II, §2, VIII-1: 41, 18–21 = IX-2: 64; CSM I: 224.
75. Laporte, *Le Rationalisme de Descartes*, 254; see 220.

independence vis-à-vis the principles? Would Descartes *here* think without principle, without system? Concerning the system, the history of interpretation of Descartes' philosophy has ended up by admitting—we know that it was not without hesitations—that the paradigm of the system not only would remain foreign to Descartes but above all that it is manifestly unsuitable to his method or his metaphysics. Concerning the principle, it would be advisable to respect the caution of Descartes' position: questioned about the "first principle," he first underlines that "the word 'principle' can be taken in several senses"; illustrating this ambiguity immediately by distinguishing the logical sense from that which allows us to reach an existence ("a *common notion* so clear and so general that it can serve as a principle for proving the existence of all the beings, or entities, to be discovered later") and the ontic sense of existence allowing us to deduce others from it ("to look for a *being* whose existence is known to us better than that of any other"); in other words, in the first sense, the principle of contradiction, and in the second, "that our soul exists," the *ego cogito* as *ego sum, ego existo.* Yet this ambiguity does not erase the Cartesian indeterminacy about the principle: besides the fact that the first principle (the ego) does not coincide with the first cause (God), the very principle of a sole first principle, origin of any deduction, appears to be put in question by Descartes' concluding remark: "I will also add that one should not require the first principle to be such that all other propositions can be reduced to it and proved by it. It is enough if it is useful for the discovery of many, and if there is no other proposition on which it depends, and none which is easier to discover. For it may be that *there is no principle in the world at all* to which alone all things can be reduced."[76] A first principle remains a first principle *for us,* according to our finitude; it is thus not assumed to allow the deduction of *any* other propositions, but it is enough for it, in order to merit this primacy, to allow the deduction of several, without having to rely on any other principle; in other words, the primacy of this principle itself remains finite and logical in the frame of the creation of eternal truths; it is never a matter of God's absolute primacy, as if one had been able to identify the first principle, the first being, and the first cause. Here also, the opposition of Descartes' successors to him appears total.

It follows that there would be nothing absurd in envisioning that a "thing" could not let itself be "reduced" (hence also deduced from and produced by) a sole ("single") principle, if at least this principle

---

76. To Clerselier, June or July 1646, IV: 444, 26—445, 3; CSMK: 290; emphasis added.

remained finite. Now, all these conditions become reunited in the case of the consciousness of the union: it can be reduced to none of the first principles that can be envisioned within the frame of our finite rationality: neither the logical principles (for example, certain of the common *naturae simplicissimae*, X: 419, 22–29; CSM I: 45), nor the ego as pure *mens*, nor God, who is incomprehensible for us, can serve as first principle or provide a principle assuring the deduction of a clear and distinct idea of the union or of the *meum corpus*. In this sense, the union remains *beyond principle*. This goes back to thinking what its status as *primitive* notion really means: a notion without precedent, without precondition, in short without any principle other than itself. The union, outside of principle, hence attests no less than an *anarchy* in Cartesian thought: the search for first principle and the establishment of the principles of philosophy leads to the discovery of an exception irreducible to the principle of a unique and first principle—a first notion that can be conceived as principle only by sensory experience, *meum corpus*.

One can specify from which principles the anarchy of the union exempts itself if one takes into consideration the interpretation that I have proposed quite a while ago of Descartes' metaphysics as a doubled onto-theo-logy.[77] First, the onto-theo-logy of the *cogitatio*, where any being finds itself led back to the rank of an *ens ut cogitatum* (anticipating the formulations of the *metaphysica generalis* as *ontologia*, ratifying the equation of the *ens* as *cogitabile*) and where the supreme being (*ens summe perfectum*) redoubles the *ens ut cogitatum* by a *\*cogitatio sui*, in order to establish a *metaphysica specialis* of the *ego cogito*. Obviously, the union does not fall under this, because it allows itself to be known only by an experience that escapes the clarity and the distinction required and produced by the *intuitus*, the accomplished form of the *cogitatio*. And it does so in twofold fashion: on the one hand, the union does not let itself be thought as an object of the *Mathesis universalis*, modeled and configured in extension; on the other hand, it becomes accessible only by the *sensus*, which imposes on the *mens* a passive thought, from somewhere other than the active spontaneity of the *cogitatio* speaking to itself, and always against its wish (*me invito*); for if the union surfaces in the *cogitatio*, it is always by coming up against it from a ground that escapes it and constrains it to passivity; the union, like the sensation that practices it, is imposed on the *cogitatio* from below and becomes a *cogitatum*, so to say, only on the surface, attesting an unthinkable

77. It has already been almost three decades, in *On Descartes' Metaphysical Prism*, especially §10, 118–27.

irreducible, all the more irreducible as it defines maybe more the ego in its depth than the transparent exercise of the *cogitatio*. One would have to go so far as to say that not only is the union never reduced to an *ens ut cogitatum* and becomes an exception to the first *metaphysica generalis*, but above all it puts into question the *metaphysica specialis* by contesting that the *cogitatio* could be grounded on it alone and reach a *\*cogitatio sui* having the rank of first principle, grounded on itself.

Second, the onto-theo-logy of the *causa*, where any being finds itself led back to the rank of an *ens ut causatum* (anticipating here still on the formulations of the *metaphysica generalis* as science of causes producing and above all giving reason to effects, in accordance with the principle of sufficient reason) and where the supreme being (*ens summe potens*) doubles the *ens ut causatum* in a *causa sui*, in order to establish a *metaphysica specialis* of the *potentia infinita*. Obviously the union does not fall under this onto-theo-logy either. First, because between soul and body there is no causality, at least no causality that would remain intelligible to us: to understand the union consists not in establishing a causal link in the *meum corpus*, but instead in admitting its established fact, and, on the basis of this factical experience, in learning to manage the involuntary movements of the body of the "disposition" by the indirect and totally heterogeneous behaviors of thoughts (playing one passion against another, distracting or provoking one thought more than another, etc.); if the union can sometimes become thinkable and manageable for us, that will never be by the direct exercise of causality, unknown from the body to the soul, illusory from the soul to the body. In this way the union essentially exempts itself from the *metaphysica generalis* of the *ens ut causatum*. Yet could one not argue, in a second phase, that the union remains compatible with the *metaphysica specialis* of the *causa sui*? In fact, does its facticity not result directly from divine omnipotence or, what amounts to the same, the establishment of nature? It probably does, but this pure fact is not enough to validate a case of exercise of the principle of sufficient reason, because here the *causa totalis*, God, provides no reason for what it establishes: that God has created us according to the union attests really to its causality without conditions, but for all that does not provide reason for this union—at least it does not provide any reason for *us*, because the efficient cause *here* does not produce any intelligibility *for us*. Quite to the contrary, the establishment of the union by nature establishes the nonintelligibility at the core of our condition; and it even threatens in this way, as we have just suggested, the self-certainty of the *ego cogito*, for we experience the union as "without why"—and that is why it rattles the principle of sufficient reason, thus puts into question any *metaphysica specialis* of the *causa sui*.

The exception to a first principle that characterizes the third primitive notion, thus its anarchy, is very clearly manifested in its double exception to the two figures of the doubled onto-theo-logy of Cartesian metaphysics, as the first five Meditations (and their Replies) settle it in 1641. The union, henceforth characterized as the facticity of an experience, remains without possible comparison and is accessible only by a diminished consciousness, exempting itself from any first principle and irreducible to the figures of the doubled onto-theo-logy. Yet, if it resists the still irresistibly growing empire of metaphysics, does it still belong to philosophy, or does it come from a "beyond philosophy" (Alquié)?[78] This strange question would find maybe the outline of a response if we were to go back to our question from the beginning: what does "not thinking of anything" mean? To think of nothing—means to think of no *thing*, not even of a *res, ne rem*. Yet, we know henceforth in regard to the union that it is not a thing, neither a thing in extension (an object), nor a thing in thought (*cosa mentale*); for it does not coincide even with me, the ego, when it is known and defined as a *mens* purely and simply. The union can be experienced only in the *res cogitans* itself unfolded all the way to the *res sentiens* that senses and, thereby, feels itself. Such a feeling has nothing to do with a thing, neither of the world of extension, nor of the world of thought. The union is not a thing: it follows that thinking of nothing could be defined as the condition of possibility of a thought of the union. *To think the union would require us to think of nothing.* Yet, if philosophy consists, in its metaphysical expression, in thinking always and first of all what is, that is to say in thinking things *inasmuch as beings*, then to think the union inasmuch as it is not a thing would become possible and thinkable only by suspending the common use of philosophy understood as metaphysics of being. This is what Descartes, it seems, literally says: "That is why people *who never philosophize* and use only their senses have no doubt that the soul moves the body and that the body acts on the soul" (III: 692, 4–6; CSMK: 227). For at stake is "the union which everyone invariably experiences in himself without philosophizing" (III: 694, 1–2; CSMK: 228). To philosophize without philosophy, would that really be to philosophize?

78. Alquié, *La Découverte métaphysique*, 311.

# 5

## Union and Unity

*§22. The Question of Exception in the Replies*

As the exception of the union imposed itself only with difficulty on Descartes himself, one should not be surprised that it seemed almost unintelligible to the majority of his readers. The main reason for this difficulty or even reluctance has to do not only with the innovation of the *corpus meum*, but with the fact that the then dominant conceptual vocabulary—that of *metaphysica* in the process of scholastic consolidation—made its correct formulation almost impossible. Descartes was perfectly aware of this when he warned Regius, who was the first victim of this powerlessness, that *"mentem corpori realiter et substantialiter esse unitam, non per situm aut dispositionem . . . , sed per verum modum unionis, qualem vulgo omnes admittunt,* etsi nulli, qualis sit, explicent, *nec ideo etiam teneris explicare*—the mind is united in a real and substantial manner to the body. You must say that they are united not by position or disposition, as you assert in your last paper—for this too is open to objection and, in my opinion, quite untrue—but by a true mode of union, as everyone agrees, *though nobody explains what this amounts to*, and so you need not do so either."[1] Moreover,

1. To Regius, January 1642, III: 493, 4–10; CSMK: 206.

Descartes often respects this reservation: philosophy only has to note the union via experience and as an establishment of nature without having to explain it; its function would rather consist in describing it, establishing continuities between thoughts and movements, neither claiming to confuse them, nor linking them up directly by a univocal causal chain. Even so he does not hesitate to become more involved in the contemporary vocabulary, by speaking here even in his warning to Regius of a union *substantialiter*, in the mode of substance. Did Descartes have a particularly clear and distinct concept of substance available, to which he could have appealed in case of difficulty more than to any other in the metaphysical vocabulary? I take its opposite as established:[2] first challenged in the *Regulae*, the concept of *substantia* actually reappears only in marginal fashion in the *Meditations* and owes its supposedly systematic (but fundamentally aporetic) exposition in the *Principles of Philosophy* precisely to the desire to translate the new philosophy into a vocabulary henceforth considered ancient, which it essentially contradicts. Now, as I will argue, it is possible that nothing stigmatizes the semantic inadequacy of *substantia* more than the innovation of the *meum corpus* and of the union. One can piece together several of Descartes' attempts, either spontaneous or under pressure from objectors, at expounding the *meum corpus* in terms of *substantia* (hence with the *substantia completa*, the union *per se*, the union *substantialiter* or the single *forma substantialis*, etc.); but all of them quickly become disqualified, if just by the silent refusal to erect the union itself finally as a (third) *substantia*. The exception of the *meum corpus* is manifested by its irreducibility to the vocabulary of the *metaphysica* in the process of constitution, more specifically to the semantic of the *substantia*. That at least will be the issue at stake in this chapter.

Even so, one will not fail to object that from 1641 onward Descartes did most certainly appeal to the vocabulary of *substantia* in order to determine the terms of the union, thus arguably having excellent reasons for doing so. He certainly did have reasons, but one can dispute their excellence. The first commentary on the use of *substantia* in the Sixth Meditation appears in a response to Hobbes. With his customary simplifying dogmatism, Hobbes suggested that the thinking thing must be cor-

---

2. Based on previous work, *Sur l'ontologie grise de Descartes*, §§12–14, 71ff.; *On Descartes' Metaphysical Prism*, §13 and §15, 150–69 and 193–205; and "Substance and Subsistence: Suárez and the Treatise on *Substantia* in the *Principles of Philosophy* I, §51–§54," in *On the Ego and on God*, chapter V, 80–99.

poreal, under the pretext that *"subjecta enim omnium actuum videntur intelligi solummodo sub ratione corporea, sive sub ratione materiae—* the subject of any act can be understood only in terms of something corporeal or in terms of matter" (VII: 173, 16–18; CSM II: 122). Descartes corrects this with a distinction, without yet getting annoyed about it: "subjecta enim omnium actuum intelliguntur quidem sub ratione substantiae *(vel etiam, si lubet,* sub ratione materiae, *nempe Metaphysicae), non autem idcirco sub ratione corporum*—the subject of any act can be understood only in terms of substance (or even, if he insists, in terms of 'matter,' i.e. metaphysical matter); but it does not follow that it must be understood in terms of a body" (175, 11–14; CSM II: 124). In this way the concept of substance comes in for a polemical reason and in direct reference to the use of *metaphysica*: acts refer to a substance and not necessarily to the body. This appeal to simple Aristotelian orthodoxy nevertheless has an aim of Cartesian orthodoxy: any act refers to *"substantia cui insit*—a substance in which it inheres" (175, 27f.; 176, 12, 19–20; CSM II: 124, trans. lightly modified); but this substance in turn is defined by what we comprehend of it, by a concept defining the acts and modes in question; accordingly an act of thought must correspond to a thinking substance (or *subjectum*) that is in no way material or corporeal, except by giving up any distinct concept: *"Postquam vero duos distinctos conceptus istarum duarum substantiarum formavimus, facile est, ex dictis in sexta Meditatione, cognoscere an una et eadem sint, an diversae.*—Once we have formed two distinct concepts of these two substances, it is easy, on the basis of what is said in the Sixth Meditation, to establish whether they are one and the same or different" (176, 26–29; CSM II: 124). And, actually, that text really did mobilize the distinction between a *substantia intelligens* (78, 25; CSM II: 54) and a *substantia corporea* (79, 3–4, 19; CSM II: 55).[3] The term *substantia* is thus introduced and confirmed polemically in order to avoid Hobbes' abuse of an unfounded use of *materia*.

We must still assess the scope of such recourse to *substantia* in 1641. Several reasons come to limit its solidity and thus its authority.

(a) First, one must recall that the ego of the *cogito*, thus the primordial *res cogitans* (28, 20 and 34, 18), is described without appealing to the concept of *substantia*, which appears later only to prove the existence of God (moreover together with the so far unused principle of

---

3. In the same way as the principle of the distinction of the ideas of soul and body, recalled in VII: 176, 26–29; CSM II: 124, comes from VII: 78, 13–20; CSM II: 54.

causality): strictly speaking, the real substrate of the modes of the *cogitatio* thus has no need to be defined as a substance in order to be and to be distinctly known. In this case at least, the concept of *substantia* remains optional.[4]

(b) The *substantia* intervenes in fact in a decisive manner only in order to prove two existences, that of God in the Third Meditation, then that of material things or *alia corpora* in the Sixth Meditation; in the two cases, the proof requires connecting these substances (the infinite one of God and the finite one of material things) with the ideas that the ego has of them via efficient causality. Yet, as we have seen (above, §4), as much as efficient causality does not raise a problem between the infinite thinking substance of God and the finite thinking substance of the ego, so much does it raise a difficulty between the finite thinking substance of the ego and the potential substances whose extended character can be neither displayed nor guaranteed by the ambiguity of efficiency. Moreover, Descartes will draw the conclusion from this in lucid fashion: substance, as *res existens*, "does not of itself have any effect on us—*hoc solum per se nos non afficit*" (*Principles of Philosophy* I, §52; CSM I: 210). A conclusion that, in all rigor, one must correct: for only the *extended* substance does not affect us, because, as we have seen, the *cogitatio* itself senses and senses itself: "*Sentire, idem est hic quod cogitare*" (I, §9 ["thinking is here identified with sensing"; CSM I: 195]).

(c) More generally, material things seem to suffer from two other impeding weaknesses, which compromise their status as substance. On the one hand, in principle and by virtue of the *natura simplicissima* of movement, they turn out to be incapable of stability, thus of a true substantiality that would be neither provisional nor variable; in particular, they do not reach individuation, neither through (changing) matter nor through form (devoid of its rank of essence). In Cartesian terms this means the suppression of any substantial form (see below, §25) and opens the field to Leibniz' inexorable critique. On the other hand, the reservation that weighs on any finite (created) substance—that is to say, that it would always require God's ordinary assistance, who alone strictly speaking merits the title of substance (*Principles of Philosophy* I, §51)—is especially valid for material things. The *res cogitans* itself is in some way unconditionally each time and as long as it thinks, even when it is mistaken or deluded. The terms of the union and thus the union

---

4. See my remarks in *On Descartes' Metaphysical Prism*, §11 and §13, 128–42 and 150–69, in *On the Ego and on God*, chapter 1, §6, and chapter 5, §1, 23–26 and 80–83, and in "Descartes hors sujet."

itself resist the vocabulary and the semantic of substance for these three reasons (that the *res cogitans* has no need to be defined by the *substantia* in order to be; that the causal demonstration does not prove the materiality of the cause of the corporeal ideas; that the corporeal things satisfy the permanence and the individuation of the *substantia* only in a very approximate fashion).

Therefore, what does Descartes hope to gain by situating the terms of the union or even the union itself within the horizon of substantiality? One could invoke the needs of the construction of a proof for the existence of material things, but besides its weaknesses (see above, §4) this proof contributes nothing to the essential discovery, that of *meum corpus*, which is not a matter of extension (see above, §§8–10). One could maybe evoke at least one argument in favor of the immortality of the soul: if the *mens* is a substance, it is absolutely distinguished from the body, which is a different substance; now death, assuming one could define it, consists in a change of form or the division of a body; thus a matter of a variation of accidents of a different substance. Now, first of all, the variation of a mode of a substance is not enough for annihilating this same substance (a dead body still is an extended substance that remains); and the variation of a mode of extension can still less annihilate a distinct substance, in this case a nonextended one, a *res cogitans;* and besides we have "no convincing evidence or precedent to suggest that any substance can perish—*Nec . . . ullum argumentum, vel exemplum, quod persuadeat aliquam substantiam posse interire*" (VII: 153, 23–25; CSM II: 109). This argument remains all the same purely logical (*logikos*, which makes it already better than the majority of the objections made by Mersenne), because it assumes to be already proven that bodies *could* be substances by full right (which is strictly speaking not the case) and that the *res cogitans* itself *should* be one (which is according to the letter not the case). And above all, it is absolutely not at all a matter of the union here.

Yet the attraction of the union by the vocabulary of the *substantia* will lead the debate into a problematic direction and probably a dead end one. It all comes from one of Arnauld's objections that is ordinary enough (it resonates with others by Hobbes and Gassendi): he notes that the distinction of body and soul via the irreducibility of their respective modes assumes that we would have a "complete and adequate knowledge—*notitia completa et adaequata*" (VII: 201, 20–21; CSM II: 141, trans. lightly modified) of them; short of which the inadequacy of the notion of the body, for example, could cause us to exclude a still open possibility—that the body could think; yet this perfect knowledge remains God's privilege. Descartes responds by distinguishing adequate knowledge that would contain "absolutely all the properties which are in the thing which is the object of knowledge—*omnes . . . proprietates quae sunt in re cognita*" and that "God alone—*solus Deus*" can have (220, 8–11; CSM II: 155) from the knowledge that is only complete (*completa*, 221, 14; CSM II: 156). For complete knowledge, the only one accessible to a finite mind that cannot measure the "infinite power of God—*infinita Dei potestas*" (220, 20; 155), requires only that one not render a notion inadequate by an abstraction that would contradict the clear and distinct idea in it; such is the case when one depends on the idea of *res extensa*, which does not clearly and distinctly comprehend the mode of the *cogitatio*, but only those of *figura et motus*. The distinction between soul and body demands only complete notions, without confusion, neither subtraction nor addition of their properties through arbitrary abstraction by the understanding. Descartes concludes from this that *the same* is true for the distinction of substances, which the complete knowledge of their modes is enough to ensure, it being understood that we cannot know the substances directly as such and without the modes: "*Neque enim substantias immediate cognoscimus, ut alibi notatum est, sed tantum ex eo quod percipiamus quasdam formas sive attributa, quae cum alicui rei debeant inesse ut existant, rem illam cui insunt vocamus* substantiam.—We do not have immediate knowledge of substances, as I have noticed elsewhere. We know them only by perceiving certain forms or attributes which must inhere in something if they are to exist; and we call the thing in which they inhere a 'substance.'"[5] In this way, substance is *also* made known by the *complete* knowledge of its attributes: "*me per rem completam nihil aliud intelligere, quam substantiam indutam iis formis sive attributis, quae sufficiunt ut ex iis agnoscam ipsam esse substantiam*—by a 'complete thing' I simply mean a substance endowed with the forms or attributes which enable me to recognize that it is a substance" (222, 1–4; CSM II: 156). A substance is thus *also* known by a *complete* notion, that of its attributes (thus of its modes). Consequently, as by definition the notion of a substance implies "*quod per se, hoc est absque ope ullius alterius substantiae possit existere*—that it can exist by itself, that

---

5. VII: 222, 5–9; CSM II: 156. Referring to the distinction already made in the Third Replies, VII: 175, 22—176, 29; CSM II: 124, and confirmed by the Fifth Replies, 360, 2–6; CSM II: 249.

is without the aid of any other substance" (226, 3–5; CSM II: 159),[6] there should be only *complete* substances here, except via abstraction.[7] Otherwise, "*mihi contradictorium videri, ut sint substantiae, hoc est, res per se subsistentes, et simul incompletae, hoc est, per se subsister non valentes*—I find it self-contradictory that they should be substances, that is, things which subsist on their own, and at the same time incomplete, that is, not possessing the power to subsist on their own" (222, 17–20; CSM II: 156–57).

From now on, with the completeness of the notion being identified with the subsistence of substance by itself, the question of the union *itself* will be able to be raised in terms of substantiality: accordingly one will say that substances that are in themselves complete and autarchic are never incomplete, *except when* one refers them to a different substance ("*sed tantum* quatenus referentur *ad aliquam aliam substantiam, cum qua* unum per se componunt—it is incomplete in so far *as it is referred* to some other substance in conjunction with which it forms something which is *a unity in its own right*," 222, 22–24; CSM II: 157). For example, the hand becomes an incomplete substance "*cum refertur*—when it is referred" to the whole body of which it is a gripping

6. "*cum unaquaeque ex ipsis absque alia potest existere*—when each of them can exist apart from the other" (Second Set of Replies, VII: 162, 11–12; CSM II: 114). See "*Per substantiam nihil aliud intelligere possumus, quam rem quae ita existit, ut nulla alia re indigeat ad existendum*—By substance we can understand nothing other than a thing which exists in such a way as to depend on no other thing for its existence" (*Principles of Philosophy* I, §51, VIII-1: 24, 21–23; CSM I: 210); and first "*substantiam, sive . . . rem quae per se apta est existere*—a substance, or . . . a thing capable of existing independently" (Third Meditation, VII: 44, 22–23; CSM II: 30).

7. The formal distinction proceeds by such an abstraction and thus has no bearing on the *entia incompleta*: "*sufficere quidem ut unum ab alio distincte et seorsim concipiatur per abstractionem intellectus rem* inadaequate *concipientis*—It is sufficient for this kind of distinction that one thing be conceived distinctly and separately from another by an abstraction of the intellect which conceives the thing *inadequately*" (First Set of Replies, VII: 120, 19–21; CSM II: 85–86). This is confirmed by: "So, to tell whether my idea has been made incomplete or *inadaequata*/inadequate by an abstraction of my mind, I merely look to see whether I have derived it, not from some thing outside myself which is more complete, but *per abstractionem intellectus*/by an intellectual abstraction from some other, richer or more complete idea which I have in myself. This intellectual abstraction consists in my turning my thought away from one part of the contents of this richer idea the better to apply it to the other part with greater attention." To Gibieuf [?], 10 January 1642, III: 474, 20—475, 5; CSMK: 201–2 [dated 19 January 1642 in the translation].

part; but it remains a complete substance, "*cum sola spectatur*—when it is considered on its own" (222, 25–27; CSM II: 157).[8] Yet such a reference remains in itself without any ontic, hence real, import demonstrated; henceforth the quasi-union that it could provide would not abolish the ontic completeness of substances in presence (the hand, the body), which remain always independent, as substances must, because "it is of the nature of substances that they should mutually exclude one another—*haec enim est natura substantiarum, quod sese mutuo excludant*" (227, 9–10; CSM II: 159). Thus, in the hypothesis of a union between substances or that which would take their place, this union would inevitably become accidental. This is how the trap of the accidental interpretation of the union is put into place as an obligatory result of its interpretation in terms of *substantia*.

### §23. *Regius and the* ens per accidens

Regius unites all the skills to be caught in this trap. As professor of medicine but not directly of philosophy at the new university of Utrecht, he could but take the contemporary vocabulary of *metaphysica* for granted without assessing its limitations. Too preoccupied with positive theses in an ontic region, he wanted to delay no further from critiquing that vocabulary. To the contrary, as one of the oldest devotees of Cartesian thought in the United Provinces (and elsewhere, considering the encounter dates to 1638), he was able to imagine that he comprehended its teachings as well as or even better than the author himself, simplifying them, radicalizing them, and, finally, distorting them. If one adds a true polemical talent to this mixture of deficiency and self-importance, it becomes almost predictable that Regius would stumble on the substantial aporia of the union and in this way make it manifest. In an argument made on 18 December 1641, he formulated (through the intermediary of the student Henri Van Loon) a thesis that sets down the aporia: "VIII. Forma specialis *est mens humana, quia per eam cum forma generali in materia corporea homo est, id quod est. Haec ad formam generalem seu materialem nullo modo potest referri: quoniam ipsa (utpote substantia incorporea) nec est corpus, nec ex motu aut quiete, magnitudine, situ*

---

8. See: "*Sic homo vestitus considerari potest, ut quid compositum ex homine et vestibus; sed vestitum esse, respectu hominis, est tantum modus, quamvis vestimenta sint substantia*—Thus a man who is dressed can be regarded as a compound of a man and clothes. But with respect to the man, his being dressed is merely a mode, although clothes are substances." *Comments on a Certain Broadsheet*, VIII-2: 351, 13–16; CSM I: 299.

*aut figura partium oriri potest. IX. Ex hac [i.e., humana mente] et cor-pore non fit unum ens per se, sed per accidens, cum singula sint* substan-tiae perfectae seu completae. *X. Cum autem dicuntur incompletae, hoc intelligendum est ratione compositi, quod ex harum unione oritur.—*VIII. The special form is the human mind, because, with a general form in a corporeal matter, the human is what he is through it. IX. It [i.e., the special form] can in no way be related to a general or a material form, because it is not itself (as incorporeal substance)[9] a body, nor can it be born from movement, rest, size, position, or the form of parts. What is produced starting from it [i.e., the human mind] and from the body is not one by itself, but by accident, because *each of* [these two] *substances is perfect and complete. X.* When one calls them all the same incomplete, one must understand this in terms of the composition born from their union."[10] Descartes rapidly came to learn of this interpreta-tion and deplored it: "In your theses you say that a human being is an *ens per accidens.* You could scarcely have said anything harder that would be more objectionable and provocative."[11] The violence of this thesis results from at least two initial misinterpretations: (i) if one be-gins by thinking the union starting by combining two preexisting terms (against its correct meaning as a *primitive* notion, which is therefore conceived only starting from itself and from it alone, according to a new beginning); (ii) if one then considers the mind and the body as substances, and these substances as quite obviously and by definition complete substances; (iii) then the union itself can only be conceived as an accidental (*per accident*) conjunction between elements that remain each *subsistens per se.* The "hard" and false conclusion results from the double error of misunderstanding the primitive character of the union and of thinking the other two terms as substances, thus as perfect and complete entities, irreducible to a real unification *per se.* In this way,

9. The same formulation "*Anima rationalis est substantia incorporea . . . a corpore sit distincta*" is found in the *Physiologia sive cognitio sanitatis* I, 1, §18, which appeared in Utrecht in 1641, the same year as the *Disputatio medica,* republished by Erik-Jan Bos, *The Correspondence between Descartes and Hen-ricus Regius* (Utrecht: Utrecht University, Publications of the Department of Philosophy—Zeno, 2002), 210.

10. *Disputatio medica de illustribus aliquot quaestionibus physiologicis* III, art. 8–10 (Utrecht: 1641), without pagination. Cited in Theo Verbeek, *Descartes and the Dutch: Early Reactions to Cartesian Philosophy, 1637–1650* (Car-bondale: Southern Illinois University Press, 1991), 105; citation completed by Erik-Jan Bos, *The Correspondence between Descartes and Henricus Regius,* 93 (emphasis added).

11. To Regius, December 1641, III: 460, 1–4; CSMK: 200; trans. modified.

Regius' thesis amasses all the misinterpretations, making it impossible to think the *meum corpus* and installing the paradigm of its inevitable misunderstanding in the vocabulary of *metaphysica*.

Faced with this conceptual and political disaster, Descartes first contemplates resorting to escape tactics, to denials. He proposes at least three of them to Regius, who, to my knowledge, will not use any of them.

(a) One could maintain that *per accidens* here did not really mean *by accident*, but only that incomplete substances behave among themselves *like* accidents, without being themselves accidents: "*Vocamus enim accidens, omne id quod adest vel abest sine subjecti corruptione, quamvis forte, in se spectatum, sit substantia, ut vestis est accidens homini. Sed te non idcirco dixisse* hominem esse ens per accidens, *et satis ostendisse, in decima thesi, te intelligere illum esse ens per se. Ibi enim dixisti animam et corpus, ratione ipsius, esse substantias incompletas; et ex hoc quod sint incompletae, sequitur illud quod componunt, esse ens per se.*—For the term 'accident' means anything which can be present or absent without its possessor ceasing to exist—though perhaps some accidents, considered in themselves, may be substances, as clothing is an accident with respect to a human being. Tell them that in spite of this you did not say *that a human being is an ens per accidens*, and you showed sufficiently, in your tenth thesis, that you understood it to be an *ens per se*. For there you said that the body and the soul, in relation to the whole human being, are incomplete substances; and it follows from their being incomplete that what they constitute is an *ens per se*" (III: 460, 14–22; CSMK: 200).[12] Obviously, this commentary serves only to reinforce the ambiguity: Are soul and body (complete) substances or incomplete

12. It is still in this way that Descartes himself presents Regius' controversial thesis in 1647 in order to distance himself from it: "*vocando scilicet* ens per accidens *id omne quod ex duabus substantiis plane diversis constaret, nec ideo negando unionem substantialem qua mens corpori conjungitur, nec utriusque partis aptitudinem naturalem ad istam unionem, ut patebat ex eo quod statim postea subjunxissent*: illas substantias dici incompletas, ratione compositi quod ex earum unione oritur; *adeo ut nihil in ipsis posset reprehendi, nisi forsan modus loquendi minus in scholis usitatus*—Certainly, by describing as contingent being everything that consists of divergent substances, nor therefore by denying the substantial union by which the mind is joined to the body, nor the natural aptitude of either part to that union, so that it subsisted from that which they steadily joined afterwards: I call them incomplete in substance, by reason of the compound that arose from their union; so that nothing can be grasped in itself except perhaps as a manner of speaking that is less used in the schools" (To Dinet, VII: 585, 22—586, 2).

(nonsubstances)? Are they simply substances? Is the union a combination? In this way, the real questions remain all the more obscured.

(b) One could also plead guilty outright and abandon the "hard" formulation: "*Sed quia verbum, ens per accidens, eo sensu [i.e., illum esse compositum ex duabus rebus realiter distinctis] non usurpatur in scolis, idcirco longe melius est . . . ut aperte fatearis te illum scolae terminum non recte intellexisse, quam ut male dissimules; ideoque, cum de re plane idem quod alii sentires, in verbis tantum discrepasse. Atque omnino ubicumque occurret occasio, tam privatim quam publice, debes profiteri te creder hominem esse* verum ens per se, non autem per accidens, *et mentem corpori realiter et substantialer esse unitam.*—But the expression *ens per accidens* is not used in that sense [namely as a composite of two really distinct things] by the scholastics. Therefore, if you cannot use the explanation which I suggested in a previous letter . . . then it is much better to admit openly that you misunderstood this scholastic expression than to try unsuccessfully to cover the matter up. You should say that fundamentally you agree with the others and that your disagreement with them was merely verbal. And whenever the occasion arises in public and in private, you should give out that you believe that a human being is *a true ens per se, and not an ens per accidens*, and that the mind is united in a real and substantial manner to the body" (III: 492, 20—493, 5; CSMK: 206). This withdrawal into the middle of nowhere obviously does not fundamentally resolve anything: What does a being by itself mean, a substantial unity between terms for which one does not decide whether they are or are not complete substances?

(c) There remains a final ruse, entirely *ad hominem* (referring to the theologian Voetius) and nevertheless, in a sense, perfectly Cartesian in intention:[13] "*majorisque est momenti ad refutandos illos qui animas mortales putant, docere istam distinctionem partium in homine, quam docere unionem; majorem me gratiam initurum esse sperabam a Theologis, dicendo hominem esse* ens per accidens, *ad designandam istam distinctionem, quam sit, respiciendo ad partium unionem, dixissem illum esse* ens per se.—But many more people make the mistake of thinking that the soul is not really distinct from the body than make the mistake

13. See the "Letter to the Dean and the Doctors of the Faculty of Theology at the Sorbonne," where Descartes promises that after him "*nemoque amplius erit in mundo, qui vel Dei existentiam, vel realem humanae animae a corpore distinctionem ausit in dubium revocare*—there will be no one left in the world who will dare to call into doubt either the existence of God or the real distinction between the human soul and body" (VII: 6, 13–16; CSM II: 6).

of admitting their distinction and denying their substantial union, and in order to refute those who believe souls to be mortal it is more important to teach the distinctness of parts in a human being than to teach their union. And so I thought I would please the theologians more by saying that a human being is an *ens per accidens*, in order to make the distinction, than if I said that he is an *ens per se*, in reference to the union of the parts" (III: 508, 27—509, 2; CSMK: 209). But this hierarchy between the union (less important theologically) and the distinction (more important theologically) first of all has no strict philosophical justification; then it does not resolve whether and how one can pass from one point of view to the other; finally, it explains nothing about the concept of the union itself. These tactical maneuvers by Descartes were not followed by Regius, most probably less through lack of prudence than through confidence in his positions and persistence in getting them to prevail.

One must thus now ask: Did Descartes ever formulate a fundamental (and not just tactical) argument to correct the union's accidental nature, as Regius proclaimed it (for want of explaining it)? It appears that he formulated at least one, on two occasions, in very similar terms. First in mid-December 1641: "*Objici tantum potest,* non esse accidentarium humano corpori, quod animae conjungatur, *sed ipsissimam ejus naturam; quia, corpore habente omnes dispositiones requisitas ad animam recipiendam, et sine quibus non est proprie humanum corpus, fieri non potest sine miraculo, ut anima illi non uniatur; atque etiam* non esse accidentarium animae, quod juncta sit corpori, *sed tantum accidentarium esse illi post mortem, quod a corpore sit sejuncta.*—It may be objected that *it is not natural for the human body to be joined to the soul*, but its very nature; because if the body has all the dispositions required to receive a soul, which it must have to be strictly a human body, then short of a miracle it must be united to a soul. Moreover, it may be objected that *it is not the soul's being joined to the body*, but only its being separated from it after death, *which is accidental* to it" (III: 460, 25—461, 6; CSMK: 200). Then, a month later, in January 1642: "*Sed quatenus homo in se totus consideratur, omnino dicimus ipsum esse unum Ens* per se, *et non per accidens; quia unio, qua corpus humanum et anima inter se conjunguntur, non est ipsi accidentaria, sed essentialis, cum homo sine ipsa non sit homo.*—But if a human being is considered in himself as a whole, we say of course that he is a single *ens per se*, and not *per accidens*; because *the union* which joins a human body and soul to each other *is not accidental to a human being, but essential, since a human being without it is not a human being*" (III: 508, 19–23;

CSMK: 209; emphasis added).[14] This twofold formulation, apparently without effect on Regius, deserves a careful commentary.

First, it never uses the problematic of substance, whether complete or incomplete, in this way extracting the question of the union from the vocabulary of *metaphysica* (here designated as that of the School), in which, under the influence of also radically scholastic objections from Hobbes, Mersenne, and Arnauld, then finally followed by Regius as simple sidekick, Descartes had allowed himself to get bogged down. In one go, he returns to the vocabulary of *meum corpus* and of *me totum* from the Sixth Meditation, even anticipating the "body of a man" and the "extended primitive notion by itself," in accordance with the vocabulary from the correspondence with Mesland and Elizabeth. In other words, any solution to the aporia in which Regius is stuck cannot come from a simple correction of formulations drawn from *substantia* and from its compositions; one must retrace one's steps (or jump ahead without turning around) by breaking with the language of substance, of accidents, of attributes, of *per se*, and so forth.

Second, the accidental nature becomes reversed: it no longer starts from substances, as a response to their potential (actually contradictory) incompleteness, but from the union itself posited at the outset, no longer obtained (or rather missed) at the end. One no longer asks whether the soul is accidental to the body or whether the body is accidental to the soul, in order to obtain a nonunion in the end; one wonders whether, the union being considered first (and hence starting from itself alone, as a truly primitive notion), it is accidental to the *mens* or accidental to the body. It is obviously not so *on the condition* of thinking the soul and the body each time *starting from the union*: the soul here means the soul of the union, that is to say the *res cogitans* that thinks *also* passively, and thus senses, later also called extended in a sense; while the body hence means the *corpus humanum* that will be named later the *body of a man* (in a sense indivisible) and that extends the *meum corpus* distinguished from the *alia corpora*, simple material things. Two years before showing it explicitly to Elizabeth, Descartes here makes the theoretical gesture that would allow him to *begin* with the union, against the interlocutors who stubbornly seek to end with it by beginning with substance (and accident); he really establishes the union as a *primitive* notion.

14. It seems to me that one must insist on developing the formulation "*ipsum esse unum Ens per se*" by translating *unum* twice: a being by itself, which is a unified being, according to the convertibility of transcendentals, which causes a being that really exists to be truly one.

Finally, and above all, the union can become a new point of departure, primitive and without other presupposition than its unified ipseity, in short an "*ipsum . . . unum Ens* per se" having available an *ipsissima natura*, only because the *corpus humanum* ensures finally and definitively its unity to the *mens*; in fact, ipseity comes to the ego only by and in the union of the "*meum corpus, sive potius me totum*—my body, or rather my whole self" (VII: 81, 24–25; CSM II: 56). Even more: a question remained without reply in the Second Meditation, which asked: "*Quidnam igitur antehac me esse putavi? Hominem scilicet. Sed quid est homo? Dicamne animal rationale? Non.*—What then did I formerly think I was? A man. But what is a man? Shall I say 'a rational animal'? No" (VII: 25, 25–27 = IX-1: 20; CSM II: 17). It finds now its response, the human appears as a *homo in se totus* because the *mens* is identified (with) itself in the essential and nonaccidental union, which gives it a *meum corpus*, a *corpus humanum* without which it would not be the *mens* of a human (but maybe that of an angel); without union, no *res cogitans* configured in all its modes, sensing and passive thought included; without union, no human body, but also no human thought; in short, without union, no response to the question "What is a human?" "because without it a human would not be a human—*cum homo sine ipsa non sit homo.*"

The body does not think, except under the heading of *corpus humanum* taken on in the union. The *res cogitans* would not think if it did not also think passively, thus it would not think truly and completely in all of its modes, if it did not also think in the union.

## §24. The ens per se, Suárez, and Descartes

And certainly Descartes, who had supported him as long as possible, ends by admitting that Regius had not only displayed imprudence in 1641, but above all, starting from the 1646 *Fundamenta Physices*, had warped Descartes' positions: "But the worst is that while in matters of physics he has followed closely whatever he thought to be in accordance with my views (though in some places he has made serious mistakes even about this), he has done just the opposite in matters of metaphysics."[15] His deviation and then final rupture in fact concern "metaphysics,"[16] where Descartes actually will have no disciple: "*nullos*

---

15. To Mersenne, 5 October 1646, IV: 510, 27—511, 2; CSMK: 296.

16. See: "Regarding the book of M. le Roy [i.e., Regius], it does not contain a word, having to do with metaphysics, that would not be directly contrary to

*unquam discipulos habui, nullos quaesivi, sed potius fugi*—I have never had any students, I have never sought any; rather I have fled them."[17] In what sense? In fact, if Regius is no less of a metaphysician than Descartes, he is so in a different way, or even more so, but without really noticing it and consequently in a more dogmatic fashion. Gauging Regius' metaphysical choices requires that one single out three of his texts, marking an equal number of discrepancies.

In 1641, when the *Disputatio medica* launches the thesis of human unity *per accidens*, Regius clearly forces Descartes to enter into a debate for which the terms are not immediately suitable for his teaching of the union.[18] As we have seen (above, §23), Descartes condemns the thesis of his student in private and, for the public, tries to soften its excess and blunt its point. Yet, because he finds himself on the terrain of the *metaphysica* and its vocabulary, he agrees once more as he did in the Replies to respond within the terms of the polemic by formulating another possible interpretation of the union *per se* in favor of the union *per accidens*. "*Utque appareat, id quod est ens per se, fieri posse per accidens, nunquid mures generantur sive fiunt per accidens ex sordibus? Et tamen sunt entia per se.*—That something which is an *ens per se* may yet come into being *per accidens* is shown by the fact that mice are generated, or come into being, *per accidens* from dirt, and yet they

---

my opinions" (To Huygens, 5 October 1646, IV: 517, 16–18; untranslated in CSMK); and "You are right in supposing that I do not share Regius' opinion [that the mind is a corporeal principle, or indeed his view that we know nothing except by appearance]; for in my writings I have said exactly the opposite" (To Mersenne, 23 November 1646, IV: 566, 13–17; CSMK: 301 [bracketed part of quote not included by Marion]). This works just fine for Regius who writes quite insolently: "And, to hide nothing from you, several people here are convinced that you have discredited your [natural] philosophy a lot by publishing your metaphysics" (To Descartes, 23 July 1645, IV: 255, 14–17).

17. To Voetius, VIII-2: 20, 6–7; untranslated in CSM/CSMK.

18. "If Descartes does not shy away from using the language of the 'school,' it is still the case that to my knowledge the sequence *ens per se/accidents*, which he inherits from Regius, appears nowhere else than in the texts linked to the Utrecht controversy," as Gilles Olivo rightly underlines in "L'homme en personne. Descartes, Suarez et la question de ens per se," in Theo Verbeek, ed., *Descartes et Regius. Autour de l'Explication de l'esprit humain* (Amsterdam: Rodopi, 1993), 71 and 76. On Regius' metaphysics, see Ferdinand Hallyn, "La *Philosophia Naturalis* de Regius et l'écriture athée," in Antony McKenna, Pierre-François Moreau, Frédéric Tinguely, eds., *Libertinage et philosophie au XVIIe siècle* (Saint-Étienne: Publications de l'Université de Saint-Étienne, 2005).

are *entia per se.*"[19] This argument refers first to a distinction by Thomas Aquinas: the pair *per se/per accidens* concerns the modes of predication, but cannot be superimposed on the difference between *ens per se (subsistens)*, known as substance, and the *ens per accidens*; in this way a substance can subsist by itself (*a white man*) and nevertheless be said to be accidental (*white* happening to *this man*); and, conversely, white, which comes as an accident to a substance, remains *in itself* white, for if whiteness is *per accidens* for the substance, it is *per se* for itself.[20] Suárez takes this difference up more clearly: "[The set] *per se* and *per accidens* is here not said according to the mode of being (*ratione essendi*) that opposes *per se* and *in alio*, a meaning according to which only substance is *per se*, everything else being said by accident, or rather accidental; no, [the set] *per se* and *per accidens* is said in relation to the unity (*in ordine ad unitatem*)."[21] It follows that any simple term (satisfying its definition and its essence) is by itself, even when it is incomplete (soul, as form) or abstract accident (whiteness), that is, the first paradox that an accident can be by itself.[22] But Suárez goes further: even a composite being can be one *per se*, for example if incompleteness (the lack of substantiality, of substrate, or of *suppositum* in a form or essence) demands intrinsically another term of the union; this is the case for the union of form to the corresponding unformed matter;[23] a fortiori it is the case for the

19. To Regius, December 1641, III: 460, 22–25; CSMK: 200; confirmed *almost* literally (if *substantialis* is equivalent to *per se*) by a well-meaning presentation to Dinet of Regius' thesis: "*vocando scilicet* ens per accidens *id omne quod ex duabus substantiis plane diversis constaret nec ideo negando* unionem substantialem *qua mens corpori conjugitur, nec utriusque partis aptitudinem naturalem ad istam unionem*—certainly, by describing as contingent being everything that consists of divergent substances, nor therefore by denying the substantial union by which the mind is joined to the body, nor the natural aptitude of either part to that union" (VII: 585, 22–26; untranslated in CSM II). It seems to me that these texts permit us to confirm that Descartes was informed about the medieval distinctions between being *per se* or *(per) accidens* on the one hand, and, on the other, the question of the unity *per se* or *per accidens*, as Olivo shows very fittingly ("L'homme en personne," 72–79), which I will complete.

20. See *In XII libros metaphysicorum Aristotelis expositio* V, 9, n. 885, ed. Cathalla (Turin: 1964), 237.

21. Suárez, *Disputatio metaphysica* IV, s. 3, n. 3, in *Opera Omnia* (Paris: Vives, 1861), XXV: 126.

22. "*hoc modo quodlibet accidens in abstracto sumptum ea consideratione est ens per se*—in this way, the contingent topic that is taken in the abstract by this consideration is being per se" (ibid., n. 7, 127).

23. Ibid., n. 8, 127–28.

human: "In fact, who would say that the human is not a being by itself? This can be proven a posteriori, for all the parts of this kind all need each other and cannot be maintained *per se* separately in any way or at least not for very long. This indicates that all are in their kind incomplete beings and are ordered *per se* to make up a certain being. This being, inasmuch as put together in this way, is a being *per se* and one *per se*."[24] That is, the second paradox of unity *per se* of two incomplete beings, which were nevertheless as beings as such *per se*, but of which the *ratio unitatis* does not coincide with the *ratio essendi*. Finally, the third paradox, even if one sticks with being one *per accidens*, one must here distinguish three cases: being one simply by aggregation (*per aggregationem*), gathering together several other beings without order or real unity; then *ens per accidens* in the strict sense, gathering together several other beings without physical union, but with an order (an army, a city, etc.); and finally the case of a "being composed of a substance and an accident, adhering to it, [it] seems much more able to name itself a being *per se*; it is the third type of being *per accidens*"; in contrast to the two others, it implies a difference neither of *subjectum* nor of accomplice and accepts a physical unity because its two elements are by force ordered one to the other by their nature.[25]

In this way, Regius' error remains very mundane, characterized by an ignorant and scientistic good sense: he imagines that unity *per se* is valid only for a substance, thus also that a nonsubstantial unity must be conceived *per accidens*, without comprehending that accidents must remain a *per se* and that two substances can just as well be united *per accidens*

---

24. "*Quis enim neget hominem esse unum per se ens? Et a posterior id declarari potest, nam omnes hujusmodi partes sibi invicem deserviunt et per se separatae aut nullo modo, aut non diu conservari; signum ergo est, illas omnes in suo genere incompleta entia et per se ordinari ad componendum ens aliquod; ergo illud ut sic compositum est ens per se et unum per se. Unde hoc satis est quod partes illae habeant naturaliter aliquem conjunctionem et copulationem, quaecumque illa sit; nam illa sufficit ut omnes eadem forma informari et convenire ad constituendum cum illa unum ens, habens unum esse simpliciter*" (ibid., n. 11, 128).

25. "*Tamen hac consideratione et comparatione ens compositum ex substantia et accidente sibi inhaerente multo magis videtur posse vocari ens per se; hoc enim est tertium genus entium per accidens, quod magis videtur recedere ab illo primo et infimo ente per aggregationem, magisque accedere ad unum per se, quia et ea, quibus constat, non distinguuntur supposito, sicut in allis, et habent inter se majorem physicam unionem, ut unum revera est in potentia ad aliud, quamvis accidentali et alterum natura sua est ordinatum ad aliud, et in unione ad aliud habet suam perfectionem correlatam*" (ibid., n. 14, 130).

(aggregates) as *per se* (human). He does not see that "in the expression *ens per se/accidens*, the question of substantiality is put out of play."[26] And Voetius most probably knew his neo-scholastic *metaphysica* no better because he engages in polemics with Regius on the same terms as he does, confusing the two registers of *per se/per accidens*—once more Descartes comes off as knowing the medievals far better.[27]

The misrepresentation of "metaphysics," first understood as the school *"metaphysica"* with the quarrel over the *per se* in 1641, is doubled in 1645 by a rupture with properly Cartesian metaphysics in the debate about the *mens corporea*: *"Quid enim tanti opus est, ut ea quae ad Metaphysicam vel Theologiam spectant scriptis tuis immisceas, cum ea non possis attingere, quin statim in alterutram partem aberres? Prius, mentem, ut substantiam a corpore distinctam, considerando, scripseras hominem esse* ens per accidens; *nunc autem econtra, considerando mentem et corpus in eodem homine arcte uniri, vis illam tantum esse* modum corporis. *Qui error multo pejor est priore.*—Why is it necessary for you to mix metaphysical and theological matters in your writings, given that you cannot touch upon such things without falling into some error or other? At first, in considering the mind as a distinct substance from the body, you write that a man is an *ens per accidens*; but then, when you observe that the mind and the body are closely united in the same man, you take the former to be only *a mode of the body*. The latter error is far worse than the former."[28] The critique of this "still worse error" by Descartes is well known: *"mentem posse a nobis sine corpore intelligi, ac proinde non esse ejus modum*—we can understand the mind apart from the body; hence it is not a mode of the body."[29] By overevaluating substantiality (in its opposition to accident) and by identifying it with any meaning *per se*, Regius also lacks the distinction

26. Olivo, "L'homme en personne," 76.

27. He also does not fail to stigmatize Regius' *ignorantia* (VIII-2: 352, 13; CSM I: 300).

28. To Regius, July 1645, IV: 250, 7–15; CSMK: 255. Descartes is here alluding to the text that will be published a year later under the title *Fundamenta physices*, in Amsterdam, in August 1646 (see Theo Verbeek, "Regius' *Fundamenta physices*," *Journal of the History of Ideas* 55.4 [1994]: 533–51). There is a similar formulation in the *[Brevis] Explicatio mentis humanae sive animae rationalis*, §1 (Utrecht, 1647): *"mens posit esse vel substantia, vel quidam substantiae corporeae modus"* (= AT VIII-2: 342, 23–24). See: "You are right in supposing that I do not share Regius' opinion that the mind is a corporeal principle . . . ; for in my writings I have said exactly the opposite." To Mersenne, 23 November 1646, IV: 566, 13–17; CSMK: 301.

29. *Comments on a Certain Broadsheet*, VIII-2: 350, 21–21; CSM I: 298.

between the substance and the mode (or the principal attribute). Everything we think becomes substance, without consideration of the distinction of the *naturae simplicissimae* or the primitive notions. The same confusion of concepts that wants to reinforce the distinction between mind and body (united by accident only in the human, made from two substances) is inverted in the contrary result of abolishing their distinction (the *mens* relying on a corporeal principle, that is to say, on an extended substance). It is not even a matter of having in this way missed what is essential for Descartes—the third primitive notion, its irreducibility to the first, the radical innovation of *meum corpus*—of which Regius obviously has no idea; it is a matter of having missed the point of departure, which Descartes moreover tries to surpass, the two first primitive notions: from the beginning of the debate Regius actually had seen nothing of what Descartes established metaphysically. Descartes thus had every reason for concluding an impossible discussion laconically: "he published a book last year [1646], titled *Fundamenta Physicae*, where he has transcribed badly and changed the order and denied several truths of metaphysics, on which all of physics must be grounded" (IX-2: 17–18 and 23–25; not translated in CSMK).

Yet the third mistake, which closes the debate, is announced in 1647 with the *Brevis explicatio mentis humanae*. The fast clarification of the *Comments on a Certain Broadsheet* manifests very clearly the common root of Regius' preceding mistakes and their sole principle: the recourse to the language of *metaphysica*, in such a way as to speak of the union only starting from *substantia*. In fact, §2 of the *Explicatio* produces all the possibilities, albeit erroneous, that such an explication offers: "So far as the nature of things is concerned, the possibility seems to be open that the mind (*mens*) can be either a substance or a mode of a corporeal substance (*vel substantia, vel quidam substantiae corporea modus*); Or, if we are to follow some philosophers, who hold that extension and thought are attributes which are present in certain substances, as in subjects, then since these attributes are not opposites but merely different (*non sit opposita, sed diversa*), there is no reason why the mind should not be a sort of attribute co-existing with extension in the same subject (*mens possit esse attributum quoddam, eidem subjecto cum extensione conveniens*), though the one attribute is not included in the concept of the other (*quamvis unum in alterius conceptu non comprehendatur*). For whatever we can conceive of (*possumus concipere*) can exist. Now, it is conceivable that the mind (*mens*) is some such item; for none of these implies a contradiction. Therefore it is possible that the mind

is some such item [i.e., comprised in the concept of another]."[30] This
strange reasoning suffers from an obvious contradiction: the rule that
everything we conceive can be (by God's omnipotence) is valid only for
what we conceive clearly and distinctly: "*Et quidem jam ad minimum
scio illas [i.e., res materiales] quatenus sunt purae Matheseos objectum,
posse existere,* quandoquidem ispas clare et distincte percipio—And at
least I now know that they [i.e., material things] are capable of existing,
in so far as they are the subject-matter of pure mathematics, *since I perceive them clearly and distinctly.*"[31] Now, according to Regius himself,
the concept of the *mens* is not included in that of extension, in the twofold sense (inseparable for Descartes) of being included there and clearly
and distinctly conceived; thus the bringing together (*convenire*) of the
two notions in a sole concept cannot be permitted, because it can be
neither conceived (*concipere*) nor comprehended (*comprehendere*). Besides, as Descartes will soon note (VIII-2: 355, 5–12; CSM I: 302), from
§5 onward Regius contradicts (*contradictoria*, 355, 12) his conclusion
of §2, by assuring us that if we can doubt the body without doubting
the mind, this proves that "in that moment (*quamdiu*) . . . we cannot say
that the mind is a mode of the body" (343, 22–23; CSM I: 295, trans.
lightly modified). This obvious contradiction follows from forgetting
to ensure the difference of terms on the basis of their clear and distinct
perception; a forgetting that leads to holding the difference between

---

30. VIII-2: 342, 22—343, 7; CSM I: 294–95. A text already known to Descartes in a manuscript version (under the title *Explicatio mentis sive animae rationalis*), it was challenged by the *Comments on a Certain Broadsheet* of 1647,
but published in Utrecht, as *Philosophia naturalis*, only in 1648 (second edition
1654), 335; *Philosophie naturelle* (Utrecht, 1687), 427, corrected.

31. VII: 71, 13–16 = IX-1, 57; CSM II: 50. Descartes himself underlines
this: "*Ubi notandum est, hanc regulam, quicquid possumus concipere, id post
esse, quamvis mea sit, et vera, quoties agitur de claro et distincto conceptu, in
quo rei possibilitas continetur, quia Deus potest omnia efficere, quae nos pos-
sibilia esse clare percipimus; non esse tamen temere usurpandam, quia facile sit,
ut quis putet se aliquam rem recte intelligere, quam tamen praejudicio aliquo
excaecatus non intelligit*—We should note that even though the rule, 'Whatever
we can conceive of can exist,' is my own, it is true only so long as we are dealing with a conception which is clear and distinct, a conception which embraces
the possibility of the thing in question, since God can bring about whatever we
clearly perceive to be possible. But we ought not to use this rule heedlessly, because it is easy for someone to imagine that he properly understands something
when in fact he is blinded by some preconception and does not understand it at
all" (351, 29—352, 61; CSM I: 299).

the concepts of *mens/cogitatio* and of extension to be like a *diversity without opposition* (*non sunt opposita, sed diversa*, 343, 1); now we precisely cannot conceive a clearer and more distinct opposition than that between two concepts that not only can be conceived one without the other (primitive notion) but cannot be brought together in a common and superior third: "*nulla major inter illa opposito esse potest, quam quod sint diversa*—there can be no greater opposition between them than the fact that they are different" (349, 13–14; CSM I: 298); therefore their diversity really leads to an opposition, except by acting as if "*unum et idem subjectum duas habere diversas naturas*—one and the same subject has two different natures" (350, 3–4; CSM I: 298). This confusion probably results from lack of attention, but from a lack of attention that one can specify: Regius does not see that if the different modes can fit together, they do fit in this way only related to a (principal) attribute, which itself alone permits identifying a substance, thus which can itself not be confused with any other (principal) attribute. From there the essential reminder: "*cavendumque est, ne per attributum nihil hic aliud intelligamus quam modum*—We must take care here not to understand the word 'attribute' to mean simply 'mode.'"[32] In short, Regius invokes against the Cartesian position a group of concepts he has not mastered.

This failure is nevertheless of interest, because §2 of the *Explicatio*, by developing the actually incompatible and never clearly discriminated hypotheses, in order to interpret the union substantially, in advance

---

32. VIII-2: 348, 19–20; CSM I: 297; see: "*verum ipsa extensio, quae est modorum illorum subjectum, in se spectata, non est substantiae corporeae modus, sed attributum, quod ejus essentiam naturamque constituit. . . . verum ipsa cogitatio, ut est internum principium, ex quo modi isti exurgunt, et cui insunt, non concipitur ut modus, sed ut attributum, quod constituit naturam alicujus substantiae, quae an sit corporea, an vero incorporea, hic quaeritur*—the extension itself—the subject of these modes—is not a mode of the corporeal substance, but an attribute which constitutes its natural essence. . . . thought itself, as the internal principle from which these modes spring and in which they are present, is not conceived as a mode, but as an attribute which constitutes the nature of a substance. Whether this substance is corporeal or incorporeal is the question at issue here" (348, 29–349, 9; CSM I: 297–98). And the attribute draws its irreducibility only from the clear and distinct perception: "*Ex hoc enim, quod unum sine alio sic intelligatur, cognoscitur non esse ejus modus, sed res vel attributum rei, quae potest absque illo subsister*—For, in virtue of the fact that one of these attributes can be distinctly understood apart from the other, we know that the one is not a mode of the other, but is a thing, or attribute of a thing, which can subsist without the other" (350, 25–29; CSM I: 299).

delineates the paths that Descartes' contemporaries or successors will attempt—in vain, it seems to me. The first, that *"mens possit esse vel substantia*—the mind can be either a substance" (342, 23; CSM I: 294), really does correspond to a thesis by Descartes, but in such a way that the *res cogitans*, conceived in this way as first primitive notion, permits no access to the union (as will be proved by Malebranche's radicalization of the antagonism between the first two primitive notions); Descartes as well does not depend on it and precisely attempts to attain the union directly as a third and radical primitive notion. The second hypothesis, which takes the *mens* as *"vel quidam substantiae corporeae modus*—or a mode of a corporeal substance" (342, 23–24; CSM I: 294), and which Regius defends, repeats Hobbes' position in the Third Objections (VII: 173, 13ff.; CSM II: 122), with countless revivals to our own day, but without consideration of the principle of clear and distinct distinction of attributes. The third is left: *"cum ea attributa non sint opposita, sed diversa, nihil obstat, quo minus mens possit esse attributum quoddam, eidem subjecto cum existensione conveniens, quamvis unum in alterius conceptu non comprehendatur*—since these attributes are not opposites but merely different, there is no reason why the mind should not be a sort of attribute co-existing with extension in the same subject, though the one attribute is not included in the concept of the other" (343, 1–4; CSM I: 294–95). Assigning thought as well as extension to a common term, although we do not have clear and distinct comprehension of it, or rather *precisely* for that reason, announces both Spinoza (with a single term, the sole *substantia absolute infinita infinitis modis* [absolute infinite substance in infinite modes], on the condition that we know only two of its attributes) and Leibniz (with an infinity of individual substances, on the condition that we do *not* have a complete individual notion of them). If each of these hypotheses for thinking the *mens* starting from substance leads to no longer being able to think the union of soul and body correctly, one must first definitely give up the point of departure offered by the first category of being, and thus leave the language of *metaphysica* behind. This is exactly and paradoxically what Descartes will do.

## §25. The Sole Substantial Form

Leaving the language of *metaphysica* can be accomplished, as we have seen, by elaborating new concepts starting from vocabulary that is more everyday (§§9–10, §21). Yet it is also possible to do so by displacing, redirecting, and overinterpreting the concepts of *metaphysica*, left apparently unchanged. That seems to be the case with the residual use of several Aristotelian formulations, which one would not have predicted as ample, formulations like *substantial form*, *soul formed by the body*, *substantial union*. One will have to admit their use and, instead of attempting to reduce it, measure the displacements their meaning undergoes and how they can, thus overdetermined, serve the Cartesian innovation of the union.

The question of the validity of these formulations could appear to have been ruled straightaway out of play, at least since 1637. That is at least what this clarification made to Regius suggests. First, by reproaching him, in private, for his useless polemical imprudence: "*Ut, de ipsis formis substantialibus et qualitatibus realibus, quid opus tibi fuit eas palam rejicere? Nunquid meministi me, in* Meteoris *p. 164, expressissimis verbis monuisse ipsas nullomodo a me rejici, aut negari, sed tantummodo non requiri ad rationes meas explicandas?*—For instance, why did you need to reject openly substantial forms and real qualities? Do you not remember that on page 164 of my *Meteorology*,[33] I said quite expressly that I did not at all reject or deny them, but simply found them unnecessary in my explanations?"[34] A different irenic denial in the *Essais* takes this up exactly: "Then, know also that in order to keep my peace with the philosophers, I have no desire to deny that which they imagine to be in bodies in addition to what I have given, such as their *substantial forms*, their *real qualities* and the like; but it seems to me that my explanations ought to be approved all the more because I shall make them depend on fewer things."[35] But this uselessness becomes specified for the public debate with Voetius by a more fully argued and hence sufficiently vivid refutation: "*Sed nullius plane actionis naturalis ratio reddi potest per illas formas substantiales, cum earum assertores fateantur ipsas esse occultas, et a se non intellectas; nam si dicant aliquam actionem procedere a forma substantiali, idem est ac si dicerent, illam procedere a re a se non intellecta, quod nihil explicat . . . Contra autem a formis illis essentialibus, quas nos explicamus, manifestae ac mathematicae rationes redduntur actionum naturalium, ut videre est de forma salis communis in meis* Meteoris—But no natural action at all can be explained by these substantial forms, since their defenders admit

33. See the anastatic reprint (Lecce: Conte Editore, 1987) and AT VI: 239, 5–12.

34. To Regius, January 1642, III: 492, 2–7; CSMK: 205.

35. *Meteorology* I, AT VI: 239, 5–12, trans. Paul J. Olscamp as *Discourse on Method, Optics, Geometry, and Meteorology* (Indianapolis: Library of Liberal Arts, 1965), 268.

that they are occult and that they do not understand them themselves. If they say that some action proceeds from a substantial form, it is as if they said that it proceeds from something which they do not understand; which explains nothing. . . . Essential forms explained in our fashion, on the other hand, give manifest and mathematical reasons for natural actions, as can be seen with regard to the form of common salt in my *Meteorology*."[36] Actually, Descartes proposed there "to show you here that this alone is sufficient to give them all the qualities that salt has," that is to say, that "the salinity of the sea consists only in those larger particles of its water which, as I have just said, are incapable of being bent like the others through the action of the fine material, or even of being agitated without the intervention of the smaller particles"; from now on in order to "understand the reason" of different kinds of knowledge of salt, he only needs to model with "shape," "parts," "movements," and "quantity/ies."[37] In short, the *naturae simplicissimae* provide reason for extended things, while the substantial forms leave them unintelligible.

A first conclusion follows from this: one must give up on substantial forms first and above all because the form does not function as substance; the form does not make the material thing intelligible, in contrast to *figura*, which the *Regulae* had already in fact and by right substituted for it: "*Quid igitur sequetur incommodi, si, caventes ne aliquod novum ens inutiliter admittamus et temere fingamus, non negemus quidem de colore quidquid aliis placuerit, sed tantum abstrahamus ab omni alio, quam quod habeat figurae naturam, et concipiamus diversitatem, quae est inter album, coeruleum, rubrum, etc., veluti illam quae*

36. To Regius, January 1642, III: 506, 8–19; CSMK: 208–09. Same argument in 1644: "*nullo modo possumus intelligere . . . quales sunt illae* formae substantiales *et qualitates reales, quas in rebus esse multi supponunt*—we cannot understand . . . the *substantial forms* and real qualities which many suppose to inhere in things" (*Principles of Philosophy* IV, §198, VIII-1: 322, 14–18; CSM I: 285). And in 1647: "*Misera illa entia (scilicet formas substantiales, et qualitates reales) nullius plane usus esse perspeximus, nisi forte ad excoecanda studiorum ingenia*—We have observed that those wretched entities (namely, substantial forms and real qualities) are clearly of no use, except perhaps for blinding the minds of students" (To Dinet, VII: 592, 4–7; not translated in CSM II).

37. *Meteorology* III, AT VI: 250, 8–10; 249, 3–8; 252, 3, respectively (= *give reason* 264, 22; *the reason why*, 262, 17; 257, 12); *figure/shape*, 249, 8; *part* 249, 8 (and 249, 16; 251, 6; 253, 21, etc.); *moving* 250, 7 (and 251, 25; 252, 9; etc.); *quantity/ies* 253, 2 (and 252, 7). See *cause* (253, 24; 257, 21, 28; 261, 16); *to cause* 252, 24; 255, 28; 264, 20); and *effect* 257, 2, 27. [English quotation in text from Olscamp, 275.]

*est inter has aut similes figuras?*—So what troublesome consequences could there be if—while avoiding the useless assumption and pointless invention of some new entity, and without denying what others have preferred to think on the subject—we simply make an abstraction, setting aside every feature of colour apart from its possessing the character of shape, and conceive of the difference between white, blue, red, etc., as being like the difference between the following figures or similar ones?"[38] There is no substantial form, first because there is no form that could ensure the thing its substantiality: the thing appears as intelligible via the *figura*, but, functioning as a simple concept available to the mind modeling and measuring, the *figura* varies according to the phenomena and their always accidental, never subsisting variations; it is hence not a substance. A second conclusion must be added to this: there is no substantial form because if it had to be produced on the occasion of a phenomenon, it would be produced as an accident: "*Quod confirmatur exemplo animae, quae est vera forma substantialis hominis; haec enim non aliam ob causam a Deo immediate creari putatur, quam quia est substantia; ac proinde, cum aliae non putentur eodem modo creari, sed tantum educi e potentia materiae, non putandum etiam est eas esse substantias.*—This is confirmed by the example of the soul, which is the true substantial form of man. For the soul is thought to be immediately created by God for no other reason than that it is a substance. Hence, since the other 'forms' are not thought to be created in this way, but merely to emerge from the potentiality of matter, they should not be regarded as substances." In short, if the human soul merits the title of substance because it is created immediately and so to say eternally by God, the other substantial forms that one assumes very prudently to arise solely from the occasion of the events of nature alone, "de novo,"[39]

38. Regula XII, AT X: 413, 11–17; CSM I: 41. See my commentary in *Sur l'ontologie grise de Descartes*, §19, 116ff.

39. To Regius, January 1642, III: 505, 16–19 and 14; CSMK: 208. See also the insistence on the nonsubstantiality of everything that falls under matter: "*Ne enim aliqua sit ambiguitas in verbo, hic est notandum, nomine* formae *substantialis, cum illam negamus, intelligi substantiam quandam materiae adjunctam, et cum ipsa totum aliquod mere corporeum componentem, quaeque non minus, aut etiam magis quam materia, sit vera substantia, sive res per se subsistens, quia nempe dicitur esse actus, illa vero tantum potentia. Hujus autem substantiae, seu formae substantialis, in rebus mere corporalibus, a materia diversae, nullibi plane in sacra scriptura mentionem fieri putamus*—To prevent any ambiguity of expression, it must be observed that when we deny *substantial forms*, we mean by the expression a certain substance joined to matter, making up with it a merely corporeal whole, and which, no less than matter and even more than

thus do not merit the title of substances; the substantial forms thus have nothing [to do with] substances. As neither a form susceptible of ensuring a substantiality, nor a substance in the strict sense, the substantial form offers, in addition to its ontic contradictions, no epistemic utility whatsoever. But then why does Descartes maintain that the human soul remains a *vera/true* substantial form?

He does so because it is an exception, but an exception that one must still identify. One can do so by noting the correction, often repeated, of the concept of *anima* by that of *mens*: "*Quod autem* animam rationalem *nomine* mentis humanae *appellet, laudo: sic enim vitat ae-quivocationem, quae est in voce animae; atque me hac in re imitatur.*—I approve of his calling the rational soul the 'human mind,' for by using this expression he avoids the ambiguity in the term 'soul,' and he is following me in this respect."[40] The ambiguity depends on the fact that the term "soul" can also cover a corporeal reality, like the material principles of vegetative, sensitive, motor life, following Aristotle's multiplying of the soul: "*Loquor autem hic de* mente *potius quam de anima, quoniam animae nomen est aequivocum, et saepe pro re corporea usurpatur.*—I use the term 'mind' rather than 'soul' since the word 'soul' is ambiguous and is often applied to something corporeal."[41] In other words, just as the majority of substantial forms do not merit the title of substance, so the majority of the occurrences of "soul" do not concern thought; thus in order for it to be able to assume *revera* the rank of substantial form, one must restrict the soul to thought, to the pure and simple *cogitatio*: "*Ego vero, animadvertens principium quo nutrimur toto genere distingui ab eo quo* cogitamus, *dixi* animae *nomen, cum pro utroque sumitur, esse aequivocum; atque ut specialiter sumatur pro* actu primo *sive* praecipua hominis forma, *intelligendum tantum esse de principio quo* cogitamus, *hocque nomine* mentis *ut plurimum appellavi ad vitandam aequivocationem.*—I, by contrast, realizing that the principle by which we are nourished is wholly different—different in kind—from that in virtue of which we *think*, have said that the term 'soul,' when it is used to refer to both these principles, is ambiguous. If we are to take 'soul' in its special sense, as meaning the 'first actuality' or 'principal form of man,' then the term must be understood to apply only to the principle

---

matter—since it is called an actuality and matter only a potentiality—is a true substance, or self-subsistent thing. Such a substance, or substantial form, present in purely corporeal things but distinct from matter, is nowhere, we think, mentioned in Holy Scripture" (ibid., III: 502, 5–15; CSMK: 207).

40. *Comments on a Certain Broadsheet*, VIII-2: 347, 5–8; CSM I: 296.
41. Second Set of Replies, VII: 161, 25–27; CSM II: 114.

in virtue of which *we think*."[42] But there is more: the reduction of the soul to the *mens*, as exclusively *res cogitans*, compensates for the inverse reduction of Aristotle's immaterial *forma* (εἶδος) to Descartes' extended *figura*; because no formal principle comes to ensure the stability of the material thing in itself, this principle can henceforth come to it only from the *cogitatio* of the human mind, from the outside. The soul must become *mens* in order for the unformed *figura* (devoid of any *forma*) to recover a formal principle of substantiality. In this way, redefined as *mens*, the sole *cogitatio* can inform any matter and any other body, precisely because it thinks it without form, as a simple *figura* regulated from the exterior by this very *cogitatio*. The *cogitatio* controls the *figura* (and the succession of figurations that alone ensure the always varying identity of the extended thing) and suppresses the *forma* (thus the possibility and the necessity of inventing a substantial form), because it thinks and organizes the extension of any material thing via models and parameters. The *mens* thinks the shapes and in this way eliminates the substantial forms.

Descartes can thus quite logically, albeit not without paradox, conclude that the *mens*, while suppressing the substantial forms (or rendering them useless) by thinking them as shapes, remains in reality the only substantial form: "*praecipua [i.e., quaestio] erat de formis substantialibus rerum materialium, quas omnes*, excepta anima rationali, *Medicus [i.e., Regius] negarat*—the principal question bears on substantial forms that the physician [i.e., Regius] had entirely denied *except for the rational soul*" (VII: 587, 11–13; untranslated in CSM II). Why can it escape the universal disqualification of substantial forms? Because it, and it alone, is not composed of parts assembled from the outside by a foreign *mens*, a thing alienated into an object for a *cogitatio*, but remains united

---

42. Fifth Set of Replies, VII: 356, 14–21. See: "*Sed quaesivi an aliquid in me esset ex iis, quae animae prius a me descriptae tribusbam, cumque non omnia quae ad ipsam retuleram in me invenirem*, sed solam cogitationem, *ideo non dixi me esse animam*, sed tantum rem cogitantem, *atque huis rei cogitanti nomen mentis, sive intellectus, sive rationis, imposui, non ut aliquid amplius significarem nomine mentis quam nomine rei cogitantis*—What I did do was inquire whether there were in me any of the features which I had previously been in the habit of attributing to the soul as previously described by men. Now I did not find within me all the attributes which I had formerly referred to the soul; *the only one* I found was *thought*, and hence I did not say I was a soul but merely *that I was a thinking thing*. In applying the term 'mind' or 'intellect' or 'reason' to the thinking thing, I did not intend to endow the term 'mind' with any more weighty significance than the phrase 'thinking thing'" (Seventh Replies, VII: 491, 13–20; CSM II: 332).

to itself and has thus an essential form that assures it a substantiality: "quae *agnoscitur* sola *esse* forma substantialis, *alias autem ex partium configuratione et motu constare*—if the soul is recognized as *merely a substantial form*, while other such forms consist in the configuration and motion of parts."[43] Thus the *mens* claims the exclusivity of the substantial form, not really so much because it would characterize itself directly as such or because it would validate such a concept, but because it eliminates all the others. If only one *forma substantialis* remains, this will be the one.

This exclusive claim to the status of *forma substantialis* is marked by the resumption of another scholastic formulation, that is to say here one belonging to *metaphysica*—that the soul informs the body. It appears all the more fully than even the *Regulae*, in other places such a radical Ockham's razor, had maintained it: "*quid sit mens hominis, quid corpus, quo modo hoc ab illa informetur*—what the human mind is, what the body is and how it is informed by the mind" (X: 411, 18–19; CSM I: 40). The *Principles* later confirms it as if in passing: "*Sciendum itaque humanam animam, etsi totum corpus informet, praecipuam*

43. To Regius, January 1642, III: 503, 9–11; CSMK: 207. Common opinion instead lets the ambiguous and not exclusively cognizing soul fall into corporeity and thus into mortality: "*e contra ex opinione affirmante* formas substantiales, *facillimum esse prolapsum in opinionem eorum qui dicunt animam humanam esse corpoream et mortalem*—on the contrary . . . it is the view which affirms *substantial forms* which allows the easiest slide to the opinion of those who maintain that the human soul is corporeal and mortal" (6–9; CSMK: 207). This confirms Marleen Rozemond's remark suggesting that the *forma substantialis* of the soul for the body is invoked by Descartes less for explaining the union than for supporting the immortality of the soul (*Descartes' Dualism*, 152ff.). Actually, Descartes never attempts to *explain* the union, which he notes in its facticity, but to conceive its status and consequences; in this case it plays the role of the sole *forma substantialis* that replaces all the others, which are all corporeal and hence mortal, while it is incorporeal and hence immortal. In other words: "*Postquam autem haec satis animadverti, et mentis ideam a corporis motusque corporei ideis accurate distinxi, omnesque* alias qualitatum realium formarumve substantialium *ideas, quas ante habueram, ex ipsis a me conflatas effictasve fuisse deprehendi, perfacile me omnibus dubiis, quae hic proposita sunt, exolvi*—But later on I made the observations which led me to make a careful distinction between the idea of the mind and the ideas of body and corporeal motion; and I found that all *those other ideas of 'real qualities' or 'substantial forms'* which I had previously held were ones which I had put together or constructed from those basic ideas. And thus I very easily freed myself from all the doubts that my critics here put forward" (Sixth Set of Replies, VII: 442, 30—443, 6; CSM II: 298).

*tamen sedem suam habere in cerebro.*—It must be realized that the human soul, while *informing* the entire body, nevertheless has its principal seat in the brain."[44] Yet, once more, from where comes this privilege of remaining the form of the body, if there are no longer any *forma* here for the extended body, but only a sequence of *figurae* varying according to their movements? It comes from the fact that the *human* soul does not think its *human* body in the manner in which it represents (other) bodies to itself: it does not form the body into a different object according to order and measure, but assimilates itself to it, while it remains entirely extended, as if willing to exercise its thought *in the mode of sensing*, that is to say following its ability that allows it to think *passively*. The "body of a man" (IV: 166, 1–2, 12; CSMK: 242–43) does not stay before the *cogitatio* like an ob-ject face to face with the *intuitus*; it is united to it as an instrument for passive thought, unified (and thus subject to the rest of extension) and indivisible (inasmuch as auxiliary and peripheral to passive thought). This portion of extension, unified as "the body of a man," becomes, from the informed object it could have remained, a part certainly thrown off center, but henceforth intrinsic to the *cogitatio*, because indispensable to its passive exercise, the *sensus*. Once more, "no longer having the same shape, they [i.e., the same bodies] are numerically the same (*eadem numero*) only because they are *informed* by the same soul"; and thus, abstracted from quantity with shape and divisible extension, "all the matter, however large or small, which as a whole is informed by the same human soul, is taken for a whole and entire human body."[45] The literal formulation "the numerical identity of the body of a man does not depend on its matter, but on its *form, which is the soul*"[46] must then not be understood as the restoration, diplomatic concession, or chance survival of a thesis that would be maintained in its customary meaning. Each of its terms has been revised; and it means henceforth that (i) while the substitution of *figura* for *forma* disqualifies *forma* in order to assure the least substance to the thing, henceforth an object; (ii) the human soul, understood as strict *mens*, does not always think extension as an object kept away from the

44. *Principles of Philosophy* IV, §189, VIII-1: 315, 23–25; CSM I: 279; omitted by Picot's translation [into French].

45. To Mesland, 9 February 1645, IV: 167, 2–3; then 168, 27–30; CSMK: 243 and 244; trans. modified. This [operates] on the eucharistic model of the union par excellence, that of a mind to a *meum corpus*, where "the soul of Jesus Christ *informs* the matter of the host" (IV: 169, 11; CSMK: 244).

46. To Mesland, 1645 or 1646, IV: 346, 20–22; CSMK: 279; emphasis added.

*intuitus*, because it can think passively, that is to say can sense, only by turning to the disposition of "the body of a man"; (iii) this *meum corpus* really does remain a portion of extension, but one that becomes indivisible (united), because its function of passivity joins it intrinsically (unifies it) to the *res cogitans*, whose final mode of sensing becomes operative only with its help. The *mens* remains the substantial form of *its* body only because without the body the mind could not think in accordance with all the modes of a *res cogitans*.

## §26. The Substantial Union without Third Substance

It now becomes possible to envision the main difficulty, which has so far been postponed so as not to tackle it without precautions: Does the union—which recovers at the end, albeit with a completely different status from that of the medievals, the exclusive title of substantial form by informing "the body of a man"—have the rank of a substance? That would be the logical conclusion in *metaphysica*: in being united to a soul, the *meum corpus* can finally be said to be by itself; acquiring in this way a circumscribed unity that subtracts it from the continually moving change of the *alia corpora* in undifferentiated extension, it remains in itself; satisfying the two characteristic privileges of substance according to the *Categories*, it here integrates itself by simply becoming one with its effectively substantial, or more exactly substantializing, form. Following the example of Gilson, one interpretive tradition has not turned away from this apparently perfectly logical consequence: "If then there is a substantial union of the soul and the body, it can consist only in the union of two substances in order to form a third out of it, soul and body being two parts of a same whole, and their unity a *unity of composition.*"[47] It goes through Jean Laporte—"Is the *union of the soul and the body* a 'primitive notion'? Assuredly, for it presupposes no other before it. Neither more nor less than thought and *extension*, it is substance"[48]—and through Martial Gueroult—"the set of all realities that constitute me: spiritual substance, extended substance, and composite substance of soul-body"[49]—in order to reach recently John

47. Étienne Gilson, "Descartes et la métaphysique scolastique," *Revue de l'université de Bruxelles* (1923–24): 31, reprinted in *Études sur le rôle de la pensée médiévale dans la constitution du système cartésien* (Paris: Vrin, 1930, 1967), 249f.

48. Laporte, *Le Rationalisme de Descartes*, 235.

49. Gueroult, *Descartes' Philosophy*, II: 117 (see the index, 309–11). Rodis-Lewis in *L'Œuvre de Descartes*, 543, also cites Jean Wahl: "a third substance

Cottingham, who is nonetheless the most exact of the commentators in the analytic tradition. He goes all the way to invoking a trialist position of substance, where the third primitive notion would hold the rank of substance, just like the first two.[50] One must oppose to this logic, which has only appearance on its side, a fact that despite its enigmatic character is recalled by conscientious readers. Commenting on the letter to Regius from mid-December 1641, Alquié underlined this fact: "*Ens per se.* One needs to notice that Descartes is all the same reluctant to say that the human being is a substance. It is characteristic to see in this entire text . . . the expression *ens per se* being substituted for *substantia.*"[51] And Denis Kambouchner points out, against Gueroult, that "this composite that constitutes 'a single whole' is never called a substance by Descartes"; in other words, "*the union* itself is here taken not as a nature or an original notion that itself *would be related* to a third substance or a species of substance, but always as a real *condition* from which all these phenomena proceed."[52] The most recent of them all, Gilles Olivo, exactly sums up the factual requirement and the rightful difficulty: "Nowhere does Descartes say of the human that he is a substance, even if thought and extension respond to substances of which they are the attributes, permitting us to know them and to distinguish them one from another. What is then known in terms of being according to the union if the human is neither a substance nor an

---

comes to superimpose itself on the two clear and distinct ideas of the soul and the body," in "Notes sur Descartes," *Revue philosophique de la France et de l'Étranger* (1937): 371.

50. John Cottingham, "Cartesian Trialism," *Mind* 94 (1985): 218–30. Rozemond rightly rejects this thesis after a detailed examination in *Descartes' Dualism*, 173f. and especially 191f.: "There is a third substance. . . . But this result is completely unacceptable" is the case only because "Descartes himself never calls the mind-body composite a substance" (ibid., 194 and 213); but above all because he never conceives the union as the result of such a composite; which is precisely what must be understood. See Lilli Alanen, "Descartes' Dualism and the Philosophy of Mind," *Revue de métaphysique et de morale* 94.3 (1989): 391–413, and Daisie Radner, "Descartes' Notion of the Union of Mind and Body," *Journal of the History of Ideas* 9.2 (1979): 159–70.

51. Note in Alquié's edition of Descartes, *Œuvres philosophiques*, vol. III (Paris: Garnier, 1973), 902, see page 914, radicalizing in this way his discussion, at the time still quite hazy, with Laporte in *La Découverte métaphysique*, chapter 15, in particular 308ff.

52. Denis Kambouchner, *L'Homme des Passions* (Paris: Albin Michel, 1995), I: 43 and 421.

accident?"⁵³ Neither substance nor accident—what ontological status should one accord to the union?

All the thinkable compromises having without doubt been tried, either by Regius and the opponents contemporary or just posterior to Descartes or by the ingenuity or blindness of modern commentators, only one radical option remains: to wonder whether the union could and *should* be known in general "in terms of being." It was Alquié who had the audacity to propose that Descartes took the new path of "renouncing any ontological system" in order to think the union, in explicit contrast to all his successors who "often extended [his teaching] onto the plane of ontology."⁵⁴ But how should one pinpoint this difference in regard to an ontological (*ontic* would be more exact) interpretation of the union in the details of the texts? We have already seen that even before *not having* described the union under the heading of *substantia*, Descartes had noted that the union would either reverse the characteristics of the first two *substantiae* (above, §§19–21) or accentuate the inadequacy of the very concept of *substantia* applied to the union (§§22–23). In this way the denial of *substantia* for the union comes after a persistent deterioration of the entire concept of substance—in the case of the union, but also as a result of the aporiae of its general definition (in the *Principles of Philosophy* I, §§51–53). The union certainly does not receive the title of substance, not at all because it would not deserve it, but instead because *substantia* no longer manages to allow it to be conceived, as it here still manages—somewhat—for the two other primitive notions. The union creates a crisis for the Cartesian concept of substance and retrospectively manifests its original inconsistency. It is not the substance that causes default to the union but the union that by surpassing its grasp marks the failure of substance. We owe it to Marjorie Grene to have uniformly marked this intrinsic weakness, "the alteration, and indeed impoverishment, of the concept of substance" according to Descartes: "My point is just this: that Descartes could save the unity of man in the face of his sharp dualism only through the radical impairment of the concept of substance."⁵⁵ Can one specify and confirm textually this "impoverishment" and this failure of substantiality in the case of the union and of the crisis that it causes for it?

53. Olivo, "L'homme en personne," 70.
54. Alquié, *La Découverte métaphysique*, 318 and 313, respectively.
55. Marjorie Grene, *Descartes among the Scholastics* (Milwaukee: Marquette University Press, 1991), 36, 40.

There is obviously an unambiguous Cartesian response: not only does the union never assume (or claim) the title of substance (it is never a question of a third substance), but it tolerates substantiality only on the condition of displacing or even of degrading it into an adverb or an adjective, by denying it the rank of substantive *for the case of the union*. The substantivized substance (designating the οὐσία πρωτή) becomes degraded into an adverbalized or adjectivized substantiality. This deterioration intervenes from the discussion with Arnauld onward: "*mentem habere vim corpus movendi, vel illi esse* substantialiter unitam—the mind has the power of moving the body, and is substantially united to it"; or "*simul etiam probavi* substantialiter *illi [i.e., corpori] esse* unitam—I also proved at the same time that the mind is substantially united with the body." And, a decisive point, understanding the union as substantial does not enter into competition with the concept of the mind as a complete thing, that is to say with the substantiality of the *mens* as a whole: "*illam esse corpori* substantialiter unitam, *quia* unio illa substantialis *non impedit quominus clarus et distinctus solius mentis tanquam rei completae conceptus habeatur*—the mind is substantially united with the body, since that substantial union does not prevent our having a clear and distinct concept of the mind on its own, as a complete thing."[56] The substantive and the adverb (or adjective) do not contradict each other, because they do not apply to the same terms.

When thus the Utrecht quarrel forces Descartes to correct Regius, he actually restricts himself to developing an already established thesis without any ad hoc improvisation in order to respond to the question of the *ens per se* or in order to reassure the conservatism of the Calvinists: "*mentem corpori realiter et* substantialiter *esse unitam, non per situm aut dispositionem*—the mind is really and *substantially* united to the body . . . and not by position or disposition"; and "*admissa ejus [i.e., animae] distinctione* unionem substantialem *negent*—once the distinction between soul and body is admitted, they deny the *substantial* union."[57] Moreover, the same formulation serves to convince the Jesuits on the same point: "*nec ideo negando* unionem substantialem *qua mens corpori conjungitur, nec utriusque partis aptitudinem naturalem ad istam unionem*—without for all that denying the *substantial* union in which the mind is joined to the body, nor the natural ability of both

56. Fourth Set of Replies, 219, 19–20; CSM II: 155, trans. lightly modified; 228, 2–3 and 228, 13–16; CSM II: 160, respectively.

57. To Regius, January 1642, III: 493, 4–5 and 508, 26–27, respectively; CSMK: 206 and 209, trans. modified in both cases.

for this union."[58] The union is not a third substance, but it is no less substantial—that is the final Cartesian formulation.

Once identified one must still understand it. Now, literally, *substantial union* means that the union neither requires nor produces a substance, and it precludes searching for a *unitive substance*, a third substance in charge of the union of the first two. Apart from the fact that it is hard to see how two substances, which by definition must remain independent, could be united and hence be abolished in a third, itself also independent and complete—which is what *unitive substance* would mean—one must instead understand via the *substantial union* that what takes on the substantial role of substance that it is *not* consists not in an unthinkable third substance but in the union itself and in it alone. In order for the union to be ensured substantially, only the union is necessary and nothing else. And precisely because no substance explains the union, but the union is explained by itself, being in itself, the union assumes in this sense any definition of substance, of which it bears the characteristics, being in itself, saying itself. It picks up again the defunct properties of substance, without becoming itself substance, but by being dressed in the array of substantiality, which is added (adjectivally) to it, as a manner of acting (adverbally). The union is not a substance, but it operates in a substantial fashion, by itself and in itself. From this results the paradox that it no longer needs a new substance for the union to prove itself substantial; or even that it is not a third substance, precisely because it turns out to be substantial.

Then from where does the union derive its substantiality? It makes itself without addition *from a* new substance, as one could have expected after the treatise on *substantia* in the *Principles of Philosophy* I, but by addition *to a* substance that is already available and established, the *mens*. The union does not attain its substantial rank by a new substance and must also itself not become one; it adds itself to the substance of the *mens* by allowing it to unify a region of extension under the authority

58. To Dinet, VII: 585, 24–26; untranslated in CSM II. Moreover, writing to another Jesuit, the expression can be applied also to the explication of the Eucharist: "it is the same body, numerically the same body, so long as it remains joined and *substantially* united with the same soul" (To Mesland, 9 February 1645, IV: 166, 18–20; CSM II: 243). It is in this sense that one must understand the exceptional upholding of this substantial form: Gilson admits the fact, wondering "whether he [i.e., Descartes] finally would not with this expression [i.e., *substantial form*] keep something of the idea," but he does not see the reason for this clearly: "It seems that it is the second hypothesis that is true." Gilson, *Études sur le rôle de la pensée médiévale*, 247.

and the aegis of a *meum corpus*. For the *mens*, as much of a substance as it is, is so not in exactly the same sense as extension. The difference has to do with the fact that the material substance consists, on the one hand, in a substrate that is as such unknowable, and, on the other hand, in a principal attribute that is knowable—but by what? Obviously by the *cogitatio*, for it alone can reason from the principal known attribute to the substance that does not affect us immediately. In this way extended substance itself testifies to a privilege of thinking substance, which implements not only the substrate that affects us only through the mediation of the principal attribute (the *cogitatio* of extension thought in this way), but also, just as obviously, a *cogitatio* thinking this relation (between principal attribute and substrate). Thought actually displays the substantiality of the *mens* in three and not in two terms: *cogito (concipio)*, *cogitatio* of extension (attribute), and substance.[59]

In contrast, the thinking substance or the *mens* is precisely accomplished only by thinking, namely, as thinking thought [*pensée pensante*] and not only as thought thought [*pensée pensée*]. In this it is opposed to material substance, which cannot on its own articulate its substrate on extension (principal attribute) and must appeal to another operator, the *cogitatio*, in order to unite them. In this way, the *mens* becomes substantial and owes its substantiality only to the fact that it thinks in action (as thinking *cogitatio* and not only as thought *cogitatio*, as attribute of a substrate). Now, the implementing of the thinking *cogitatio* depends on the modes according to which it is practiced. Thus, the *mens* substantializes itself proportionate to the modes of its thinking thought. In this way, it can vary the span, according to which it limits itself to the active modes of the *cogitatio* (doubt, pure understanding, will and imagination), or rather is opened to its passive mode, the *sensus*, so as to think *by receiving* the *cogitata*, without producing them. In this case, it becomes also, besides the pure *mens*, the *meum corpus*. Yet, because this *meum corpus* ensures to the *mens* one of its modes of thought, its *sensus*, and because this mode, although necessitating a peripheral addition, belongs by right to the essential definition of the *cogitatio*, thus to the thinking substance, the *meum corpus* in this way added (united to the *mens*) belongs to it *substantially*, just as much as the other modes of the *res cogitans*. The union absolutely does not have as definition to add a new substance that is in any case unthinkable to the two others; its function is to add

59. See on this disputable parallelism between the two substances (thought and extension) my analysis in *On Descartes' Metaphysical Prism*, §13, "The Egological Deduction of Substance," 155ff.

*substantially* to the *res cogitans* what it lacks in its unstable substance. This final mode is the most unstable, but is also absolutely indispensable, in other words *substantial*, for making the *mens* that of a human, the *sensus*, the only mode that would allow it to think finally passively.

And this substantial union in no way contradicts the real distinction of the *mens* and the body, as Descartes does not stop repeating to the readers who do not stop doubting it: in fact, the *mens* remains a complete substance even without the body; except that this *mens*, which would no longer be united or not yet substantially united to the *sensus*, could think only partially, namely actively, maybe like an angel, but surely not like a human being. Without body or rather without *its body* (*meum corpus*), the *mens* would remain a substance, but a substance thinking narrowly, restricted to what its active thought can produce, autarchic and hence orphaned by the sensory, blind, deaf, anesthetized, literally *insensible*. Between a *mens* without or with *sensus*, the difference thus depends not on substantiality (which remains established in both cases), but on the scope and span of this thought—only active, or active *and* also really passive—it being understood that a thought that is both passive and active is superior to a thought that is only passive. The *mens* reduced to its active modes remains a substance; but it can also enlarge its substantiality in its passive mode of the *sensus*, and being substantially united to a *meum corpus*, still form the same and single substance, henceforth enlarged to the body, or rather to *its* body. The body of the union becomes participating party of the substantiality, even if the soul is substance already without it and the union never is. That a *mens* without body remains a substance in turn does not imply that a body remains a substance without the union. Or rather, this body will not remain a substance except by ceasing to have the rank of *meum corpus*, this body made mine by the union; dead, it will (again) become a substance by common right by dispersing itself into pure and simple extension, without unity because without union to a *mens*, substance because more substantial. A body, but not mine, can be actively known in this way like any other portion of extension, but never passively felt. Faced with this, a *mens* without *meum corpus* would then become not an incomplete *res* (because without body), but a *res* that is much less *cogitans*: without *meum corpus*, the ego would think much less, because it would not think passively—being reduced to activity.[60]

---

60. "The soul is conceived to be essentially active" (Baker and Morris, eds., *Descartes' Dualism*, 122): an essentially disputable thesis, albeit indisputably Spinozist.

The substantial union of the soul and the body (of the *mens* and the *meum corpus*) hence designates and documents Descartes' final discovery: thinking implies also thinking passively; passivity comes to the *res cogitans* only with (so to say) the connection of an external peripheral to the central unit, which allows it to work no longer only actively, by organizing what its hard drive contains—the active modes of doubt, of the understanding, of the will, and of the imagination, operating by attention, effort, and decision—but by treating everything that the senses can put at its disposal; in short, no longer to think as "*solus in mundo*—alone in the world" (VII: 42, 22; CSM II: 29), "*meque solum alloquendo et penitius inspiciendo*—conversing with myself and scrutinizing myself" (34, 16–17; CSM II: 24), but to treat and interpret the pieces of information that arrive passively "*vel invito . . . velim, . . . nolim*—whether I want to or not" (38, 16–17; CSM II: 26), "*me non cooperante, sed saepe etiam invito*—are produced without my cooperation and often even against my will" (79, 13–14; CSM II: 55).

This emerges as the privilege of the union: to make possible "*in me passiva quadam facultas* sentiendi—a certain passive faculty in me of sensing" (79, 7–8; CSM II: 55), by which "*ista sensuum perceptiones* adveniunt—these perceptions *come* from the senses" (81, 20–21; CSM II: 56) to me as so many events. Indeed it is an event and not, especially not, a substance—this is how Descartes actually thinks the union. The union is accomplished (as the sudden and so to say disjointed existence of the cognizing ego was accomplished), *quoties* and *quamdiu*, each time and as long as it thinks it is, or whatever else it thinks, at least provided that while thinking what it thinks, it thinks that it thinks, itself and no other. But this union is not accomplished if the ego thinks only in general (according to its primary modes, all active), it requires also, in order to be produced, that the ego think passively, because a thinkable thought comes to it (*advenire*, 75, 20; CSM II: 52), sent (*emittere*, 80, 3; CSM II: 55) also from elsewhere (*aliunde*, 75, 21; 80, 3; CSM II: 52, 55). This is what the new Cartesian definition of death, by cessation of corporeal emission not by dissolution of the soul, confirms very clearly. In fact, when this emission "ceases" (XI: 330, 17; CSM I: 329) coming from elsewhere (because the body can no longer "move" itself and thus ceases to emit signals that serve the soul in order to make its passive thoughts), the soul "absents itself" (330, 16; CSM I: 329) from reception, closes the hearing. It no longer has anything to do with the body, which has stopped emitting and thus no longer plays the role of *meum corpus*. Death (of a *meum corpus* that has become again a simple part of physical extension of the *alia corpora*) therefore intervenes when nothing of thinkable reflecting intervenes any longer. Death is defined as the advent of the nonevent. One must thus also consider, at this point—with attention and once more—two particularities of the language, two terms that are rare in French and hapax legomenon in Descartes.

First, "the sudden and unexpected arrival of the impression [*l'arrivement subit et inopiné de l'impression*]" (*Passions of the Soul*, §72, XI: 381, 22–23; CSM I: 353): it is a matter of "surprise," which provokes wonder [*l'admiration*], thus the first passive thought, the one that permits and determines all the others, as the simplest (no object is here yet identified), which produces the others by additional specifications (knowledge of the object, temporalization, possession, etc.); this "arrival [*arrivement*]" should not be understood as a simple arrival [*arrivée*]—regular, continuous, thus for example like the advent of water, of air, or of electricity that a simple switch would restore for our convenience; here, the impression does not arrive for our convenience, because it comes "by reason of surprise" (381, 22; CSM I: 353), *invito, velim nolim* (uninvited, willy-nilly). The impression that the soul will transform into passive thought arrives on its own rhythm, at its own pleasure, without forewarning. It is a matter not of an arrival (foreseen by the arrival schedules at the train station), but of a delivery [*un arrivage*], which is decided by the nightly catch, its result unforeseen, its transport by chance, and so forth. In these irregular impressions, come from anywhere, it is the world itself and entirely that becomes a "sudden and unexpected arrival" (381, 23; CSM I: 353) of *commodo et incommoda*. The world appears no longer as the totality of extension in movement and changing forms, but able to be calculated and modeled by the *inspectio mentis*; it comes as an ensemble of events that can never be repeated and never foreseen, which determine thought *aliunde* (from elsewhere) as an instance of synthesis, if one still wants to [use this term], but as *passive* syntheses, to speak like Husserl. The ego does not constitute the world as a total object, it receives it as an affection always open to the possible, the opening to the world becoming, in passive thought, a *being-in-the-world*, to use Heidegger's expression.

This is confirmed by the second hapax: describing desire, Descartes notes that "when we are assured that what we desire will come about [*aviendra*], then although we still want it to come about [*avienne*] we are no longer agitated by the passion of desire" (§166, XI: 457, 7–10; CSM I: 389). He introduces in this way the *verb* "*avenir*/to come," still used in the seventeenth century, the deverbal forming the substantive "*avenir*/future": *avenir* designates first an action, a mode of "coming" [*venir*]. What mode? The mode, as the dictionary Littré says, of what befalls, thus what drops down, what imposes itself and emerges at its own moment, in its manner and thus not in mine. What befalls me constrains me to think: it imposes itself on the one who does not see it until after the fact, without anticipation, neither thus the least a priori, thus at least at the moment, without submitting itself to the a priori conditions of experience. That means that what comes does not lend itself to thought like an object. It gives itself as such, but not as that which I could constitute as an object. It is thus by definition exempt from the precept of the Second Regula, which demanded "*Circa illa tantum objecta . . . versari, ad quorum certam et indubitatam cognitionem nostra ingenia videntur sufficiere*—to attend only to those objects of which our minds seem capable of having certain and indubitable cognition."[61] The passions, and thus the passive thought that implements them by welcoming them, accordingly surpass the initial undertaking of the objectification of experience. To know passively, in particular to heal the passions, comes down to admitting the "arrivals [*arrivements*]" which "come [*éviennent*]" like pure events. Therefore, in order to think them, one must give up on clarity and distinction, at least of the kind that objectification requires, but also on certainty, if not, at the second degree, the certainty of "self-satisfaction." The *Passions of the Soul* in the end are opposed to the enterprise of the *Regulae*, drowning its prohibitions and annulling its boundaries.

If Descartes refuses obstinately to qualify the union by title of substance, if thus any reproach against it seems less founded and less intelligent than the one of "substantialization," nevertheless repeated ad nauseam by the whole history of reception, if to the contrary his whole effort consisted maybe in restricting the field of application of *substantia* (first to the benefit of the object, then of God's nonunivocity, finally to that of passive thought), he does so in a heroic effort of surpassing what he had himself first of all established—the rules defining the a priori conditions of possibility of experience and, hence, of the *objects* of experience. The union is not a substance, because I am not an object. But neither is God nor the world. What horizon was accordingly opened that Descartes' successors so quickly closed down again? What advance did he glimpse that they did not suspect, at least until Kant?

61. Regula II, AT X: 362, 2–4; CSM I: 10.

# 6

## Passion and Passivity

### §27. *From Action and Passion to Cause*

Thus the question of "my body—*meum corpus*" can be resolved or even be raised only within the horizon of passivity. Yet passivity must itself be defined in such a sense that it could also and above all contribute to defining the passivity of the *res cogitans*.

Now, according to Descartes, it is precisely in regard to this passivity of thought that the limits of previous metaphysics are best revealed: "The defects of the sciences we have from the ancients are nowhere more apparent than in their writings on the passions. This topic, about which knowledge has always been keenly sought, does not seem to be one of the more difficult to investigate since everyone feels passions in himself and so has no need to look elsewhere for observations to establish their nature. And yet the teachings of the ancients about the passions are so meagre and for the most part so implausible that I cannot hope to approach the truth except by departing from the paths they have followed. That is why I shall be obliged to write just as if I were considering a topic that no one had dealt with before me."[1] No doubt, Descartes opens

1. *Passions of the Soul*, §1, AT XI: 327, 9—328, 5; CSM I: 328.

his final treatise as he opened his first, the *Regulae*, with a frank polemic against the ancients, that is to say, against Aristotle. Yet the stakes of this polemic would still need to be clarified: In what does the failure of the ancients consist? The reply is not obvious and the most common understanding of this polemic really does not hold up under examination. In fact, we have developed the custom of situating Descartes' originality in his "intention . . . to explain the passions only as a natural philosopher [physicist], and not as a rhetorician or even as a moral philosopher."[2] He is taken to have substituted a mechanistic or even materialist doctrine for the moralizing rhetoric of his predecessors. Now, besides being anachronistic and simplistic, this opposition immediately suffers from at least two weaknesses.

First, this restriction of the description of the soul to what a "physicist" could know about it literally cites just one of the theses of Aristotle, who also attributes the consideration of the soul to a "physicist": "ταῦτα ἤδη φυσικοῦ τὸ θεωρῆσαι περὶ ψυχῆς—hence a physicist would define an affection of the soul differently from a dialectician."[3] Then, Descartes himself actually does not stick to what a "physicist" could say about the passions. Certainly physiology and thus physics play a role in this explanation: according to §3, one must attribute to our body only "anything . . . we see can also exist in wholly inanimate bodies" (this is what §§4–16 will actually study); but from this principle also follows that anything that cannot be conceived as belonging to an extended body "must be attributed to our soul"[4] (which is what §§17–21 will develop); in such a way that the real description of the passions (§§30–50) brings together what the "physicist" says about the physiology of the body (thus the "movements of the blood and the spirits which cause" the passions "in so far as they relate to the body,"[5] §§96–138) with what belongs to the soul, that is to say precisely the passive thoughts that are here called the passions. And neither the first half of the second

2. Response to Second Letter, Preface to *Passions of the Soul*, AT XI: 326, 13–15; CSM I: 327.

3. Aristotle, *On the Soul*, I.1, 403a28, ed. Jonathan Barnes, *The Complete Works of Aristotle* (Princeton: Princeton University Press, 1984), I: 643. The opposition to rhetoric becomes confirmed by another celebrated remark: "It is evidently equally foolish to accept probable reasoning from a mathematician and to demand from a rhetorician demonstrative proofs" (*Nicomachean Ethics*, I.3, 1094b26; Barnes, 1730).

4. *Passions of the Soul*, §3, 329, 5–6 and 9–10, respectively; CSM I: 329.

5. *Passions of the Soul*, §96, 401, 2–3; CSM I: 362 and §137, 429, 23–24; CSM I: 376, respectively.

part nor the third part of the treatise is written by a "physicist," even if they depend on what he has written in the first part (§§4–16) and in the second (§§96–138)—they aim respectively to "pursue virtue diligently" (§148) and to teach "wisdom" (§212), that is to say, what a "moral philosopher," if not a "rhetorician," writes.[6]

One must thus search elsewhere for the issue justifying the reproach that Descartes here addresses to the ancients and the supposedly radical opposition resulting from it. In fact, §1 seems to sketch a response: the promise of treating "a topic that no one had dealt with before me" is here immediately explained: "In the first place, I note that"; the reader expects a thesis that contradicts head-on what previous philosophy supported; yet, what does one read? Precisely an *agreement* with "the philosophers": "I note that whatever takes place or occurs is generally called by philosophers a 'passion' with regard to the subject to which it happens and an 'action' with regard to that which makes it happen. Thus, although an agent and patient are often quite different, an action and passion must always be a single thing which has these two names on account of the two different subjects to which it may be related."[7] The action consists in a subject ("which acts"), the passion in a different subject ("to which happens" what happens), but these two "very different" subjects are "a single thing." Two postulates go together but must be distinguished: first the duality of subjects, then the uniqueness of the "thing."

For the first Descartes clearly assumes it: "*Semper autem existimavi unam et eadem rem esse, quae, cum refertur ad terminum a quo, voca-*

6. *Passions of the Soul*, §148, 442, 10; CSM I: 382; §212, 488, 17; CSM I: 404 and §1, 328, 5–13; CSM I: 328, respectively. That physiology ("physics") plays a central role, but not exclusively in the *Passions*, which adduce also the irreducible role of the soul (and thus of "moral philosophy"), should all the less surprise as the *Discourse on Method* had already marked a difference between on the one hand "questions in physics . . . particularly the explanation of the movement of bodies," and on the other, "some difficulties pertaining to medicine, and also the difference between our soul and that of the beasts" (AT VI: 1, 10–14; CSM I: 111). See my commentary in the preface to Vincent Aucante, *La Philosophie médicale de Descartes* (Paris: PUF, 2006). What we understand today by "medicine" falls solely under what Descartes understands by "the questions of physics," while what Descartes understands by "medicine," but which concerns the different notions of the soul (human, animal), would fall under what we call (without precision) philosophy. See especially Claude Romano's illuminating comments in "Les trois médicines de Descartes," *XVII siècle* 217.4 (2002): 675–96 (and Caps' clarification in *Les "médecins cartesiens,"* 48ff.).

7. *Passions of the Soul*, §1, 328, 5–13; CSM I: 328.

*tur actio, cum vero ad terminum* ad quem *sive* in quo *recipitur, vocatur passio: adeo ut plane repugnet, vel per minimum temporis momentum, passionem esse sine actione.*—I have always thought that it is one and the same thing which is called an activity in relation to a *terminus a quo* [the source of the action], and a passivity in relation to a *terminus ad quem* or *in quo* [the destination of the action or its locus of reception]. If so, it is contradictory that there should be a passivity without an activity for even a single moment."[8] He achieves this all the more easily as he can appeal without further complication to Suárez: "Action and passion are really joined in a single movement or change in such a way that the action cannot be separated from the passion nor the passion from the action, even by the absolute power [of God]; for the sign for this is that they are actually not distinguished according to the nature of the thing. . . . The first premise is also proven because it is contradictory that a passion would be produced in some subject or other without it proceeding from some agent, for there is no effect without cause. . . . And, reciprocally, an action cannot come from a subject (this is precisely the issue in question) without producing there at the same time a passion, for if it is produced starting from a subject it finds its end in a subject and is produced in this same [subject]; thus there is a passion and reception on the part of such a subject; hence the passion and such an action are absolutely inseparable."[9] Yet the inseparability of action and of passion does not yet decide what they share in common: is it a matter of an *idem subjectum,* of a link between cause and effect (as for Suárez), or of a *una et eadem res* and of a *single thing* (as Descartes suggests)? What does it mean that a single thing is related to two *subjecta,* substrates, ὑποκείμενα? The inseparability of action and passion leads by its very

8. To Hyperaspistes, August 1641, AT III: 428, 17–22; CSMK: 193 [the bracketed renderings of the Latin are explanatory notes by CSMK].

9. Suárez: "*Actio et passio ita conjunguntur realiter in uno motu seu mutatione, ut nec actio a passione, nec passio ab actione separabilis sit, etiam de potentia absoluta [Dei]; ergo signum est non distingui actualiter ex natura rei . . . Antecedens autem probatur, quia repugnat passionem fieri in aliquo subjecto, quin ab aliquo agente procedat, quia non potest esse effectus sine causa . . . E converso etiam non potest esse actio ex subjecto (de hoc enim est sermo), quin hoc ipso inferat passionem, nam si ex subjecto fit, in subjecto recipitur terminus ejus, et in eodem fit; ergo est passio et receptio ex parte talis subjecti; sunt ergo omnino inseparabiles passio et talis actio.*" *Disputationes metaphysicae,* XLIX, s. 1, n. 9, in O.o., vol. 26, 900, which Gilson cites wrongly as *D.M.* XLVIII, *Index scolastico-cartesien* [1913] (Paris: Vrin, 1913, 1979), 7–8, a mistake reproduced by Alquié, in *Descartes. Œuvres philosophiques,* III: 952.

vagueness to wondering about the second postulate, which concerns the uniqueness of the "thing."

Here Descartes (and Suárez) rejoin Aristotle in order to oppose him. He was the first to recognize that "indeed something is found in common between the two terms, one appears to be acting, the other being acted upon," for "action and passion are in a certain manner (πῶς) the same [according to genus], in another way [according to species] different and heterogeneous one from the other."[10] But in Aristotle's case the inseparability rests on a common term, or rather a common act, because it is precisely a matter of ἐνέργεια, of the rise of two terms relative to each other into the same εἶδος, because first relative to the formation and essence of a single thing. Not only "is it not absurd that the actualization (ἐνέργεια) of one thing should be in another" but "it seems in fact that the ἐνέργεια of actions is found in what suffers and what it exerts its effect on."[11] Here, action and passion as categories of being refer to an οὐσία,[12] whose single ἐνέργεια they implement. Or, more exactly, the unique ἐνέργεια of a single and same thing resumes the otherwise heterogeneous relation of action and passion in its ontically assured unity. Now, such a reference of terms to the relationship to ἐνέργεια is enough to manifest Descartes' genuine opposition to the "ancients": it is a matter not of the identity of action and passion, a point on which he is in perfect agreement with the "philosophers" (in this case Suárez), but of the justification of this identity. Like Suárez, Descartes can only resort to the relation of cause to effect or to an *una et eadem res*, composed in static fashion of two "subjects," because, since his polemic against Aristotle in the *Regulae*, he no longer has the least access open to him to anything like an οὐσία or, a fortiori, to the ἐνέργεια that it implements starting from itself.[13] Furthermore, not only does Descartes (and

10. Aristotle, *On the Soul*, III.4, 429b25 and *Of Generation and Corruption*, I.7, 324a4, respectively. [Translations here and below are of Marion's French, which is quite different from the English translation of Aristotle's text.]

11. Aristotle, *Physics* III.3, 202b6 and *On the Soul*, II.2, 414a12, respectively. See also: "For it is in the passive factor that the actuality (ἐνέργεια) of the active or motive factor is realized" (*On the Soul*, III.2, 426a4–5; Barnes, 677) and "The active and the passive imply an active and a passive capacity and the actualization of the capacities (ἐνεργείας τὰσ τῶν δυνάμεων)" (*Metaphysics* Δ.15, 1021a13–16; Barnes, 1612).

12. Passion and action actually first go back to an οὐσία (see *Categories* 4, 1b25–2a4).

13. I here take for granted the anti-Aristotelian critique completed from the outset by the *Regulae ad directionem Ingenii*, for which I have established the results in *Sur l'ontologie grise de Descartes*, especially §§13–14 and §28.

most probably already Suárez) no longer have available what would ensure the unity (and not only the correlation or addition) of action and passion, but by establishing between them a relation of efficient causality he is scarcely able to *oppose* the two terms at the very moment of making them interact. For the paradox of efficient causality always depends on this: it manages to join two terms in contiguity and within the moment that hence appear all the more irreducibly different—an inert body acting on another, God creating eternal truths, the infinite allowing the finite, a will provoking a movement or a thought, and so forth. The same is true in the case of species in an exemplary manner: the action comes either from the body on the soul (in the case of the passions of the soul), or from the will on thought (in the case of active thoughts), or from the soul on the body (in the case of free actions), but in all these cases action and passion, which cannot be separated, nevertheless link together two terms that not only are irretrievably distinct from one another but opposed to each other.

That is why Descartes, when defining passion and action without reference to the οὐσία, can attribute a very broad definition to them: "whatever takes place or newly comes about."[14] In fact, broadening this definition permits him to encompass in the passions even imaginings without "conspicuous and determinate" external cause, provided that "our will is not used in forming them," thus passions "if the word is understood in a more general sense."[15] It appears too wide only in comparison with the relationship that remains restricted and precisely referred to the οὐσία in the *Categories*, but remains just broad enough for what Descartes understands here, namely, the accidental nature of what happens in perfect facticity, the "first encounter with some object

14. *Passions of the Soul,* §1, AT XI: 328, 6; CSM I: 328, trans. lightly modified.

15. *Passions of the Soul,* §21, XI: 345, 11; 344, 21–22 and 345, 9–10, respectively; CSM I: 336. The same broadening of the passion in the simple absence of action comes up again in §28: "We may call them [i.e., the passions of the soul] 'perceptions' if we use this term *generally* to signify all the thoughts which are not actions of the soul or volitions" (349, 19–22; CSM I: 339). Or at §41: "of the two kinds of thought I have distinguished in the soul—the first its actions, i.e. its volitions, and the second its passions, taking this word *in its most general sense* to include every kind of perception" (359, 16–21; CSM I: 343). See also: "Consequently, the term 'passion' can be applied in *general* to all the thoughts which are thus aroused in the soul by cerebral impressions alone, without the concurrence of its will, and therefore without any action of the soul itself; for whatever is not an action is a passion" (To Elizabeth, 6 October 1645, IV: 310, 16–21; CSM I: 270).

[which] surprises us and that we find novel," with things that "may happen," in short with the "event" in general, once named in an admirable hapax "the sudden and unexpected arrival [*arrivement*] of the impression which changes the movements of the spirits."[16] Understood in this way, passion will no longer make the thing (that is to say, rather the οὐσία) play with itself, in the rise toward its ἐνέργεια, because Descartes has eliminated these notions, in perfect conformity with his critique of the definition of movement by power and by act; passion will henceforth attempt to describe and to order the *effects* of what happens to the soul, whatever they might be and from wherever they might arrive (they actually prove to be legion, §§27–28). Passivity, which is at play in the passions of the soul, designates "all the thoughts which are not actions of the soul" (§28, 349, 20–21; CSM I: 339), in other words all events [*événements*], any advent [*avènement*], and any "arrival [*arrivement*]" that its facticity imposes on the *res cogitans*. From now on, passion points to the mode of thought in which the *res cogitans* thinks passively without "generally" exercising the cause of its own thought. What does it mean for the ego to think without causing its thought, "without it,"[17] thinking without wanting to, thinking under the hold of a causality

---

16. *Passions of the Soul*, §53, XI: 373, 5–6; CSM I: 350; §145, 438, 15; CSM I: 380; §166, 457, 10 (with the rare verb *avenir*!); CSM I: 389; and finally §72, 381, 22–24; CSM I: 353, respectively. Obviously such a broadening by abstraction from the οὐσία and of its ἐνέργεια can also be understood as a "*reducing* of passion to what is solely and effectively perceived by the soul" (Guénancia, *L'Intelligence du sensible*, 204), in the sense of a reduction of passivity to the effect of causal efficacy.

17. *Passions of the Soul*, §13, XI: 338, 23; CSM I: 333; see "against our volition" (339, 7; CSM I: 333), "without the help of the soul" (§16, 341, 11; CSM I: 334), "without any contribution from our will" (341, 23; CSM I: 335). Already To Elizabeth: "Consequently, the term 'passion' can be applied in general to all the thoughts which are thus aroused in the soul by cerebral impressions alone, *without the concurrence of its will*" (6 October 1645, IV: 310, 16–18; CSM I: 270). The anxiety already present in the *etiam invito*, which already lurks in the *Meditations*, reappears here in grand style: "*Et praeterea experior illas [i.e., ideas] non a mea voluntate nec proinde a me ipso pendere; saepe enim vel invito observantur: ut jam, sive velim, sive nolim, sentio calorem, et ideo puto sensum illum, sive ideam caloris, a re a me diversa, nempe ab ignis cui assideo calore, mihi advenire*—in addition I know by experience that these ideas do not depend on my will, and hence that they do not depend simply on me. Frequently I notice them even when I do not want to: now, for example, I feel the heat whether I want to or not, and this is why I think that this sensation or idea of heat comes to me from something other than myself, namely the heat of the fire by which I am sitting" (VII: 38, 15–20; CSM II: 26, among other occurrences).

submitted to and received, thinking under influence, thinking *as an effect*? This emerges as the unsettling stake of the inquiry that gives rise to the whole treatise of *The Passions of the Soul*, which is devoted entirely to "*still two* other causes, which depend solely on the body" (§12, 337, 5; CSM I: 332). Here, the onto-theo-logy of the *ens ut causatum* extends its shadow and its authority to the very heart of the onto-theo-logy of the *ens ut cogitatum*, under the proclaimed *leitmotiv* of the "cause."[18] The sole question henceforth becomes: "What are the first causes of the passions"?[19]

### §28. To Think Passively, or Thought as Passion

The link of causality, which is substituted for the relationship between two categories connected to the same οὐσία (or rather a category of relation between two inseparable predications connected to the same οὐσία), should not lead us to imagine anachronistically that Descartes here raises the question of the causality between soul and body, acting reciprocally on each other. The union does not have to be explained, because, as we have seen, Descartes admits it as a fact and a fact of reason (see above, §21 and §26) without needing to submit it to causality. Here it is a matter neither of the causality of the soul on the body, nor even of that of the body on the soul, but an issue of determining, within and from the point of view of the *res cogitans*, how (by what causes) the *cogitationes* can come to the ego without its being at their initiative and thus despite itself. Now, at this point of the inquiry, nothing prejudges the origin of these entirely passive *cogitationes*; and this passivity will actually be explained by (or be applied to) several equally possible and active causes: either the objects of extension, or *meum corpus*, or the movements of spirits. Moreover the soul, when it tries to act on its body or on the other bodies, does so neither directly nor consciously (*Passions of the Soul*, §41), because some of its thoughts remain passive even in this action. One must thus consider the dimensions of this passivity.

What cause should one assign to the passivity of the *res cogitans*?

18. *Passions of the Soul*: "one of the causes" (§12, XI: 337, 4), "The other cause" (§14, 339, 17); §19, 343, 12–13; §21, 344, 15–16; 345, 11; §23, 346, 6; §24, 347, 14; "no next cause" and "also by other causes" (§25, 344, 20 and 24); §27, 349, 14; §29, 350, 24, 26; §34, 354, 24; §37, 357, 13, 17, 24; §38, 358, 9; §39, 358, 19; §40, 359, 6, 7 (starting from the "effects of passions").

19. *Passions of the Soul*, §51, 371, 8, opening of the second part (distinguishing "the ultimate and most proximate cause of the passions" from "their first causes," 371, 10 and 15; CSM I: 349).

The response seems self-evident: the body, because there is no "subject which acts more directly upon our soul than the body to which it is joined" (§2, 328, 18–20; CSM I: 328). But how should one define this body? Is it an issue of the *meum corpus*, which as we know Descartes understood since the Sixth Meditation as we today understand the flesh (*Leib*) in contrast with the extended bodies of the physical world (*Körper*)? The first response seems ambiguous: among "anything we experience as being in us," if what "we cannot conceive in any way as capable of belonging to a body must be attributed to our soul" (§3, 329, 4–10; CSM I: 329; in such a way that "every kind of thought present in us belongs to the soul," §4, 329, 16–17; CSM I: 329)—then, to the contrary, everything that can be found both "in us" and also "in wholly inanimate bodies"[20] must be ascribed to "our body."[21] Does Descartes here confuse what he had previously distinguished? Obviously not, because the "inanimate bodies" remain distinct from what is found "in us"; but precisely, elements are found "in us" that do not belong to the soul, which thinks by itself: in this way "all the heat and all the movements present in us, in so far as they do not depend on thought, belong solely to the body" (§3, 329, 23–26; CSM I: 329). In other words, my body, *meum corpus*, is defined as that which, in the soul and "in us," results not from thought (thinking spontaneously) but from the movements of inanimate bodies. Besides, from the moment that these movements will end in extension, from the moment that "the mechanism of which our body is composed" and "the corporeal principle underlying all these movements" are dissolved, when "this heat ceases and the organs which bring about bodily movement decay,"[22] we die—our soul will no longer have the link via the *meum corpus* to extension, henceforth immobile and

20. *Passions of the Soul*, §3, 329, 6; CSM I: 329; see "since we do not doubt that there are inanimate bodies which can move in as many different ways as our bodies" (§4, 329, 17–20; CSM I: 329).

21. *Passions of the Soul*, §3, 329, 7; CSM I: 329, in opposition to "a body" (329, 9), "the body" (329, 26).

22. *Passions of the Soul*, §7, 331, 12–13; CSM I: 330; §8, 333, 11–12; CSM I: 331; §5, 330, 17–18; CSM I: 329, respectively (see §6, 330, 24–25; CSM I: 329). My body interferes with the *mens* by affecting it (more precisely by rendering it passive in this way and able to be affected) only as long as it is being supported by the movements that as movements belong necessarily to extension and that accordingly render it homogeneous to the *mens*, although we experience it "in us" (§3). We have our body (*meum corpus*, *Leib*) only as long as we need it, as long as "while we are alive" (§8, 333, 8–9) the movements of inanimate extension (and the heat that goes with them, §8, 333, 9; CSM I: 331; §107, 407, 25; CSM I: 366; §122, 418, 12–14; CSM I: 371) affect us with passive thoughts.

inert, and will remain deprived of passivity. The activity of the "inanimate bodies" ("in differences in the movements produced in the sense
organs by their objects") constitutes in this way a first cause of passivity,
the most external one.[23] It is nevertheless rightly being credited to the
*meum corpus*, because it alone conveys via a second cause the effects
of the first: "the unequal agitation of the spirits and differences in their
parts," that is to say, the internal dispositions of spirits in the whole
*meum corpus*.[24] The bodies and my body accordingly act within extension, but also starting from the extension "against our soul" (§2, 328,
19; CSM I: 328).

The excursus of §§2–16 also allows us to begin to disentangle "the
functions" of the soul and for the first time to comprehend why there
are two of them. That is, to the question raised by §3, what "do we
experience" as "being in us," §17 responds that "there is nothing in us
which we must attribute to our soul except our thoughts."[25] Yet, henceforth, we can and we must distinguish two kinds of thoughts: first, as
in §3, what "we experience"[26] depends only on our soul, on thoughts,
but now understood in the specific sense of actions, of "volitions," in
other words, active thoughts. As to what in §3 had to be "attributed
only to our body," without doubt it is not being directly credited to
the soul in §17 (because that would be to confuse the simple material and intellectual natures); but what had already been said to be "in
us" now produces "perceptions or modes of knowledge present in us,"
because the soul receives them "always . . . from the things that are represented by them"; and these types of knowledge take on the status of
"passions," because, even if they remain "always" thoughts in the soul,
"often it is not our soul which makes them such as they are."[27] In other

23. *Passions of the Soul*, §12, 337, 6–8 (the activity analyzed in §12–13);
CSM I: 332–33.

24. *Passions of the Soul*, §14, 339, 17–19; CSM I: 334. It is thus really a
matter of "two . . . causes, which depend solely on the body," one acting via the
mediation of the other (§12, 337, 5).

25. *Passions of the Soul*, §3, 329, 5; CSM I: 329 (= §2, 328, 26; CSM I:
328); §3, 329, 4–5; CSM I: 329; and §17, 342, 10–11; CSM I: 335, respectively.

26. *Passions of the Soul*, §17, 342, 15; CSM I: 335, responding to §3, 329,
4–5; CSM I: 329: "anything we experience as being in us."

27. *Passions of the Soul*, respectively §3, 329, 6–7; CSM I: 329 and §17, 342,
18–22; CSM I: 335 (the second "in us" of §17, 342, 19 responding to the second "in us" of §3, 329, 8). The main restriction, that "often" the soul does not
make (does not cause) the perceptions, is found again *a contrario* in §51: "they
[i.e., the passions] may sometimes be caused by an action of the soul which
sets itself to conceive some object or other" (371, 15–17; CSM I: 349; see §41,

words, there are active thoughts in us (called "willed"), but also passive thoughts from the fact that "inanimate bodies" conveyed by the *meum corpus* act on my soul (these passive thoughts are called "passions"). In short, the soul is not limited to thinking only those thoughts that it "makes . . . such as they are," but also those that it "receives from things" (§17, 342, 20–22; CSM I: 335) and that are passive.

Yet, a new question arises from this result: what perceptions merit the name of passions? Is it enough that a thought comes to the soul without its activity for us to be able to qualify it as passion? Putting the question another way, where is the boundary between active thoughts and passive thoughts to be drawn? Is the passivity of thought reduced to representations produced by affectivity or to those that accompany moral practice? Before anything else one must note that the field of passivity straightaway retreats before the will. And for several reasons. (a) In fact, the will is exerted over "the actions of the soul" (like loving God) no less than over "our body," thus in the end over "our thought" inasmuch as it is applied to "some object which is not material" (§18, 343, 1–4; CSM I: 335). (b) Then, as "it is certain that we cannot will anything without thereby perceiving that we are willing it," the action of willing is immediately equivalent to a corresponding perception of the will (this "is really one and the same thing"). We certainly prefer indicating it as "whatever is most noble," thus as a volition, but this volition covers just as much a perception of the will.[28] Will and perception

---

360, 1–2; CSM I: 343: "except when it [i.e., the will] is itself their cause [i.e., of the passions]"). This can be understood either as a re-conversion by the will of thoughts first passive (§19f.), or as the control of certain passions (§§45–50).

28. *Passions of the Soul*, §19, 343, 15–18, then 21–22 and 23; CSM I: 335–36. This conversion of the will into idea or perception of this will, thus extension of the will into the domain of perception, constitutes one of Descartes' ancient and constant theses. Thus: "I have never said that all our thoughts are in our power, but only that *if there is anything absolutely in our power, it is our thoughts*, that is to say, those which come from our will and free choice" (To Mersenne, 3 December 1640, AT III: 249, 4–8; CSMK: 160, commenting on the *Discourse on Method*, AT VI: 25, 23–24; CSM I: 123: "nothing lies entirely within our power except our thoughts"). And especially: "I claim that we have ideas not only of all that is in our intellect, but also of all that is in the will. For we cannot will anything without knowing that we will it, nor could we know this except by means of an idea; but I do not claim that the idea is different from the act itself" (To Mersenne, 28 January 1642; III: 295, 22–27; CSMK: 172). And also: "*Hic voluntatis et intellectus functiones confunduntur: neque enim voluntatis est intelligere, sed tantum velle; ac quamvis nihil unquam velimus, de quo non aliquid aliquo modo intelligamus, ut jam ante concessi, plura tamen*

are hence interchangeable in the idea of what I want; the passion of an action (the idea of the will) passes accordingly under the control and the regime of action. (c) But we cannot neglect to push the argument further. For in the final account certain other perceptions depend on the will, starting with doubt; accordingly, does the argument of the evil genius not impose itself (it is pedagogically, psychologically, but not theoretically true) by an act of the will: "*non male agam, si,* voluntate *plane in contrarium versa, me ipsum fallam*—it will be a good plan to turn my *will* in completely the opposite direction and deceive myself"?[29] (d) As for the imagination, it depends first on attention, which itself also depends on the will to apply it: "When our soul applies itself to imagine something non-existent—as in thinking about an enchanted palace or a chimera—and also when it applies itself to consider something that is purely intelligible and not imaginable—for example, in considering its own nature—the perceptions it has of these things depend chiefly on the volition which makes it aware of them. That is why we usually regard these perceptions as actions rather than passions."[30] This reprisal of productive imagination (already Kantian, and not only reproductive, like the Aristotelian one) moreover had already been acquired earlier: "But when the soul uses the will to determine itself to some thought which is not just intelligible but also imaginable, this thought makes a new impression in the brain; this is not a passion within the soul, but an action—and this is properly called imagination."[31] Thus, even the imagination can be converted into action, because it depends on the will.

---

*eadem de re nos posse velle quam cognoscere*—Here there is a confusion between the functions of the intellect and the will. The function of the will is not to understand, but only to will; and though, as I agreed before, we never will anything of which we have no understanding at all, yet experience shows clearly that about any given thing our will may extend further than our knowledge" (To Hyperaspistes, August 1641, AT III: 432, 3–8; CSMK: 195). The boundary between will (action) and perception (passion) becomes thus here essentially porous, if not effaced.

29. First Meditation, AT VII: 22, 12–14; CSM II: 15.
30. *Passions of the Soul,* §20, XI: 344, 4–13; CSM I: 336.
31. To Elizabeth, 6 October 1645, AT IV: 311, 8–13; CSMK: 271. This is confirmed by *Passions of the Soul* in §19 ("the perceptions of our volitions and of all the imaginings or other thoughts which depend on them," 343, 13–15; CSM I: 335), §43 ("When we want to imagine something we have never seen, this volition has the power to make the gland move in the way required," 361, 4–6; CSM I: 344), §80 ("Moreover, in using the world 'willingly' I am not speaking of desire . . . but of the assent by which we . . . imagine a whole, of which we take ourselves to be a part," 387, 18–23; CSM I: 356). The same is

As a consequence, must one conclude that all the modes of the *res cogitans*, namely, doubt, the will, and the imagination, belong to the will and not to perception, thus to action and not to passion? One could nevertheless invoke one case of resistance to this empire of action, namely, the understanding. For this purpose one often invokes an apparently very clear declaration by Descartes: "*Intellectio enim proprie mentis passio est, et volitio ejus actio.*—For strictly speaking, understanding is the passivity of the mind and willing is its activity."[32] Yet this declaration is precisely not without ambiguity. It sounds in fact like *a common position of the school philosophy*, which raises immediately a reservation, if not to say an objection, from Descartes: "sed, *quia nihil unquam volumus, quin simul intelligamus, et vix etiam quicquam intelligimus, quin simul etiam velimus, ideo non facile in iis passionem ab actione distinguimus*—but because we cannot will anything without understanding what we will, and we scarcely ever understand something without at the same time willing something, we do not easily distinguish in this matter passivity from activity."[33] This text should surprise us more than it usually does, for at issue is not only Descartes' current position (which we have just seen above), underlining that any

---

true for memory, over which imagination presides: "Thus, when the soul wants to remember something, this volition makes the gland . . . driving the spirits towards different regions of the brain until they come upon the one containing traces left by the object we want to remember" (§42, 360, 10–15; CSM I: 344). One can recover a sketch of this hold of the will on the attention from the Fourth Meditation: "*Nam, quamvis eam in me infirmitatem esse experiar, ut non possim semper uni et eidem cognitioni defixus inhaerere*, possum *tamen attenta et saepius iterata meditatione* efficere, *ut ejusdem, quoties usus exiget, recorder, atque ita habitum quemdam non errandi acquiram*—Admittedly, I am aware of a certain weakness in me, in that I am unable to keep my attention fixed on one and the same item of knowledge at all times; but by attentive and repeated meditation I am nevertheless *able to make* myself remember it as often as the need arises, and thus get into the habit of avoiding error" (VII: 62, 2–7; IX-1, 55; CSM II: 43).

32. To Regius, May 1641, III: 372, 12–13; CSMK: 182. See also: "I regard the difference between the soul and its ideas as the same as that between a piece of wax and the various shapes it can take. Just as it is not an activity but a passivity in the wax to take various shapes, so, it seems to me, it is a passivity in the soul to receive one or other idea, and only its volitions are activities. It receives its ideas partly from objects which come into contact with the senses, partly from impressions in the brain, and partly from prior dispositions in the soul and from movements of the will" (To Mesland, 2 May 1644, AT IV: 113, 22—114, 4; CSMK: 232).

33. To Regius, May 1646, AT III: 372, 13–16; CSMK: 182; emphasis added.

will is really equivalent to the perception of this will, thus to a passion, in such a way that any action could be converted into passion. Here the argument goes further, because it then draws out what is reciprocal to the first thesis: almost (*vix*) everything that we understand (*intelligimus*), we also will, thus any passion (perception, namely, perception of understanding) can be confused with an action (that of willing what we understand). Not only does this will encompass the perception of this will (and the action swamp the passion), but in turn almost (*vix*) all perception of the understanding implies willing what has been understood (and the passion of understanding is converted into an action of the will that wills what the understanding has understood). A radical lack of distinction between passion and the will *even in the case of the understanding* hence ensues. The mode of the *cogitatio* that the understanding constitutes (the *intellectus* such as it operates in the Second and Third Meditations as pure and without imagination or sensation) thus is not exempt from the grasp of the will in it, which would reduce it from passion to action, as has been the case already for doubt, imagination (and memory).[34] Would the *res cogitans* thus think only under the direct or indirect rule of the will, hence only actively?

Even if Descartes affirms without ambiguity that "various perceptions or modes of knowledge present in us may be called its passions [i.e., those of the soul], in a general sense, for it is often not our soul

---

34. One must take up again here, in detail, the intellectual role (in the sense of *intellectu*) of the will across the entire text of the *Meditations*—if just to recognize first of all that it does not produce error ("*nulla . . . in ipsa voluntate . . . falsitat*—as for the will . . . one need not worry about falsity," VII: 37, 17–20; CSM II: 26), then that it even "puts together" the ideas (*componere*, 43, 8; CSM II: 29), finally and above all that it interferes with the understanding ("*latius patet*," 58, 21; CSM II: 40) or even allows itself to be determined by it ("*magna . . . propensio*—a great inclination," 59, 1–3; CSM II: 41). At the very least it is not self-evident that the understanding constitutes an exception to the other *modi cogitandi* and that one could without further precaution maintain Gueroult's erroneous thesis, which says: "The three authorities, understanding, imagination, and sense perception, are not and cannot be on the same plane, in some sort of equality. The understanding is always subject, which is never the case for imagination or sense perception" (in Guénancia, *L'Intelligence du sensible*, 354). Not only is doubt and especially the will lacking in this enumeration of *modi cogitandi*, not only is the term "subject" unknown to Descartes in this sense, but it is not a matter of equality or inequality, not even of a primacy of the will, but of a much more essential question: Can one, according to Descartes, think passively or wouldn't the *res cogitans* always become active, at least in a tangential sense?

which makes them such as they are,"[35] he does not reach this result without difficulty. Thus he still maintains the equivalence between passivity and affection in 1644, accordingly restricting the former to the latter: *"affectus, sive animi pathemata, hoc est, quatenus sunt confusae quaedam cogitationes, quas mens non habet a se sola, sed ab eo quod a corpore, cui intime conjuncta est, aliquid patiatur*—simply as emotions or passions of the soul, that is, as confused thoughts, which the mind does not derive from itself alone but experiences as a result of something happening to the body with which it is closely conjoined."[36] It actually always remains possible *not* to think the passivity of thought radically in the case of thoughts that have come from the exterior, if only by appealing to the reasons that Augustine, for example, enumerates: "these mental motions, which the Greeks call πάθη, while some of our own writers [i.e., of the Latins], like Cicero, call them perturbations, some others call them affections or affects, while finally others, like this final one [i.e., Apuleius], call them passions, following the Greek expression."[37] Actually from the *Discourse on Method* onward

35. *Passions of the Soul,* §17, XI: 342, 17–21; CSM I: 335.

36. *Principles of Philosophy* IV, §190, VIII-1: 317, 24–27; CSM I: 281. See I, §48: *"commotiones, sive animi pathemata, quae nec ad solam mentem, nec etiam ad solum corpus referri debent, quaeque . . . ab arcta et intima mentis nostrae cum corpore unione proficiscuntur,"* which *"ab arcta et intima mentis nostrae cum corpore unione proficiscuntur*—emotions or passions of the mind which do not consist of thought alone . . . we also experience within ourselves certain other things which must not be referred either to the mind alone or to the body alone. These arise . . . from the close and intimate union of our mind with the body" (VIII-1: 23, 17–18 and 15–17; CSM I: 209); and II, §2, 41, 18–19; CSM I: 224: *"mens est conscia non a se sola proficisci, nec ad se posse pertinere ex eo solo quod sit res cogitans*—The mind is aware that these sensations do not come from itself alone, and that they cannot belong to it simply in virtue of its being a thinking thing." But to observe that the thoughts do not come to the *mens* by itself is not the same thing as to see that by welcoming them, the *mens* begins to think passively. Regarding the development from the *Principles* to the *Passions,* see Gilles Olivo, "Descartes critique du dualisme cartésien ou l'homme des *Principia*: union de l'âme et du corps et vérités éternelles dans les *Principia* IV, 188–189," in Jean-Robert Armogathe, Giulia Belgioioso, eds., *Descartes. Principia philosophiae (1644–1994).*

37. "*de his animi motibus, quae Graeci* πάθη*, nostri autem quidam, sicut Cicero, perturbationes* [see *Tusculanes* IV.3, 8; 5, 10, etc.]*, quidam affectiones vel affectus* [Quintilian, *Institutiones Oratoris,* VI.2, 2]*, quidam vero, sicut iste* [Apuleius, *De deo Socratis,* XII]*, de Graeco expressione passiones vocant.*" Augustine, *De civitate Dei,* IX.4, 1; *City of God,* 361, trans. modified.

Descartes takes the side of the term "passion,"[38] a fundamental decision that every translator should respect. This is at least what is pointed out by the *Praefatiuncula ad lectorum* that Henri Desmarets adds to the Latin translation of the *Passions of the Soul*, which his son publishes in the same year of 1650: "although the term 'affects' could maybe have been employed with better Latinity, I have nevertheless preferred to maintain that of the 'passions' in order to remain closer to the principles followed by the author."[39] In fact, Descartes' decision leaves no doubt: one must recognize for passivity in general—under the title of "passion"—the entirety of the thoughts that the *cogitatio* accomplishes without having recourse to the activity of the will, without any action on its part, in short the whole of passive thought: "Consequently, the term 'passion' can be applied *in general* to all the *thoughts* which are thus aroused *in the soul* by cerebral impressions alone, *without the concurrence of the will*, and therefore *without any action* of the soul itself; for whatever is not an action is a passion."[40] This formulation of 1645 will be developed in 1650 by another that is just as clear: "On the other hand, the various perceptions or modes of knowledge present in us may be called its passions, *in a general sense, for it is often not our soul which makes them* such as they are."[41]

This passivity has two characteristics.

(a) It is really a matter of a passivity of the *res cogitans*, of the soul as *mens*, inasmuch as it thinks, and not, as for example in Saint Thomas, of an accidental passivity, depending on the fact that the soul becomes linked to a body: "wherefore passion properly so called cannot be in the

---

38. See: "no cares or passions" (VI: 11, 10; CSM I: 116); "internal passions" (55, 18, 27; CSM I: 139); "the natural movements which express passions" (58, 18; CSM I: 140). But it is translated in all three cases by *affectus*.

39. "*Et ausim sane dicere illos [i.e., conceptus] non potuisse ab alio quam ab homine Gallo satis feliciter exprimi. Id me movit ut, cum nomen* Affectuum *latinius forte posset usurpari, maluerim tamen* Passionum *vocere retinere, quo Authoris ipsius principiis magis inhaererem*" (*Passiones animae, per Renatum Des Cartes Gallice ab ipso concscriptae, nunc autem in exterorum gratiam Latina versione civitate donatae ab H.D.M.I.U.L.*, Amsterdam, 1650, cited in AT XI: 490, reprinted by Conte Editore, Lecce, 1997). On this preface and this translation, see Paul Dibon, "En marge de la Préface à la traduction latine des *Passions de l'âme*," *Studia Cartesiana* 1 (Amsterdam, 1979).

40. To Elizabeth, 6 October 1645, AT IV: 310, 16–21; CSMK: 270.

41. *Passions of the Soul*, §17, AT XI: 342, 17–21; CSM I: 335. One will note, in these two final texts, the adversarial nuance ("But," "on the other hand")—Descartes makes a choice.

soul, save accidentally, in so far, to wit, as the composite is passive."[42] In short, it is a matter of passions *of the soul*, and not of the accident of the soul or of the body (in whatever way one understands it). At stake are passions of the soul, because the soul, as such, as *res cogitans*, thinks not only actively, but *also passively*; and because it hence needs the passions in order to deploy all the forms of its *cogitatio*, which alone are qualified for allowing it to practice its *passive* thought.

(b) This passivity matters so much that one must describe it by referring back to at least three concepts: "we may define them *generally* as those perceptions, sensations or emotions of the soul which we refer particularly to it, and which are *caused*, maintained and strengthened by some movement of the spirits."[43] It is really a matter of "perceptions," because "we use this term *generally* to signify all the thoughts which *are not at all actions* of the soul or volitions" (349, 20–23; CSM I: 339, trans. lightly modified), in this case thoughts that are "confused and obscure" (350, 3; CSM I: 339). It is also a matter of "sensations, because they are *received* into the soul in the same way as the objects of the external senses" (350, 4–6; CSM I: 339), without that implying any clear and distinct knowledge. Finally it is a matter of "emotions," a term that is applied to "all the changes which *occur* [lit. *arrive*] *in the soul*, that is, to all the various thoughts that *come to it*" (350, 9–10; CSM I: 339). In three graduated ways, these terms mark the involuntary nature, the reception, and the event-character [*événementialité*] of definitively passive thought, that is to say, thought that is situated in the soul but without arising from it.

The passions of the soul thus do not first of all or particularly give rise to a question of ethics or of physiology, but to an epistemic question, which asks how sensation is to be integrated into the *cogitatio*; which also elicits a question of rational psychology that seeks to integrate sensation into the *cogitatio*; which in the end leads to an investigation of special metaphysics—how to unfold all the operations of the *res cogitans*? It will certainly be necessary to take positions in ethics or physiology, but they will intervene only as replies and contributions to a single issue—that of defining the *cogitatio* that the *res cogitans* can think only by allowing it to come to it from *elsewhere*.

---

42. "*Passio proprie dicta non potest competere animae nisi per accidens, inquantum scilicet* compositum patitur." Thomas Aquinas, *Summa Theologiae* I-II, q.22, a.1, resp., trans. Fathers of the English Dominican Province as *Summa Theologica* (Westminster, UK: Christian Classics, 1948), 691.

43. *Passions of the Soul*, §27, AT XI: 349, 12–17; CSM I: 338–39.

## §29. All That the Soul Senses

To come from elsewhere means for this mode of the *cogitatio* to depend on causes other than the single one that is proper and internal to it, namely, its will. The *res cogitans* actually experiences a different cause from the one that its will exercises *ad extra* in centrifugal fashion: the cause or causes *ad intra* that in centripetal fashion are exercised by the movements of the animal spirits acting on the pineal gland and, via their intermediary, the movements of the bodies of the world (the "objects") affecting the *meum corpus*. "Perceptions, sensations or emotions of the soul which we refer particularly to it, and which are *caused, maintained and strengthened* by some movement of the spirits" (§27, 349, 12–16; CSM I: 338–39). Also, "the principal effect of all the human passions as they *move* and *dispose* the soul to *want* the things for which they prepare the body" (§40, 359, 8–10; CSM I: 343). First of all, one must take exteriority in its vagueness and all its generality; for one would not be able to doubt that "all our perceptions, both those that refer to objects outside us and those we refer to various states of our body, are indeed passions with respect to our soul, so long as we use the term 'passion' in its *most general* sense." Why thus at times "restrict the term to signify only perceptions which refer to the soul itself" (§25, 347, 25—348, 3; CSM I: 337–38)? Because passivity varies according to the measure or the degree of exteriority of that to which it is related. Accordingly we can distinguish at least three degrees of passivity according to which the ego identifies the (more or less external) origin of the cause that renders the soul passive: either objects outside of us, extended bodies in the world (§23); or "our body" (§24), *corpus meum*; or finally (§25) "our soul."

In the first case, the cause that passively causes the *res cogitans* to sense a lived [experience] of consciousness comes from something other than the thinking self: one must hence "relate" this lived experience of consciousness to an intentional object in the world, according to noetic-noematic correlation; just as light is referred to a torch or sound to a bell. Here passivity is measured by the exteriority of the extension.

In the second case, the cause that passively causes us to sense a lived experience of consciousness comes certainly from something other than the sole *res cogitans*, but nevertheless not from a thing that would all the same be foreign and external to it, because it is a matter of *meum corpus* "*arctisseme conjunctum et quasi permixtum*—closely joined and, as it were, intermingled"[44] with me: here the lived experience of

---

44. Sixth Meditation, AT VII: 81, 3–4; CSM II: 56.

consciousness cannot be "referred" with an intentional gap to some external object or other, which "my body," intimately united to the *mens*, obviously is not; in this way pain, especially hunger and thirst (see above, chapter 2, §8), are felt "as being in our limbs, and not as being in objects outside us."[45] Here passivity is measured by the intimacy of the union of the soul to *meum corpus*, without exteriority.

The third case is left, where the perceptions are "referred especially to the soul" in order to form the passions "in its most proper and most specific signification." It is a matter of a case where "no proximate cause," that is to say one external to the soul itself, can be found: neither the nerves nor the objects that exercise a causality through them affect the pineal gland and, through it, the soul; the soul is always being affected by the movements of spirits "agitated in various ways," but from nothing external (neither object nor cause) that passes via the nerves, only by "traces of various impressions" left "fortuitously" by real former impressions of spirits. In other words, the spirits that agitate the gland and thereby affect the soul do not themselves depend on any external cause, or any foreign object; nor do they come from (active) volitions of the soul; spirits are moved only from the fact of living memory, but empty of certain of their old movements, of the simple *trace* of a vanished exteriority. In other words the soul here is subject to a passion that comes neither from the exteriority (of the world), nor from the intimacy (of *meum corpus*), nor from an action (of the will), but solely from the "shadow and picture" of exteriority.[46]

Would it then be a matter only of the simple *trace* of a passion? An essential paradox intervenes here: these perceptions, which are aroused only by traces, quite to the contrary constitute the most reliable and indisputable of the passions; in fact, any perception referring to an object can deceive, inasmuch as it more or less differs from this object (in attributing to it a property that it does not have); in the same way perception referring to *meum corpus* can deceive me (for example by making me locate the pain in a missing limb, etc.); in turn, if it is a matter of referring perceptions to the soul and to it alone, directly, then these perceptions "are so close and so internal to our soul that it cannot possibly feel them unless they are truly as it feels them to be" (§26, 348, 25–27; CSM I: 338). Accordingly, "even if we are asleep and dreaming,

---

45. *Passions of the Soul*, §24, XI: 347, 2–3; CSM I: 337.
46. *Passions of the Soul*, respectively §29, 350, 16–17; §21, 345, 7–8; §25, 347, 20; §21, 344, 24, 25; 345, 1; 345, 13–14 (= §26: "shadow or picture," 348, 17–18; CSM I: 338).

we cannot feel sad, or moved by any other passion, unless the soul truly has this passion within it" (349, 4–7; CSM I: 338). When dreaming, whether sleeping or awake, I can certainly be deceived about the perception of objects in the world or sensations of states of *meum corpus*; but I cannot be deceived in the passion that affects my soul—here sadness. For even without external cause or movement of spirits by the nerves, it is enough for me to be affected by sadness in order for me really to be sad, in the strictest sense of this passion. At stake is not just the fact, already noted, that sensation, taken as such, does not deceive, or even the paradox that the sensing of sensation attests and shows itself always to be absolutely true, even if the sensed content can deceive.[47] At issue here is rather the privilege of the passions, which one cannot doubt, not only because "everyone feels passions in himself,"[48] they remain intimate to him by this very sensing, but because by sensing them *in* us, we sense them *as* us, we *sense ourselves in them*. To sense oneself—this appears in fact as the strange phenomenon (that Descartes describes in detail several times) of a passion that "arrives when we happen to *feel ourselves* sad or joyful without being able to say why" (§51, 372, 2–3; CSM I: 349, trans. lightly modified). It is a matter of a passion that can occur without the action of "some object or other" or "by the mere temperament of the body" (371, 17–18; CSM I: 349), but for which it is enough that "impressions" come "fortuitously" (372, 1) into the brain, that is to say, as previously, via *traces* of past movements of the spirits, not at all by actually present movements: in this sense, it [the passion] is situated nearest to the soul and to the soul alone.

One can find confirmation for the fact that the soul senses only itself—at least tangentially—in this figure of passion in an apparently ambiguous formulation that Descartes employs at least twice: "our mind wanders idly [*nonchalamment*] without applying itself to anything of its own accord," or "when the soul does not determine itself to anything of its own accord, but idly [*nonchalamment*] follows the impressions that happen to be in the brain."[49] Must one understand this to mean that the soul is determined by nothing that belongs to itself? Or that it decides to determine nothing by itself and thus, once more, to bracket

47. Regula XII, AT X: 423, 1–30 and *"videor videre,"* Second Meditation, VII: 29, 11–19 (see above, chapter 3, §§15–16), respectively.

48. *Passions of the Soul*, §1, XI: 327, 14–15; CSM I: 328.

49. *Passions of the Soul*, §21, XI: 345, 4–5; CSM I: 136, and To Elizabeth, 6 October 1645, IV: 311, 5–8; CSMK: 271, respectively.

itself? In fact, one must understand that, in its supposed nonchalance, the soul decides not to decide, in other words not to assign a cause (neither a body of the world, nor my own body) to the passion it undergoes, to assign it "no subject,"[50] in such a way that this passion refers itself to nothing other than itself; thus becoming the pure indubitable sensation inasmuch as felt, the passion, without other cause or substrate than itself, accomplishes a perfect auto-affection, where, as it senses *itself* and itself alone, it becomes the sole phenomenalization of the soul sensing itself by itself. One sees from this that the soul would not sense any thing (through passion as perception of objects of the world) if it did not first of all and at the same time sense its *meum corpus* (via the emotion of sensations of suffering, of need, of pleasure, thirst, hunger, etc., in fact by movements of spirits); but also that the soul would not sense the *meum corpus* if it did not experience itself in the end, or rather first, itself, in the pure sensing of self. In the strict sense, having sensations does not mean so much sensing something other than oneself, or even experiencing one's flesh (*meum corpus*), as it does sensing *oneself*, sensing oneself feeling and sensing that only this passion of the self gives the ego an access to its phenomenality.

One could raise an objection to this: in describing sadness in this way (§§26 and 51), or even joy as much as sadness (§51), as a sensation of self by self, a proof of the self and a quasi auto-affection, does one not confuse what Descartes nevertheless distinguishes with the greatest care? He actually opposes (in §91), on the one hand, "this joy, which is a passion" and which consists of the joy "that the soul has from the good which the impressions of the brain represent to it as its own," from, on the other hand, "the purely intellectual joy that arises in the soul through an action of the soul alone and which may be said to be a pleasant emotion which *the soul arouses in itself*, in which consists the enjoyment it has from the good which its understanding represents to it as its own." Yet here still the text to which one believes one is objecting could well have an intention opposite to what one endows it with because, as soon as the distinction between two joys is indicated (either passion coming from the body and the movements of spirits or purely intellectual coming from the understanding and its representations), he clarifies immediately that "it is *true* that, while the soul is joined to the

---

50. *Passions of the Soul*, §51, 372, 3, *sujet* here in the sense of ὑποκείμενον [the idiomatic expression is untranslated in CSM I: 349, which says "without being able to say why"].

body, this intellectual joy can scarcely fail to be accompanied by the joy which is a passion."[51] Why does passionate joy (and sadness) come almost always ("often")[52] to interfere with intellectual joy? Because, if the understanding sees ("observes") that we possess a good, imagination (and without doubt also, at the same time, the will) provokes immediately a movement of spirits in the brain, which thus arouses inevitably a passion (§91, 397, 11–18; CSM I: 361). In fact, these two joys share what is essential—the enjoyment [*jouissance*] of a good as possessed, thus possessed in itself, thus an enjoyment *of self*. They differ only in the means that ensure this enjoyment of self—either from a pure representation to the understanding or from impressions on the brain, with the understanding that in the two cases it is a matter of a passion being exercised on the soul (representative perception or emotion by the movements of spirits). Yet what is essential precisely remains, namely, the enjoyment of self by possession of a good. And often enjoyment of self has enough force in order for the quasi-occasional objects of this enjoyment, objects that I possess nevertheless and by the intermediary of which I possess myself and sense myself, to vanish into vagueness "without being able to observe so distinctly the good or evil which causes this feeling" (§93, 398, 9–11; CSM I: 361). In the lack of distinction of its causes, which responds to the vanishing of any "subject" (§51, 372, 3), joy not only becomes indistinctly intellectual and also emotion, but can be born from sadness.

In fact, as the surprising §147 explains, sadness and joy can always live together in the same emotion of the same soul, for we can feel a joy at the pleasure of feeling all sorts of passions "aroused in us," because they give us all and each an enjoyment of self by possession of a good. I

51. *Passions of the Soul*, §91, 397, 8–11; emphasis added; CSM I: 361, trans. modified. I here take account of Rodis-Lewis' reading (in her edition of the *Passions of the Soul* [Paris: Vrin, 1966]), revising that of AT XII (see the additional notes of the 1974 revision, 722). The same distinction and same self-affection is found in §147: "internal emotions which are produced in the soul only by the soul itself. In this respect they differ from its passions, which always depend on some movement of the spirits" (440, 23–27; CSM I: 381). And the same unification of opposites appears in §93: "When intellectual joy or sadness arouses the corresponding passion, its cause is quite obvious" (398, 3–5; CSM I: 361).

52. *Passions of the Soul*, §93, 398, 8; CSM I: 361. See: "Although these emotions of the soul [i.e., interior emotions that are only aroused in the soul by the soul itself] are *often* joined with the passions which are *similar* to them, they *frequently* occur with others, and they may even originate in those to which they are opposed" (§147, 440, 27—441, 3; CSM I: 381).

enjoy myself (and am thus joyous) and this joy can at times "as readily originate in sadness as in any of the other passions" (like the adventures in a novel or in the theater, the dying of one's wife, a burial ceremony, etc.).[53] This is very probably a matter of one of the "internal emotions which are produced in the soul only by the soul itself" (440, 24–25; CSM I: 381), different from "passions, which always depend on some movement of the spirits" (440, 26–27; CSM I: 381); but precisely it is the passions, which arrive the most "fortuitously" and the most "non-chalantly," that can all the better come closest to the purely intellectual joy of a soul *sensing itself*. In this way, the phenomenon of joy is unified (with sadness, but also between emotion and intellectual representation) in the unique passive experience of the auto-affection of the *res cogitans* by it in itself. The passion of joy, which is distinguished only with difficulty from purely intellectual joy, in fact reveals the most radical passivity—neither the passivity that comes from the exterior in order to be applied to objects (like the perception of the things of the world), nor the one that comes from internal movements of *meum corpus* in order to be applied to it, nor even the one that comes from these same movements in order to be applied to the soul (the passions in the narrow sense), but (in *fourth* position) the one that comes from the soul's enjoyment of itself thanks to the possession of a good. Joy assures the soul a radical passivity, because it comes to it from itself and from itself alone; the autonomy of enjoyment of self results from the passivity of the affection of self by self: "a pleasant emotion which the soul arouses *in itself by itself*" (§91, 397, 5–6; CSM I: 361, trans. modified), one of the "internal emotions which are produced *in the soul only by the soul itself*" (§147, 440, 23–24; CSM I: 381), "a kind of joy . . . the sweetest of all joys, because its cause depends *only on ourselves*" (§190, 471, 19–21; CSM I: 396). In this way the mode of passive thought repeats the experience of self that the *cogito, sum* performed in the mode first (but not solely) of active thought (*intellectus*, doubt, will). Or, in other words, this auto-affection returned on itself repeats, precisely in the mode of passivity, what the *causa sui* accomplished in the active mode according to efficient causality. In both cases, joy repeats or imitates one of Descartes' onto-theo-logical attempts in order to ensure a first principle (and a highest being) to being in general.

53. *Passions of the Soul*, §147, 441, 22 and 23–24, respectively; CSM I: 381. The theater comes in at §94, 399, 25 and §147, 441, 17. See also §63: "A good done by ourselves gives us an internal satisfaction, which is the sweetest of all the passions" (377, 18–20; CSM I: 351–52).

Starting from this passivity that is so radical that it becomes an auto-affection, that is to say a declination of the *cogito, sum* in the mode of passive thought, it becomes possible to comprehend the shared and restricted definition of passions: "perceptions, sensations or emotions of the soul which we refer particularly to it, and which are caused, maintained and strengthened by some movement of the spirits" (§27, 349, 12–16; CSM I: 338–39). It is thus a matter of thoughts for which the cause comes not from active thought, but from "movements of the spirits," which cause, make endure ("maintain"), and reinforce ("strengthen") thought that has become passive in this way. One must underline that thought results from the movement of spirits in two ways. First, in the moment when they cause this thought, then beyond these movements and as long as the emotion produced by them endures: "the passions are not only caused but also maintained and strengthened by some particular movement of the spirits."[54] This second manner, moreover, plays an essential role, because it ensures a deployment of passions in duration, or rather manifests that the passions master duration and allow a permanence of the *mens*, which it does not have available when it relies on its basic (and very short) attention: "the utility of all the passions consists simply in the fact that they strengthen and *prolong* thoughts in the soul which it is good for the soul to preserve and which otherwise might easily be erased from it" (§74, 383, 17–20; CSM I: 354). In fact, the union links the soul and *meum corpus* so intimately that what had been united once upon a time is repeated at each new occurrence of one of the terms (either some such movement of spirits or some such emotion), according to "the principle which underlies everything I have written about them—namely, that our soul and body are so linked that once we have joined some bodily action with a certain thought, the one does not occur thereafter without the other occurring too."[55] As long as attention, this feeble faculty of the pure understanding alone, cannot endure, so long can the *mens* "persist in this volition" (§52, 372, 19–20;

---

54. *Passions of the Soul*, §46, 363, 16–18; CSM I: 345. See §160: "the same movement of the spirits which serves to strengthen a thought" (451, 13–14; CSM I: 386). This duality of functions corresponds to that of the "causes," which modify the course of spirits toward the members and muscles, on the one hand, the "differences in the movements produced in the sense organs by their objects" (causality in the moment), on the other hand, "the unequal agitation of the spirits and differences in their parts [i.e., that of the muscles]" (§12, 337, 7–8; CSM I: 332–33 and §14, 339, 18–19; CSM I: 334, respectively).

55. *Passions of the Soul*, §136, 438, 20–25; CSM I: 375 (see §16, which consists only of explaining this "principle," 341, 11—342, 5; CSM I: 334–35).

CSM I: 349), that of keeping its thoughts for a time, provided that the movements of the spirits "strengthen and prolong" them (§74, 383, 18; CSM I: 354). What the understanding is not able to do with its attention, endure in a thought, the *mens* can do with corporeal movements: once more a paradox of the communication of idioms between the two principal attributes of the two substances (see above, chapter 4, §19).

Even so, this support for the duration of the passion by the movements of the spirits presupposes and prolongs the instantaneous causality that these movements exercise on these thoughts, which have become their effects. The definition of the passions underlines this very strongly: "the principal effect of all the human passions is that they move and *dispose the soul to want* the things for which they prepare the body."[56] The passions *cause desire* for the things that they prepare also and in parallel fashion in the body: just as the movements of bodies (automatic movements or reflexes of *corpus meum* or of machines) make me do what is useful for me, so the passions make me wish for this useful thing that these corporeal movements will turn out to produce. Passion marks a thought in me that is thought not at my initiative, but "against" (§2, 328, 19) my will, at the initiative of corporeal movements (of spirits). The will that fixes my attention in some thought or other no longer comes from me, but comes to me from elsewhere into myself, in order to *make me think* what I would not have wanted to think by myself. The best example of such a volition coming from the *meum corpus* or even from corporeal things, in order to make me wish, whether I want it or not, is the passion of love, precisely because it is intrinsically defined by the will as an "emotion of the soul caused by a movement of the spirits, which *impels the soul to join itself willingly* to objects that appear to be agreeable to it."[57] The double meaning of "will" becomes much

56. *Passions of the Soul*, §40, 359, 7–10; CSM I: 343. See §52: "The function of all the passions consists solely in this, that they *dispose our soul to want* the things which nature deems useful for us . . . ; and the same agitation of the spirits which normally causes the passions" also disposes the body to make movements which help us to attain these things" (372, 17–23; CSM I: 349). And §74: "they strengthen and *prolong* thoughts in the soul" (383, 18; CSM I: 354). That is also the sense of "formation and strengthening" (§104, 406, 2; CSM I: 365), "maintain and strengthen" (§106, 407, 1–2; CSM I: 365); "strengthen and *preserve*" (§70, 380, 26f.; CSM I: 353); the "disposition/condition" in §94 (399, 17–18; CSM I: 362), "disposes the soul to wish" (§86, 392, 23; CSM I: 358).

57. *Passions of the Soul*, §79, 387, 3–6; CSM I: 356. See §81: "we also join to it willingly the things" (388, 13–14; CSM I: 356). See: "I know no other definition of love save that it is a passion which makes us join ourselves willingly to some object" (To Chanut, 1 February 1647, IV: 611, 1–3; CSMK: 310).

clearer if one follows the somewhat earlier argument that Descartes addresses to Chanut: if one considers "purely intellectual or rational" love (not yet passion), it is certainly a matter of being joined to a good "by one's will," by "the movement of one's will," but always one that "accompanies the knowledge" of this good as a good; in this case the will, which follows the understanding, remains mine. These "movements of the will" remain "rational thoughts." But, as soon as one passes to the realm of the passions, the thought that fixes the beloved object for me becomes "a confused thought, aroused in the soul by some motion of the nerves," which "disposes" our soul and "inclines the soul to join to itself willingly the object presented to it." But this second will is not at all rational, because I can experience it (actually be submitted to it passively, because I do not produce it actively) even when I am actually not aware of any object worthy of love.[58] The will (especially the will to unite myself to what appears to me as a good, but maybe is not one) to which I submit in the passion of love is distinguished from the will that I actively want in the rational judgment precisely by the fact that in this case I am its author, the author and the cause. Not only can this will "most easily conquer the passions," but there it retains "the control that we have over our volitions"[59]—understood in the sense of volitions imposed from elsewhere, which are imposed on me passively, in short, volitions whose will goes against me and in the name of the movements of bodies.

How should one describe these volitions that go against the grain, that render the *mens* passive? One could describe them as "pseudo-volitions," if they did not often precisely will more strongly than the voluntary and rational volitions.[60] One could speak of "vicariousness of reason in the determination of the will,"[61] if it were not to the contrary a different, passionate, will that would exercise by vicariousness the role of reason itself, and not only the role of intellectual reason. One could surely highlight the explication that Descartes himself provides of what it is "to join or separate oneself willingly": "Moreover, in using the word 'willingly' I am not speaking of desire, which is a completely separate passion relating to the future. I mean rather the *consent* by

58. To Chanut, 1 February 1647, 601, 14–15, 23, 25, 26; 602, 3–4, 6 and 27f.; 603, 5, 10–11, respectively; CSM I: 306–7.

59. *Passions of the Soul*, §48, 366, 26–27; CSM I: 347 and §152, 445, 17; CSM I: 384, respectively.

60. Alquié, in his edition of *Œuvres philosophiques*, III: 984.

61. Kambouchner, *Descartes et la philosophie morale*, 100.

which we consider ourselves henceforth as joined with what we love."[62] Consent admits the inclination that the corporeal movements impose on my mind to be a volition, while in fact it is not a matter of *my* will, although it is really a matter of *a* will; I consent, as one consents to a protectorate or a colonization, to lending my will to a foreign power, of which it becomes the auxiliary as much as the guarantor. In the volition that the corporeal movements cause, incite, dispose, and strengthen, it is thus still most probably an issue of *my* will, solely and uniquely, but enlisted, submitted, and rented out to these movements come from elsewhere. The passivity of thought here reaches its accomplishment: even "these movements of the will which constitute love, joy, sadness and desire,"[63] in short, all the principal passions (and thus in fact *all* the passions) are being subverted by a passivity come from elsewhere. The passions render *even the will* passive, which nevertheless defines what is most proper to me.[64]

## §30. Generosity, or the Will as Passion

Now, it is precisely the recovery of the will itself by passivity, the "consent" of the will to let itself will from elsewhere, in short the decision no longer not only to think actively, but even *to want* actively, which will allow us, by one of these *reversals* of the order of reasoning so characteristic of the genuine reasoning of order according to Descartes, to confer on the will the status of an action of the ego, which all the same imposes a passion on it by itself—a passion caused by the will inasmuch as it remains nevertheless absolutely active.

It would have been simpler, in any case more in conformity with the neo-Stoicism of the time, to envision that the will could simply counter the dominant passivity of the passions by a counteraction against them. Yet Descartes seems reasonably skeptical about the power that

---

62. *Passions of the Soul,* §80, 387, 17–22; CSM I: 356, trans. lightly modified. I depend here on Alexandre Delamarre, "Du consentement. Remarques sur *les passions de l'âme,* §40," in Jean Deprun and Jean-Luc Marion, eds., *La Passion de la raison. Hommage à Ferdinand Alquié* (Paris: PUF, 1983), which underlines the conceptual status of the consent, which is not the "will *of someone other* in myself: the alterity of the quasi-will is the retrospective appearance of *my* only will" (141).

63. To Chanut, 1 February 1647, AT IV: 602, 3–5; CSMK: 306.

64. To Christina, 20 November 1647: "so there remains only the will, which is absolutely within our disposal" (AT V: 83, 8–9; CSMK: 325, see also above, §28, 209ff.).

people would have to "equip the will to fight with its proper weapons," convinced that "the will, lacking the power to produce the passions directly," would not be able to be modified except "indirectly through the representations of things which are usually joined with the passions we wish to have and opposed to the passions we wish to reject." Any "effort"[65] thus consists more modestly in not attempting to modify the passions directly (by opposing an autonomous will to the volitions come from elsewhere, that is to say, the movements of the spirits), but modifying these movements by stimulating other external objects in order to cause other movements, thus other representations. The first part of the treatise concludes in this way.

Yet, by describing first the primitive passions and above all by developing a particular passion, that of generosity, the two other parts follow a more subtle and more paradoxical path, which also proves much more effective. Let us suppose the definition and the general mechanism of the passion: it exercises a counterwill (from elsewhere) on the (autonomous) will and one more powerful than it; in fact and in the majority of cases, the soul can neither reverse the connection of forces, nor avoid the passivity of the passion. Only one solution remains: to make this passivity itself perform to the profit of the (autonomous) will and no longer to its debit. In other words, it would be necessary for a certain passion to come not from elsewhere (movement of spirits caused by the body or by the *meum corpus*), but well and truly from the very activity of the (autonomous) will, in such a way as to place this passivity in the service and as a reinforcement of the activity of the autonomous will. In this way, what would remain *formally* a passion (movements of spirits acting on the soul) would come *in fact* from the representation of the active will and lead back to it. Let us note, by anticipation, that the same will be true for the case of the love of God; as such, the love of God could not be displayed in a passion, because we cannot represent God to ourselves by an idea that is of the type of often confused images that the passions produce; but we have all the same an imaginable representation available, if not of God, at least of our very love of God; and this imagination allows us to constitute the mechanism of a passion: "For although we cannot *imagine* anything in God, who is the object of our love, we can *imagine our love* itself, which consists in our wanting to unite ourselves to some object, that is, we can consider

65. *Passions of the Soul*, §48, AT XI: 367, 3; CSM I: 347; §47, 365, 27–29; CSM I: 346; §45, 362, 26—363, 1; CSM I: 345; and §50, 370, 11 or 16; CSM I: 348, respectively.

ourselves in relation to God as a minute part of all the immensity of the created universe." There will thus really be a perception, a feeling, or an emotion, in short an imagination, certainly not of God but of our union with him, in such a way that "the idea of such a union by itself is sufficient to produce heat around the heart and cause a violent passion."[66] The idea alone (and alone imaginable) of our union with God (literally the only idea of our love of God, himself by definition unimaginable) is enough to launch the movements of spirits, which make up the power of passion. On this example, one clearly sees a vaster project emerging: to conceive a perception (imagined, passive, but indisputable) of the will (autonomous, in act, active) that can launch the movements of the spirits, which exert passivity on the soul, but also confer on it the power of a passion—in such a way that the activity of the will becomes the origin of a passivity, thus produces a passion of the soul to the benefit of this very activity.[67]

In order to form a notion of this model of a *passion of activity*, Descartes will invent generosity by setting up characteristics for it that differentiate it decisively from both *magnanimitas* and μεγαλοψυχία.

(a) First, generosity comes from wonder by the intermediary of esteem (and of contempt);[68] yet wonder is precisely produced without corporeal idea, because without any idea at all, since we experience "some new object" and one that "surprises us" and even "before we know it"—or thus by the mere appearance of an outline, "the first image of the objects before us."[69] In fact, wonder (thus generosity) bears less on a representable object than on a process, an event, which passes and must be thought as *passing*, a "surprise, i.e. the sudden and unexpected arrival" of the "event" as "rare."[70] It is so radically a matter of a pas-

---

66. To Chanut, 1 February 1647, AT IV: 610, 5–16; CSMK: 310.

67. Guénancia formulates this perfectly: "For the volitions to have the force of moving the soul as much as the passions to which this force is natural, it will be necessary that the soul by its effort and its address transform them into its own passions, that it manage to be moved by its own representations as much as and even more than by the objects of its passions, precisely in order to be moved less by them. Generosity will manifest the power of the soul to constitute its own free will as object of the strongest of passions." *L'Intelligence du sensible*, 259.

68. Generosity consists in esteeming oneself, thus depends on esteem (*Passions of the Soul*, §§151–53); but esteem and contempt "are merely species of wonder" (§150, AT XI: 444, 12–13; CSM I: 383).

69. *Passions of the Soul*, §53, 373, 5–6, then 10–11; CSM I: 350, trans. lightly modified; and §78, 386, 15–16; CSM I: 355, respectively.

70. Ibid., respectively §72, 381, 22–24; CSM I: 353 (see "sudden surprise," §70, 380, 18; CSM I: 353; "surprise," §73, 382, 26; CSM I: 354); §166, 457,

sion of exteriority, of surprise, of expectation or lack of knowledge, that it almost escapes representation, at least in the sense of the imaginative representation of an object.[71] Henceforth, no passion derived from wonder (thus generosity) will have need for a representation in the strict sense, with a minimum of image: accordingly, as our union with God replaces the impossible image of God in order to form the passion of the love of God, in the same way the "use of our free will" in general would be able to replace some volition or other linked to some object or other, unimaginable or too abstract (good and evil, will or divine providence, etc.) in order to form the passion of generosity.

(b) This passion, which nevertheless requires no imagination, also does not require an object different from the soul itself; it is characterized by its self-reference, because wonder can be reflected on itself, as much as esteem and contempt (which deploy it) "are chiefly noteworthy when we *refer them to ourselves*, i.e. when it is our own merit for which we have esteem or contempt"; in other words, if "we may have esteem or contempt for *ourselves*,"[72] this passion exerts passivity, although it does not for all that question the autonomy and even less the autarchy of the ego. Even in the state of passivity, that is to say, when it shall submit to the passion of generosity, constraining its will to want the object of generosity passively, even at this very moment the ego will undergo only the pressure of a *self*-evaluation, of a passivity come from itself.

---

10; CSM I: 389 (where one should note the unusual use of the verb—not simply the mundane substantive—*avenir*: "And when we are assured that what we desire *will come about* [*aviendra*], then although we will want it to *come about* [*aviene*] we are no longer agitated by the passion of desire, which made us await the *outcome* [*l'événement*] with concern," 457, 7–11); and finally: "For we wonder only at what appears to us *unusual* and extraordinary. . . . The other passions may serve to make us take note of things which appear good or evil, but we will only wonder at things which merely appear *unusual*" (§75, 384, 6–7 and 19–22; CSM I: 354 and 355).

71. Carole Talon-Hugon characterizes precisely this passion as caused by "the unknown and the remarkable." *Les Passions rêvées par la raison. Essai sur la théorie des passions de Descartes et de quelques-uns de ses contemporains* (Paris: Vrin, 2002), 203. See my analysis in *Cartesian Questions*, chapter 5, §5, 111–14.

72. *Passions of the Soul*, §151, 444, 26—445, 3; CSM I: 383 and §54, 373, 23–24; CSM I: 350, respectively. See "*Self*-satisfaction" (§63, 377, 16; CSM I: 351 = §190, 471, 13; CSM I: 356); "for what reason anyone ought to have esteem or contempt for *himself*" (§152, 445, 12–13; CSM I: 384); "which causes a person's *self*-esteem to be as great as it may legitimately be" (§153, 445, 27f.; CSM I: 384).

(c) Finally and very logically, the relation between the ego undergoing this passion and the object of this passion can remain (so strangely) internal only if this self-reference draws its power of influencing the soul from its privilege of accomplishing itself without gap in representation and efficiency, but with the immediacy of sensing. One can probably sometimes understand such a sensing as sensation (empirical sensing), but, more radically and in order to ensure this first meaning, one must here understand it as the affection of the self for the self of the *res cogitans*: it is neither via representation nor via a concept, nor via an image that the generous person knows that he wants or can make (good) use of his free will, but because he senses it: "in his feeling within himself a firm and constant resolution to use it well."[73] The passion of generosity therefore does not *link* the cause (image, corporeal movement) to the effect (volition imposing itself on the passivity of the soul); it *identifies* them, because the soul *senses* the will that affects it not only as its own, but as itself. A remarkable convergence ensues between two modalities of the *cogitatio*, at first glance quite different: just as the ego of the *cogito* ends up experiencing the *cogitatio* in general and its own *ego sum, ego existo* as a sensing, an auto-affection of self by itself thinking (see above, chapter 3, §§15–16), in the same way generosity ends up causing the ego to be affected (that is to say, submitted to a passion) by itself under the form of its self-esteem, without external object or image from elsewhere. As the *cogitatio* ends up by affecting itself in the *ego sum, ego existo* (to the point of seeming a *cogitatio sui*), so the will ends by affecting itself in generosity (to the point of seeming a will in itself). The cohesion of the Cartesian ego appears in this all the more powerful.

Three privileges thus characterize generosity by comparison with the other passions: in contrast to them generosity has no need of an image, no need for a (self-referential) external object, nor any need for verification of this object (immediate sensing). But these three privileges all derive from a fourth characteristic: generosity implements the will, which, by virtue of these three same privileges (without image, without external object, by pure sensing), appears as the very ipseity of the ego. For nothing belongs irreducibly to the ego or defines its ipseity as much

---

73. *Passions of the Soul*, §153, 446, 5–7; CSM I: 384. See: "this feeling *about themselves*" (§154, 446, 13–14; CSM I: 384); "do not feel *themselves* capable" (§156, 447, 24–25; CSM I: 385); "feeling *oneself* weak or irresolute" (§159, 450, 4–5; CSM I: 386, trans. lightly modified); "the peace of mind and inner satisfaction *felt in themselves* by those who know they always do their best" (To Christina, 20 November 1647, V: 85, 21–23; CSMK: 326, trans. lightly modified).

as that which depends on it; now, only its thoughts truly depend on it; but among these thoughts only the volitions depend on it absolutely. Must one hence conclude from this that the ego identifies itself with its volitions? Most probably not, because not all the volitions reach their goal (through lack of power), and above all, because not all of them will the good (through lack of knowledge).[74] Thus only the *intention* of its volitions remain properly and legitimately speaking the ego's own: "only one thing in us which could give us good reason for esteeming ourselves, namely, the exercise of our free will and the control we have over our volitions."[75] We must distinguish carefully here between a will to the second level (volition$_2$), named the "exercise of our free will," and the volitions to the first level (volitions$_1$), often called simply "our volitions," which remain only partially our responsibility—in proportion to our ignorance of the good, to our weakness of execution. This distinction appears often and without any possible confusion: "The first consists in his knowing that nothing truly belongs to him but this freedom to dispose his volitions"—where the "disposition" (volition$_2$) governs the "volitions" (volition$_1$).[76] When one "holds in high esteem the liberty and absolute control over ourselves," one actually esteems the hold of volition$_2$ ("liberty and control") over volitions$_1$ ("oneself/ourselves").[77] Or also: "The volition we *feel* in ourselves always to make good use of our free will"[78] attests to a volition$_2$ to make use of free will as volition$_1$; and above all, this formulation indicates that the soul senses only

74. "*ratione cognitionis et potentiae*—in virtue of the knowledge and power" (Fourth Meditation, VII: 57, 17; CSM II: 40).

75. *Passions of the Soul*, §152, XI: 445, 15–17; CSM I: 384.

76. *Passions of the Soul*, §153, 446, 2–3; CSM I: 384. See: "But knowledge is often beyond our powers; and so there remains only our will [volition$_2$], which is absolutely within our disposal [volition$_1$]" (To Christina, 20 November 1647, V: 83, 6–9; CSMK: 325). Must one distinguish the consideration of its "use" (XI: 445, 16; CSM I: 384; 452, 31; CSM I: 387) from that of its "good use" (To Christina, 20 November 1647, V: 84, 15 and 20–21; CSMK: 325; 85, 16; CSMK: 326; see *Passions of the Soul*, §153, XI: 446, 5–7; CSM I: 384; §155, 447, 17; CSM I: 385), as Maria Nowersztern suggests in "Ne pas être sujet? *Similitudo Dei*: la liberté et son usage, des *Meditationes* aux *Passions de l'âme*," *Les Études philosophiques* 96.1 (2011): 71–83?

77. *Passions of the Soul*, §203, XI: 481, 22–23; CSM I: 401.

78. *Passions of the Soul*, §158, 449, 14–15; CSM I: 386. See §153: "his *feeling* within himself a firm and constant resolution to use it well" (446, 5–7; CSM I: 384). And: "the peace of mind and inner satisfaction *felt* by those who know they always do their best" (To Christina, 20 November 1647, V: 85, 21–23; CSMK: 326).

volition$_2$, because it senses *itself* only there, while the volitions$_1$ (of the first level) remain to a large extent foreign to it (under the influence of corporeal movements, lacking knowledge and power, etc.).

Accordingly, a passion is constituted, where "the same movement of spirits which serves to strengthen a thought" can strengthen the one caused as much in the case of the ordeal as in the case of generosity, because in both cases the soul becomes affected by "the good opinion we have of ourselves."[79] In generosity *also* the soul remains passive, because the corporeal movements here really come to "strengthen" (§74, 383, 18; CSM I: 354) a thought accordingly come from elsewhere, willed by a counter-volition$_1$; but, paradoxically, this thought represents a volition$_2$, itself identical to the soul (by an original sensing) and entirely free of its resolution to use (or even to use well) its volitions$_1$. The soul submits passively to the passion that the representation of its activity via the movements that come from elsewhere provokes in it. There is thus an exception to the principle that "the will lacks the power to produce the passions directly":[80] the passion that the will provokes by itself when it wonders at and loves itself for the good use that it is able to make of its free will, and that this representation (without imagination) provides it, like the other passions, affects it from the exterior, although it actually is provided by what remains the most proper to it, its volition$_2$ of using its volitions$_1$ well. In short, the will takes control of passion again by provoking its own passion, or rather by provoking (in itself) a passion stimulated by its own activity as will to the second level. The will, by passing from the first to the second level, becomes so perfectly identical to itself that it stimulates in itself passion for its own action, passion for itself, active insofar as it is passion. More than any other action or passion, generosity verifies in the end that it is really "a single thing, which has these two names" (§1, 328, 12; CSM I: 328).

## §31. *Virtue and Passion*

This result hence validates the initial intention of the treatise *The Passions of the Soul* perfectly. But it only manages to do so by leading to

79. *Passions of the Soul*, §160, 451, 13–14 and 17–18; CSM I: 386. See "the movement which produces humility, whether of the virtuous or of the vicious kind, is made up of those of wonder, of sadness, and of self-love mingled with hatred for the faults that give rise to self-contempt" (451, 24—452, 2; CSM I: 387). It is remarkable that the very same movements would provoke and maintain opposing moral passions.

80. *Passions of the Soul*, §47, 365, 27–29; CSM I: 346, trans. lightly modified.

an extreme hubris. Yet how would one avoid it, when generosity relies on wonder and love of oneself, of a *self* taken on its own in the most irreducible and inalienable way, and when this ownness furthermore consists in a *power* to determine the self (volition₂)? Understood in this way as the self's identification with a power over the self, generosity confers on the ego an autonomy (a "self-satisfaction") that nothing would appear to curb. One could even distinguish three forms of this hubris, which is manifested in (a) a redefinition of the likeness to God, (b) a distinction between beatitude and the highest good, and finally (c) an at least implicit demand for the *causa sui*.

The argument about an image and likeness of the *res cogitans* to God goes back to at least 1641: "*ex hoc uno quod Deus me creavit, valde credibile est me quodammodo ad imaginem et similitudinem ejus factum esse*—the mere fact that God created me is a very strong basis for believing that I am somehow made in his image and likeness." But while Descartes first refers this likeness to the thought of self in general ("*illamque similitudinem, in qua Dei idea continentur, a me percipi per eandem facultatem, per quam ego ipse a me percipior*—[I perceive] that likeness, which includes the idea of God, by the same faculty which enables me to perceive myself"), he quickly starts to relate it to the will: "*Sola est voluntas, sive arbitrii libertas, quam tantam in me experior, ut nullius majoris ideam apprehendam; adeo ut illa praecipue sit, ratione cujus imaginem quandam et similitudinem Dei me referre intelligo*—It is only the will, or freedom of choice, which I experience with me to be so great that the idea of any greater faculty is beyond my grasp; so much so that it is above all in virtue of the will that I understand myself to bear in some way the image and likeness of God."[81] Nevertheless, he does not yet draw the consequences from this that now become necessary: to resemble the infinite God via an infinite will (or at least one of the sort that nothing greater than it could be conceived), or actually

81. Third Meditation, VII: 51, 18–20 and 21–23 (= IX: 1, 41); CSM II: 35, then Fourth Meditation, 57, 11–15 (= IX: 1, 45); CSM II: 40, respectively. See: "*Voluntas vero infinita quodammodo dici potest, quia nihil unquam advertimus, quod alicujus alterius voluntatis, vel immensae illius quae in Deo est, objectum esse possit, ad quod etiam nostra non se extendat*—The will, on the other hand, can in a certain sense be called infinite, since we observe without exception that its scope extends to anything that can possibly be an object of any other will—even the immeasurable will of God" (*Principles of Philosophy* I, §35, VIII-1: 18, 13–16; CSM I: 204). For a more detailed exposition of the infinite dimension of the human will and its likeness to God, one can refer to my documentation in *Sur la théologie blanche de Descartes*, §17, especially 402ff.

through the use of the free will itself reduced to its most proper and inalienable domain, "the disposition" (volition$_2$) to the second level of finite volitions of the first level (volitions$_1$), means to imitate his independence and self-determination at least partially: "It [i.e., the exercise of our free will] renders us *in a certain way like God* by making us *masters of ourselves*, provided we do not lose the rights it gives us through timidity." In other words, control is reversed via the negation of its contrary, subjection: "Now free will is in itself the noblest thing we can have, since it makes us in a way equal to God and seems to exempt us from being his subjects; and so its correct use is the greatest of all the goods we possess; indeed there is nothing that is more our own or that matters more to us."[82] Without having to give in to anachronism, one can say that the ego turns the divine model against itself or, at least, that it becomes exposed to the danger of such a reversal.

In this respect one should not underestimate the discussion about the definition of beatitude and the highest good. Descartes twice leads it back to the use of volition$_2$. To Elizabeth, he underlines that "there is a difference between happiness, the supreme good, and the final end or goal towards which our actions ought to tend. For happiness is not the supreme good, but presupposes it, being the contentment or satisfaction of the mind which results from possessing it. The end of our actions, however, can be understood to be one or the other."[83] Beatitude concerns my mind and its "contentment" or its "satisfaction," while the highest good goes back to things outside of me, that is to say, actually to things, to other beings, to their properties and their hierarchy. Beatitude is part of the autonomy of the ego, while the highest good keeps it in a situation of heteronomy. It is hence self-evident that morality will focus on beatitude, especially if the autonomy of volition$_2$ ("contentment") permits its accomplishment: "happiness consists solely in contentment of

82. *Passions of the Soul*, §152, XI: 445, 20–23; CSM I: 384, and To Christina, 20 November 1647, V: 85, 13–20; CSMK: 326. On the theological tradition of a human likeness to God by the will (thus infinite will), see, among others, my sketch "L'image de la liberté," in Rémi Brague, ed., *Saint Bernard et la philosophie* (Paris: PUF, 1992) (with the complement of "Réponse à J.-L. Vieillard-Baron à propos d'une hypothèse sur saint Bernard et l'image de Dieu," *Philosophie* 42 [1994]).

83. To Elizabeth, 18 August 1645, IV: 275, 1–8; CSMK: 261. See To Elizabeth, 4 August 1645: "there is a difference between *l'heur* and *la béatitude*. The former depends only on outward things . . . but beatitude consists, it seems to me, in a perfect contentment of mind and inner satisfaction" (IV: 264, 2–9; CSMK: 257, trans. lightly modified).

mind—that is to say, in contentment in general. . . . in order to achieve a contentment which is solid, we need to pursue virtue—that is to say, to maintain a firm and constant will to bring about everything we judge to be the best, and to use all the power of our intellect in judging well."[84] Beatitude, far from depending on the highest good, must—or at the very least should have to—depend only on the free will: "a beatitude that depends *entirely* on our free will." For what is essential consists in the fact that beatitude may be reached "without any assistance *from elsewhere.*"[85]

To Christina Descartes clarifies another distinction that still leads to the same result. Without doubt, if one considers "the goodness of each thing . . . it is evident that God is the supreme good." Even so, if one considers goods in the strict sense and "in relation to ourselves" only "those that we *possess* or have the power to acquire," that is to say if we consider the highest good only from the point of view of *possession*, thus of the autonomy of the ego, then only what we can eventually possess as our own can claim this rank, our will of wanting the good (volition$_2$). It follows that the highest good "consists only in a firm will to do well and the contentment which this produces." For, exactly, a highest good remains a good only if we can attain it, possess it, and gain it as a good; now, "there remains only our will, which is absolutely within our disposal," thus our will and its control become the sole instance of the highest good for us. The will can implement the highest good as a good in our "power," because at least it would be "within our disposal."[86] Such a disposal of the highest good by the will continues and radicalizes the autonomy of the infinite will. It is finally extended, as if in the shadow cast by its light, by a kind of figure of the *causa sui*.

In fact, these two movements both go back to the circularity of what occurs actively, because it is a matter of an act of the will, and of the will by itself—that is to say of a certain imitation of the *causa sui*. It is hence no accident that this formulation appears *almost* literally at least once in the *Passions of the Soul*: "The satisfaction of those who steadfastly pursue virtue is a habit of their soul which is called 'tranquillity' and

84. To Elizabeth, 18 August 1645, IV: 277, 15–25; CSMK: 262.

85. To Elizabeth, 1 September 1645, IV: 281, 19–20 and 21–22, respectively; CSMK: 262, trans. modified. Can Descartes really reconcile these two declarations, (a) that "happiness is not the supreme good, but presupposes it" (IV: 275, 4–5; CSMK: 261) and (b) that "happiness . . . depends entirely on our free will" (IV: 281, 19–20; CSMK: 262)?

86. To Christina, 20 November 1647, V: 82, 7–9, 22–24 and 29–31; then 83, 8–9 and 83, 2 and 9, respectively; CSMK: 324–25; trans. modified.

'peace of mind.' But the fresh satisfaction we gain when we have just performed an action we think good is a passion—a kind of joy which I consider to be the sweetest of all joys, because *its cause depends only on ourselves.*[87] Virtue profits from a constancy in satisfaction that the passion of joy does not have, when it arises anew with each good action; nevertheless, satisfaction in both cases always arises not only from the fact that the resolution (volition$_2$) to use our free will (volition$_1$) really confers on the ego an absolute control over its morality (which remains good at the second level, even if it can fail at the first level, by lack of science or power), but from the fact that through this reduction, the ego can produce *by itself* and as efficient cause a satisfaction *of self* that acts *on itself* as a passion. In contrast with volitions$_1$, which are rendered fallible by their contingency and which are enlisted in phenomenal determinism, volition$_2$ defines a so to say noumenal autonomy which is implemented by "good will"[88] and of which the ego can always "make good use" at least in intention. Accordingly, this ego can always, as a cognizing being (and *cogitatio sui*), be affected with self-contentment by self-causing the passion of generosity. Accordingly, failing to produce (*efficere*) its own existence starting from its essence as the divine *causa sui* does, the ego manages to self-cause for itself the passion of a perfect moral activity, thus to self-procure for itself a perfect "satisfaction." This *causa sui*, reduced to morality in this way, certainly only from afar imitates the divine *causa sui* that is immediately ontological (in the sense of *metaphysica generalis*), and in no way would be able to abolish the gap that separates the ego from God. Yet it opens the path to a drift and a hubris: if it depends only on the ego to obtain, like an efficient cause, the (moral) satisfaction of having used its will well (to the second level), what sharing between good and evil still remains thinkable? What limit can one still pose to the "self-satisfaction" that inspires the ego to the passion of self-love? Or would one have to anticipate the consent without exception that Nietzsche's Amen without exception will claim to accomplish quite a bit later? Certainly, the satisfaction of the ego in the state of generosity admits a criterion for itself; it depends on "only one thing in us which could give us good reason for esteeming ourselves, namely, the exercise of our free will and the control that we have over

---

87. *Passions of the Soul,* §190, XI: 471, 14–21; CSM I: 396. See maybe also: "A good *done by ourselves* gives us an internal satisfaction, which is the sweetest of all the passions" (§63, 377, 18–20; CSM I: 351–52).

88. *Passions of the Soul,* for example §154, 446, 22; CSM I: 384; §187, 470, 5; CSM I: 395; §192, 473, 9–10; CSM I: 397. See "a firm will to do well" (To Christina, 20 November 1647, V: 82, 30; CSMK: 324).

our volitions"; but how exactly should one measure these reasons for esteeming oneself, how could one truly decide what "causes a person's self-esteem to be as great as it may *legitimately* be"? For in the end, [as concerns] judgments about the use of volitions, "*we* refer them to *ourselves*, i.e. . . . . it is *our own merit for which we have esteem.*"[89] Does not the ego henceforth remain in the final account the sole and unique judge of the esteem that it itself merits, thus of the satisfaction that it causes itself, hence of the passion with which it affects itself? The *causa sui* accordingly in morality stays unfailingly circular. The ego seems neither always able, nor thus always obligated, not to find in itself not only the greatest "satisfaction" and greatest thinkable "contentment," but also to find in itself its highest good. Is there a principle of limitation (and of regulation) of self-esteem or of the passion (love, joy, wonder) that the activity of the will provokes (at the second level of intention)?

It is certainly necessary, because Descartes confers on generosity not only the rank of a passion, but also that of a virtue. Against Aristotle and Saint Thomas Aquinas, for whom the passions do not have moral qualification, whether good or bad, but fall under sensibility,[90] Descartes postulates in the decisive §§160–61 of the *Passions of the Soul* that if the "virtues are habits in the soul" producing thoughts, these thoughts sometimes become stimulated by the "movements of spirits," just like the passions, with the consequence that certain thoughts "are both actions of virtue and at the same time passions of the soul."[91] In other

---

89. *Passions of the Soul*, §152, AT XI: 445, 25–27; CSM I: 384; §153, 446, 1; CSM I: 384; §151, AT XI: 445, 1–3; CSM I: 381. We should also not forget the difficulty of esteeming another good correctly in general, independently of the difficulty of a self-estimation: a confused representation of a good now overestimated linked to the union, forgetfulness of "the way in which it is referred to us," etc. (see To Christina, 20 November 1647, V: 84, 30—85, 27; CSMK: 325–26).

90. "πάθη μὲν οὖν οὐκ εἰσὶν οὔθ' αἱ ἀρεταὶ οὔθ' αἱ κακίαι, ὅτι οὐ λεγόμεθα κατὰ τὰ πάθη σπουδαῖοι ἢ ψαῦλοι—Now neither the excellences nor the vices are *passions*, because we are not called good or bad on the ground of our passions" (Aristotle, *Nicomachean Ethics* II.5, 1105b28–30; Barnes, 1746); "*Respondeo dicendum quod virtus moralis non potest esse passio*—I respond by saying that the moral virtue cannot be a passion" (Aquinas, *Summa Theologiae*, I-I, q. 59, a. 1, resp.), first because passion is a movement of sensibility, while virtue is a mode of the *habitus*, which potentially allows a movement; then because the passions are as such morally neutral, inasmuch as they are not referred by reason to good or evil; finally because virtue goes from reason to the appetite, while (sometimes at least) passion goes from the appetite to reason.

91. *Passions of the Soul*, §161, XI: 453, 15 and 16–17; CSM I: 387–88. See §160: "But it may be questioned whether generosity and humility, which are vir-

words, the fact that a thought becomes reinforced (or even totally produced) by corporeal movements is not enough to forbid it the rank
of virtue. Even as *habitus* the virtues can rely on passivity granted a
physiological support derived from *meum corpus*. The exercise of free
will and the passion that it can arouse, namely generosity, thus becomes
in principle qualified (or at least qualifiable) as a virtue, and hence the
first of the virtues, being the first of the passions and the only one still
available to volition$_2$. Declarations regarding this are not missing: "it
[i.e., the highest good] consists solely in virtue, because this is the only
good, among all those we can possess, which depends entirely on our
free will." And: "But I make a distinction between the supreme good—
which consists in the exercise of virtue, or, what comes to the same,
the possession of all those goods whose acquisition depends upon our
free will—and the satisfaction of mind which results from that acquisition." Or also: "there remains only our will, which is absolutely within
our disposal. . . . This by itself constitutes all *the virtues*; . . . that it is
which constitutes the supreme good."[92] Accordingly, the wise person
must experience the passion of generosity and also attain the highest
virtue by it—he or she must "arouse the passion of generosity in himself
and then acquire the virtue, since this virtue is, as it were, the key to all
the other virtues."[93]

The problem seems in the end very simple. If the generous person
"feels within himself a firm and constant resolution to use it [i.e., the
free disposal of his volitions] well—that is, never to lack the will to
undertake and carry out whatever *he judges to be best*. To do that is to
pursue *virtue* in a perfect manner" (§153, 446, 5–10; CSM I: 384), then
he will not really pursue virtue except if his passion arises really from
an exact and normative judgment of truth about "the best things" to do.
Is there such a criterion, an operation or a reference that would allow

---

tues, can also be passions. For their movements are less apparent, and it seems
that virtue is not so closely associated with passion as vice is. Yet I see no reason
why the same movement of the spirits which serves to strengthen a thought
which has bad foundations might not also strengthen one that is well-founded"
(451, 7–16; CSM I: 386). The difficulty does not lie in knowing how generosity
can be a passion, but in how, being a passion, it can also become a virtue (as
Talon-Hugon underlines in *Les Passions rêvées par la raison*, 243).

92. Respectively, To Elizabeth, 18 August 1645, IV: 276, 11–14; CSMK:
261; To Elizabeth, 6 October 1645, IV: 305, 11–15; CSMK: 268; To Christina,
20 November 1647, V: 83, 8–19; CSMK: 325.

93. *Passions of the Soul*, §161, XI: 454, 5–7; CSM I: 388, trans. lightly
modified.

the generous person to know whether he has "legitimately" made good use of his free will (volition$_2$) even for decisions strained by the lack of knowledge or power (volition$_1$)? There are actually at least two.

The first criterion depends directly on generosity. In fact, the generous person knows that he can "legitimately" esteem in himself (as truly his) nothing but the "good use" of his free will; he thus operates for himself a kind of reduction of volition$_1$ to volition$_2$ (intention, "good will"); but, by the most obvious and basic justice, he admits also other "free causes" (§162, 454, 17f. and passim; CSM I: 388), or rather he admits the others as such free causes: he has "this knowledge and this feeling about [him]self" that "any other person can have . . . *about himself.*"[94] Consequently, the generous person must esteem other people just as much as he esteems himself and *reciprocally*: good use is decided "legitimately" as that of "good will" and nothing else, otherwise one sinks into esteem for "all the other goods," which cannot be multiplied and fall under competition due to their rarity, leading to pride, hatred, contempt, jealousy, and anger.[95] To esteem oneself as volition$_2$ leads to esteeming other people solely by their use of the same volition$_2$, therefore to making generous people "have esteem for everyone [i.e., other people]" (§156, 448, 10; CSM I: 385). Accordingly, the generous person is verified to be generous by seeing whether he escapes pride, vanity, but also vicious humility and self-contempt, all the vices linked to the will of wanting something else (and other goods) than the good use of his free will. In a word, esteem of the other becomes the criterion for esteem of self. The first criterion thus depends on the community of generous people.[96]

But this community itself also relies more directly on the doctrine of love than on the definition of the virtuous passion of generosity.[97] For

94. *Passions of the Soul*, §154, 446, 13–15; CSM I: 384. See "the virtuous will for which alone they esteem themselves, and which they suppose *also* to be present, or at least capable of being present, in every other person" (§154, 447, 3–5; CSM I: 384); and: "since others have free will *just as much as* we do, they may use it *just as well as* we use ours" (§155, 447, 16–17; CSM I: 385).

95. *Passions of the Soul*, §158, 449, 19–27; CSM I: 386; see §157 and §164, passim.

96. The one where "they esteem nothing more highly than doing good to others and disregarding their own self-interest" (*Passions of the Soul*, §156, 447, 25—448, 2; CSM I: 385).

97. The development that follows completes but especially corrects other analyses of the Cartesian doctrine of love, where I had not yet sufficiently seen its positive role as final criterion of good use of volition$_2$ (thus *Sur la théologie blanche de Descartes*, §17, 422ff. and *Cartesian Questions*, chapter 6, 118–38).

love always presupposes a norm: that of loving a good to the extent of its perfection: "It is the nature of love to make one consider oneself and the object loved as a single whole of which one is but a part; and *to transfer the care one previously took of oneself* to the preservation of this whole. One keeps for oneself only a part of one's care, a part which is great or little in proportion to whether one thinks oneself a larger or smaller part of the whole to which one has given one's affection." Or, even more exactly: "We may, I think, more reasonably distinguish kinds of love according to the *esteem* which we have for the object we love, as compared with ourselves." To love consists in uniting myself via the will to a good so as to form a whole with it, of which I myself form a part. What part? This is where an estimation comes in, just as in generosity: I must in fact *estimate* whether I constitute a lesser, an equal, or a main part within that whole: "For when we have *less* esteem for it *than for ourselves*, we have only a simple affection for it; when we esteem it *equally with ourselves*, that is called 'friendship'; and when we have *more esteem* for it, our passion may be called 'devotion.'"[98] Depending on the esteem, one will not love as fully a flower, a bird, or a horse (simple affection), people (friendship) and one's wife or one's children, one's sovereign or especially God (devotion). All depends on the honesty with which "we consider *ourselves*" in regard to "the whole thing" loved, either that "one prefers oneself" to it (fairly if one constitutes the majority of this whole, otherwise unfairly), or that, because "we have much more esteem for him than for ourselves," "we prefer the thing loved [*over ourselves*] so strongly that we are not afraid to die in order to preserve it." Having devotion to a lesser good attests to a "very disordered mind,"[99] as does having only simple friendship for a sovereign or for God: love consists just in establishing this hierarchy, which in the end consists in a hierarchy of esteem. Love thus fixes a norm for esteem and consequently for generosity.

In particular, devotion culminates in charity. In fact, not only does "charity require that each of the two should *value* his friend above himself"; but this movement of charity brings about the same effect as generosity, which it actually accomplishes perfectly, namely, "the inner satisfaction which always accompanies good actions, and especially

---

98. Respectively, To Chanut, 1 February 1647, IV: 611, 25—612, 2; CSMK: 311; then *Passions of the Soul*, §83, XI: 389, 28—390, 2 and 390, 2-7; CSM I: 357.

99. *Passions of the Soul*, §83, XI: 390, 24, 28, 23 and 29-30; then 390, 9; CSM I: 357-58.

actions which proceed *from a pure affection for others which has no reference to oneself,* that is, from the Christian virtue called charity."[100] And at issue is the love of God even beyond love "of others than oneself."[101] For even if we cannot experience a passion for God (which would involve imaginings, while God cannot be imagined), at least we can, by a "very attentive meditation," successively "consider that he is . . . a thing that thinks," then "the infinity of his power," "the extent of his providence," and the "infallibility of his decrees," in order to arrive at "such an extreme joy"[102] that, this time far from wishing "to exempt ourselves from being his subjects,"[103] each generous person, esteeming God as such in all his perfections, "thinks that the knowledge with which God has honoured him is enough by itself to make his life worth while. Joining himself willingly entirely to God, he loves him so perfectly that he desires nothing at all except that the will of God should be done."[104] To do the will *of God* paradoxically constitutes the best use of my free will, because in *this* case alone I know that I esteem this use "legitimately": loving God, I form a "whole" with him in which obviously I have to esteem him more than me, and, according to this criterion, I must prefer him to myself, thus prefer his will to mine. On this condition generosity finds a norm. It stops running the danger not only of a hubris of "self-contentment," but above all of an illusion of autonomy and autarchic accomplishment.

Henceforth, a passion really can become the highest of virtues. And the principle is verified that "the philosophy that I study does not at all teach me to reject the use of the passions."[105] Moreover, having been elevated to the dignity of one of the forms of passive thought in general, probably the most powerful one, the passions become the place and tool of virtue, precisely in their occasional *excess*: "the philosophy that

100. To Chanut, 1 February 1647, IV: 612, 14–15; CSMK: 311, and To Elizabeth, 6 October 1645, IV: 308, 27—309, 4; CSMK: 269–70, respectively.

101. *Passions of the Soul*, §82, XI: 389, 14–15; CSM I: 357.

102. To Chanut, 1 February 1647, respectively IV: 608, 7 (see 609, 7 and VII: 52, 12), 12, 24, 26 and 28; 609, 8; CSMK: 309, trans. lightly modified.

103. To Christina, 20 November 1647, V: 85, 15–16; CSMK: 326; which corresponds to "far from being so injurious and ungrateful to God as to want to take his place" (To Chanut, 1 February 1647, IV: 609, 8–10; CSMK: 309).

104. To Chanut, 1 February 1647, IV: 609, 10–15; CSMK: 309–10, trans. lightly modified. On the love of God to the point of doing his will, see Vincent Carraud, "Descartes: le droit de la charité," in Guido Canziani and Yves Charles Zarka, eds., *L'interpretazione nei secoli XVIII e XVIII* (Milan: Franco Angeli, 1993).

105. To Brasset, 31 March 1649, V: 332, 2–3; untranslated in CSMK.

I cultivate is not so barbarous or so fierce that it rejects the use of the *passions*; to the contrary, it is in it alone that I place all the sweetness and bliss of this life. And while there are many of these passions whose excess is vicious, there are all the same some others that I *esteem* all the more, the more excessive they are; and I place gratitude among these as much as among the virtues."[106] Gratitude has value only starting from generosity, and it belongs as much to the virtues as to the passions, by its very excess. Passive thought accordingly brings the *cogitatio* to its very end.

106. To Newcastle, March or April 1648, V: 135, 5–13; untranslated in CSMK.

## Conclusion

### §32. *Descartes' Advance*

The inquiry pursued here about passive thought as it occupies the final period of Descartes' research leads to several clear conclusions.

(a) One must reread the two parts of the Sixth Meditation, reconciling them synchronically with each other: the demonstration of the existence of other, material and extended, bodies can only fail (as was historically the case) if it is not based on the recognition (albeit unfolded after it) of the union of the *mens* with *its* body (*meum corpus*). This union alone allows us to establish the efficient causality of external sensations based on *the proof of the passivity of thought* (chapters 1 and 2).

(b) A third term is freed up between the thinking substance and the extended substance. It does not substantially add any new substance, although it qualifies the union adjectivally as substantial: *my body, meum corpus*, in opposition to other bodies that are extended; *my body* still belongs to the *mens*, but to the *mens* thinking within the mode of sensation, to the *mens* modified by the exercise of its passivity. This third term can in the end come to ground the existence of material bodies (of extended things), because by right this term had never been doubted, not even by the First Meditation, despite the Cartesian hesitations that actually continue all the way to 1641 (chapter 3).

(c) The *meum corpus* acquires its complete specificity by *being qualified as a third primitive notion*, at the price of a radical (but not contradictory) rewriting of the table of the simple natures. As primitive notion, called "the union," the *meum corpus* marks its primordiality by reversing and crossing the properties of the other two primitive notions: in its case the soul becomes extended, the body becomes in its case indivisible, and it is all the better known as it is known without clear and distinct idea, through a pure sensing, where the (intentional) "attention" (of an object) is dispelled to the benefit of a (nonintentional) "respite," a pure experience of the self (chapter 4).

These new questions (*meum corpus*, third primitive notion of "the union," lack of attention, primordial sensing of the self) become spontaneously understood or rather immediately misunderstood by Descartes' interlocutors, as much by his supposed disciples (Regius, Arnauld) as by his proclaimed adversaries (Hobbes, Gassendi, Voetius, etc.), because they straightaway attempt to conceive them within the scholastic vocabulary of substance (of accidents, of attributes, of efficient causality, etc.), in short, according to the table of Aristotelian categories (despite its having been already subverted by that of the simple natures in the *Regulae*). From this follows not only the impossibility of understanding Descartes' advances but even the distortion of his own innovations by Descartes himself, which he sometimes tries to retranslate into the terms of *substantia* out of pedagogical concern or for greater polemic effectiveness. But above all it has as a result the covering over of innovations by any number of aporiae. These aporiae inevitably result from the attempts to reduce the new concepts to the ancient scholastic topics. In this way questions are born without historical foundation in Descartes (and survive all the way into contemporary discussions): the interaction between thought and matter, the parallel between representation and the object, the possibility of free will, and so forth. That this covering over had begun even during Descartes' lifetime and that it was able to be pursued almost without interruption (except maybe Rousseau, in a sense Kant, Maine de Biran, and some others) to our own day makes all the more obvious what it dissimulates (chapter 5).

Finally, one must understand *The Passions of the Soul* (and all the French writings that prepare it in the correspondence with Elizabeth, Chanut, and Christina) first as a reformulation or even a counterformulation within a vocabulary that is no longer substantialist but as new as it is French (not Latin, not scholastic), not only as a doctrine of morality based on physiological grounds (the longstanding dominant tendency), but especially as research into the precise functioning of passivity in the exercise of the *res cogitans*: *the* passion of the soul *first of all means the passivity of the cogitatio carried to its highest level of precision.* Within the context of a passivity intrinsic and essential to the *cogitatio* (and not one that is accidental or degenerate), the question of virtue must be posed and resolved within the terms of a *virtuous* passivity, in other words, a virtue provoked by a passion, but the passion of perfect activity—that of the good use of the free will (generosity). Morality consists not in eliminating the passivity of the *cogitatio*, but in integrating activity within it, including even the activity of virtue (chapter 6).

These conclusions, obviously on the condition that they are accepted, in turn raise another question: Does the radical innovation they claim—that passivity defines a mode and probably the most privileged mode of the *cogitatio*—remain compatible with the previous determinations of the *res cogitans*? In other words, can the modes of the *cogitatio* all be practiced starting from only one single comprehension of the ego? Putting the question differently, can one reconcile the active modes of the *cogitatio* (doubt, understanding, will, imagination) with its passive mode without radically having to revise the definition of the *res (substantia) cogitans* that supports them? Or does the difference of modes maintain the unity of the ego and its status as principle? If that were the case, then Descartes would have had to institute not only two, but really *three* beginnings for his whole philosophical journey. The first beginning is introduced with the ego and the methodical constitution of objects (beginning with the *Regulae* up to the *Essays*)—in this way it knows everything that is not itself or rather everything that faces it within extension, real or imagined. But it does not for all that know itself, because the constitution of objects and of the single science does not absolutely require the knowledge of the one who implements the method: the method has no other grounding than itself. From there we move to a second beginning: the method itself can fall under the blow of doubt, if this hyperbolic doubt is based, as its dark side, on the creation of the eternal truths, the bright side of the incomprehensibility of the infinite (1630). Henceforth the question of the grounding of finite science, a grounding that transcends *humana sapientia*, becomes necessary. The ego of metaphysics precisely transforms the incomprehensibility of the infinite into this grounding (1641) because it manages to recognize the infinite as the horizon and the condition of possibility of the finite exercise of the *cogitatio*. Yet, as we have seen, the finitude of the *res cogitans* poses the question of the limitations of its exercise, in other

words of its activity: the deployment of the modalities of the *cogitatio*
as *finite* requires integrating into them sensation in its own right as the
highest mode of passivity. Now it is one of the signs of Descartes' greatness as a first-rate thinker[1] to have understood and developed that
the integration of sensation as passivity into the *res cogitans* demands
far more than the cursory addition of empirical character, the raw and
incontestable supposition of sense data, to the clarity and distinction of
actively produced ideas—as if it were sufficient to double the *mens* by
unquestioned "kinds of knowledge" in order to justify the noncritical
doubling (with which the majority of those, from Locke to Hume, passing via Malebranche and Condillac, will be content, whom, probably
by antinomy, one calls empiricists, although they accept and impose a
priori sensation itself). Descartes saw and accepted that the integration
of sensation into the *res cogitans* demands far more than admitting the
inoperative receptivity of a supposedly simple sensible given, that it actually demands no less than a complete overhaul of the *res cogitans*, not
only starting from a different perceived thing, but *starting from a passivity* henceforth primordial, because it governs the relationship of the
*cogitatio* to itself. In short, the *res cogitans* can really include sensation
among the modes of the *cogitatio* only because this *cogitatio* experiences itself, when it comes down to it, through the *sensing of self*. As
much the sensing of self of the theoretical ego ("*At certe videre video,
audire, calescere. Hoc falsum esse non potest; hoc est proprie in me
sentire appelatur; atque hoc praecise sic sumptum nihil aliud est quam
cogitare.*— And it is certain that I see myself seeing, that I see myself
hearing, that I see myself warming myself. This cannot be false; what is
called 'sensing within myself' is strictly just this, and in this restricted
sense of the term it is simply thinking")[2] as that of practice ("one cannot feel [*oneself*] sad, or moved by any other passion, unless the soul

---

1. Maybe one can distinguish third-rate philosophers who have the already rare greatness of starting a single new beginning to reach their "intuition,"
their distinction, or their *instauratio magna* (like Spinoza, Berkeley, Schopen-
hauer, Bergson, etc.); second-rate philosophers who manage, because the thing
itself demands it of them, to accomplish two beginnings, thus a "second sailing"
(like Plato, Leibniz, Nietzsche, etc.); and finally first-rate philosophers whom the
thing itself forces to establish at least three new beginnings (as maybe Descartes,
Kant, Husserl, etc.). The case of Heidegger remains to be examined (one should
keep in mind that it is a matter *not* of a hierarchy among philosophers but of
characterizing their styles).

2. Second Meditation, AT VII: 29, 14–18; CSM II: 19, retranslated by
author [English modified to reflect the French rather than the Latin].

truly has *this passion within itself*")[3] or even that of generosity, which is moral ("this knowledge and this *feeling*").[4] Thus, rather than taking passivity as self-evident, as the supposed empiricists limit themselves to doing, rather than turning it into a simple activity that would come from elsewhere and not from the ego (a passive thought for me but still and continually produced actively by someone else, whether that would be God, another person, or even a thing in the world), Descartes takes sensation really seriously and sees it as the intrinsic and not accidentally passive modality of my *cogitatio*: sensation appears as the passivity that the fact of being exposed to exteriority forces on the *mens*. But this is not some anonymous and abstract exteriority in general, rather it is a matter of the only one that "the union" permits, that is to say, the ego who thinks by *sensing*, because, more radically, it knows and experiences itself as being (and knowing) according to *corpus meum*, in other words, according to its flesh (*Leib*).

One must thus admit at least three beginnings, thus three forms of the ego, while it remains each time a principle: the principle of methodical knowledge (thinking according to the understanding and the imagination), the principle of metaphysical self-knowledge (thinking according to doubt, understanding, and will), finally the principle of passive thought to the point of the *cogitatio* as passion (thinking according to sensation, but in response to the will).

One must also draw the inevitable consequence from this: no reading of Descartes can present itself as trustworthy or claim to be adequate—not even by far—without reconstituting these three beginnings and giving them a coherent interpretation, without limiting oneself to choosing among them, as was historically so often the case, one or the other period leaving unmentioned whichever seems the least intelligible or the most incompatible with it. If Descartes had to think the ego successively as principle of a methodical science of objects, then as principle of a metaphysical grounding, and finally as principle of a primordial passivity, did he do so because each attempt failed, because not one of them was sufficient to fulfill the function of principle and it was necessary to take up its establishment anew? Or rather, to the contrary, does the triple repetition of the principle remain perfectly coherent, or does it even reinforce a coherence so far remaining undecided? How was

3. *Passions of the Soul*, §26, XI: 349, 4–7; CSM I: 338, trans. lightly modified.

4. Ibid., §154, 446, 13; CSM I: 384.

Descartes able to do what he had to do—to determine three forms for the function of principle assumed or demanded by the ego?

A response to this question has already been sketched: the unity of the Cartesian metaphysics comes from its double onto-theo-logical constitution, which first articulates an ontology (*metaphysica generalis*) of being as *cogitatum* with a *metaphysica specialis* (via a *psychologia rationalis*) where the being ego of the *\*cogitatio sui* assumes the function of first principle; then an ontology (*metaphysica generalis*) of being as *causa* or *causatum* where the divine being of the *causa sui* ensures the role of first principle (*metaphysica specialis* via *theologia rationalis*). But one can again ask how these two onto-theo-logical constitutions relate to each other—as parallel, concurrent, hierarchical, or in some other fashion? We are able to respond to this first of all by taking permission from the two meanings of the concept of "principle" admitted by Descartes: either, first, "principle" designates that which "confirms the truth . . . by . . . a reasoning," for example, the principle of non-contradiction; or, second, "the first principle is that our soul exists, because there is nothing whose existence is better known to us."[5] This literally Cartesian doubling of "principle" nevertheless is not enough to clarify and even less to justify the duality of the onto-theo-logies. First because only one text documents it. Then because it can be applied in two different ways. Either one will retain the opposition between truth confirming the reasoning and existence, and one will say that the first meaning of the principle returns to a non-contradiction, thus to the onto-theo-logy of the *cogitatio*, whereas the second returns to the onto-theo-logy of the *causa*, because it implements existence. Or one will insist that the two meanings of "principle" meet in each of the two terms of each of the two onto-theo-logies: first a logical principle (either that of non-contradiction or the principle of causality or that of sufficient reason) for the *metaphysica generalis*, then an existence (a supreme being, either the ego or the *\*cogitatio sui*, or the God of the *causa sui*). In this way the double sense of "principle" does not exactly cover the doubling of the onto-theo-logical constitution and, consequently, cannot reinforce the cohesion, leaving the plurality of meanings of the ego as first principle undetermined. Moreover, another obvious and major difficulty is added to this dual ambiguity: how could one ensure the coherence of

5. To Clerselier, June or July 1646, IV: 444, 12, 17–18 and 23–25, respectively; CSMK: 290. The present discussion extends and in a sense corrects my development in *On Descartes' Metaphysical Prism*, §10, 118–27.

*three* meanings of first beginning by relying on only two terms (whether the two Cartesian meanings of "first principle," the two determinations of *metaphysica* as *generalis* and as *specialis*, the two dimensions of each onto-theo-logy, or the two onto-theo-logies themselves)?

A final hypothesis nevertheless remains possible, which reconciles the duality of elements of *metaphysica* and the threefold meaning of the ego as "first principle." In fact, in order to articulate the first onto-theo-logy with the second, it would be necessary that the first meaning of the ego as "first principle" is articulated with its simple status of *causatum* in the second onto-theo-logy, where precisely the *causa sui* exercises by power the "first principle." In other words, a form of the ego would be necessary where the *cogitatio* is practiced actively (by doubt, understanding, will, and imagination) and also passively (under the influence of an external cause, thus thinking via sensation). How could we fail to see that the ego of the union consists precisely in the articulation of these two postures of the *cogitatio*? Inasmuch as it wills and, more particularly, wills to the second level to use its will well, the ego imitates the divine causality the most closely to the point where we have to speak of a temptation of the *causa sui*.[6] Yet, inasmuch as it thinks by receiving its thoughts of objects passively from its *meum corpus* or even from its own sensing of self, this same ego experiences itself as caused by other authorities (whatever they might be) and thus as a thinker even more radically passive than by the understanding. Thus the final state of the ego, in Descartes' third beginning, does not come to *augment* the heterogeneity of its constitution(s) of metaphysics, as if beyond being as *cogitatio/cogitationes* and being as *causa/causatum* it had risked a third meaning of being [*de l'étant*] in its being [*être*], but instead *absorbs* it. The final meaning of the ego *conjoins* in itself the two meanings of the being of being and, more modestly, the modes of the *cogitatio*, that the two preceding meanings (each partial anyway) had opposed, or better juxtaposed: activity (*cogitatio* through doubt, understanding, will, and imagination) and passivity (*cogitatio* through sensation). The ego, at least when it manages to implement all its modalities of *cogitatio*, here including the most problematic one of sensation, also manages to unify the two onto-theo-logies which, so far, were more juxtaposed than they were articulated in Descartes' explicitly metaphysical writings. More than a belated and undecided moral development, the ego of passivity appears thus as the most fully achieved accomplishment of Cartesian metaphysics.

6. See above, chapter 6, §29.

A final question remains: If my analyses have some validity—if thus passivity and activity have an equally primordial status in the exercise of thought—why did none of Descartes' successors (at least none of the most noteworthy ones) all the way to Rousseau, who knew him, and Nietzsche and Husserl, who barely knew him, take up his analysis and pursue his breakthrough? Why did especially Spinoza, Malebranche, and probably also Leibniz construct their doctrines of the passions as an always active recovery of affects? From where does the advance come to him that has kept Descartes misunderstood and solitary for so long? Is it explained by the reservation of its unveiling: "*quamvis istam philosophiam nondum totam ostendam, existimo tamen, ex iis quae jam dedi, facile posse intelligi qualis sit futura—*although I have not yet revealed the whole of my philosophy, I think that the samples I have already produced make it easy to understand what it will be like"?[7] But he had really "given" enough of it so that the rest could end up manifesting itself. Or rather is it the case that he had already finished by "passing beyond the limits of philosophizing that I have prescribed for myself"?[8] In any case, he preceded us. Merleau-Ponty had truly seen and recognized this, all the more significantly because it was *in fine*: "Human body. Descartes. The Cartesian idea of the human body as human *non-closed*, open inasmuch as governed by thought—is perhaps the most profound idea of the soul and the body. It is the soul intervening in a body that is *not of the in itself* (if it were, it would be closed like an animal body), that can be a body and living—human only by reaching completion in a 'view of itself' which is thought—."[9]

7. To Dinet, VII: 602, 24–26; CSM II: 397.
8. To Silhon?, 4 April 1648, V: 139, 9–10; untranslated in CSMK.
9. Maurice Merleau-Ponty, *The Visible and the Invisible*, trans. Alphonso Lingis (Evanston, IL: Northwestern University Press, 1968), 234.

# Index of Names